D0091403

Understanding the War on Terror

FOREIGN AFFAIRS BOOKS

American Foreign Policy: Cases and Choices (2003)*

America and the World: Debating the New Shape of International Politics (2002)*

The Middle East in Crisis (2002)*

The Rise of China (2002)*

How Did This Happen? Terrorism and the New War (2002) Public Affairs

The American Encounter:
The United States and the Making of the Modern World (1997) BasicBooks

The Clash of Civilizations? The Debate (1996)*

*To order, call W.W. Norton & Company at 800-233-4830 or
visit www.wwnorton.com

COUNCIL ON FOREIGN RELATIONS

Iran: Time for a New Approach (2004)
Zbigniew Brzezinski and Robert M. Gates, co-chairs

Iraq: One Year After* (2004)
Thomas Pickering and James R. Schlesinger, co-chairs

Renewing the Atlantic Partnership (2004)
Henry A. Kissinger and Lawrence H. Summers, co-chairs

Climate Change: Debating America's Policy Options (2004)
David G. Victor

Giving Meaning to "Never Again":
Seeking an Effective Response to the Crisis in Darfur and Beyond* (2004)
Cheryl O. Igiri and Princeton N. Lyman

What Works in Girls' Education:
Evidence and Policies from the Developing World (2004)
Barbara Herz and Gene B. Sperling

Download these reports for free at www.cfr.org or order the user-friendly print editions by
calling the Brookings Bookstore at 800-275-1447 or going to www.brookings.org.

*Only available online at www.cfr.org

Understanding the War on Terror

A Foreign Affairs Book

FOREIGN AFFAIRS / Council on Foreign Relations

NEW YORK

Distributed by
W.W. Norton & Company
500 Fifth Avenue
New York, New York 10110

Founded in 1921, the Council on Foreign Relations is an independent,
national membership organization and a nonpartisan center for scholars dedicated to
producing and disseminating ideas so that individual and corporate members,
as well as policymakers, journalists, students, and interested citizens in the United States
and other countries, can better understand the world and the foreign policy choices
facing the United States and other governments. The Council does this by convening meetings;
conducting a wide-ranging Studies program; publishing *Foreign Affairs*, the preeminent
journal covering international affairs and U.S. foreign policy; maintaining a diverse
membership; sponsoring Independent Task Forces; and providing up-to-date information
about the world and U.S. foreign policy on the Council's website, www.cfr.org.

**The Council takes no institutional position on policy issues and has no
affiliation with the U.S. government. All statements of fact and expressions of opinion
contained in its publications are the sole responsibility of the author or authors.**

The Council's bimonthly magazine, *Foreign Affairs*, has been America's leading
publication on international affairs and foreign policy for over 80 years.
With a circulation of 130,000 worldwide, *Foreign Affairs* has long been the most
influential forum for important new ideas, analysis, and debate on significant
global issues. To subscribe, or for more information, visit www.foreignaffairs.org.

Foreign Affairs books are distributed by W.W. Norton (www.wwnorton.com).

Copyright © 2005 by the Council on Foreign Relations®, Inc.
All rights reserved. Printed in the United States of America.

This book may not be reproduced in whole or in part, in any form
beyond the reproduction permitted by Sections 107 and 108 of the U.S. Copyright
Law Act (17 U.S.C. Sections 107 and 108) and excerpts by reviewers for the
public press, without express written permission from the Council on Foreign Relations.
For information, write to the Publications Office, Council on Foreign Relations,
58 East 68th Street, New York, NY 10021.

Contents

Introduction

Gideon Rose

9/11 AND AFTER

ON THE MORNING of September 11, 2001, the United States awoke to find itself at war. If that much was clear, however, many other things were not—including the nature of the enemy, the location of the battleground, and the strategy and tactics necessary for victory. This collection tries to shed light on those crucial topics and put the nation's most important security challenge in proper perspective.

When the first plane crashed into the World Trade Center at 8:46 AM, most people thought it was an accident. When the second plane hit 17 minutes later, it became clear that something was horribly wrong, a feeling soon confirmed by the crash at the Pentagon. Then the collapse of the twin towers on live television turned the disaster into one of the signal tragedies in American history.

During the 1990s, with the Cold War won and the economy booming, the United States had relaxed, releasing the tension it had sustained for decades. The attacks of September 11 changed all of that, thrusting the country back into history with a vengeance. The public was so unprepared for such a catastrophe, however, that the universal first reaction was shock and confusion, followed quickly by uncontrollable grief and anger.

The notion that such a calamity could have been caused by a few lightly armed young men dispatched by a religious zealot sitting in a cave half a world away simply did not compute. Indeed, it is still hard for many to accept even now, years later, when it is supported by overwhelming evidence. From that first morning on, accordingly, the country has been dead set on getting the people responsible and making sure it never happens again—but has been less sure about just who those people are and how to prevent another attack.

As soon as they heard about the crashes, a few government officials and terrorism experts were confident the culprit was Osama bin Laden, a renegade Saudi extremist operating out of Afghanistan. His organization had been responsible for several previous attacks on American targets, including the bombings of the U.S. embassies in Kenya and Tanzania in 1998 and the U.S.S. *Cole* in Yemen in 2000, and it was known to be looking for other opportunities to strike. Bin Laden and his group, in this view, represented the changing nature of national security threats that the United States faced in the new millennium: not traditional interstate rivalries, but amorphous transnational forces driven by ideology and culture as much as old-fashioned material interests.

Unlike most of the wild speculation that day, this hunch proved correct, and Washington soon began planning how to strike back. When the Islamic radicals who controlled Afghanistan refused to give bin Laden up they were added to the enemies list, and a lightning military campaign soon routed both the Taliban "hosts" and their al Qaeda "guests."

At this point, however, things began to get murky. Bin Laden and his top deputies managed to escape during the fighting and disappeared deep into their mountain redoubts. Their organization, meanwhile, turned out to be only part of a much larger problem, the bloody spearhead of a global movement with broader appeal and greater resources than almost anyone had realized. Suddenly, radical Islamists seemed to be everywhere one looked, from Southeast Asia to Western Europe to New York and Florida. And viewed with newly anxious eyes, America's open society now seemed appallingly vulnerable, easy prey for a determined enemy.

If the first stages of the country's response to the September 11 attacks had seemed relatively obvious, therefore, the next steps appeared less so. What should be done about al Qaeda fugitives still at large? Where besides Afghanistan did what the Bush administration had come to call the "war on terror" need to be fought, and how? What had to be done to get better intelligence on the enemy and provide for what was now referred to as "homeland security"?

Introduction

As these questions were being mulled, the Bush administration decided to launch another military campaign, this one designed to topple Saddam Hussein's regime in Iraq. The administration's central argument for the war was the need to eliminate the dangers posed by Saddam's unconventional weapons programs. It chose to present the conflict, however, as a crucial battle in the broader war on terror, citing supposed links between Iraq and al Qaeda and arguing that the roots of Islamist terrorism lay in Middle Eastern tyranny and could be cut off by the spread of democracy throughout the region.

At the time, national security professionals generally agreed that Saddam's weapons programs were threatening and needed to be dealt with—even though they disagreed over how to do it and though in retrospect their worries proved to have been largely unfounded. The administration's attempts to link Iraq to the war on terror, however, were met with skepticism not only after the fall of Baghdad but beforehand as well.

Saddam Hussein's Iraq may indeed have technically been a state sponsor of terror, the professionals knew, yet its activity in this area in general, and with regard to al Qaeda in particular, was not very significant. Apart from using Afghanistan as a base, radical Islamist terrorists did not rely much on state sponsors, and Iraq would rank low on any list of countries where al Qaeda had a presence or from which it received support. And as for the notion that Islamic radicalism could be countered through political liberalization, many professionals were open to the idea in principle but doubtful about whether in practice an invasion of Iraq would lead to a liberal democratic outcome there, let alone one that could trigger a domino effect throughout the region.

Ironically, the postwar troubles in Iraq have lent some perverse legitimacy to the administration's original claims that the country was connected to the war on terror, as radical jihadists have become key players in the insurgency against the occupation and as the difficulties the United States has encountered there have encouraged its enemies throughout the region. Like the Israeli-Palestinian conflict, therefore, the situation in Iraq now clearly affects the struggle against radical Islamism even as events in each area continue to follow their own internal dynamic.

Gideon Rose

DEFINING THE STRUGGLE

IN TRYING TO MAKE SENSE of what happened that September morning, the country is lucky to be able to draw on the extraordinary efforts of the National Commission on Terrorist Attacks Upon the United States, more popularly known as the 9/11 Commission. The first selection in this volume, taken from the commission's Final Report, is a minute-by-minute narrative of the attacks themselves. The second and third selections are statements prepared by the Commission's staff that provide an introduction to al Qaeda and a snapshot of how the attacks were planned and executed. Anyone interested in learning more about 9/11 itself should read the Final Report in its entirety.

The mental world the hijackers inhabited is so alien to us, however, that entering into it requires not only cold facts but also imaginative reconstruction. The essay by Michael Scott Doran thus explores the intricacies of radical Islamist ideology. The attacks were designed to hurt the United States, he argues, but even more to provoke a massive reaction—one that would polarize the Islamic world, discredit its corrupt authoritarian regimes, and pave the way for the victory of the pure and faithful. Alan Cullison, meanwhile, fleshes out the picture of the enemy by using documents found on an abandoned computer to evoke the daily life of al Qaeda operatives in Afghanistan and elsewhere.

Fareed Zakaria then places radical Islamism in its historical context, locating its origins not in Islam as a religion nor in centuries-old trends but rather in the failed political development of the modern Middle East. The key to ultimate victory, he argues, is finding a way to help the countries of the Muslim world enter modernity in dignity and peace. Ladan Boroumand and Roya Boroumand complement Zakaria by placing al Qaeda's ideology in a broader intellectual context; they argue that it is best understood as a modern totalitarian challenge to both traditional Islam and democracy. And Walter Laqueur places the hijackers' methods in perspective, showing where the attacks fit in the history of terrorism and political violence.

Although 9/11 took the public by surprise, something like it had been dreaded by the small community of professionals inside the government who had been tracking the emergence of al Qaeda over the previous decade. Another staff statement from the 9/11 Commission therefore provides background on how the White House handled the issue from the first World Trade Center attack in 1993 to the second one eight years later. George W. Bush's speech to Congress and the nation on September 20, 2001, set out the guidelines for the more aggressive American approach that followed 9/11, and Michael E. O'Hanlon's article analyzes the administration's actions through the Afghan campaign.

The "Bush doctrine" famously sought to draw a line between those "with us" and "with the terrorists," but some of the toughest questions have concerned relations with countries that don't fall neatly into either category. Stephen Philip Cohen's analysis of Pakistan and F. Gregory Gause's treatment of Saudi Arabia show the difficulties in dealing with states caught in the middle, while John Gershman's discussion of Southeast Asia explores how the radical Islamist challenge is playing out in Muslim states outside the Middle East. Thomas Carothers, finally, describes the inherent contradictions in the Bush administration's attempt to promote democracy in the Muslim world while relying on authoritarian governments for critical help in taking the fight to the enemy—to which Undersecretary of State Paula Dobriansky responds by denying that the administration has been forced to make any unpleasant tradeoffs.

THE ROAD AHEAD

ONE OF THE MOST worrying features of the crisis has been the revelations it has prompted regarding just how inadequate are the systems designed to keep Americans safe. Stephen Flynn suggests a variety of useful measures that could be taken to help secure U.S. borders, where massive flows of trucks, ships, goods, and people simply overwhelm the agencies charged with overseeing them. The real challenge, he shows, will be finding some way of policing globalization so as to reap its benefits without being left naked in the face of its dangers. Probing the intelligence failure that allowed the attackers to go undetected, Richard Betts finds that reform is easy to pontificate about but hard to implement—and probably not very useful in any event.

Faced with an unconventional fight against unconventional enemies, the Bush administration devised a number of unconventional responses, including controversial rules for handling suspects and prisoners with little regard for the niceties of traditional legal procedure. Kenneth Roth argues that in its zeal the administration has trespassed on fundamental rights that should remain inviolate, while Ruth Wedgwood counters that the administration has responded appropriately to unprecedented conditions.

Just how aggressively the administration should wage the conflict in general, actually, has been an issue from the beginning. Michael Howard argues, for example, that the very concept of a "war on terror" is mistaken, because such terminology predisposes policymakers toward overly militarized responses to situations that are best handled primarily through non-military means. Grenville Byford, meanwhile, takes issue with the notion that terror is the defining feature of the crisis. What matters is not how the United States was struck but that it was struck at all, he argues, and recognizing that old-fashioned national security interests are in play would help clarify and focus the task at hand.

Max Boot, finally, criticizes those who would limit the struggle to al Qaeda alone. The 9/11 attack was the culmination of decades of challenges to U.S. interests from Middle East radicals, he argues, and the failure to respond to those challenges forcefully in the past only emboldened the enemy. Iraq did indeed deserve to be considered as part of the larger conflict, in Boot's view, although less because of its direct ties to al Qaeda or 9/11 than because of the need to end America's tradition of regional appeasement once and for all.

More than three years after 9/11, figuring out the status of the war it spawned remains difficult. The lack of any further attacks inside the United States is encouraging, but the persistence of the threat is not. Jessica Stern argues that al Qaeda has managed to survive and adapt to new circumstances, and Paul Pillar offers suggestions for how the struggle should be waged now that the enemy is dispersed rather than concentrated. Reuel Marc Gerecht claims that the war in Iraq has helped the war against Islamic radicalism, but James Fallows argues that it has hurt it by squandering attention, resources, and international good will. Barton Gellman and Dafna Linzer, tracking the tradeoffs that had to be made as the government shifted gears to move from one fight to the other, provide evidence for Fallows' case. What is clear is that the struggle continues and is destined to top the American national security agenda for years to come.

I
The Enemy

We Have Some Planes

TUESDAY, SEPTEMBER 11, 2001, dawned temperate and nearly cloudless in the eastern United States. Millions of men and women readied themselves for work. Some made their way to the Twin Towers, the signature structures of the World Trade Center complex in New York City. Others went to Arlington, Virginia, to the Pentagon. Across the Potomac River, the United States Congress was back in session. At the other end of Pennsylvania Avenue, people began to line up for a White House tour. In Sarasota, Florida, President George W. Bush went for an early morning run.

For those heading to an airport, weather conditions could not have been better for a safe and pleasant journey. Among the travelers were Mohamed Atta and Abdul Aziz al Omari, who arrived at the airport in Portland, Maine.

INSIDE THE FOUR FLIGHTS

BOARDING THE FLIGHTS *Boston: American 11 and United 175.* Atta and Omari boarded a 6:00 A.M. flight from Portland to Boston's Logan International Airport.[1]

When he checked in for his flight to Boston, Atta was selected by a computerized prescreening system known as CAPPS (Computer Assisted Passenger Prescreening System), created to identify passengers who should be subject to special security measures. Under security rules in place at the time, the only consequence of Atta's selection by CAPPS was that his checked bags were held off the plane until it was confirmed that he had boarded the aircraft. This did not hinder Atta's plans.[2]

Atta and Omari arrived in Boston at 6:45. Seven minutes later, Atta apparently took a call from Marwan al Shehhi, a longtime colleague who was at another terminal at Logan Airport. They spoke for three minutes.3 It would be their final conversation.

Between 6:45 and 7:40, Atta and Omari, along with Satam al Suqami, Wail al Shehri, and Waleed al Shehri, checked in and boarded American Airlines Flight 11, bound for Los Angeles. The flight was scheduled to depart at 7:45.4

In another Logan terminal, Shehhi, joined by Fayez Banihammad, Mohand al Shehri, Ahmed al Ghamdi, and Hamza al Ghamdi, checked in for United Airlines Flight 175, also bound for Los Angeles. A couple of Shehhi's colleagues were obviously unused to travel; according to the United ticket agent, they had trouble understanding the standard security questions, and she had to go over them slowly until they gave the routine, reassuring answers.5 Their flight was scheduled to depart at 8:00.

The security checkpoints through which passengers, including Atta and his colleagues, gained access to the American 11 gate were operated by Globe Security under a contract with American Airlines. In a different terminal, the single checkpoint through which passengers for United 175 passed was controlled by United Airlines, which had contracted with Huntleigh USA to perform the screening.6

In passing through these checkpoints, each of the hijackers would have been screened by a walk-through metal detector calibrated to detect items with at least the metal content of a .22-caliber handgun. Anyone who might have set off that detector would have been screened with a hand wand—a procedure requiring the screener to identify the metal item or items that caused the alarm. In addition, an X-ray machine would have screened the hijackers' carry-on belongings. The screening was in place to identify and confiscate weapons and other items prohibited from being carried onto a commercial flight.7 None of the checkpoint supervisors recalled the hijackers or reported anything suspicious regarding their screening.8

While Atta had been selected by CAPPS in Portland, three members of his hijacking team—Suqami, Wail al Shehri, and Waleed al Shehri—were selected in Boston. Their selection affected only the handling of their checked bags, not their screening at the checkpoint. All five men cleared the checkpoint and made their way to the gate for American 11. Atta, Omari, and Suqami took their seats in business class (seats 8D, 8G, and 10B, respectively). The Shehri brothers had adjacent seats in row 2 (Wail in 2A, Waleed in 2B), in the first-class cabin. They boarded American 11 between 7:31 and 7:40. The aircraft pushed back from the gate at 7:40.[9]

Shehhi and his team, none of whom had been selected by CAPPS, boarded United 175 between 7:23 and 7:28 (Banihammad in 2A, Shehri in 2B, Shehhi in 6C, Hamza al Ghamdi in 9C, and Ahmed al Ghamdi in 9D). Their aircraft pushed back from the gate just before 8:00.[10]

Washington Dulles: American 77. Hundreds of miles southwest of Boston, at Dulles International Airport in the Virginia suburbs of Washington, D.C., five more men were preparing to take their early morning flight. At 7:15, a pair of them, Khalid al Mihdhar and Majed Moqed, checked in at the American Airlines ticket counter for Flight 77, bound for Los Angeles. Within the next 20 minutes, they would be followed by Hani Hanjour and two brothers, Nawaf al Hazmi and Salem al Hazmi.[11]

Hani Hanjour, Khalid al Mihdhar, and Majed Moqed were flagged by CAPPS. The Hazmi brothers were also selected for extra scrutiny by the airline's customer service representative at the check-in counter. He did so because one of the brothers did not have photo identification nor could he understand English, and because the agent found both of the passengers to be suspicious. The only consequence of their selection was that their checked bags were held off the plane until it was confirmed that they had boarded the aircraft.[12]

All five hijackers passed through the Main Terminal's west security screening checkpoint; United Airlines, which was the responsible air carrier, had contracted out the work to Argenbright Security.[13] The checkpoint featured closed-circuit television that recorded all passengers, including the hijackers, as they were screened. At 7:18, Mihdhar and Moqed entered the security checkpoint.

Mihdhar and Moqed placed their carry-on bags on the belt of the X-ray machine and proceeded through the first metal detector. Both set off the alarm, and they were directed to a second metal detector. Mihdhar did not trigger the alarm and was permitted through the checkpoint. After Moqed set it off, a screener wanded him. He passed this inspection.[14]

About 20 minutes later, at 7:35, another passenger for Flight 77, Hani Hanjour, placed two carry-on bags on the X-ray belt in the Main Terminal's west checkpoint, and proceeded, without alarm, through the metal detector. A short time later, Nawaf and Salem al Hazmi entered the same checkpoint. Salem al Hazmi cleared the metal detector and was permitted through; Nawaf al Hazmi set off the alarms for both the first and second metal detectors and was then hand-wanded before being passed. In addition, his over-the-shoulder carry-on bag was swiped by an explosive trace detector and then passed. The video footage indicates that he was carrying an unidentified item in his back pocket, clipped to its rim.[15]

When the local civil aviation security office of the Federal Aviation Administration (FAA) later investigated these security screening operations, the screeners recalled nothing out of the ordinary. They could not recall that any of the passengers they screened were CAPPS selectees. We asked a screening expert to review the videotape of the hand-wanding, and he found the quality of the screener's work to have been "marginal at best." The screener should have "resolved" what set off the alarm; and in the case of both Moqed and Hazmi, it was clear that he did not.[16]

At 7:50, Majed Moqed and Khalid al Mihdhar boarded the flight and were seated in 12A and 12B in coach. Hani Hanjour, assigned to seat 1B (first class), soon followed. The Hazmi brothers, sitting in 5E and 5F, joined Hanjour in the first-class cabin.[17]

Newark: United 93. Between 7:03 and 7:39, Saeed al Ghamdi, Ahmed al Nami, Ahmad al Haznawi, and Ziad Jarrah checked in at the United Airlines ticket counter for Flight 93, going to Los Angeles. Two checked bags; two did not. Haznawi was selected by CAPPS. His checked bag was screened for explosives and then loaded on the plane.[18]

The four men passed through the security checkpoint, owned by United Airlines and operated under contract by Argenbright Security. Like the checkpoints in Boston, it lacked closed-circuit television surveillance so there is no documentary evidence to indicate when the hijackers passed through the checkpoint, what alarms may have been triggered, or what security procedures were administered. The FAA interviewed the screeners later; none recalled anything unusual or suspicious.[19]

The four men boarded the plane between 7:39 and 7:48. All four had seats in the first-class cabin; their plane had no business-class section. Jarrah was in seat 1B, closest to the cockpit; Nami was in 3C, Ghamdi in 3D, and Haznawi in 6B.[20]

The 19 men were aboard four transcontinental flights.[21] They were planning to hijack these planes and turn them into large guided missiles, loaded with up to 11,400 gallons of jet fuel. By 8:00 A.M. on the morning of Tuesday, September 11, 2001, they had defeated all the security layers that America's civil aviation security system then had in place to prevent a hijacking.

THE HIJACKING OF AMERICAN 11

AMERICAN AIRLINES FLIGHT 11 provided nonstop service from Boston to Los Angeles. On September 11, Captain John Ogonowski and First Officer Thomas McGuinness piloted the Boeing 767. It carried its full capacity of nine flight attendants. Eighty-one passengers boarded the flight with them (including the five terrorists).[22]

The plane took off at 7:59. Just before 8:14, it had climbed to 26,000 feet, not quite its initial assigned cruising altitude of 29,000 feet. All communications and flight profile data were normal. About this time the "Fasten Seatbelt" sign would usually have been turned off and the flight attendants would have begun preparing for cabin service.[23]

At that same time, American 11 had its last routine communication with the ground when it acknowledged navigational instructions from the FAA's air traffic control (ATC) center in Boston. Sixteen seconds after that transmission, ATC instructed the aircraft's pilots to climb to 35,000 feet. That message and all subsequent attempts to contact the flight were not acknowledged. From this and other evidence, we believe the hijacking began at 8:14 or shortly thereafter.[24]

Reports from two flight attendants in the coach cabin, Betty Ong and Madeline "Amy" Sweeney, tell us most of what we know about how the hijacking happened. As it began, some of the hijackers—most likely Wail al Shehri and Waleed al Shehri, who were seated in row 2 in first class—stabbed the two unarmed flight attendants who would have been preparing for cabin service.[25]

We do not know exactly how the hijackers gained access to the cockpit; FAA rules required that the doors remain closed and locked during flight. Ong speculated that they had "jammed their way" in. Perhaps the terrorists stabbed the flight attendants to get a cockpit key, to force one of them to open the cockpit door, or to lure the captain or first officer out of the cockpit. Or the flight attendants may just have been in their way.[26]

At the same time or shortly thereafter, Atta—the only terrorist on board trained to fly a jet—would have moved to the cockpit from his business-class seat, possibly accompanied by Omari. As this was happening, passenger Daniel Lewin, who was seated in the row just behind Atta and Omari, was stabbed by one of the hijackers—probably Satam al Suqami, who was seated directly behind Lewin. Lewin had served four years as an officer in the Israeli military. He may have made an attempt to stop the hijackers in front of him, not realizing that another was sitting behind him.[27]

The hijackers quickly gained control and sprayed Mace, pepper spray, or some other irritant in the first-class cabin, in order to force the passengers and flight attendants toward the rear of the plane. They claimed they had a bomb.[28]

About five minutes after the hijacking began, Betty Ong contacted the American Airlines Southeastern Reservations Office in Cary, North Carolina, via an AT&T airphone to report an emergency aboard the flight. This was the first of several occasions on 9/11 when flight attendants took action outside the scope of their training, which emphasized that in a hijacking, they were to communicate with the cockpit crew. The emergency call lasted approximately 25 minutes, as Ong calmly and professionally relayed information about events taking place aboard the airplane to authorities on the ground.[29]

At 8:19, Ong reported: "The cockpit is not answering, somebody's stabbed in business class—and I think there's Mace—that we can't breathe—I don't know, I think we're getting hijacked." She then told of the stabbings of the two flight attendants.[30]

At 8:21, one of the American employees receiving Ong's call in North Carolina, Nydia Gonzalez, alerted the American Airlines operations center in Fort Worth, Texas, reaching Craig Marquis, the manager on duty. Marquis soon realized this was an emergency and instructed the airline's dispatcher responsible for the flight to contact the cockpit. At 8:23, the dispatcher tried unsuccessfully to contact the aircraft. Six minutes later, the air traffic control specialist in American's operations center contacted the FAA's Boston Air Traffic Control Center about the flight. The center was already aware of the problem.[31]

Boston Center knew of a problem on the flight in part because just before 8:25 the hijackers had attempted to communicate with the passengers. The microphone was keyed, and immediately one of the hijackers said, "Nobody move. Everything will be okay. If you try to make any moves, you'll endanger yourself and the airplane. Just stay quiet." Air traffic controllers heard the transmission; Ong did not. The hijackers probably did not know how to operate the cockpit radio communication system correctly, and thus inadvertently broadcast their message over the air traffic control channel instead of the cabin public-address channel. Also at 8:25, and again at 8:29, Amy Sweeney got through to the American Flight Services Office in Boston but was cut off after she reported someone was hurt aboard the flight. Three minutes later, Sweeney was reconnected to the office and began relaying updates to the manager, Michael Woodward.[32]

At 8:26, Ong reported that the plane was "flying erratically." A minute later, Flight 11 turned south. American also began getting identifications of the hijackers, as Ong and then Sweeney passed on some of the seat numbers of those who had gained unauthorized access to the cockpit.[33]

Sweeney calmly reported on her line that the plane had been hijacked; a man in first class had his throat slashed; two flight attendants had been stabbed—one was seriously hurt and was on oxygen while the other's wounds seemed minor; a doctor had been requested; the flight attendants were unable to contact the cockpit; and there was a bomb in the cockpit. Sweeney told Woodward that she and Ong were trying to relay as much information as they could to people on the ground.[34]

At 8:38, Ong told Gonzalez that the plane was flying erratically again. Around this time Sweeney told Woodward that the hijackers were Middle Easterners, naming three of their seat numbers. One spoke very little English and one spoke excellent English. The hijackers had gained entry to the cockpit, and she did not know how. The aircraft was in a rapid descent.35

At 8:41, Sweeney told Woodward that passengers in coach were under the impression that there was a routine medical emergency in first class. Other flight attendants were busy at duties such as getting medical supplies while Ong and Sweeney were reporting the events.36

At 8:41, in American's operations center, a colleague told Marquis that the air traffic controllers declared Flight 11 a hijacking and "think he's [American 11] headed toward Kennedy [airport in New York City].They're moving everybody out of the way. They seem to have him on a primary radar. They seem to think that he is descending."37

At 8:44, Gonzalez reported losing phone contact with Ong. About this same time Sweeney reported to Woodward, "Something is wrong. We are in a rapid descent . . . we are all over the place." Woodward asked Sweeney to look out the window to see if she could determine where they were. Sweeney responded: "We are flying low. We are flying very, very low. We are flying way too low." Seconds later she said, "Oh my God we are way too low." The phone call ended.38

At 8:46:40, American 11 crashed into the North Tower of the World Trade Center in New York City.39 All on board, along with an unknown number of people in the tower, were killed instantly.

THE HIJACKING OF UNITED 175

UNITED AIRLINES FLIGHT 175 was scheduled to depart for Los Angeles at 8:00. Captain Victor Saracini and First Officer Michael Horrocks piloted the Boeing 767, which had seven flight attendants. Fifty-six passengers boarded the flight.40

United 175 pushed back from its gate at 7:58 and departed Logan Airport at 8:14. By 8:33, it had reached its assigned cruising altitude of 31,000 feet. The flight attendants would have begun their cabin service.41

The flight had taken off just as American 11 was being hijacked, and at 8:42 the United 175 flight crew completed their report on a "suspicious transmission" overheard from another plane (which turned out to have been Flight 11) just after takeoff. This was United 175's last communication with the ground.[42]

The hijackers attacked sometime between 8:42 and 8:46. They used knives (as reported by two passengers and a flight attendant), Mace (reported by one passenger), and the threat of a bomb (reported by the same passenger). They stabbed members of the flight crew (reported by a flight attendant and one passenger). Both pilots had been killed (reported by one flight attendant). The eyewitness accounts came from calls made from the rear of the plane, from passengers originally seated further forward in the cabin, a sign that passengers and perhaps crew had been moved to the back of the aircraft. Given similarities to American 11 in hijacker seating and in eyewitness reports of tactics and weapons, as well as the contact between the presumed team leaders, Atta and Shehhi, we believe the tactics were similar on both flights.[43]

The first operational evidence that something was abnormal on United 175 came at 8:47, when the aircraft changed beacon codes twice within a minute. At 8:51, the flight deviated from its assigned altitude, and a minute later New York air traffic controllers began repeatedly and unsuccessfully trying to contact it.[44]

At 8:52, in Easton, Connecticut, a man named Lee Hanson received a phone call from his son Peter, a passenger on United 175. His son told him: "I think they've taken over the cockpit—An attendant has been stabbed—and someone else up front may have been killed. The plane is making strange moves. Call United Airlines—Tell them it's Flight 175, Boston to LA." Lee Hanson then called the Easton Police Department and relayed what he had heard.[45]

Also at 8:52, a male flight attendant called a United office in San Francisco, reaching Marc Policastro. The flight attendant reported that the flight had been hijacked, both pilots had been killed, a flight attendant had been stabbed, and the hijackers were probably flying the plane. The call lasted about two minutes, after which Policastro and a colleague tried unsuccessfully to contact the flight.[46]

At 8:58, the flight took a heading toward New York City.[47]

At 8:59, Flight 175 passenger Brian David Sweeney tried to call his wife, Julie. He left a message on their home answering machine that the plane had been hijacked. He then called his mother, Louise

Sweeney, told her the flight had been hijacked, and added that the passengers were thinking about storming the cockpit to take control of the plane away from the hijackers.[48]

At 9:00, Lee Hanson received a second call from his son Peter:

It's getting bad, Dad—A stewardess was stabbed—They seem to have knives and Mace—They said they have a bomb—It's getting very bad on the plane-Passengers are throwing up and getting sick-The plane is making jerky movements—I don't think the pilot is flying the plane—I think we are going down—I think they intend to go to Chicago or someplace and fly into a building—Don't worry, Dad—If it happens, it'll be very fast—My God, my God.[49]

The call ended abruptly. Lee Hanson had heard a woman scream just before it cut off. He turned on a television, and in her home so did Louise Sweeney. Both then saw the second aircraft hit the World Trade Center.[50]

At 9:03:11, United Airlines Flight 175 struck the South Tower of the World Trade Center.[51] All on board, along with an unknown number of people in the tower, were killed instantly.

THE HIJACKING OF AMERICAN 77

AMERICAN AIRLINES FLIGHT 77 was scheduled to depart from Washington Dulles for Los Angeles at 8:10. The aircraft was a Boeing 757 piloted by Captain Charles F. Burlingame and First Officer David Charlebois. There were four flight attendants. On September 11, the flight carried 58 passengers.[52]

American 77 pushed back from its gate at 8:09 and took off at 8:20. At 8:46, the flight reached its assigned cruising altitude of 35,000 feet. Cabin service would have begun. At 8:51, American 77 transmitted its last routine radio communication. The hijacking began between 8:51 and 8:54. As on American 11 and United 175, the hijackers used knives (reported by one passenger) and moved all the passengers (and possibly crew) to the rear of the aircraft (reported by one flight attendant and one passenger). Unlike the earlier flights, the Flight 77 hijackers were reported by a passenger to have box cutters. Finally, a passenger reported that an announcement had been made by the "pilot" that the plane had been hijacked. Neither of the firsthand accounts mentioned any stabbings or the threat or use of either a bomb or Mace, though both witnesses began the flight in the first-class cabin.[53]

At 8:54, the aircraft deviated from its assigned course, turning south. Two minutes later the transponder was turned off and even primary radar contact with the aircraft was lost. The Indianapolis Air Traffic Control Center repeatedly tried and failed to contact the aircraft. American Airlines dispatchers also tried, without success.[54]

At 9:00, American Airlines Executive Vice President Gerard Arpey learned that communications had been lost with American 77. This was now the second American aircraft in trouble. He ordered all American Airlines flights in the Northeast that had not taken off to remain on the ground. Shortly before 9:10, suspecting that American 77 had been hijacked, American headquarters concluded that the second aircraft to hit the World Trade Center might have been Flight 77. After learning that United Airlines was missing a plane, American Airlines headquarters extended the ground stop nationwide.[55]

At 9:12, Renee May called her mother, Nancy May, in Las Vegas. She said her flight was being hijacked by six individuals who had moved them to the rear of the plane. She asked her mother to alert American Airlines. Nancy May and her husband promptly did so.[56]

At some point between 9:16 and 9:26, Barbara Olson called her husband, Ted Olson, the solicitor general of the United States. She reported that the flight had been hijacked, and the hijackers had knives and box cutters. She further indicated that the hijackers were not aware of her phone call, and that they had put all the passengers in the back of the plane. About a minute into the conversation, the call was cut off. Solicitor General Olson tried unsuccessfully to reach Attorney General John Ashcroft.[57]

Shortly after the first call, Barbara Olson reached her husband again. She reported that the pilot had announced that the flight had been hijacked, and she asked her husband what she should tell the captain to do. Ted Olson asked for her location and she replied that the aircraft was then flying over houses. Another passenger told her they were traveling northeast. The Solicitor General then informed his wife of the two previous hijackings and crashes. She did not display signs of panic and did not indicate any awareness of an impending crash. At that point, the second call was cut off.[58]

At 9:29, the autopilot on American 77 was disengaged; the aircraft was at 7,000 feet and approximately 38 miles west of the Pentagon.[59] At 9:32, controllers at the Dulles Terminal Radar Approach Control "observed a primary radar target tracking eastbound at a high rate of speed." This was later determined to have been Flight 77.

At 9:34, Ronald Reagan Washington National Airport advised the Secret Service of an unknown aircraft heading in the direction of the White House. American 77 was then 5 miles west-southwest of the Pentagon and began a 330-degree turn. At the end of the turn, it was descending through 2,200 feet, pointed toward the Pentagon and downtown Washington. The hijacker pilot then advanced the throttles to maximum power and dove toward the Pentagon.[60]

At 9:37:46, American Airlines Flight 77 crashed into the Pentagon, traveling at approximately 530 miles per hour.[61] All on board, as well as many civilian and military personnel in the building, were killed.

THE BATTLE FOR UNITED 93

AT 8:42, United Airlines Flight 93 took off from Newark (New Jersey) Liberty International Airport bound for San Francisco. The aircraft was piloted by Captain Jason Dahl and First Officer Leroy Homer, and there were five flight attendants. Thirty-seven passengers, including the hijackers, boarded the plane. Scheduled to depart the gate at 8:00, the Boeing 757's takeoff was delayed because of the airport's typically heavy morning traffic.[62]

The hijackers had planned to take flights scheduled to depart at 7:45 (American 11), 8:00 (United 175 and United 93), and 8:10 (American 77). Three of the flights had actually taken off within 10 to 15 minutes of their planned departure times. United 93 would ordinarily have taken off about 15 minutes after pulling away from the gate. When it left the ground at 8:42, the flight was running more than 25 minutes late.[63]

As United 93 left Newark, the flight's crew members were unaware of the hijacking of American 11. Around 9:00, the FAA, American, and United were facing the staggering realization of apparent multiple hijackings. At 9:03, they would see another aircraft strike the World Trade Center. Crisis managers at the FAA and the airlines did not yet act to warn other aircraft.[64] At the same time, Boston Center realized that a message transmitted just before 8:25 by the hijacker pilot of American 11 included the phrase, "We have some planes."[65]

No one at the FAA or the airlines that day had ever dealt with multiple hijackings. Such a plot had not been carried out anywhere in the world in more than 30 years, and never in the United States. As news of the hijackings filtered through the FAA and the airlines, it does not seem to have occurred to their leadership that they needed to alert other aircraft in the air that they too might be at risk.[66]

United 175 was hijacked between 8:42 and 8:46, and awareness of that hijacking began to spread after 8:51. American 77 was hijacked between 8:51 and 8:54. By 9:00, FAA and airline officials began to comprehend that attackers were going after multiple aircraft. American Airlines' nationwide ground stop between 9:05 and 9:10 was followed by a United Airlines ground stop. FAA controllers at Boston Center, which had tracked the first two hijackings, requested at 9:07 that Herndon Command Center "get messages to airborne aircraft to increase security for the cockpit." There is no evidence that Herndon took such action. Boston Center immediately began speculating about other aircraft that might be in danger, leading them to worry about a transcontinental flight—Delta 1989—that in fact was not hijacked. At 9:19, the FAA's New England regional office called Herndon and asked that Cleveland Center advise Delta 1989 to use extra cockpit security.[67]

Several FAA air traffic control officials told us it was the air carriers' responsibility to notify their planes of security problems. One senior FAA air traffic control manager said that it was simply not the FAA's place to order the airlines what to tell their pilots.[68] We believe such statements do not reflect an adequate appreciation of the FAA's responsibility for the safety and security of civil aviation.

The airlines bore responsibility, too. They were facing an escalating number of conflicting and, for the most part, erroneous reports about other flights, as well as a continuing lack of vital information from the FAA about the hijacked flights. We found no evidence, however, that American Airlines sent any cockpit warnings to its aircraft on 9/11. United's first decisive action to notify its airborne aircraft to take defensive action did not come until 9:19, when a United flight dispatcher, Ed Ballinger, took the initiative to begin transmitting warnings to his 16 transcontinental flights: "Beware any cockpit intrusion—Two a/c [aircraft] hit World Trade Center." One of the flights that received the warning was United 93. Because Ballinger was still responsible for his other flights as well as Flight 175, his warning message was not transmitted to Flight 93 until 9:23.[69]

By all accounts, the first 46 minutes of Flight 93's cross-country trip proceeded routinely. Radio communications from the plane were normal. Heading, speed, and altitude ran according to plan. At 9:24, Ballinger's warning to United 93 was received in the cockpit. Within two minutes, at 9:26, the pilot, Jason Dahl, responded with a note of puzzlement: "Ed, confirm latest mssg plz—Jason."[70]

The hijackers attacked at 9:28. While traveling 35,000 feet above eastern Ohio, United 93 suddenly dropped 700 feet. Eleven seconds into the descent, the FAA's air traffic control center in Cleveland received the first of two radio transmissions from the aircraft. During the first broadcast, the captain or first officer could be heard declaring "Mayday" amid the sounds of a physical struggle in the cockpit. The second radio transmission, 35 seconds later, indicated that the fight was continuing. The captain or first officer could be heard shouting: "Hey get out of here—get out of here—get out of here."[71]

On the morning of 9/11, there were only 37 passengers on United 93—33 in addition to the 4 hijackers. This was below the norm for Tuesday mornings during the summer of 2001. But there is no evidence that the hijackers manipulated passenger levels or purchased additional seats to facilitate their operation.[72]

The terrorists who hijacked three other commercial flights on 9/11 operated in five-man teams. They initiated their cockpit takeover within 30 minutes of takeoff. On Flight 93, however, the takeover took place 46 minutes after takeoff and there were only four hijackers. The operative likely intended to round out the team for this flight, Mohamed al Kahtani, had been refused entry by a suspicious immigration inspector at Florida's Orlando International Airport in August.[73]

Because several passengers on United 93 described three hijackers on the plane, not four, some have wondered whether one of the hijackers had been able to use the cockpit jump seat from the outset of the flight. FAA rules allow use of this seat by documented and approved individuals, usually air carrier or FAA personnel. We have found no evidence indicating that one of the hijackers, or anyone else, sat there on this flight. All the hijackers had assigned seats in first class, and they seem to have used them. We believe it is more likely that Jarrah, the crucial pilot-trained member of their team, remained seated and inconspicuous until after the cockpit was seized; and once inside, he would not have been visible to the passengers.[74]

At 9:32, a hijacker, probably Jarrah, made or attempted to make the following announcement to the passengers of Flight 93: "Ladies and Gentlemen: Here the captain, please sit down keep remaining sitting. We have a bomb on board. So, sit." The flight data recorder (also recovered) indicates that Jarrah then instructed the plane's autopilot to turn the aircraft around and head east.[75]

The cockpit voice recorder data indicate that a woman, most likely a flight attendant, was being held captive in the cockpit. She struggled with one of the hijackers who killed or otherwise silenced her.[76]

Shortly thereafter, the passengers and flight crew began a series of calls from GTE airphones and cellular phones. These calls between family, friends, and colleagues took place until the end of the flight and provided those on the ground with firsthand accounts. They enabled the passengers to gain critical information, including the news that two aircraft had slammed into the World Trade Center.[77]

At 9:39, the FAA's Cleveland Air Route Traffic Control Center overheard a second announcement indicating that there was a bomb on board, that the plane was returning to the airport, and that they should remain seated.[78] While it apparently was not heard by the passengers, this announcement, like those on Flight 11 and Flight 77, was intended to deceive them. Jarrah, like Atta earlier, may have inadvertently broadcast the message because he did not know how to operate the radio and the intercom. To our knowledge none of them had ever flown an actual airliner before.

At least two callers from the flight reported that the hijackers knew that passengers were making calls but did not seem to care. It is quite possible Jarrah knew of the success of the assault on the World Trade Center. He could have learned of this from messages being sent by United Airlines to the cockpits of its transcontinental flights, including Flight 93, warning of cockpit intrusion and telling of the New York attacks. But even without them, he would certainly have understood that the attacks on the World Trade Center would already have unfolded, given Flight 93's tardy departure from Newark. If Jarrah did know that the passengers were making calls, it might not have occurred to him that they were certain to learn what had happened in New York, thereby defeating his attempts at deception.[79]

At least ten passengers and two crew members shared vital information with family, friends, colleagues, or others on the ground. All understood the plane had been hijacked. They said the hijackers wielded knives and claimed to have a bomb. The hijackers were wearing red bandanas, and they forced the passengers to the back of the aircraft.[80]

Callers reported that a passenger had been stabbed and that two people were lying on the floor of the cabin, injured or dead—possibly the captain and first officer. One caller reported that a flight attendant had been killed.[81]

One of the callers from United 93 also reported that he thought the hijackers might possess a gun. But none of the other callers reported the presence of a firearm. One recipient of a call from the aircraft recounted specifically asking her caller whether the hijackers had guns. The passenger replied that he did not see one. No evidence of firearms or of their identifiable remains was found at the aircraft's crash site, and the cockpit voice recorder gives no indication of a gun being fired or mentioned at any time. We believe that if the hijackers had possessed a gun, they would have used it in the flight's last minutes as the passengers fought back.[82]

Passengers on three flights reported the hijackers' claim of having a bomb. The FBI told us they found no trace of explosives at the crash sites. One of the passengers who mentioned a bomb expressed his belief that it was not real. Lacking any evidence that the hijackers attempted to smuggle such illegal items past the security screening checkpoints, we believe the bombs were probably fake.[83]

During at least five of the passengers' phone calls, information was shared about the attacks that had occurred earlier that morning at the World Trade Center. Five calls described the intent of passengers and surviving crew members to revolt against the hijackers. According to one call, they voted on whether to rush the terrorists in an attempt to retake the plane. They decided, and acted.[84]

At 9:57, the passenger assault began. Several passengers had terminated phone calls with loved ones in order to join the revolt. One of the callers ended her message as follows: "Everyone's running up to first class. I've got to go. Bye."[85]

The cockpit voice recorder captured the sounds of the passenger assault muffled by the intervening cockpit door. Some family members who listened to the recording report that they can hear the voice of a loved one among the din. We cannot identify whose voices can be heard. But the assault was sustained.[86]

In response, Jarrah immediately began to roll the airplane to the left and right, attempting to knock the passengers off balance. At 9:58:57, Jarrah told another hijacker in the cockpit to block the door. Jarrah continued to roll the airplane sharply left and right, but the assault continued. At 9:59:52, Jarrah changed tactics and pitched the nose of the airplane up and down to disrupt the assault. The recorder captured the sounds of loud thumps, crashes, shouts, and breaking glasses and plates. At 10:00:03, Jarrah stabilized the airplane.[87]

Five seconds later, Jarrah asked, "Is that it? Shall we finish it off?" A hijacker responded, "No. Not yet. When they all come, we finish it off." The sounds of fighting continued outside the cockpit. Again, Jarrah pitched the nose of the aircraft up and down. At 10:00:26, a passenger in the background said, "In the cockpit. If we don't we'll die!" Sixteen seconds later, a passenger yelled, "Roll it!" Jarrah stopped the violent maneuvers at about 10:01:00 and said, "Allah is the greatest! Allah is the greatest!" He then asked another hijacker in the cockpit, "Is that it? I mean, shall we put it down?" to which the other replied, "Yes, put it in it, and pull it down."[88]

The passengers continued their assault and at 10:02:23, a hijacker said, "Pull it down! Pull it down!" The hijackers remained at the controls but must have judged that the passengers were only seconds from overcoming them. The airplane headed down; the control wheel was turned hard to the right. The airplane rolled onto its back, and one of the hijackers began shouting "Allah is the greatest. Allah is the greatest." With the sounds of the passenger counterattack continuing, the aircraft plowed into an empty field in Shanksville, Pennsylvania, at 580 miles per hour, about 20 minutes' flying time from Washington, D.C.[89]

Jarrah's objective was to crash his airliner into symbols of the American Republic, the Capitol or the White House. He was defeated by the alerted, unarmed passengers of United 93.

Endnotes

1. No physical, documentary, or analytical evidence provides a convincing explanation of why Atta and Omari drove to Portland, Maine, from Boston on the morning of September 10, only to return to Logan on Flight 5930 on the morning of September 11. However, Atta reacted negatively when informed in Portland that he would have to check in again in Boston. Michael Touhey interview (May 27, 2004). Whatever their reason, the Portland Jetport was the nearest airport to Boston with a 9/11 flight that would have arrived at Logan in time for the passengers to transfer to American Airlines Flight 11, which had a scheduled departure time of 7:45 A.M. See Tom Kinton interview (Nov. 6, 2003); Portland International Jetport site visit (Aug. 18, 2003).

Like the other two airports used by the 9/11 hijackers (Newark Liberty International Airport and Washington Dulles International Airport), Boston's Logan International Airport was a "Category X" airport: i.e., among the largest facilities liable to highest threat, and generally subject to greater security requirements. See FAA report, "Civil Aviation Security Reference Handbook," May 1999, pp. 117-118. Though Logan was selected for two of the hijackings (as were both American and United Airlines), we found no evidence that the terrorists targeted particular airports or airlines. Nothing stands out about any of them with respect to the only security layer that was relevant to the actual hijackings: checkpoint screening. See FAA briefing materials, "Assessment and Testing Data for BOS, EWR, and IAD," Oct. 24, 2001. Despite security problems at Logan (see, e.g., two local Fox 25 television investigative reports in February and April 2001, and an email in August 2001 from a former FAA special agent to the agency's leadership regarding his concerns about lax security at the airport), no evidence suggests that such issues entered into the terrorists' targeting: they simply booked heavily fueled east-to-west transcontinental flights of the large Boeing aircraft they trained to fly that were scheduled to take off at nearly the same time. See Matt Carroll, "Fighting Terror Sense of Alarm; Airlines Foiled Police Logan Probe," *Boston Globe*, Oct. 17, 2001, p. B1.

2. CAPPS was an FAA-approved automated system run by the airlines that scored each passenger's profile to identify those who might pose a threat to civil aviation. The system also chose passengers at random to receive additional security scrutiny. Ten out of the 19 hijackers (including 9 out of 10 on the two American Airlines flights) were identified via the CAPPS system. According to the procedures in place on 9/11, in addition to those flagged by the CAPPS algorithm, American's ticket agents were to mark as "selectees" those passengers who did not provide correct responses to the required security questions, failed to show proper identification, or met other criteria. See FAA report, "Air Carrier Standard Security Program," May 2001, pp. 75–76; FAA record of interview, Donna Thompson, Sept. 23, 2001; Chuck Severance interview (Apr. 15, 2004); Jim Dillon interview (Apr. 15, 2004); Diane Graney interview (Apr. 16, 2004). It appears that Atta was selected at random. See Al Hickson briefing (June 8, 2004).

3. The call was placed from a pay phone in Terminal C (between the screening checkpoint and United 175's boarding gate). We presume Shehhi made the call, but we cannot be sure. Logan International Airport site visit (Aug. 15, 2003); see also FBI response to Commission briefing request no. 6, undated (topic 11).

4. Flight 11 pushed back from Gate 32 in Terminal B at 7:40. See AAL response to the Commission's February 3, 2004, requests, Mar. 15, 2004.

5. See UAL letter, "Flight 175-11Sep01 Passenger ACI Check-in History," July 11, 2002. Customer service representative Gail Jawahir recalled that her encounter with the Ghamdis occurred at "shortly before 7 A.M.," and when shown photos of the hijackers, she indicated that Mohand al Shehri resembled one of the two she checked in (suggesting they were Banihammad and Shehri). However, she also recalled that the men had the same last name and had assigned seats on row 9 (i.e., the Ghamdis), and that account has been adopted here. In either case, she almost certainly was dealing with one set of the Flight 175 hijackers. See FBI reports of investigation, interviews of Gail Jawahir, Sept. 21, 2001; Sept. 28, 2001. Even had the hijackers been unable to understand and answer the two standard security questions, the only consequence would have been the screening of their carry-on and checked bags for explosives. See FAA report, "Air Carrier Standard Security Program," May 2001, p. 76.

6. For Flight 11, two checkpoints provided access to the gate. The second was opened at 7:15 A.M. The FAA conducted many screener evaluations between September 11, 1999, and September 11, 2001. At the primary checkpoints, in aggregate, screeners met or exceeded the average for overall, physical search, and X-ray detection, while falling below the norm for metal detection. No FAA Special Assessments (by "red teams") were done at Logan security checkpoints during the two years prior to September 11, 2001. See FAA briefing materials, "Assessment and Testing Data for BOS, EWR, and IAD," Oct. 24, 2001.

7. See Air Transport Association/Regional Airlines Association (ATA/RAA) report, "Air Carriers Checkpoint Operations Guide," Aug. 1999; FAA report, "Air Carrier Standard Security Program," May 2001, appendix VI.

8. Mary Carol Turano interview (Mar. 11, 2004); FBI reports of investigation, interview of Nilda Cora, Oct. 4, 2001; interview of William Thomas, Sept. 14, 2001; interview of Jennifer Gore, Sept. 12, 2001; interview of Claudia Richey, Sept. 15, 2001; interview of Rosarito Rivera, Sept. 25, 2001.

9. See TSA report, "Selectee Status of September 11th Hijackers," undated. For boarding and seating information, see AAL record, SABRE information on Flight 11, Sept. 11, 2001. These boarding times from the American system are approximate only; for Flight 11, they indicated that some passengers "boarded" after the aircraft had pushed back from the gate. See AAL response to the Commission's February 3, 2004, requests, Mar. 15, 2004.

10. See TSA report, "Selectee Status of September 11th Hijackers, "undated; see also UAL letter, "Flight 175-11 Sep01 Passenger ACI Check-in History," July 11, 2002.

11. The Hazmis checked in at 7:29; the airline has not yet been able to confirm the time of Hanjour's check-in. However, it had to have taken place by 7:35, when he appears on the checkpoint videotape. See AAL record, SABRE information for Flight 77, Sept. 11, 2001; AAL response to the Commission's February 3, 2004, requests, Mar. 15, 2004; Metropolitan Washington Airports Authority videotape, Dulles main terminal checkpoints, Sept. 11, 2001.

12. See TSA report, "Selectee Status of September 11th Hijackers," undated; see also FAA report, "Selectee List AALA #77," undated; FBI report of investigation, interview of Vaughn Allex, Sept. 12, 2001; Vaughn Allex interview (July 13, 2004).

13. The FAA conducted many screener evaluations at Dulles between September 11, 1999, and September 11, 2001. While the test results for physical search exceeded the national average, both the metal detector and X-ray results were below average. See FAA briefing materials, "Assessment and Testing Data for BOS, EWR, and IAD," Oct. 24, 2001.

14. Metropolitan Washington Airports Authority videotape, Dulles main terminal checkpoints, Sept. 11, 2001; see also Tim Jackson interview (Apr. 12, 2004).

15. Metropolitan Washington Airports Authority videotape, Dulles main terminal checkpoints, Sept. 11, 2001; see also Tim Jackson interview (Apr. 12, 2004).

16. For investigation findings, see FAA report, "American Airlines Flight #77: Hijacking and Crash into the Pentagon, Sept. 11, 2001," undated. For screener evaluations, see Tim Jackson interview (Apr. 12, 2004).

17. See AAL record, SABRE information for Flight 77, Sept. 11, 2001; AAL response to the Commission's February 3, 2004, requests, Mar. 15, 2004.

18. UAL record, Flight 93 EWR bag loading status, Sept. 11, 2001; UAL record, Flight 93 EWR ACI passenger history, Sept. 11, 2001; UAL record, Flight 93 EWR full bag history, Sept. 11, 2001; TSA report, "Selectee Status of September 11th Hijackers," undated; FBI report, "The Final 24 Hours," Dec. 8, 2003.

19. The FAA conducted many screener evaluations at Newark between September 11, 1999, and September 11, 2001. Detection rates for metal detection, physical searches, and X-rays all met or exceeded the national averages. See FAA briefing materials, "Assessment and Testing Data for BOS, EWR, and IAD," Oct. 24, 2001; see also FAA report, "United Airlines Flight 93, September 11, 2001, Executive Report," Jan. 30, 2002.

20. UAL record, Flight 93 EWR ACI passenger history, Sept. 11, 2001; see also FBI report, "The Final 24 Hours," Dec. 8, 2003.

21.While Flights 11 and 77 were at or slightly above the average number of passengers for the respective flights that summer, Flights 175 and 93 were well below their averages. We found no evidence to indicate that the hijackers manipulated the passenger loads on the aircraft they hijacked. Financial records did not reveal the purchase of any tickets beyond those the hijackers used for themselves. See FBI response to Commission briefing request no. 6, undated (topic 8); AAL report, "Average Load Factor by Day-of-Week," undated (for Flights 11 and 77 from June 11, 2001, to Sept. 9, 2001); AAL response to the Commission's supplemental document requests, Jan. 20, 2004; UAL report, Flight 175 BOS-LAX Load Factors, undated (from June 1, 2001, to Sept. 11, 2001); UAL report, "Explanation of Load Factors," undated.

22. See AAL response to the Commission's February 3, 2004, requests, Mar. 15, 2004; AAL record, Dispatch Environmental Control/Weekly Flight Summary for Flight 11, Sept. 11, 2001; AAL report, "Flight Attendant Jump Seat Locations During Takeoff And Flight Attendant Typical Cabin Positions During Start of Cabin Service," undated; AAL report, "Passenger Name List, Flight 11/September 11," undated.

23. Commission analysis of NTSB and FAA air traffic control and radar data. See AAL record, Dispatch Environmental Control/Weekly Flight Summary for Flight 11, Sept. 11, 2001; NTSB report, "Flight Path Study-American Airlines Flight 11," Feb. 19, 2002; Bill Halleck and Peggy Houck interview (Jan. 8, 2004).The initial service assignments for flight attendants on American 11 would have placed Karen Martin and Bobbi Arestegui in first class; Sara Low and Jean Roger in business class; Dianne Snyder in the midcabin galley; Betty Ong and Amy Sweeney in coach; and Karen Nicosia in the aft galley. Jeffrey Collman would have been assigned to work in coach, but to assist in first class if needed. See AAL report, "Flight Attendant Jump Seat Locations During Takeoff And Flight Attendant Typical Cabin Positions During Start of Cabin Service," undated; Bob Jordan briefing (Nov. 20, 2003).

24. NTSB report, Air Traffic Control Recording-American Airlines Flight 11, Dec. 21, 2001; NTSB report, Air Traffic Control Recording-United Airlines Flight 175, Dec. 21, 2001. Given that the cockpit crew of American 11 had been acknowledging all previous instructions from air traffic control that morning within a matter of seconds, and that when the first reporting of the hijacking was received a short time later (the 8:19 call from Betty Ong) a number of actions had already been taken by the hijackers, it is most likely that the hijacking occurred at 8:14 A.M.

25. An early draft of an executive summary prepared by FAA security staff for the agency's leadership referred to an alleged report of a shooting aboard Flight 11.We believe this report was erroneous for a number of reasons- there is no evidence that the hijackers purchased firearms, use of a gun would be inconsistent with the otherwise common tactics employed by the hijackers, the alleged shooting victim was seated where witness accounts place the stabbing victim (9B), and, most important, neither Betty Ong nor Amy Sweeney, the only two people who communicated to the ground from aboard the aircraft, reported the presence of a gun or a shooting. Both reported knives and stabbings. AAL transcript, telephone call from Betty Ong to Nydia Gonzalez, Sept. 11, 2001; AAL transcript, telephone call from Nydia Gonzalez to Craig Marquis, Sept. 11, 2001; AAL transcript, telephone call from Nancy Wyatt to Ray Howland, Sept. 11, 2001; Michael Woodward interview (Jan. 25, 2004).The General

Accounting Office looked into the gun story and was unable to corroborate it. GAO report, summary of briefing re investigation, Aug. 30, 2002.

26. Craig Marquis interview (Nov. 19, 2003); Michael Woodward interview (Jan. 25, 2004); Jim Dillon interview (Apr. 15, 2004). See also AAL transcript, telephone call from Betty Ong to Nydia Gonzalez, Sept. 11, 2001. At the time of the hijacking, American Airlines flight attendants all carried cockpit keys on their person. See Craig Marquis, Craig Parfitt, Joe Bertapelle, and Mike Mulcahy interview (Nov. 19, 2003).

27. AAL transcript, telephone call from Nydia Gonzalez to Craig Marquis, Sept. 11, 2001; Obituary, "Daniel Lewin," *Washington Post*, Sept. 22, 2001, p. B7.

28. AAL transcript, telephone call from Betty Ong to Nydia Gonzalez, Sept. 11, 2001; AAL transcript, telephone call from Nydia Gonzalez to Craig Marquis, Sept. 11, 2001. Regarding the claim of a bomb, see Michael Woodward interview (Jan. 25, 2004).

29. Calls to American's reservations office are routed to the first open line at one of several facilities, among them the center in Cary, N.C. See Nydia Gonzalez interview (Nov. 19, 2003). On standard emergency training, see FAA report, "Air Carrier Standard Security Program," May 2001, pp. 139j-1390; Don Dillman briefing (Nov. 18, 2003); Bob Jordan briefing (Nov. 20, 2003). The call from Ong was received initially by Vanessa Minter and then taken over by Winston Sadler; realizing the urgency of the situation, he pushed an emergency button that simultaneously initiated a tape recording of the call and sent an alarm notifying Nydia Gonzalez, a supervisor, to pick up on the line. Gonzalez was paged to respond to the alarm and joined the call a short time later. Only the first four minutes of the phone call between Ong and the reservations center (Minter, Sadler, and Gonzalez) was recorded because of the time limit on the recently installed system. See Nydia Gonzalez interview (Nov. 19, 2003); Nydia Gonzalez testimony, Jan. 27, 2004.

30. AAL transcript, telephone call from Betty Ong to Nydia Gonzalez, Sept. 11, 2001.

31. See Nydia Gonzalez interview (Nov. 19, 2003); Craig Marquis interviews (Nov. 19, 2003; Apr. 26, 2004); AAL record, Dispatch Environmental Control/Weekly Flight Summary for Flight 11, Sept. 11, 2001; AAL transcript, telephone call from Bill Halleck to BOS ATC, Sept. 11, 2001. The Air Carrier Standard Security Program required airlines to immediately notify the FAA and FBI upon receiving information that an act or suspected act of airplane piracy was being committed.

32. See FAA recording, Boston Air Route Traffic Control Center, position 46R, at 8:25 A.M.; Air Traffic Control Recording-American Airlines Flight 11, Dec. 21, 2001. Starting at 8:22, Amy Sweeney attempted by airphone to contact the American Airlines flight services office at Logan, which managed the scheduling and operation of flight attendants. Sweeney's first attempt failed, as did a second at 8:24. When she got through to Nunez, the latter thought she had reported her flight number as 12. Michael Woodward, supervisor at the Boston office, hearing that a problem had been reported aboard an American airplane, went to American's gate area at Logan with his colleague Beth Williams. Woodward noted that the morning bank of flights had all departed Boston and the gate area was quiet. He further realized that Flight 12 had not even departed yet, so he and Williams returned to the office to try to clarify the situation. See

FBI report, "American Airlines Airphone Usage," Sept. 20, 2001; Michael Woodward interview (Jan. 25, 2004).The phone call between Sweeney and Woodward lasted about 12 minutes (8:32–8:44) and was not taped. See AAL email, Woodward to Schmidt, "Flight 11 Account of events," Sept. 19, 2001; AAL notes, Michael Woodward handwritten notes, Sept. 11, 2001; FBI report of investigation, interview of Michael Woodward, Sept. 13, 2001; AAL report, interview of Michael Woodward, Sept. 11, 2001; AAL transcript, telephone call from Nancy Wyatt to Ray Howland, Sept. 11, 2001.

33. See AAL transcript, telephone call from Nydia Gonzalez to Craig Marquis, Sept. 11, 2001; NTSB report, "Flight Path Study-American Airlines Flight 11," Feb. 19, 2002; AAL transcript, telephone call from Nydia Gonzalez to Craig Marquis, Sept. 11, 2001; AAL transcript, telephone call from Nancy Wyatt to Ray Howland, Sept. 11, 2001.

34. Michael Woodward interview (Jan. 25, 2004).

35. AAL transcript, telephone call from Nydia Gonzalez to Craig Marquis, Sept. 11, 2001; Michael Woodward interview (Jan. 25, 2004); AAL, Michael Woodward notes, Sept. 11, 2001. Also at this time American Airlines completed its "lockout" procedure for Flight 11, which restricted access to information about a hijacked flight in accordance with the Air Carrier Standard Security program. See FAA report, "Air Carrier Standard Security Program," May 2001, p. 110.

36. AAL transcript, telephone call from Nancy Wyatt to Ray Howland, Sept. 11, 2001; Michael Woodward interview (Jan. 25, 2004).

37. AAL transcript, telephone call from Nydia Gonzalez to Craig Marquis, Sept. 11, 2001.

38. Ibid.; Michael Woodward interview (Jan. 25, 2004).

39. NTSB report, "Flight Path Study-American Airlines Flight 11," Feb. 19, 2002.

40.The 56 passengers represented a load factor of 33.33 percent of the airplane's seating capacity of 168, below the 49.22 percent for Flight 175 on Tuesdays in the three-month period prior to September 11, 2001. See UAL report, Flight 175 BOS-LAX Load Factors, undated (from June 1, 2001, to Sept. 11, 2001). Nine passengers holding reservations for Flight 175 did not show for the flight. They were interviewed and cleared by the FBI. FAA report, "Executive Summary," Sept. 12, 2001; FAA report, "Executive Summary, Chronology of a Multiple Hijacking Crisis, September 11, 2001," Sept. 17, 2001; UAL record, Flight 175 ACARS report, Sept. 11, 2001; UAL record, Flight 175 Flight Data Recap, Sept. 11, 2001.

41. FAA report, "Executive Summary," Sept. 12, 2001; FAA report, "Executive Summary, Chronology of a Multiple Hijacking Crisis, September 11, 2001," Sept. 17, 2001; NTSB report, "Flight Path Study-United Airlines 175," Feb. 19, 2002; NTSB report, Air Traffic Control Recording-United Airlines Flight 175, Dec. 21, 2001. At or around this time, flight attendants Kathryn Laborie and Alfred Marchand would have begun cabin service in first class; with Amy King and Robert Fangman in business class; and with Michael Tarrou, Amy Jarret, and Alicia Titus in economy class. See UAL report, "Flight 175 Flight Attendant Positions/Jumpseats," undated. United flight attendants, unlike those at American, did not carry cockpit keys. Instead, such keys were stowed

in the cabin—on Flight 175, in the overhead bin above seats 1A and 1B in first class. See Don Dillman briefing (Nov. 18, 2003); Bob Jordan briefing (Nov. 20, 2003).

42.Asked by air traffic controllers at 8:37 to look for an American Airlines 767 (Flight 11), United 175 reported spotting the aircraft at 8:38. At 8:41, the flight crew reported having "heard a suspicious transmission" from another aircraft shortly after takeoff, "like someone keyed the mike and said everyone stay in your seats." See NTSB report, Air Traffic Control Recording-United Airlines Flight 175, Dec. 21, 2001.

43. See Marc Policastro interview (Nov. 21, 2003); FBI reports of investigation, interview of Lee Hanson, Sept. 11, 2001; interview of Marc Policastro, Sept. 11, 2001; interview of Louise Sweeney, Sept. 28, 2001; interview of Ronald May, Sept. 11, 2001. On both American 11 and United 175, Boeing 767 double-aisled aircraft, the hijackers arrayed themselves similarly: two seated in first class close to the cockpit door, the pilot hijacker seated close behind them, and at least one other hijacker seated close behind the pilot hijacker. Hijackers were seated next to both the left and right aisles. On American 77 and United 93, Boeing 757 single-aisle aircraft, the pilot hijacker sat in the first row, closest to the cockpit door. See FBI report, "Summary of Penttbom Investigation," Feb. 29, 2004, pp. 67–69; AAL schematics for Flight 11 and Flight 77; UAL schematics for Flight 175 and Flight 93.

44. NTSB report, "Flight Path Study-United Airlines 175," Feb. 19, 2002; NTSB report, Air Traffic Control Recording-United Airlines Flight 175, Dec. 21, 2001.

45. See FBI report of investigation, interview of Lee Hanson, Sept. 11, 2001.

46. Flight crew on board UAL aircraft could contact the United office in San Francisco (SAMC) simply by dialing *349 on an airphone. See FBI report of investigation, interview of David Price, Jan. 24, 2002.At some point before 9:00, SAMC notified United's headquarters of the emergency call from the flight attendant. See Marc Policastro interview (Nov. 21, 2003); FBI report of investigation, interview of Marc Policastro, Sept.11, 2001; Rich Miles interiew (Nov. 21, 2003).

47. NTSB report, "Flight Path Study-United Airlines 175," Feb. 19, 2002.

48. See FBI reports of investigation, interview of Julie Sweeney, Oct. 2, 2001; interview of Louise Sweeney, Sept. 28, 2001.

49. See FBI report of investigation, interview of Lee Hanson, Sept. 11, 2001.

50. See ibid.; interview of Louise Sweeney, Sept. 28, 2001.

51. NTSB report, "Flight Path Study-United Airlines 175," Feb. 19, 2002.

52. AAL report, "Flight Attendant Jump Seat Locations During Takeoff And Flight Attendant Typical Cabin Positions During Start of Cabin Service," undated; AAL email,Young to Clark, "Flight Crews," Sept. 12, 2001; AAL record, Dispatch Environmental Control/Weekly Flight Summary for Flight 11, Sept. 11, 2001.

53. AAL record, System Operations Command Center (SOCC) log, Sept. 11, 2001, p. 2; NTSB report, "Flight Path Study-American Airlines Flight 77," Feb. 19, 2002. Flight attendant Renee May would likely have started working in the first-class galley; Michele Heidenberger would have been in the aft galley; Jennifer

Lewis would have been in first class; and Kenneth Lewis would have been in the main cabin. On cabin service, see AAL report, "Flight Attendant Jump Seat Locations During Takeoff And Flight Attendant Typical Cabin Positions During Start of Cabin Service," undated. For cruising altitude, see NTSB report, "Flight Path Study-American Airlines Flight 77," Feb. 19, 2002. On events in the cabin, see FAA recording, Indianapolis Air Traffic Control Center, position HNN R, Sept. 11, 2001; FBI report of investigation, interview of Theodore Olson, Sept. 11, 2001; FBI report of investigation, interview of Ronald and Nancy May, Sept. 12, 2001; AAL record, Dispatch Environmental Control/Weekly Flight Summary for Flight 11, Sept. 11, 2001.

54. Air traffic control notified American's headquarters of the problem, and the airline began attempts to contact the flight by 8:59 via ACARS. See NTSB report, "Flight Path Study-American Airlines Flight 77," Feb. 19, 2002. On American 11, the transponder signal was turned off at 8:21; on United 175, the code was changed at 8:47; on American 77, the signal was turned off at 8:56; and on United 93, the signal was turned off at 9:41. See FAA report, "Summary of Air Traffic Hijack Events: September 11, 2001," Sept. 17, 2001; Richard Byard interview (Sept. 24, 2003); Linda Povinelli interview (Sept. 24, 2003); see also NTSB report, Air Traffic Control Recording-American Airlines Flight 77, Dec. 21, 2001; AAL record, Dispatch Environmental Control/Weekly Flight Summary for Flight 11, Sept. 11, 2001.

55. Gerard Arpey interview (Jan. 8, 2004); Larry Wansley interview (Jan. 8, 2004); AAL record, System Operations Command Center (SOCC) log, Sept. 11, 2001.

56. FBI report, "American Airlines Airphone Usage," Sept. 20, 2001; FBI report of investigation, interview of Ronald and Nancy May, Sept. 12, 2001.

57. The records available for the phone calls from American 77 do not allow for a determination of which of four "connected calls to unknown numbers" represent the two between Barbara and Ted Olson, although the FBI and DOJ believe that all four represent communications between Barbara Olson and her husband's office (all family members of the Flight 77 passengers and crew were canvassed to see if they had received any phone calls from the hijacked flight, and only Renee May's parents and Ted Olson indicated that they had received such calls). The four calls were at 9:15:34 for 1 minute, 42 seconds; 9:20:15 for 4 minutes, 34 seconds; 9:25:48 for 2 minutes, 34 seconds; and 9:30:56 for 4 minutes, 20 seconds. FBI report, "American Airlines Airphone Usage," Sept. 20, 2001; FBI report of investigation, interview of Theodore Olson, Sept. 11, 2001; FBI report of investigation, interview of Helen Voss, Sept. 14, 2001; AAL response to the Commission's supplemental document request, Jan. 20, 2004.

58. FBI report, "American Airlines Airphone Usage," Sept. 20, 2001; FBI report of investigation, interview of Theodore Olson, Sept. 11, 2001.

59. See FAA report, "Report of Aircraft Accident," Nov. 13, 2001; John Hendershot interview (Dec. 22, 2003); FAA report, "Summary of Air Traffic Hijack Events: September 11, 2001," Sept. 17, 2001; NTSB report, "Flight Path Study-American Airlines Flight 77," Feb. 19, 2002; Commission analysis of radar data.

60. See FAA report, "Summary of Air Traffic Hijack Events: September 11, 2001," Sept. 17, 2001; NTSB report, "Flight Path Study-American Airlines Flight 77," Feb. 19, 2002; FAA report, "Report of Aircraft Accident," Nov. 13, 2001.

61. See NTSB report, "Flight Path Study-American Airlines Flight 77," Feb. 19, 2002;TSA report, "Criminal Acts Against Civil Aviation for 2001," Aug. 20, 2002, p. 41.

62. The flight attendant assignments and seating included Chief Flight Attendant Deborah Welsh (first class, seat J1 at takeoff); Sandra Bradshaw (coach, seat J5);Wanda Green (first class, seat J4); Lorraine Bay (coach, seat J3); and CeeCee Lyles (coach, seat J6). See UAL response to Commission questions for the record, Apr. 5, 2004; FAA report, "Chronology of the September 11 Attacks and Subsequent Events Through October 24, 2001," undated; UAL records, copies of electronic boarding passes for Flight 93, Sept. 11, 2001; Bob Varcadipane interview (May 4, 2004); Newark Tower briefing (May 4, 2004).

63. Although the flight schedule indicates an 8:00 A.M. "departure," this was the time the plane left the gate area. Taxiing from the gate to the runway normally took about 15 minutes. Bob Varcadipane interview (May 4, 2004); Newark Tower briefing (May 4, 2004).

64. Commission analysis of FAA air traffic control data. On the FAA's awareness of multiple hijackings, see AAL transcript, telephone call from Nydia Gonzalez to Craig Marquis, Sept. 11, 2001; Craig Marquis interview (Nov. 19, 2003); AAL record, System Operations Command Center (SOCC) log, Sept. 11, 2001; UAL System Operations Control briefing (Nov. 20, 2003); Rich Miles interview (Nov. 21, 2003); UAL report, "Timeline: Dispatch/SMFDO Activities-Terrorist Crisis," undated.

65. FAA audio file, Boston Center, position 46R, 8:24:38 and 8:24:56; Peter Zalewski interview (Sept. 23, 2003).

66. On September 6, 1970, members of the Popular Front for the Liberation of Palestine hijacked a Pan American Boeing 747, a TWA Boeing 707, and a Swissair DC-8. On September 9, a British airliner was hijacked as well. An attempt to hijack an Israeli airliner was thwarted. The Pan American plane landed in Cairo and was blown up after its passengers were released. The other three aircraft were flown to Dawson Field, near Amman, Jordan; the passengers were held captive, and the planes were destroyed. The international hijacking crisis turned into a civil war, as the Jordanian government used force to restore its control of the country. See FAA report, Civil Aviation Reference Handbook, May 1999, appendix D.

The FAA knew or strongly suspected that Flight 11 was a hijacking 11 minutes after it was taken over; Flight 175, 9 minutes after it was taken over. There is no evidence to indicate that the FAA recognized Flight 77 as a hijacking until it crashed into the Pentagon.

67. FAA audio file, Herndon Command Center, line 5114, 9:07:13; FAA audio file, Herndon Command Center, position 15, 9:19. At 9:07, Boston Air Traffic Control Center recommended to the FAA Command Center that a cockpit warning be sent to the pilots of all commercial aircraft to secure their cockpits. While Boston Center sent out such warnings to the commercial flights in its sector, we could find no evidence that a nationwide warning was issued by the ATC system.

Excerpts From the 9/11 Commission Report

68. Ellen King interview (Apr. 5, 2004). FAA air traffic control tapes indicate that at 9:19 the FAA Air Traffic Control System Command Center in Herndon ordered controllers to send a cockpit warning to Delta 1989 because, like American 11 and United 175, it was a transcontinental flight departing Boston's Logan Airport.

69. For American Airlines' response, see AAL briefing (Apr. 26, 2004). For Ballinger's warnings, see Ed Ballinger interview (Apr. 14, 2004). A companywide order for dispatchers to warn cockpits was not issued until 9:21. See UAL report, "Timeline: Dispatch/SMFDO Activities-Terrorist Crisis," undated. While one of Ballinger's colleagues assisted him, Ballinger remained responsible for multiple flights. See Ed Ballinger interview (Apr. 14, 2004). American Airlines' policy called for the flight dispatcher to manage only the hijacked flight, relieving him of responsibilities for all other flights. On American Airlines' policy, see Craig Marquis, Craig Parfitt, Joe Bertapelle, and Mike Mulcahy interview (Nov. 19, 2003). United Airlines had no such "isolation" policy. UAL System Operations Control briefing (Nov. 20, 2003).

70. On FDR, see NTSB report, "Specialist's Factual Report of Investigation-Digital Flight Data Recorder" for United Airlines Flight 93, Feb. 15, 2002; on CVR, see FBI report, "CVR from UA Flight #93," Dec. 4, 2003; Commission review of Aircraft Communication and Reporting System (ACARS) messages sent to and from Flight 93 (which indicate time of message transmission and receipt); see UAL record, Ed Ballinger ACARS log, Sept. 11, 2001. At 9:22, after learning of the events at the World Trade Center, Melody Homer, the wife of co-pilot Leroy Homer, had an ACARS message sent to her husband in the cockpit asking if he was okay. See UAL record, ACARS message, Sept. 11, 2001.

71. On FDR, see NTSB report, "Specialist's Factual Report of Investigation-Digital Flight Data Recorder" for United Airlines Flight 93, Feb. 15, 2002; on CVR, see FBI report, "CVR from UA Flight #93," Dec. 4, 2003; FAA report, "Summary of Air Traffic Hijack Events: September 11, 2001," Sept. 17, 2001; NTSB report, Air Traffic Control Recording-United Airlines Flight 93, Dec. 21, 2001.

72. The 37 passengers represented a load factor of 20.33 percent of the plane's seating capacity of 182, considerably below the 52.09 percent for Flight 93 on Tuesdays in the three-month period prior to September 11 (June 11-September 4, 2001). See UAL report, Flight 93 EWR-SFO load factors, undated. Five passengers holding reservations for Flight 93 did not show for the flight. All five were interviewed and cleared by the FBI. FBI report, "Flight #93 'No Show' Passengers from 9/11/01," Sept. 18, 2001.

73. INS record, Withdrawal of Application for Admission for Mohamed al Kahtani, Aug. 4, 2001.

74. See FAA regulations, Admission to flight deck, 14 C.F.R. § 121.547 (2001); UAL records, copies of boarding passes for United 93, Sept. 11, 2001. One passenger reported that ten first-class passengers were aboard the flight. If that number is accurate, it would include the four hijackers. FBI report of investigation, interview of Lisa Jefferson, Sept. 11, 2001; UAL record, Flight 93 passenger manifest, Sept. 11, 2001. All but one of the six passengers seated in the first-class cabin communicated with the ground during the flight, and none mentioned anyone from their cabin having gone into the cockpit before the hijacking. Moreover, it is unlikely that the highly regarded and experienced pilot

and co-pilot of Flight 93 would have allowed an observer into the cockpit before or after takeoff who had not obtained the proper permission. See UAL records, personnel files of Flight 93 pilots. For jumpseat information, see UAL record, Weight and Balance Information for Flight 93 and Flight 175, Sept. 11, 2001; AAL records, Dispatch Environmental Control/Weekly Flight Summary for Flight 11 and Flight 77, Sept. 11, 2001.

75. Like Atta on Flight 11, Jarrah apparently did not know how to operate the communication radios; thus his attempts to communicate with the passengers were broadcast on the ATC channel. See FBI report, "CVR from UA Flight #93," Dec. 4, 2003. Also, by 9:32 FAA notified United's headquarters that the flight was not responding to radio calls. According to United, the flight's nonresponse and its turn to the east led the airline to believe by 9:36 that the plane was hijacked. See Rich Miles interview (Nov. 21, 2003); UAL report, "United dispatch SMFDO activities-terrorist crisis," Sept. 11, 2001.

76. In accordance with FAA regulations, United 93's cockpit voice recorder recorded the last 31 minutes of sounds from the cockpit via microphones in the pilots' headsets, as well as in the overhead panel of the flight deck. This is the only recorder from the four hijacked airplanes to survive the impact and ensuing fire. The CVRs and FDRs from American 11 and United 175 were not found, and the CVR from American Flight 77 was badly burned and not recoverable. See FBI report, "CVR from UA Flight #93," Dec. 4, 2003; see also FAA regulations, 14 C.F.R. §§ 25.1457, 91.609, 91.1045, 121.359; Flight 93 CVR data. A transcript of the CVR recording was prepared by the NTSB and the FBI.

77. All calls placed on airphones were from the rear of the aircraft. There was one airphone installed in each row of seats on both sides of the aisle. The airphone system was capable of transmitting only eight calls at any one time. See FBI report of investigation, airphone records for flights UAL 93 and UAL 175 on Sept. 11, 2001, Sept. 18, 2001.

78. FAA audio file, Cleveland Center, position Lorain Radar; Flight 93 CVR data; FBI report, "CVR from UA Flight #93," Dec. 4, 2003.

79. FBI reports of investigation, interviews of recipients of calls from Todd Beamer, Sept. 11, 2001, through June 11, 2002; FBI reports of investigation, interviews of recipients of calls from Sandy Bradshaw, Sept. 11, 2001, through Oct. 4, 2001. Text messages warning the cockpit of Flight 93 were sent to the aircraft by Ed Ballinger at 9:24. See UAL record, Ed Ballinger's ACARS log, Sept. 11, 2001.

80. We have relied mainly on the record of FBI interviews with the people who received calls. The FBI interviews were conducted while memories were still fresh and were less likely to have been affected by reading the accounts of others or hearing stories in the media. In some cases we have conducted our own interviews to supplement or verify the record. See FBI reports of investigation, interviews of recipients of calls from Todd Beamer, Mark Bingham, Sandy Bradshaw, Marion Britton, Thomas Burnett, Joseph DeLuca, Edward Felt, Jeremy Glick, Lauren Grandcolas, Linda Gronlund, CeeCee Lyles, Honor Wainio.

81. FBI reports of investigation, interviews of recipients of calls from Thomas Burnett, Sept. 11, 2001; FBI reports of investigation, interviews of recipients of calls from Marion Britton, Sept. 14, 2001, through Nov. 8, 2001; Lisa Jefferson interview (May 11,

2004); FBI report of investigation, interview of Lisa Jefferson, Sept. 11, 2001; Richard Belme interview (Nov. 21, 2003).

82. See Jere Longman, *Among the Heroes-United Flight 93 and the Passengers and Crew Who Fought Back* (Harper-Collins, 2002), p. 107; Deena Burnett interview (Apr. 26, 2004); FBI reports of investigation, interviews of recipients of calls from Jeremy Glick, Sept. 11, 2001, through Sept. 12, 2001; Lyzbeth Glick interview (Apr. 22, 2004). Experts told us that a gunshot would definitely be audible on the CVR. The FBI found no evidence of a firearm at the crash site of Flight 93. See FBI response to Commission briefing request no. 6, undated (topic 11). The FBI collected 14 knives or portions of knives at the Flight 93 crash site. FBI report, "Knives Found at the UA Flight 93 Crash Site," undated.

83. FBI response to Commission briefing request no. 6, undated (topic 11); FBI reports of investigation, interviews of recipients of calls from Jeremy Glick, Sept. 11, 2001, through Sept. 12, 2001.

84. See FBI reports of investigation, interviews of recipients of calls from United 93.

85. FBI reports of investigation, interviews of recipients of calls from United 93. For quote, see FBI report of investigation, interview of Philip Bradshaw, Sept. 11, 2001; Philip Bradshaw interview (June 15, 2004); Flight 93 FDR and CVR data. At 9:55:11 Jarrah dialed in the VHF Omni-directional Range (VOR) frequency for the VOR navigational aid at Washington Reagan National Airport, further indicating that the attack was planned for the nation's capital.

86. Flight 93 FDR and CVR data.

87. Ibid.

88. Ibid.

89. Ibid. The CVR clearly captured the words of the hijackers, including words in Arabic from the microphone in the pilot headset up to the end of the flight. The hijackers' statements, the clarity of the recording, the position of the microphone in the pilot headset, and the corresponding manipulations of flight controls provide the evidence. The quotes are taken from our listening to the CVR, aided by an Arabic speaker.

Overview of the Enemy

9/11 Commission Staff Statement No. 15

ROOTS OF AL QAEDA

IN THE 1980S a large number of Muslims from the Middle East traveled to Afghanistan to join the Afghan people's war against the Soviet Union, which had invaded in 1979. Usama Bin Ladin was a significant player in this group, then known as the "Afghan Arabs." A multimillionaire from a wealthy Saudi family, Bin Ladin used his personal wealth and connections to rich Arab contributors to facilitate the flow of fighters into Afghanistan.

He provided extensive financing for an entity called the "Bureau of Services" or Maktab al Khidmat. This Bureau operated a recruiting network in Muslim communities throughout the Middle East, Southeast Asia, Western Europe, and the United States. It provided travel funds and guest houses in Pakistan for recruits and volunteers on the road to the Afghan battlefield. Bin Ladin also used his financial network to set up training camps and procure weapons and supplies for Arab fighters. Major Afghan warlords who led forces in the battle against the Soviets also benefited from the use of these camps. Following the defeat of the Soviets in the late 1980s, Bin Ladin formed an organization called "The Foundation," or al Qaeda. Al Qaeda was intended to serve as a foundation upon which to build a global Islamic army.

In 1989, the regime in Sudan, run by a military faction and an Islamic extremist organization called the National Islamic Front, invited Bin Ladin to move there. He sent an advance team to Sudan in 1990 and moved there in mid-1991. Bin Ladin brought resources to Sudan, building roads and helping finance the government's war against separatists in the south. In return, he received permission to establish commercial enterprises and an operational infrastructure to support terrorism.

By 1992, Bin Ladin was focused on attacking the United States. He argued that other extremists, aimed at local rulers or Israel, had not gone far enough; they had not attacked what he called "the head of the snake," the United States. He charged that the United States, in addition to backing Israel, kept in power repressive Arab regimes not true to Islam. He also excoriated the continued presence of U.S. military forces in Saudi Arabia after the Gulf War as a defilement of holy Muslim land.

In Sudan, Bin Ladin built upon the al Qaeda organization he had established back in Afghanistan. Al Qaeda had its own membership roster and a structure of "committees" to guide and oversee such functions as training terrorists, proposing targets, financing operations, and issuing edicts—purportedly grounded in Islamic law—to justify al Qaeda actions.

Included in the structure were:

- *The* Shura *or* Advisory Council, *an inner circle of Bin Ladin's close associates, most of whom had longstanding ties with him going back to the formative days in Afghanistan;*
- *A* Sharia *and Political Committee responsible for issuing fatwas— edicts purporting to be grounded in Islamic Law directing or authorizing certain actions—including deadly attacks;*
- *A Military Committee responsible for proposing targets, gathering ideas for and supporting operations, and managing training camps;*
- *A Finance Committee responsible for fundraising and budgetary support for training camps, housing costs, living expenses, travel, and the movement of money allocated to operations;*
- *A Foreign Purchases Committee responsible for acquiring weapons, explosives, and technical equipment;*
- *A Security Committee responsible for physical protection, intelligence collection and counterintelligence; and*
- *An Information Committee in charge of propaganda.*

This organizational structure should not be read as defining a hierarchical chain of command for specific terrorist operations. It served as a means for coordinating functions and providing material support to operations. But once a specific operation was decided upon it would be assigned to a carefully selected clandestine cell, headed by a senior al Qaeda operative who reported personally to Bin Ladin.

With al Qaeda as its foundation, Bin Ladin sought to build a broader Islamic army that also included terrorist groups from Egypt, Libya, Algeria, Saudi Arabia and Oman, Tunisia, Jordan, Iraq, Lebanon, Morocco, Somalia, and Eritrea. Not all groups from these states agreed to join, but at least one from each did. With a multinational council intended to promote common goals, coordinate targeting, and authorize asset sharing for terrorist operations, this Islamic force represented a new level of collaboration among diverse terrorist groups.

Bin Ladin set up training camps and weapons and supply depots in Sudan. He used them to support al Qaeda and other members of the Islamic army. Bin Ladin's operatives used positions in his businesses as cover to acquire weapons, explosives, and technical equipment such as surveillance devices. To facilitate these activities, Sudanese intelligence officers provided false passports and shipping documents. At this time al Qaeda's operational role was mainly to provide funds, training, and weapons for attacks carried out by allied groups.

Contrary to popular understanding, Bin Ladin did not fund al Qaeda through a personal fortune and a network of businesses. Instead, al Qaeda relied primarily on a fundraising network developed over time. Bin Ladin never received a $300 million inheritance. From about 1970 until approximately 1994, he received about $1 million per year—a significant sum, but hardly a $300 million fortune that could be used to fund a global jihad. According to Saudi officials and representatives of the Bin Ladin family, Bin Ladin was divested of his share of his family's wealth. Bin Ladin owned a number of businesses and other assets in Sudan, although most were small or not economically viable.

LAUNCHING ATTACKS ON THE UNITED STATES

A DECEMBER 1992 explosion outside two hotels in Aden, Yemen—a stopover for U.S. troops en route to Somalia—killed one Australian tourist but no Americans. U.S. intelligence would learn four years later that the attack was carried out by a Yemeni terrorist group whose leader was close to Bin Ladin, and whose members reportedly trained at a Bin Ladin–funded camp in Sudan that was run by a member of the al Qaeda Military Committee.

In October 1993, two Black Hawk helicopters were shot down and 18 U.S. soldiers were killed in Mogadishu, Somalia. U.S. intelligence learned in the ensuing years that Bin Ladin's organization had been heavily engaged in assisting warlords who attacked U.S. forces in Somalia. The head of the al Qaeda Military Committee, from a command center set up in Nairobi, Kenya, reportedly sent scores of trainers into Somalia, including experts in the use of rocket propelled grenades, the same kind of weapon used to shoot down the helicopters. Operatives dispatched to Somalia were told their mission was "to kill U.S. troops, incite violence against U.S. personnel, and undermine the success of the U.S. mission." Sources have described several of these operatives bragging that their work had caused the defeat of the Americans. Bin Ladin and his senior associates touted the subsequent withdrawal of U.S. forces from Somalia in March 1994 as a victory for the mujahidin and a demonstration that the Americans could be forced to retreat.

Two additional attacks on U.S. forces in Saudi Arabia took place during 1995–96 for which the evidence of Bin Ladin's involvement is ambiguous.

On November 13, 1995, a car bomb exploded in Riyadh outside the Office of Program Management of the U.S.-trained Saudi Arabian National Guard. Five Americans and two officials from India were killed. Saudi authorities arrested four suspects, whom they quickly convicted and beheaded. The Saudis televised confessions of three perpetrators indicating that their actions had been influenced by Bin Ladin, but there was no charge that Bin Ladin was directly involved. Later, in a March 1997 CNN interview, Bin Ladin denied responsibility for the attack but said he was sorry he had not been a participant.

By this time U.S. intelligence learned that a year-and-a-half before the bombing of the Saudi National Guard facility, al Qaeda leaders and members of other aligned groups had decided to attack U.S. targets in Saudi Arabia and directed a team to ship explosives there. The shipment was a case study in collaboration: Bin Ladin supplied the money for purchasing the explosives; the Sudanese Ministry of Defense served as the conduit for bringing them into Sudan; they were stored briefly in the warehouse of one of Bin Ladin's business facilities; transported in a Bin Ladin company truck under the cover of Ministry of Defense invoice papers; moved to a warehouse provided by the Ministry of Defense at Port Sudan on the Red Sea; and then transported on a Bin Ladin–owned boat to Islamic army operatives residing in Yemen. From there they were moved by land to the eastern part of Saudi Arabia. Bin Ladin and his organization's role in this attack remains unclear. The attack, however, was consistent with the described purpose of the shipment.

On June 26, 1996, an explosion ripped through a building in the Khobar Towers apartment complex housing U.S. Air Force personnel in Dhahran, Saudi Arabia. Nineteen Americans were killed and 372 others were injured. Subsequent investigation concluded that the attack had been carried out by a Saudi Shia Hezbollah group with assistance from Iran. Intelligence obtained shortly after the bombing, however, also supported suspicions of Bin Ladin's involvement. There were reports in the months preceding the attack that Bin Ladin was seeking to facilitate a shipment of explosives, to Saudi Arabia. On the day of the attack, Bin Ladin was congratulated by other members of the Islamic army.

In light of the historical animosity between Shia and Sunni Muslims, the confirmation of the Hezbollah role in the attack led many to conclude that Bin Ladin's Sunni-populated organization would not have been involved. Later intelligence, however, showed far greater potential for collaboration between Hezbollah and al Qaeda than many had previously thought. A few years before the attack, Bin Ladin's representatives and Iranian officials had discussed putting aside Shia-Sunni divisions to cooperate against the common enemy. A small group of al Qaeda operatives subsequently traveled to Iran and Hezbollah camps in Lebanon for training in explosives, intelligence, and security. Bin Laden reportedly showed particular interest in Hezbollah's truck bombing tactics in Lebanon in 1983 that had killed 241 U.S. Marines. We have seen strong but indirect evidence that his organization did in fact play some as yet unknown role in the Khobar attack.

Bin Ladin also explored possible cooperation with Iraq during his time in Sudan, despite his opposition to Hussein's secular regime. Bin Ladin had in fact at one time sponsored anti-Saddam Islamists in Iraqi Kurdistan. The Sudanese, to protect their own ties with Iraq, reportedly persuaded Bin Ladin to cease this support and arranged for contacts between Iraq and al Qaeda. A senior Iraqi intelligence officer reportedly made three visits to Sudan, finally meeting Bin Ladin in 1994. Bin Ladin is said to have requested space to establish training camps, as well as assistance in procuring weapons, but Iraq apparently never responded. There have been reports that contacts between Iraq and al Qaeda also occurred after Bin Ladin had returned to Afghanistan, but they do not appear to have resulted in a collaborative relationship. Two senior Bin Ladin associates have adamantly denied that any ties existed between al Qaeda and Iraq. We have no credible evidence that Iraq and al Qaeda cooperated on attacks against the United States.

Whether Bin Ladin and his organization had roles in the 1993 attack on the World Trade Center and the thwarted Manila plot to blow up a dozen U.S. commercial aircraft in 1995 remains a matter of substantial uncertainty.

Ramzi Yousef, who was a lead operative in both plots, trained in camps in Afghanistan that were funded by Bin Ladin and used to train many al Qaeda operatives. Whether he was then or later became a member of al Qaeda remains a matter of debate, but he was at a minimum part of a loose network of extremist Sunni Islamists who, like Bin Ladin, began to focus their rage on the United States. Khalid Sheikh Mohammed, who provided some funding for Yousef in the 1993 WTC attack and was his operational partner in the Manila plot, later did join al Qaeda and masterminded the al Qaeda 9/11 attack. He was not, however, an al Qaeda member at the time of the Manila plot. A number of other individuals connected to the 1993 and 1995 plots or to some of the plotters either were or later became associates of Bin Ladin. We have no conclusive evidence, however, that at the time of the plots any of them was operating under Bin Ladin's direction.

What is clear is that these plots were major benchmarks in the evolving Islamist threat to the United States and foreshadowed later attacks that were indisputably carried out by al Qaeda under Bin Ladin's direction. Like the later attacks, they were aimed at demolishing symbols of American power and killing enormous numbers of Americans. Like Bin Ladin, Yousef was willing to employ any means to achieve these ends, and contemplated use of non-conventional weapons. In one of his television interviews Bin Ladin characterized Ramzi Yousef as a "symbol and a teacher" that would drive Muslims suffering from U.S. policy to "transfer the battle into the United States."

In May 1996, Bin Ladin left Sudan and moved back to Afghanistan. His departure resulted from a combination of pressures from the United States, other western governments, and Egypt, Saudi Arabia, and Libya, all three of which faced indigenous terrorist groups supported by Bin Ladin. The pressure on Sudan intensified in April 1996 when the UN sanctioned Sudan for harboring individuals from the group that had attempted to assassinate Egyptian President Mubarak in June 1995.

At the time of Bin Ladin's move to Afghanistan, the U.S. intelligence community had uncovered many details of his financial and business structures and their use to support terrorist groups. It was not until later in 1996, however, after he was back in Afghanistan, that new sources disclosed the nature of his organizational structure, his commitment to attacking the United States, and the involvement of his organization in attacks that had already been carried out.

CHANGING FORTUNES IN AFGHANISTAN

BIN LADIN'S DEPARTURE from Sudan marked a setback for him. The Saudi government had frozen his assets three years earlier, and the Sudanese government expropriated his assets there after he left Sudan. The financial stresses contributed to strained relations with some of his associates, who used the move back to Afghanistan as an occasion to break from al Qaeda.

There were, nonetheless, some benefits to the move. In an effort to reduce external pressures, Sudan had made some efforts to keep Bin Ladin under control and prohibited him from making public diatribes. Afghanistan's lack of a central government gave him greater latitude to promote his own agenda. Moreover, al Qaeda had never entirely left the region: even when headquartered in Sudan, it had used Pakistan and Afghanistan as a regional base and training center supporting Islamic insurgencies in Tajikistan, Kashmir, and Chechnya.

In August 1996, Bin Ladin made public his war against the United States. In his "Declaration of Holy War on the Americans Occupying the Country of the Two Sacred Places" (Mecca and Medina in Saudi Arabia), Bin Ladin called on Muslims worldwide to put aside their differences and join in deadly attacks against U.S. forces to compel their withdrawal from the Arabian Peninsula.

A month after this declaration, the Taliban, an Afghan faction supported by Pakistan, seized control of Kabul, the nation's capital. Bin Ladin began cementing his ties with the Taliban, and they soon forged a close alliance. The Taliban paid a great price for this alliance in the form of outside pressure, isolation, UN sanctions, and, after 9/11, the destruction of its regime. But prior to 9/11, the Taliban also benefited from its relationship with al Qaeda: Bin Ladin provided significant financial support to the Taliban, and supplied hundreds, if not thousands, of fighters to support the Taliban in its ongoing war against other factions in northern Afghanistan. From al Qaeda's perspective, the alliance provided a sanctuary in which to train and indoctrinate recruits, import weapons, forge ties with other jihad groups and leaders, and plan terrorist operations. Al Qaeda fighters could travel freely within the country; enter and exit without visas or any immigration procedures; and enjoy the use of official Afghan Ministry of Defense license plates. Al Qaeda also used the Afghan state-owned Ariana Airlines to courier money into the country.

There were also ideological ties. Both the Taliban and Bin Ladin espoused the vision of a pure Islamic state. Bin Ladin reportedly swore an oath of loyalty to Taliban leader Mullah Omar. Relations between Bin Ladin and the Taliban leadership were sometimes tense, and some Taliban leaders opposed the al Qaeda presence. In the end, however, Mullah Omar never broke with Bin Ladin and al Qaeda.

Similarly, Pakistan did not break with the Taliban until after 9/11, although it was well aware that the Taliban was harboring Bin Ladin. The Taliban's ability to provide Bin Ladin a haven in the face of international pressure and UN sanctions was significantly facilitated by Pakistani support. Pakistan benefited from the Taliban–al Qaeda relationship, as Bin Ladin's camps trained and equipped fighters for Pakistan's ongoing struggle with India over Kashmir.

By early 1998, Bin Ladin was also in the early stages of what would become a merger of his al Qaeda and another major terrorist group, the Egyptian Islamic Jihad. On February 23, 1998, Bin Ladin and the leader of the Egyptian Islamic Jihad, Ayman Zawahiri, published a *fatwa* that announced a "ruling to kill the Americans and their allies." It was also signed by the heads of three other groups, but their signatures were more a matter of show than substance. Unlike earlier statements, this *fatwa* explicitly instructed followers to kill "civilians and military." The decree said this ruling was "an individual duty for every Muslim who can do it in any country in which it is possible to do it."

NEW ATTACKS ON THE UNITED STATES

ON AUGUST 7, 1998 nearly simultaneous truck bombs ravaged the U.S. embassies in the East African capitals of Nairobi, Kenya and Dar es Salaam, Tanzania. The Nairobi embassy was destroyed, and 213 people were killed, including 12 Americans. About 5,000 people were injured. In Dar es Salaam 11 more were killed, none of them American, and 85 were injured.

U.S. intelligence learned a few months later that the targeting of the U.S. embassy in Nairobi began in late 1993. It was one of more than a dozen potential targets analyzed by a team residing with the same Nairobi cell used to provide assistance to the Somalis. In January 1994, al Qaeda leaders concluded that the U.S. embassy in Nairobi would be easy to attack. Preparations for the attack did not begin in earnest until late spring 1998, and the bombs were only assembled a few days before the attacks. By the night before the embassy bombing, all al Qaeda members except the suicide squads and a few people assigned to clean up the evidence trail had left East

Africa. Bin Ladin and other al Qaeda leaders in Afghanistan had also left for the countryside in expectation of U.S. retaliation.

The attacks on the U.S. embassies in East Africa in the summer of 1998 demonstrated a new operational form—they were planned, directed, and executed by al Qaeda, under the direct supervision of Bin Ladin and his chief aides.

On October 12, 2000, an explosives-laden boat tore through the side of the *U.S.S. Cole* anchored in Aden, Yemen. Seventeen members of the *Cole* crew were killed, and another 39 were wounded. In the course of the ensuing investigation, U.S. officials learned that an earlier attempt to attack a U.S. warship had been made in January 2000, aimed at the *U.S.S. The Sullivans*, but had failed because the boat was overloaded with explosives and sank. The boat was salvaged, a new martyr crew was selected, and the attack was successfully executed ten months later.

The operational commander of the attack was Abd al-Rahim al-Nashiri, who had previously assisted one of the East African embassy bombers. He had arrived in Yemen in late 1999 to supervise the purchase of the boat used in the attack, and to direct the casing and execution of the attacks. Nashiri was assisted by an al Qaeda member close to Bin Ladin, Tawfiq bin Attash ("Khallad"), who supplied the explosives used in the attack.

This attack followed the operational pattern demonstrated in the East African embassy bombings—it was directed by key al Qaeda operatives, using equipment and explosives purchased with al Qaeda funds, and executed by members of al Qaeda willing to be martyrs for the cause. By mid-November 2000, U.S. investigators were aware of the roles Nashiri and Khallad had played in the attack, and that they were senior al Qaeda operatives. The one part that could not be ascertained at the time was whether the attack had been carried out under direct orders from Bin Ladin himself. This could not be confirmed until Nashiri and Khallad were captured in November 2002 and April 2003, respectively.

At the same time, however, two disrupted Millennium plots demonstrate that Bin Ladin remained willing to provide support to attacks initiated by more independent actors. Neither intended Millennium attack was a traditional al Qaeda operation: rather, both were planned and orchestrated by independent extremist groups which received training and assistance from al Qaeda–affiliated figures. One was a plot to destroy hotels and tourist sites in Amman, Jordan. It was planned and carried out by a Palestinian radical and his partner, an American citizen, who sought to kill Americans. The other was the attempted bombing of Los Angeles International Airport. It was orchestrated by Ahmed Ressam, who conceived and prepared for the attack on his own. Ressam commented after his arrest that he had offered to let Bin Ladin claim credit for the attack, in return for providing Ressam future funding. Both Ressam and the Jordanian cell took what they needed from al Qaeda–associated camps and personnel, but did not follow the traditional al Qaeda top-down planning and approval model.

TERRORIST TRAINING CAMPS

MANY OF THE OPERATIVES in the African Embassy and *Cole* attacks attended training camps in Afghanistan, as did all 19 of the 9/11 hijackers. There was a mutually reinforcing relationship between the camps and terrorist operations: the camps provided operatives for terrorist attacks, and successful attacks boosted camp recruitment and attendance. The training at al Qaeda and associated camps was multifaceted in nature. A worldwide jihad needed terrorists who could bomb embassies or hijack airliners, but it also needed foot soldiers for the Taliban in its war against the Northern Alliance, and guerrillas who could shoot down Russian helicopters in Chechnya or ambush Indian units in Kashmir. Thus, most recruits received training that was primarily geared toward conventional warfare. Terrorist training was provided mostly to the best and most ardent recruits.

The quality of the training provided at al Qaeda and other jihadist camps was apparently quite good. There was coordination with regard to curriculum, and great emphasis on ideological and religious indoctrination. Instruction underscored that the United States and Israel were evil, and that the rulers of Arab countries were illegitimate.

The camps created a climate in which trainees and other personnel were free to think creatively about ways to commit mass murder. According to a senior al Qaeda associate, various ideas were floated by mujahidin in Afghanistan: taking over a launcher and forcing Russian scientists to fire a nuclear missile at the United States; mounting mustard gas or cyanide attacks against Jewish areas in Iran; dispensing poison gas into the air conditioning system of a targeted building; and, last but not least, hijacking an aircraft and crashing it into an airport terminal or nearby city.

Trainees in the camps did not focus solely on causing the deaths of enemies. Bin Ladin portrayed "martyrdom" in the service of jihad as a highly desirable fate, and many recruits were eager to go on suicide missions.

As time passed and al Qaeda repeatedly and successfully hit U.S. targets, Bin Ladin became a legendary figure among jihadists both inside and outside of Afghanistan. He lectured at the camps. His perceived stature and charisma reinforced the zeal of the trainees. Bin Ladin also personally evaluated trainees' suitability for terrorist operations. The camps were able to operate only because of the worldwide network of recruiters, travel facilitators, and document forgers who vetted would-be trainees and helped them get in and out of Afghanistan. There are strong indications that elements of both the Pakistani and Iranian governments frequently turned a blind eye to this transit through their respective countries.

We can conservatively say that thousands of men, perhaps as many as 20,000, trained in Bin Ladin–supported camps in Afghanistan between his May 1996 return and September 11, 2001. Of those, only a small percentage went on to receive advanced terrorist training.

FUNDING AL QAEDA IN AFGHANISTAN

AFTER ESTABLISHING ITSELF in Afghanistan, al Qaeda relied on well-placed financial facilitators and diversions of funds from Islamic charities. The financial facilitators raised money from witting and unwitting donors, primarily in the Gulf countries, and particularly in Saudi Arabia. The facilitators also appeared to rely heavily on certain imams at mosques, also primarily in the Gulf countries, who were willing to divert mandatory charitable donations known as *zakat*. Al Qaeda also collected money from employees of corrupted charities.

Operatives either penetrated specific foreign branch offices of large, international charities, particularly those with lax external oversight and ineffective internal controls, or controlled entire smaller charities, including access to their bank accounts.

There is no convincing evidence that any government financially supported al Qaeda before 9/11 (other than limited support provided by the Taliban after Bin Ladin first arrived in Afghanistan). Some governments may have turned a blind eye to al Qaeda's fundraising activities. Saudi Arabia has long been considered the primary source of al Qaeda funding, but we found no evidence that the Saudi government as an institution or senior officials within the Saudi government funded al Qaeda. Still, al Qaeda found fertile fundraising ground in the Kingdom, where extreme religious views are common and charitable giving is essential to the culture and, until recently, subject to very limited oversight. The United States has never been a primary source of al Qaeda funding, although some funds raised in the United States likely made their way to al Qaeda. No persuasive evidence exists that al Qaeda relied on the drug trade as an important source of revenue, or funded itself through trafficking in diamonds from African states engaged in civil wars.

After raising money, al Qaeda frequently moved its money by *hawala*, an informal and ancient trust-based system for transferring funds. Al Qaeda also used couriers as a secure, albeit slower, way to move funds. Bin Ladin relied on the established *hawala* networks operating in Pakistan, the United Arab Emirates, and throughout the Middle East to transfer funds efficiently. *Hawaladars* associated with al Qaeda may have used banks to move and store money, as did various al Qaeda fundraisers and operatives outside of Afghanistan, but there is little evidence that Bin Ladin or his core al Qaeda members used banks during this period.

Al Qaeda's money was distributed as quickly as it was raised—what was made was spent. The CIA estimates that al Qaeda spent $30 million annually, including paying for terrorist operations, maintaining terrorist training camps, paying salaries to jihadists, contributing to the Taliban, funding fighters in Afghanistan, and sporadically contributing to related terrorist organizations. The largest expense was payments to the Taliban, which totaled an estimated $10–20 million per year. Actual terrorist operations were relatively cheap. Although there is evidence that al Qaeda experienced funding shortfalls as part of the cyclical fundraising process (with more money coming during the holy month of Ramadan), we are not aware of any evidence indicating that terrorist acts were interrupted as a result.

AL QAEDA TODAY

SINCE THE SEPTEMBER 11 attacks and the defeat of the Taliban, al Qaeda's funding has decreased significantly. The arrests or deaths of several important financial facilitators have decreased the amount of money al Qaeda has raised and increased the costs and difficulty of raising and moving that money. Some entirely corrupt charities are now out of business, with many of their principals killed or captured, although some charities may still be providing support to al Qaeda. Moreover, it appears that the al Qaeda attacks within Saudi Arabia in May and November of 2003 have reduced—perhaps drastically—al Qaeda's ability to raise funds from Saudi sources. Both an increase in Saudi enforcement and a more negative perception of al Qaeda by potential donors have cut its income.

At the same time, al Qaeda's expenditures have decreased as well, largely because it no longer provides substantial funding to the Taliban or runs a network of training camps in Afghanistan. Despite the apparent reduction in overall funding, it remains relatively easy for al Qaeda to find the relatively small sums required to fund terrorist operations.

Prior to 9/11, al Qaeda was a centralized organization which used Afghanistan as a war room to strategize, plan attacks, and dispatch operatives worldwide. Bin Ladin approved all al Qaeda operations, often selecting the targets and operatives. After al Qaeda lost Afghanistan after 9/11, it fundamentally changed. The organization is far more decentralized. Bin Ladin's seclusion forced operational commanders and cell leaders to assume greater authority; they are now making the command decisions previously made by him.

Bin Ladin continues to inspire many of the operatives he trained and dispersed, as well as smaller Islamic extremist groups and individual fighters who share his ideology. As a result, al Qaeda today is more a loose collection of regional networks with a greatly weakened central organization. It pushes these networks to carry out attacks, and assists them by providing guidance, funding, and training in skills such as bomb-making or urban combat.

Al Qaeda remains extremely interested in conducting chemical, biological, radiological, or nuclear attacks. In 1994, al Qaeda operatives attempted to purchase uranium for $1.5 million; the uranium proved to be fake. Though this attempt failed, al Qaeda continues to pursue its strategic objective of obtaining a nuclear weapon. Likewise, it remains interested in using a radiological dispersal device or "dirty bomb," a conventional explosive designed to spread radioactive material. Documents found in al Qaeda facilities contain accurate information on the usage and impact of such weapons. Al Qaeda had an ambitious biological weapons program and was making advances in its ability to produce anthrax prior to September 11. According to Director of Central Intelligence George Tenet, al Qaeda's ability to conduct an anthrax attack is one of the most immediate threats the United States is likely to face. Similarly, al Qaeda may seek to conduct a chemical attack by using widely-available industrial chemicals, or by attacking a chemical plant or a shipment of hazardous materials.

The Intelligence Community expects that the trend toward attacks intended to cause ever higher casualties will continue.

Al Qaeda and other extremist groups will likely continue to exploit leaks of national security information in the media, open-source information on techniques such as mixing explosives, and advances in electronics. It may modify traditional tactics in order to prevent detection or interdiction by counterterrorist forces. Regardless of the tactic, al Qaeda is actively striving to attack the United States and inflict mass casualties.

Outline of the 9/11 Plot

9/11 Commission Staff Statement No. 16

ORIGINS OF THE 9/11 ATTACKS

THE IDEA for the September 11 attacks appears to have originated with a veteran jihadist named Khalid Sheikh Mohammed (KSM). A Kuwaiti from the Baluchistan region of Pakistan, KSM grew up in a religious family and claims to have joined the Muslim Brotherhood at the age of 16. After attending college in the United States, he went to Afghanistan to participate in the anti-Soviet jihad. Following the war, he helped run a non-governmental organization in Pakistan assisting the Afghan mujahidin.

KSM first came to the attention of U.S. authorities as a result of the terrorist activity of his nephew Ramzi Yousef, the mastermind of the 1993 World Trade Center bombing. KSM provided a small amount of funding for that attack. The following year, he joined Yousef in the Philippines to plan what would become known as the "Bojinka" operation, the intended bombing of 12 U.S. commercial jets over the Pacific in a two-day period. That plot unraveled, however, when the Philippine authorities discovered Yousef's bomb-making equipment in Manila in January 1995. During the course of 1995, Yousef and two of his co-conspirators in the Bojinka plot were arrested overseas and were brought to the United States for trial, but KSM managed to elude capture following his January 1996 indictment for his role in the plot.

By the middle of 1996, according to his account, KSM was back in Afghanistan. He had met Usama Bin Ladin there in the 1980s. Now, in mid-1996, KSM sought to renew that acquaintance, at a point when Bin Ladin had just moved to Afghanistan from the

Sudan. At a meeting with Bin Ladin and Mohamed Atef, al Qaeda's Chief of Operations, KSM presented several ideas for attacks against the United States. One of the operations he pitched, according to KSM, was a scaled-up version of what would become the attacks of September 11. Bin Ladin listened, but did not yet commit himself.

BIN LADIN APPROVES THE PLAN

ACCORDING TO KSM, the 1998 East Africa embassy bombings demonstrated to him that Bin Ladin was willing to attack the United States. In early 1999, Bin Ladin summoned KSM to Kandahar to tell him that his proposal to use aircraft as weapons now had al Qaeda's full support. KSM met again with Bin Ladin and Atef at Kandahar in the spring of 1999 to develop an initial list of targets. The list included the White House and the Pentagon, which Bin Ladin wanted; the U.S. Capitol; and the World Trade Center, a target favored by KSM.

Bin Ladin quickly provided KSM with four potential suicide operatives: Nawaf al Hazmi, Khalid al Mihdhar, Walid Muhammad Salih bin Attash, also known as Khallad, and Abu Bara al Taizi. Hazmi and Mihdhar were both Saudi nationals—although Mihdhar was actually of Yemeni origin—and experienced mujahidin, having fought in Bosnia together. They were so eager to participate in attacks against the United States that they already held U.S. visas. Khallad and Abu Bara, being Yemeni nationals, would have trouble getting U.S. visas compared to Saudis. Therefore, KSM decided to split the operation into two parts. Hazmi and Mihdhar would go to the United States, and the Yemeni operatives would go to Southeast Asia to carry out a smaller version of the Bojinka plot.

In the fall of 1999, training for the attacks began. Hazmi, Mihdhar, Khallad, and Abu Bara participated in an elite training course at the Mes Aynak camp in Afghanistan. Afterward, KSM taught three of these operatives basic English words and phrases and showed them how to read a phone book, make travel reservations, use the Internet, and encode communications. They also used flight simulator computer games and analyzed airline schedules to figure out flights that would be in the air at the same time.

KUALA LUMPUR

FOLLOWING THE TRAINING, all four operatives for the operation traveled to Kuala Lumpur, Malaysia. Khallad and Abu Bara were directed to study airport security and conduct surveillance on U.S. carriers, and Hazmi and Mihdhar were to switch passports in Kuala Lumpur before going on to the United States. Khallad—who traveled to Kuala Lumpur ahead of Hazmi and Mihdhar—attended a prosthesis clinic in Kuala Lumpur. He then flew to Hong Kong aboard a U.S. airliner and was able to carry a box cutter, concealed in his toiletries bag, onto the flight. He returned to Kuala Lumpur, where Hazmi and Mihdhar arrived during the first week in January 2000. The al Qaeda operatives were hosted in Kuala Lumpur by Jemaah Islamiah members Hambali and Yazid Sufaat, among others. When Khallad headed next to a meeting in Bangkok, Hazmi and Mihdhar decided to join him to enhance their cover as tourists.

Khallad had his meetings in Bangkok and returned to Kandahar. Khallad and Abu Bara would not take part in a planes operation; in the spring of 2000, Bin Ladin cancelled the Southeast Asia part of the operation because it was too difficult to coordinate with the U.S. part. Hazmi and Mihdhar spent a few days in Bangkok and then headed for Los Angeles, where they would become the first 9/11 operatives to enter the United States on January 15, 2000.

FOUR STUDENTS IN HAMBURG

WHILE KSM WAS deploying his initial operatives for the 9/11 attacks to Kuala Lumpur, a group of four Western-educated men who would prove ideal for the attacks were making their way to the al Qaeda camps in Afghanistan. The four were Mohamed Atta, Marwan al Shehhi, Ziad Jarrah, and Ramzi Binalshibh. Atta, Shehhi, and Jarrah would become pilots for the 9/11 attacks, while Binalshibh would act as a key coordinator for the plot.

Atta, the oldest of the group, was born in Egypt in 1968 and moved to Germany to study in 1992 after graduating from Cairo University. Shehhi was from the United Arab Emirates (UAE) and entered Germany in 1996 through a UAE military scholarship program. Jarrah was from a wealthy family in Lebanon and went to Germany after high school to study at the University of Greifswald. Finally, Binalshibh, a Yemeni, arrived in Germany in 1995.

Atta and Binalshibh were the first of the four to meet, at a mosque in Hamburg in 1995. In 1998, Atta and Binalshibh moved into a Hamburg apartment with Shehhi, who had been studying in Bonn; after several months, the trio moved to 54 Marienstrasse, also in Hamburg. How Shehhi came to know Atta and Binalshibh is not clear. It is also unknown just how and when Jarrah, who was living in Greifswald, first encountered the group, but we do know that he moved to Hamburg in late 1997.

By the time Atta, Shehhi, and Binalshibh were living together in Hamburg, they and Jarrah were well known among Muslims in Hamburg and, with a few other like-minded students, were holding extremely anti-American discussions. Atta, the leader of the group, denounced what he described as a global Jewish movement centered in New York City which, he claimed, controlled the financial world and the media. As time passed, the group became more extreme and secretive. According to Binalshibh, by sometime in 1999, the four had decided to act on their beliefs and to pursue jihad against the Russians in Chechnya.

THE HAMBURG STUDENTS JOIN AL QAEDA

As BINALSHIBH is the only one of the four still alive, he is the primary source for an explanation of how the Hamburg group was recruited into the 9/11 plot. Binalshibh claims that during 1999, he and Shehhi had a chance meeting with an individual to whom they expressed an interest in joining the fighting in Chechnya. They were referred to another individual named Mohamedou Ould Slahi—an al Qaeda member living in Germany. He advised them that it was difficult to get to Chechnya and that they should go to Afghanistan first. Following Slahi's advice, between November and December of 1999, Atta, Jarrah, Shehhi, and Binalshibh went to Afghanistan, traveling separately.

When Binalshibh reached the camps in Kandahar, he found that Atta and Jarrah had already pledged *bayat*, or allegiance, to Bin Ladin, and that Shehhi had already left for the UAE to prepare for the anti-U.S. mission the group had been assigned. Binalshibh followed suit, pledging *bayat* to Bin Ladin in a private meeting. Binalshibh, Atta, and Jarrah met with Bin Ladin's deputy, Mohamed Atef, who directed them to return to Germany and enroll in flight training. Atta was chosen as the emir, or leader, of the mission. He met with Bin Ladin to discuss the targets: the World Trade Center, which represented the U.S. economy; the Pentagon, a symbol of the U.S. military; and the U.S. Capitol, the perceived source of U.S. policy in support of Israel. The White House was also on the list, as Bin Ladin considered it a political symbol and wanted to attack it as well. KSM and Binalshibh have both stated that, in early 2000, Shehhi, Atta, and Binalshibh met with KSM in Karachi for training that included learning about life in the United States and how to read airline schedules.

By early March 2000, all four new al Qaeda recruits were back in Germany. They began researching flight schools in Europe, but quickly found that training in the United States would be cheaper and faster. Atta, Shehhi, and Jarrah obtained U.S. visas, but Binalshibh—the sole Yemeni in the group—was rejected repeatedly. In the spring of 2000, Atta, Shehhi, and Jarrah prepared to travel to the United States to begin flight training. Binalshibh would remain behind and help coordinate the operation, serving as a link between KSM and Atta.

CALIFORNIA

WHILE THE HAMBURG operatives were just joining the 9/11 plot, Nawaf al Hazmi and Khalid al Mihdhar were already living in the United States, having arrived in Los Angeles on January 15, 2000. It has not been established where they stayed during the first two weeks after their arrival. They appear to have frequented the King Fahd Mosque in Culver City, possibly staying in an apartment nearby. Much remains unknown about their activities and associates while in Los Angeles and our investigation of this period of the conspiracy is continuing.

KSM contends that he directed the two to settle in San Diego after learning from a phone book about language and flight schools there. Recognizing that neither Hazmi nor Mihdhar spoke English or was familiar with Western culture, KSM instructed these operatives to seek help from the local Muslim community.

As of February 1, 2000, Hazmi and Mihdhar were still in Los Angeles, however. That day, the two al Qaeda operatives met a Saudi named Omar al Bayoumi. Bayoumi told them that he lived in San Diego and could help them if they decided to move there. Within a few days, Hazmi and Mihdhar traveled to San Diego. They found Bayoumi at the Islamic Center and took him up on his offer to help them find an apartment. On February 5, Hazmi and Mihdhar moved into a unit they rented in Bayoumi's apartment complex in San Diego. While it is clear that Bayoumi helped them settle in San Diego, we have not uncovered evidence that he did so knowing that they were terrorists, or that he believed in violent extremism.

Hazmi and Mihdhar also received assistance from various other individuals in the Muslim community in San Diego. Several of their new friends were foreign students in their early 20's who worshipped at the Rabat Mosque in La Mesa. One of them, an illegal immigrant named Mohdar Abdullah, became particularly close to Hazmi and Mihdhar and helped them obtain driver's licenses and enroll in schools. When interviewed by the FBI after 9/11, Abdullah denied knowing about the operatives' terrorist plans. Before his recent deportation to Yemen, however, Abdullah allegedly made various claims to individuals incarcerated with him about having advance knowledge of the operatives' 9/11 mission, going so far as to tell one inmate that he had received instructions to pick up the operatives at Los Angeles International Airport, and had driven them from Los Angeles to San Diego. Abdullah and others in his circle appear to have held extremist sympathies.

While in San Diego, Hazmi and Mihdhar also established a relationship with Anwar Aulaqi, an imam at the Rabat Mosque. Aulaqi reappears in our story later. Another San Diego resident rented Hazmi and Mihdhar a room in his house. An apparently law abiding citizen with close contacts among local police and FBI personnel, the operatives' housemate saw nothing in their behavior to arouse suspicion. Nor did his law enforcement contacts ask him for information about his tenants.

Hazmi and Mihdhar were supposed to learn English and then enroll in flight schools, but they made only cursory attempts at both. Mihdhar paid for an English class that Hazmi took for about a month. The two al Qaeda operatives also took a few short flying lessons. According to their flight instructors, they were interested in learning to fly jets and did not realize that they had to start training on small planes. In June 2000, Mihdhar abruptly returned to his family in Yemen, apparently without permission. KSM was very displeased and wanted to remove him from the operation, but Bin Ladin interceded, and Mihdhar remained part of the plot.

THE HAMBURG GROUP ARRIVES IN THE UNITED STATES

ON THE EAST COAST, in May and June 2000, the three operatives from Hamburg who had succeeded in obtaining visas began arriving in the United States. Marwan al Shehhi arrived first, on May 29, 2000, at Newark Airport in New Jersey. Mohamed Atta arrived there five days later, on June 3. He and Shehhi had not yet decided where they would train. They directed inquiries to flight schools in New Hampshire and New Jersey, and, after spending about a month in New York City, visited the Airman Flight School in Norman, Oklahoma, where Zacarias Moussaoui would enroll the following February. For some reason, Atta and Shehhi decided not to enroll there. Instead, they went to Venice, Florida, where Ziad Jarrah had already started his training at Florida Flight Training Center, having arrived in the United States on June 27. Atta and Shehhi enrolled in a different flight school, Huffman Aviation, and began training almost daily. In mid-August, Atta and Shehhi both passed the Private Pilot Airman test. Their instructors described Atta and Shehhi as aggressive and rude, and in a hurry to complete their training.

Meanwhile, Jarrah obtained his single engine private pilot certificate in early August 2000. In October, Jarrah went on the first of five foreign trips he would take during his time in the United States. He returned to Germany to visit his girlfriend, Aysel Senguen, the daughter of Turkish immigrants, whom Jarrah had met in 1996 and married in a 1999 Islamic ceremony not recognized under German law.

THE FOURTH PILOT: HANI HANJOUR

BY THIS POINT, in the fall of 2000, three 9/11 pilots were progressing in their training. It was clear, though, that the first two assigned to the operation, Hazmi and Mihdhar, would not learn to fly aircraft. It proved unnecessary to scale back the operation, however, because a young Saudi with special credentials arrived at an al Qaeda camp in Afghanistan.

Hani Hanjour had studied in the United States intermittently since 1991, and had undergone enough flight training in Arizona to obtain his commercial pilot certificate in April 1999. His friends there included individuals with ties to Islamic extremism. Reportedly a devout Muslim all his life, Hanjour worked for a relief agency in Afghanistan in the 1980s. By 2000, he was back in Afghanistan where he was identified among al Qaeda recruits at the al Faruq camp as a trained pilot and who should be sent to KSM for inclusion in the plot.

After receiving several days of training from KSM in Karachi, Hanjour returned to Saudi Arabia on June 20, 2000. There he obtained a U.S. student visa on September 25, before traveling to the UAE to receive funds for the operation from KSM's nephew, a conspirator named Ali Abdul Aziz Ali. On December 8, 2000, Hanjour traveled to San Diego to join Nawaf al Hazmi, who had been alone since Mihdhar's departure six months earlier.

Once Hanjour arrived in San Diego and joined Hazmi, the two quickly relocated to Arizona, where Hanjour had spent most of his previous time in the United States. On December 12, 2000, they were settling in Mesa, Arizona, and Hanjour was ready to brush up on his flight training. By early 2001, he was using a Boeing 737 simulator. Because his performance struck his flight instructors as sub-standard, they discouraged Hanjour from continuing, but he persisted. He and Hazmi then left the Southwest at the end of March, driving across the country in Hazmi's car. There is some evidence indicating that Hanjour may have returned to Arizona in June of 2001 to obtain additional flight training with some of his associates in the area.

9/11 OPERATIVES ON THE MOVE

BACK IN FLORIDA, the Hamburg pilots—Atta, Shehhi, and Jarrah—continued to train. By the end of 2000, they also were starting to train on jet aircraft simulators. Around the beginning of the New Year, all three of them left the United States on various foreign trips. Jarrah took the second and third of his five foreign trips, visiting Germany and Beirut to see his girlfriend and family respectively. On one trip, Jarrah's girlfriend returned with him to the United States and stayed with him in Florida for ten days, even observing one of Jarrah's training sessions at flight school.

While Jarrah took these personal trips, Atta traveled to Germany for an early January 2001 meeting with Ramzi Binalshibh. Atta reported that the pilots had completed their training and were awaiting further instruction from al Qaeda. After the meeting, Atta returned to Florida and Binalshibh headed to Afghanistan to brief the al Qaeda leadership. As soon as Atta returned to Florida, Shehhi took his foreign trip, an unexplained eight-day sojourn to Casablanca.

After Atta and Shehhi returned to Florida, they moved on to the Atlanta area, where they pursued some additional training. The two rented a small plane with a flight instructor and may have visited a flight school in Decatur, Georgia. By February 19, Atta and Shehhi were on the move again, traveling to Virginia Beach, Virginia. Here is a shot of Atta on February 20, withdrawing $4,000 from his account at a SunTrust Bank branch in Virginia Beach. A bit later, Jarrah spent time in Georgia as well, staying in Decatur in mid-March. At the end of March, he left again for Germany to visit his girlfriend.

At about this time, Hanjour and Hazmi were driving from Arizona toward the East Coast. After being stopped for speeding in Oklahoma on April 1, they finally arrived in Northern Virginia. At the Dar al Hijra mosque in Falls Church, they met a Jordanian man named Eyad al Rababah, possibly through Anwar Aulaqi, the imam whom they had known in San Diego and who, in the interim, also had moved east in early 2001.

With Rababah's help, Hanjour and Hazmi were able to find a room in an apartment in Alexandria, Virginia. When they expressed interest in the greater New York area, Rababah suggested they accompany him to Connecticut, where he was in the process of moving. On May 8, the group—which by now included al Qaeda operatives Ahmad al Ghamdi and Majed Moqed—traveled to Fairfield, Connecticut. The next day, Rababah took them to Paterson, New Jersey to have dinner and see the area. Soon thereafter, they moved into an apartment in Paterson. At this time, we have insufficient basis to conclude that Rababah knew the operatives were terrorists when he assisted them. As for Aulaqi, there is reporting that he has extremist ties, and the circumstances surrounding his relationship with the hijackers remain suspicious. However, we have not uncovered evidence that he associated with the hijackers knowing that they were terrorists.

While Hanjour and Hazmi were settling in New Jersey, Atta and Shehhi were returning to Southern Florida. We have examined the allegation that Atta met with an Iraqi intelligence officer in Prague on April 9. Based on the evidence available—including investigation by Czech and U.S. authorities plus detainee reporting—we do not believe that such a meeting occurred. The FBI's investigation places him in Virginia as of April 4, as evidenced by this bank surveillance camera shot of Atta withdrawing $8,000 from his account. Atta was back in Florida by April 11, if not before. Indeed, investigation has established that, on April 6, 9, 10, and 11, Atta's cellular telephone was used numerous times to call Florida phone numbers from cell sites within Florida. We have seen no evidence that Atta ventured overseas again or re-entered the United States before July, when he traveled to Spain and back under his true name. Shehhi, on the other hand, visited Cairo between April 18 and May 2. We do not know the reason for this excursion.

THE MUSCLE HIJACKERS

WHILE THE PILOTS trained in the United States, Bin Ladin and al Qaeda leaders in Afghanistan started selecting the muscle hijackers—those operatives who would storm the cockpit and control the passengers on the four hijacked planes. (The term "muscle" hijacker appears in the interrogation reports of 9/11 conspirators KSM and Binalshibh, and has been widely used to refer to the non-pilot hijackers.) The so-called muscle hijackers actually were not physically imposing, as the majority of them were between 5'5" and 5'7" in height and slender in build. In addition to Hazmi and Mihdhar, the first pair to enter the United States, there were 13 other muscle hijackers, all but one from Saudi Arabia. They were Satam al Suqami, Wail and Waleed al Shehri (two brothers), Abdul Aziz al Omari, Fayez Banihammad (from the UAE), Ahmed al Ghamdi, Hamza al Ghamdi, Mohand al Shehri, Saeed al Ghamdi, Ahmad al Haznawi, Ahmed al Nami, Majed Moqed, and Salem al Hazmi (the brother of Nawaf al Hazmi).

The muscle hijackers were between 20 and 28 years of age and had differing backgrounds. Many were unemployed and lacked higher education, while a few had begun university studies. Although some were known to attend prayer services regularly, others reportedly even consumed alcohol and abused drugs. It has not been determined exactly how each of them was recruited into al Qaeda, but most of them apparently were swayed to join the jihad in Chechnya by contacts at local universities and mosques in Saudi Arabia.

By late 1999 and early 2000, the young men who would become the muscle hijackers began to break off contact with their families and pursue jihad. They made their way to the camps in Afghanistan, where they volunteered to be suicide operatives for al Qaeda. After being picked by Bin Ladin himself for what would become the 9/11 operation, most of them returned to Saudi Arabia to obtain U.S. visas. They then returned to Afghanistan for special training on how to conduct hijackings, disarm air marshals, and handle explosives and knives. Next KSM sent them to the UAE, where his nephew, Ali Abdul Aziz Ali, and another al Qaeda member, Mustafa al Hawsawi, would help them buy plane tickets to the United States.

In late April 2001, the muscle hijackers started arriving in the United States, specifically in Florida, Washington, DC, and New York. They traveled mostly in pairs and were assisted upon arrival by Atta and Shehhi in Florida or Hazmi and Hanjour in DC and New York. The final pair, Salem al Hazmi and Abdulaziz al Omari, arrived New York on June 29 and likely were picked up the following day by Salem's brother, Nawaf, as evidenced by Nawaf's minor traffic accident while heading east on the George Washington Bridge.

Finally, on July 4, Khalid al Mihdhar, who had abandoned Nawaf al Hazmi back in San Diego 13 months earlier, re-entered the United States. Mihdhar promptly joined the group in Paterson, New Jersey.

SUMMER OF PREPARATIONS

IN ADDITION TO assisting the newly-arrived muscle hijackers, the pilots busied themselves during the summer of 2001 with cross-country surveillance flights and additional flight training. Shehhi took the first cross-country flight, from New York to San Francisco and on to Las Vegas on May 24. Jarrah was next, traveling from Baltimore to Los Angeles and on to Las Vegas on June 7. Then, on June 28, Atta flew from Boston to San Francisco and on to Las Vegas. Each flew first class, in the same type of aircraft he would pilot on September 11.

In addition to the test flights, some of the operatives obtained additional training. In early June, Jarrah sought to fly the "Hudson Corridor," a low altitude "hallway" along the Hudson River that passed several New York landmarks, including the World Trade Center. Hanjour made the same request at a flight school in New Jersey.

The 9/11 operatives were now split between two locations: southern Florida and Paterson, New Jersey. Atta had to coordinate the two groups, especially with Nawaf al Hazmi, who was considered Atta's second-in-command for the entire operation. Their first in-person meeting probably took place in June, when Hazmi flew round-trip between Newark and Miami.

The next step for Atta was a mid-July status meeting with Binalshibh at a small resort town in Spain. According to Binalshibh, the two discussed the progress of the plot, and Atta disclosed that he would still need about five or six weeks before he would be able to provide the date for the attacks. Atta also reported that he, Shehhi, and Jarrah had been able to carry box cutters onto their test flights; they had determined that the best time to storm the cockpit would be about 10-15 minutes after takeoff, when they noticed that cockpit doors were typically opened for the first time. Atta also said that the conspirators planned to crash their planes into the ground if they could not strike their targets. Atta himself planned to crash his aircraft into the streets of New York if he could not hit the World Trade Center. After the meeting, Binalshibh left to report the progress to the al Qaeda leadership in Afghanistan, and Atta returned to Florida on July 19.

In early August, Atta spent a day waiting at the Orlando airport for one additional muscle hijacker intended for the operation, Mohamed al Kahtani. As noted in Staff Statement No. 1, Kahtani was turned away by U.S. immigration officials and failed to join the operation. On August 13, another in-person meeting of key players in the plot apparently took place, as Atta, Nawaf al Hazmi, and Hanjour gathered one last time in Las Vegas. Two days later, the FBI learned about the strange behavior of Zacarias Moussaoui, who was now training on flight simulators in Minneapolis.

THE FINAL DAYS

IN ADDITION TO their last test flights and Las Vegas trips, the conspirators had other final preparations to make. Some of the pilots took practice flights on small rented aircraft, and the muscle hijackers trained at gyms. The operatives also purchased a variety of small knives that they may have used during the attacks. While we can't know for sure, some of the knives the terrorists bought may have been these, which were recovered from the Flight 93 crash site. On August 22, Jarrah attempted to buy four Global Positioning System (GPS) units from a pilot shop in Miami. Only one unit was available, and Jarrah purchased it along with three aeronautical charts.

Just over two weeks before the attacks, the conspirators purchased their flight tickets. Between August 26 and September 5, they bought tickets on the Internet, by phone, and in person. Once the ticket purchases were made, the conspirators returned excess funds to al Qaeda. During the first week in September, they made a series of wire transfers to Mustafa al Hawsawi in the UAE, totaling about $26,000. Nawaf al Hazmi attempted to send Hawsawi the debit card for Mihdhar's bank account, which still contained approximately $10,000. (The package containing the card would be intercepted after the FBI found the Express Mail receipt for it in Hazmi's car at Dulles Airport on 9/11.)

The last step was to travel to the departure points for the attacks. The operatives for American Airlines Flight 77, which would depart from Dulles and crash into the Pentagon, gathered in Laurel, Maryland, about 20 miles from Washington, DC. The Flight 77 team stayed at a motel in Laurel during the first week of September and spent time working out at a nearby gym. On the final night before the attacks, they stayed at a hotel in Herndon, Virginia, close to Dulles Airport. Further north, the operatives for United Airlines Flight 93, which would depart from Newark and crash in Stony Creek Township, Pennsylvania, gathered in Newark. Just after midnight on September 9, Jarrah received this speeding ticket as he headed north through Maryland along Interstate 95, towards his team's staging point in New Jersey.

Atta continued to coordinate the teams until the very end. On September 7, he flew from Fort Lauderdale to Baltimore, presumably to meet with the Flight 77 team in Laurel, Maryland. On September 9, he flew from Baltimore to Boston. By this time, Marwan al Shehhi and his team for Flight 175 had arrived in Boston, and Atta was seen with Shehhi at his hotel. The next day, Atta picked up Abdul Aziz al Omari, one of the Flight 11 muscle hijackers, from his Boston hotel and drove to Portland, Maine. For reasons that remain unknown, Atta and Omari took a commuter flight to Boston during the early hours of September 11 to connect to Flight 11. As shown here, they cleared security at the airport in Portland and boarded the flight that would allow them to join the rest of their team at Logan Airport.

The Portland detour almost prevented Atta and Omari from making Flight 11 out of Boston. In fact, the luggage they checked in Portland failed to make it onto the plane. Seized after the September 11 crashes, Atta and Omari's luggage turned out to contain a number of telling items, including: correspondence from the university Atta attended in Egypt; Omari's international driver's license and passport; a video cassette for a Boeing 757 flight simulator; and this folding knife and pepper spray, presumably extra weapons the two conspirators decided they didn't need.

On the morning of September 11, after years of planning and many months of intensive preparation, all four terrorist teams were in place to execute the attacks of that day.

FINANCING OF THE 9/11 PLOT

WE ESTIMATE that the 9/11 attacks cost somewhere between $400,000 and $500,000 to execute. The operatives spent over $270,000 in the United States, and the costs associated with Zacarias Moussaoui—who is discussed at greater length below—were at least $50,000. Additional expenses included travel to obtain passports and visas; travel to the United States; expenses incurred by the plot leader and facilitators outside the United States; and expenses incurred by the people selected to be hijackers but who ultimately did not participate. For many of these expenses, we have only fragmentary evidence and/or unconfirmed detainee reports and can make only a rough estimate of costs. Our $400,000–$500,000 estimate does not include the cost of running the camps in Afghanistan where the hijackers were recruited and trained, or the cost of that training.

We have found no evidence that the Hamburg group received funds from al Qaeda before late 1999. They apparently supported themselves before joining the conspiracy. Thereafter, according to KSM, they each received $5,000 to pay for their return to Germany from Afghanistan plus funds for travel from Germany to the United States. KSM, Binalshibh, and plot facilitator Mustafa al Hawsawi, each received money—perhaps $10,000—to cover their living expenses while they fulfilled their roles in the plot.

In the United States, the operatives' primary expenses consisted of flight training, living expenses (room, board and meals, vehicles, insurance, etc.), and travel (casing flights, meetings, and the flights on 9/11). All told, about $300,000 was deposited into the 19 hijackers' bank accounts in the United States. They received funds in the United States through a variety of unexceptional means. Approximately $130,000 arrived via a series of wire transfers from Ali Abdul Aziz Ali, who sent approximately $120,000 from Dubai, and Binalshibh, who sent just over $10,000 from Germany. Shown here is the receipt for the largest wire transfer sent to the conspirators in the United States, $70,000 that Ali wired Marwan al Shehhi on September 17, 2000, just when Shehhi, Atta and Jarrah were in the middle of their flight training. In addition to receiving funds by wire, the operatives brought significant amounts of cash and travelers checks with them into the United States, the largest amount coming with the 13 muscle hijackers who began arriving in April 2001. Finally, several of the operatives relied on accounts in overseas financial institutions, which they accessed in the United States with ATM and credit cards.

The conspiracy made extensive use of banks in the United States, both branches of major international banks and smaller regional banks. All of the operatives opened accounts in their own names, using passports and other identification documents. There is no evidence that they ever used false social security numbers to open any bank accounts. Their transactions were unremarkable and essentially invisible amidst the billions of dollars flowing around the world every day.

No credible evidence exists that the operatives received substantial funding from any person in the United States. Specifically, there is no evidence that Mihdhar and Hazmi received funding from Saudi citizens Omar al Bayoumi and Osama Bassnan, or that Saudi Princess Haifa al Faisal provided any funds to the conspiracy either directly or indirectly.

To date, the U.S. government has not been able to determine the origin of the money used for the 9/11 attacks. Compelling evidence traces the bulk of the funds directly back to KSM, but from where KSM obtained the money remains unknown at this time. Ultimately the question is of little practical significance. Al Qaeda had many avenues of funding and a pre-9/11 annual budget estimated at $30 million. If a particular source of funds had dried up, al Qaeda could have easily found enough money to fund an attack that cost $400,000–$500,000 over nearly two years.

A CLOSER LOOK AT SPECIFIC ASPECTS OF THE PLOT

GIVEN THE CATASTROPHIC results of the 9/11 attacks, it is tempting to depict the plot as a set plan executed to near perfection. This would be a mistake. The 9/11 conspirators confronted operational difficulties, internal disagreements, and even dissenting opinions within the leadership of al Qaeda. In the end, the plot proved sufficiently flexible to adapt and evolve as challenges arose.

INITIAL CHANGES IN THE PLOT

AS ORIGINALLY ENVISIONED, the 9/11 plot involved even more extensive attacks than those carried out on September 11. KSM maintains that his initial proposal involved hijacking ten planes to attack targets on both the East and West coasts of the United States. He claims that, in addition to the targets actually hit on 9/11, these hijacked planes were to be crashed into CIA and FBI headquarters, unidentified nuclear power plants, and the tallest buildings in California and Washington State. The centerpiece of his original proposal was the tenth plane, which he would have piloted himself. Rather than crashing the plane into a target, he would have killed every adult male passenger, contacted the media from the air, and landed the aircraft at a U.S. airport. He says he then would have made a speech denouncing U.S. policies in the Middle East before releasing all of the women and children passengers.

KSM concedes that this ambitious proposal initially received only a lukewarm response from the al Qaeda leadership in view of the proposal's scale and complexity. When Bin Ladin finally approved the operation, he scrapped the idea of using one of the hijacked planes to make a public statement but provided KSM with four operatives, only two of whom ultimately would participate in the 9/11 attacks. Those two operatives, Nawaf al Hamzi and Khalid al Mihdhar, had already acquired U.S. visas in their Saudi passports by the time they were picked for the operation. According to KSM, both had obtained visas because they wanted to participate in an operation against the United States, having been inspired by a friend of theirs who was a suicide bomber in the August 1998 attack on the U.S. embassy in Kenya.

It soon became clear to KSM that the other two operatives, Khallad bin Attash and Abu Bara al Taizi—both of whom had Yemeni, not Saudi, documentation—would not be able to obtain U.S. visas. Khallad, in fact, had already been turned down in April 1999, at about the same time that Hazmi and Mihdhar acquired their U.S. visas in Saudi Arabia.

Although he recognized that Yemeni operatives would not be able to travel to the United States as readily as Saudis like Hazmi and Mihdhar, KSM wanted Khallad and Abu Bara to take part in the operation. Accordingly, by mid-1999, KSM made his first major adjustment, splitting the plot into two parts so that Yemeni operatives could participate without having to obtain U.S. visas. He focused in particular on Southeast Asia because he believed it would be easier for Yemenis to travel there than to the United States.

The first part of the operation would remain as originally planned—operatives including Hazmi and Mihdhar would hijack commercial flights and crash them into U.S. targets. The second part, however, would now involve using Yemeni operatives in a modified version of the Bojinka plot: operatives would hijack U.S. commercial planes flying Pacific routes from Southeast Asia and explode them in mid-air instead of crashing them into particular targets. (An alternate scenario, according to KSM, involved flying planes into U.S. targets in Japan, Singapore or Korea.) All planes in the United States and in Southeast Asia, however, were to be crashed or exploded more or less simultaneously, to maximize the psychological impact of the attacks.

Khallad has admitted casing a flight between Bangkok and Hong Kong in early January 2000 in preparation for the revised operation. According to his account, he reported the results from this mission to Bin Ladin and KSM. By April or May 2000, however, Bin Ladin had decided to cancel the Southeast Asia part of the planes operation because he believed it would be too difficult to synchronize the hijacking and crashing of flights on opposite sides of the globe. Deprived of the opportunity to become a suicide operative, Khallad was re-deployed, first helping KSM communicate with Hazmi in California and later assisting in the *Cole* bombing, much as Binalshibh was assigned to assist the Hamburg pilots after failing to obtain a visa himself.

Hazmi and Mihdhar were particularly ill-prepared to stage an operation in the United States. Neither had any significant exposure to Western culture; Hazmi barely spoke English, and Mihdhar spoke none. Given this background, KSM had real concerns about whether they would be able to fulfill their mission. In fact, he maintains that the only reason the two operatives were included in the 9/11 plot was their prior acquisition of visas and Bin Ladin's personal interest in having them participate.

Unlike the other 9/11 hijackers—who were instructed to avoid associating with others in the local Muslim community—Hazmi and

Mihdhar received specific permission from KSM to seek assistance at mosques when they first arrived in the United States. According to KSM, he also directed them to enroll in English language classes as soon as possible so that they could begin flight training right away. As KSM tells it, Hazmi and Mihdhar attempted to enroll in three language schools upon arriving in Los Angeles but failed to attend classes at any of them. Once they moved to San Diego, Hazmi enrolled in English classes and, a little later, both took some flight training, but they failed to make progress in either area.

According to their flight instructors, Hazmi and Mihdhar said they wanted to learn how to control an aircraft in flight, but took no interest in take-offs or landings. One Arabic-speaking flight instructor has recalled that the two were keen on learning to fly large jets, particularly Boeing aircraft. When the instructor informed them that, like all students, they would have to begin training on single engine aircraft before learning to fly jets, they expressed such disappointment that the instructor thought they were either joking or dreaming.

KSM says now that he was surprised by the failure of Hazmi and Mihdhar to become pilots. This failure, however, had little impact on the plot. The setback occurred early enough to permit further adjustment. Al Qaeda's discovery of new operatives—men with English language skills, higher education, exposure to the West, and, in the case of Hani Hanjour, prior flight training—soon remedied the problem.

ADDITIONAL SAUDI PARTICIPANTS IN THE PLOT

IN ADDITION TO the reassignment of operatives, the plot saw a variety of potential suicide hijackers who never participated in the attacks. These al Qaeda members either backed out of their assignment, had trouble acquiring the necessary travel documentation, or were removed from the operation by al Qaeda leadership.

According to KSM, al Qaeda intended to use 25 or 26 hijackers for the 9/11 plot, as opposed to the 19 who actually participated. Even as late as the summer of 2001, KSM wanted to send as many operatives as possible to the United States in order to increase the chances for successful attacks, contemplating as many as seven or more hijackers per flight. We have identified at least nine candidate hijackers slated to be part of the 9/11 attacks at one time or another:

• Ali Abd al Rahman al Faqasi al Ghamdi and Zuhair al Thubaiti were both removed from the operation by al Qaeda leadership.

• Khalid Saeed Ahmad al Zahrani and Saeed Abdullah Saeed al Ghamdi, whom we discussed in Staff Statement No. 1, failed to acquire U.S. visas.

• Saeed al Baluchi and Qutaybah al Najdi both backed out after Najdi was stopped and briefly questioned by airport security officials in Bahrain.

• Saud al Rashid and Mushabib al Hamlan apparently withdrew under pressure from their families in Saudi Arabia.

• And, as discussed in Staff Statement No. 1, Mohamed Mani Ahmad al Kahtani was denied entry by U.S. officials at the airport in Orlando on August 4, 2001.

For the most part, these operatives appear to have been selected by Bin Ladin in Afghanistan and assigned to KSM in much the same manner as the others. All nine were Saudi nationals. A tenth individual, a Tunisian named Abderraouf Jdey, may have been a candidate to participate in the 9/11 attack, or he may have been a candidate to participate in a later attack. He withdrew, and we will discuss him later in connection with plans involving Moussaoui. None of these potential hijackers succeeded in joining the 19.

INTERNAL DISAGREEMENT:
ATTA, JARRAH AND MOUSSAOUI

INTERNAL DISAGREEMENT among the 9/11 plotters may have posed the greatest potential vulnerability for the plot. It appears that, during the summer of 2001, friction developed between Atta and Jarrah—two of the three Hamburg pilots—and that Jarrah may even have considered dropping out of the operation. What is more, it appears as if KSM may have been preparing another al Qaeda operative, Zacarias Moussaoui, to take Jarrah's place.

Jarrah was different from the other Hamburg pilots, Atta and Shehhi. Given his background and personality, Jarrah seemed a relatively unlikely candidate to become an al Qaeda suicide operative. From an affluent family, he studied at private, Christian schools in Lebanon before deciding to study abroad in Germany. He knew the best nightclubs and discos in Beirut, and partied with fellow students in Germany, even drinking beer—a clear taboo for any religious Muslim. His serious involvement with his girlfriend, Aysel Senguen, and close family ties resulted in almost daily telephone conversations with them while he was in the United States. He took five overseas trips within a ten-month span before September 11.

Jarrah also appears to have projected a friendly, engaging personality while in the United States. Here he is, hair frosted, proudly displaying the pilot's certificate he received during his flight training in Florida. Yet, this is the same person who, only a year earlier, had journeyed from Hamburg to Afghanistan and pledged to become one of Bin Ladin's suicide operatives.

Both KSM and Binalshibh have reported that Atta and Jarrah clashed over the extent of Jarrah's autonomy and involvement in planning the operation. Binalshibh believes the dispute stemmed, at least in part, from Jarrah's frequent visits to and contact with his girlfriend and his family. Further, unlike Atta and Shehhi—who had attended flight school together—Jarrah spent much of his time in the United States alone. Binalshibh was supposed to have trained with Jarrah but failed to obtain a U.S. visa. As a result, according to Binalshibh, Jarrah felt isolated and excluded from decision-making. Binalshibh claims he had to mediate between Atta and Jarrah.

Jarrah's final trip to see his girlfriend, from July 25 to August 5, 2001, is of particular interest. In contrast to his prior trips, this time Senguen bought him a one-way ticket to Germany. Moreover, it appears that Atta drove him to the airport in Miami, another unusual circumstance suggesting that something may have been amiss. Finally, according to Binalshibh, who met Jarrah at the airport in Duesseldorf, Jarrah said he needed to see Senguen right away. When he had time to meet with Binalshibh a few days later, the two of them had an emotional conversation during which Binalshibh encouraged Jarrah to see the plan through.

Perhaps the most significant evidence that Jarrah was reconsidering his participation in the 9/11 plot resides in communications that took place between KSM and Binalshibh in mid-July 2001. During the spring and summer of 2001, KSM had a number of conversations that appear to have concerned the 9/11 plot. Both KSM and Binalshibh confirm discussing the plot during their mid-July conversation, which occurred just a few days before Jarrah embarked on his last trip to Germany. At this point, Binalshibh had just returned from his meeting with Atta in Spain and was now reporting to KSM on the status of the plot. Concerned that Jarrah might drop out of the operation, KSM emphasized to Binalshibh the importance of ensuring peace between Jarrah and Atta. In the course of discussing this concern and the potential delay of the plot, moreover, KSM instructed Binalshibh to send "the skirts" to "Sally"—a coded reference instructing Binalshibh to send funds to Zacarias Moussaoui. Atta and Jarrah were referred to as an unhappy couple. KSM warned that if Jarrah "asks for a divorce, it is going to cost a lot of money."

There is good reason to believe that KSM wanted money sent to Moussaoui to prepare him as a potential substitute pilot in the event Jarrah dropped out. Moussaoui attended al Qaeda training camps in Afghanistan. Sent to Malaysia in September 2000 by Bin Ladin and KSM to obtain pilot training, Moussaoui told terrorist associates there about his plans to crash a plane into the White House. He came to the United States in February 2001—armed with the fruits of Atta's flight school research—and started taking flight lessons at the Airman Flight School in Norman, Oklahoma, but stopped that training by early June. Shortly after he received $14,000 from Binalshibh in early August, however, Moussaoui rushed into an intensive flight simulator course at Pan Am International Flight Academy in Eagan, Minnesota. At about this same time, he also purchased two knives and inquired of two GPS manufacturers whether their units could be converted for aeronautical use—actions that closely resembled those of the 9/11 hijackers during their final preparations for the attacks. Moussaoui's August 16, 2001, arrest ended his simulator training and may have prevented him from joining the 9/11 operation.

The reports of the interrogations of Binalshibh and KSM regarding Moussaoui are not entirely consistent. According to Binalshibh, he understood that KSM was instructing him to send the money to Moussaoui in July 2001 as part of the 9/11 plot. Moreover, recounting a post-9/11 discussion he had with KSM in Kandahar, Binalshibh says KSM referred to Moussaoui as if he had been part of the 9/11 plot, noting that Moussaoui was arrested because he was not sufficiently discreet and had been an exception to Bin Ladin's strong overall record of choosing the right operatives for the plot.

KSM, on the other hand, denies that Moussaoui was ever intended to be part of the 9/11 operation and was slated instead to participate in a so-called "second wave" of attacks on the West Coast after September 11. KSM also claims that Moussaoui never had any contact with Atta in the United States, and we have seen nothing to the contrary. Notably, however, KSM also claims that by the summer of 2001 he was too busy with the 9/11 plot to plan the second wave attacks. Moreover, he admits that only three potential pilots were recruited for the alleged second wave, Moussaoui, Abderraouf Jdey, also known as Faruq al Tunisi (a Canadian passport holder), and Zaini Zakaria, also known as Mussa. By the summer of 2001, both Jdey and Zaini already had backed out of the operation. The case of Jdey holds particular interest, as some evidence indicates that he may have been selected for the planes operation at the same time as the Hamburg group.

In any event, Moussaoui's arrest did not cause the plot any difficulty. Jarrah returned to the United States on August 5 and, as subsequent events would demonstrate, clearly was resolved to complete the operation.

TIMING AND TARGETS

THE CONSPIRATORS' selection of both the date and the targets for the attacks provides another opportunity to examine the plot from within. Although Atta enjoyed wide discretion as tactical commander, Bin Ladin had strong opinions regarding both issues. The date of the attacks apparently was not chosen much more than three weeks before September 11. According to Binalshibh, when he met with Atta in Spain in mid-July, Atta could do no more than estimate that he would still need five to six weeks before he could pick a date. Then, in a mid-August phone call to Binalshibh, Atta conveyed the date for the attacks, which Binalshibh dutifully passed up his chain of command in a message personally delivered to Afghanistan by Hamburg associate Zakariya Essabar in late August.

Bin Ladin had been pressuring KSM for months to advance the attack date. According to KSM, Bin Ladin had even asked that the attacks occur as early as mid-2000, after Israeli opposition party leader Ariel Sharon caused an outcry in the Middle East by visiting a sensitive and contested holy site in Jerusalem that is sacred to both Muslims and Jews. Although Bin Ladin recognized that Atta and the other pilots had only just arrived in the United States to begin their flight training, the al Qaeda leader wanted to punish the United States for supporting Israel. He allegedly told KSM it would be sufficient simply to down the planes and not hit specific targets. KSM withstood this pressure, arguing that the operation would not be successful unless the pilots were fully trained and the hijacking teams were larger.

In 2001, Bin Ladin apparently pressured KSM twice more for an earlier date. According to KSM, Bin Ladin first requested a date of May 12, 2001, the seven-month anniversary of the *Cole* bombing. Then, when Bin Ladin learned from the media that Sharon would be visiting the White House in June or July 2001, he attempted once more to accelerate the operation. In both instances, KSM insisted that the hijacker teams were not yet ready.

Other al Qaeda detainees also confirm that the 9/11 attacks were delayed during the summer of 2001, despite Bin Ladin's wishes. According to one operative, Khalid al Mihdhar disclosed that attacks had been delayed from May until July, and later from July until September. According to another al Qaeda member in Kandahar that summer, a general warning—much like the alert issued in the camps two weeks before the *Cole* bombing and ten days before the eventual 9/11 attacks—was issued in July or early August of 2001. As a result of this warning, many al Qaeda members dispersed with their families, internal security was increased, and Bin Ladin dropped out of sight for about 30 days until the alert was cancelled.

KSM claims he did not inform Atta or the other conspirators that Bin Ladin wanted to advance the date because he knew they would move forward when they were ready. Atta was very busy organizing the late arriving operatives, coordinating the flight teams, and finalizing the targets. In fact, target selection appears to have influenced the timing of the attacks. As revealed by an Atta-Binalshibh communication at this time, recovered later from a computer captured with KSM, Atta selected a date after the first week of September so that the United States Congress would be in session.

According to KSM, the U.S. Capitol was indeed on the preliminary target list he had initially developed with Bin Ladin and Atef in the spring of 1999. That preliminary list also included the White House, the Pentagon, and the World Trade Center. KSM claims that while everyone agreed on the Capitol, he wanted to hit the World Trade Center whereas Bin Ladin favored the Pentagon and the White House.

Binalshibh confirms that Bin Ladin preferred the White House over the Capitol, a preference he made sure to convey to Atta when they met in Spain in the summer of 2001. Atta responded that he believed the White House posed too difficult a target, but that he was waiting for Hani Hanjour and Nawaf al Hazmi to assess its feasibility. On July 20, Hanjour—likely accompanied by Hazmi—rented a plane and took a practice flight from Fairfield, New Jersey, to Gaithersburg, Maryland, a route that would have allowed them to fly near Washington, DC. When Binalshibh pressed Atta to retain the White House as a target during one of their communications in early August, Atta agreed but said he would hold the Capitol in reserve as an alternate target, in case the White House proved impossible. Based on another exchange between Atta and Binalshibh, as late as September 9—two days before the attacks—the conspirators may still have been uncertain about which Washington target they would strike.

DISSENT AMONG AL QAEDA LEADERS

THE ATTITUDE OF the al Qaeda leadership toward the 9/11 plot represents one last area for insight. As Atta made his final preparations during the summer of 2001, dissent emerged among al Qaeda leaders in Afghanistan over whether to proceed with the attack. Although access to details of the plot was carefully guarded, word started to spread during the summer of 2001 that an attack against the United States was imminent. According to KSM, he was widely known within al Qaeda to be planning some kind of operation against the United States. Many were even aware that he had been preparing operatives to go to the

United States, as reported by a CIA source in June 2001. Moreover, that summer Bin Ladin made several remarks hinting at an upcoming attack, which spawned rumors throughout the jihadist community worldwide. For instance, KSM claims that, in a speech at the al Faruq training camp in Afghanistan, Bin Ladin specifically urged trainees to pray for the success of an upcoming attack involving 20 martyrs.

With news of an impending attack against the United States gaining wider circulation, a rift developed within al Qaeda's leadership. Although Bin Ladin wanted the operation to proceed as soon as possible, several senior al Qaeda figures thought they should follow the position taken by their Afghan host, Taliban leader Mullah Omar, who opposed attacking the United States. According to one al Qaeda member, when Bin Ladin returned after the general alert in late July, he spoke to his confidants about problems he was having with Omar's unwillingness to allow any further attacks against the United States from Afghanistan.

KSM claims that Omar opposed attacking the United States for ideological reasons but permitted attacks against Jewish targets. KSM denies that Omar's opposition reflected concern about U.S. retaliation but notes that the Taliban leader was under pressure from the Pakistani government to keep al Qaeda from engaging in operations outside Afghanistan. While some senior al Qaeda figures opposed the 9/11 operation out of deference to Omar, others reportedly expressed concern that the U.S. would respond militarily.

Bin Ladin, on the other hand, reportedly argued that attacks against the United States needed to be carried out immediately to support the insurgency in the Israeli occupied territories and to protest the presence of U.S. military forces in Saudi Arabia. Bin Ladin also thought that an attack against the United States would reap al Qaeda a recruiting and fundraising bonanza. In his thinking, the more al Qaeda did, the more support it would gain. Although he faced opposition from many of his most senior advisers—including Shura council members Shaykh Saeed, Sayf al Adl, and Abu Hafs the Mauritanian—Bin Ladin effectively overruled their objections, and the attacks went forward.

Somebody Else's Civil War

Michael Scott Doran

> *Call it a city on four legs*
> *heading for murder. ...*
> *New York is a woman*
> *holding, according to history,*
> *a rag called liberty with one hand*
> *and strangling the earth with the other.*
> —Adonis [Ali Ahmed Said],
> *"The Funeral of New York," 1971*

IN THE WEEKS AFTER the attacks of September 11, Americans repeatedly asked, "Why do they hate us?" To understand what happened, however, another question may be even more pertinent: "Why do they want to provoke us?"

David Fromkin suggested the answer in *Foreign Affairs* back in 1975. "Terrorism," he noted, "is violence used in order to create fear; but it is aimed at creating fear in order that the fear, in turn, will lead somebody else—not the terrorist—to embark on some quite different program of action that will accomplish whatever it is that the terrorist really desires." When a terrorist kills, the goal is not murder itself but something else—for example, a police crackdown that will create a rift between government and society that the terrorist can then exploit for revolutionary purposes. Osama bin Laden sought—and has received—an international military crackdown, one he wants to exploit for his particular brand of revolution.

Bin Laden produced a piece of high political theater he hoped would reach the audience that concerned him the most: the *umma*, or universal Islamic community. The script was obvious: America, cast as the villain, was supposed to use its military might like a car-

---

This article originally appeared in the January/February 2002 issue of *Foreign Affairs*.

toon character trying to kill a fly with a shotgun. The media would see to it that any use of force against the civilian population of Afghanistan was broadcast around the world, and the *umma* would find it shocking how Americans nonchalantly caused Muslims to suffer and die. The ensuing outrage would open a chasm between state and society in the Middle East, and the governments allied with the West—many of which are repressive, corrupt, and illegitimate— would find themselves adrift. It was to provoke such an outcome that bin Laden broadcast his statement following the start of the military campaign on October 7, in which he said, among other things, that the Americans and the British "have divided the entire world into two regions—one of faith, where there is no hypocrisy, and another of infidelity, from which we hope God will protect us."

Polarizing the Islamic world between the *umma* and the regimes allied with the United States would help achieve bin Laden's primary goal: furthering the cause of Islamic revolution within the Muslim world itself, in the Arab lands especially and in Saudi Arabia above all. He had no intention of defeating America. War with the United States was not a goal in and of itself but rather an instrument designed to help his brand of extremist Islam survive and flourish among the believers. Americans, in short, have been drawn into somebody else's civil war.

Washington had no choice but to take up the gauntlet, but it is not altogether clear that Americans understand fully this war's true dimensions. The response to bin Laden cannot be left to soldiers and police alone. He has embroiled the United States in an intra-Muslim ideological battle, a struggle for hearts and minds in which al Qaeda had already scored a number of victories—as the reluctance of America's Middle Eastern allies to offer public support for the campaign against it demonstrated. The first step toward weakening the hold of bin Laden's ideology, therefore, must be to comprehend the symbolic universe into which he has dragged us.

AMERICA, THE HUBAL OF THE AGE

BIN LADEN'S October 7 statement offers a crucial window onto his conceptual world and repays careful attention. In it he states, "Hypocrisy stood behind the leader of global idolatry, behind the

Hubal of the age—namely, America and its supporters." Because the symbolism is obscure to most Americans, this sentence was widely mistranslated in the press, but bin Laden's Muslim audience understood it immediately.

In the early seventh century, when the Prophet Muhammad began to preach Islam to the pagan Arab tribes in Mecca, Hubal was a stone idol that stood in the Kaaba—a structure that Abraham, according to Islamic tradition, originally built on orders from God as a sanctuary of Islam. In the years between Abraham and Muhammad, the tradition runs, the Arabs fell away from true belief and began to worship idols, with Hubal the most powerful of many. When bin Laden calls America "the Hubal of the age," he suggests that it is the primary focus of idol worship and that it is polluting the Kaaba, a symbol of Islamic purity. His imagery has a double resonance: it portrays American culture as a font of idolatry while rejecting the American military presence on the Arabian peninsula (which is, by his definition, the holy land of Islam, a place barred to infidels).

Muhammad's prophecy called the Arabs of Mecca back to their monotheistic birthright. The return to true belief, however, was not an easy one, because the reigning Meccan oligarchy persecuted the early Muslims. By calling for the destruction of Hubal, the Prophet's message threatened to undermine the special position that Mecca enjoyed in Arabia as a pagan shrine city. With much of their livelihood at stake, the oligarchs punished Muhammad's followers and conspired to kill him. The Muslims therefore fled from Mecca to Medina, where they established the *umma* as a political and religious community. They went on to fight and win a war against Mecca that ended with the destruction of Hubal and the spread of true Islam around the world.

Before the Prophet could achieve this success, however, he encountered the Munafiqun, the Hypocrites of Medina. Muhammad's acceptance of leadership over the Medinese reduced the power of a number of local tribal leaders. These men outwardly accepted Islam in order to protect their worldly status, but in their hearts they bore malice toward both the Prophet and his message. Among other misdeeds, the treacherous Munafiqun abandoned Muhammad on the battlefield at a moment when he was already woefully outnumbered. The Hypocrites were apostates who accepted true belief but then rejected it, and as such they were regarded as worse than the infidels who had never embraced Islam to begin with. Islam can understand just how difficult it is for a pagan to leave behind all the beliefs and personal connections that he or she once held dear; it is less forgiving of those who accept the truth and then subvert it.

In bin Laden's imagery, the leaders of the Arab and Islamic worlds today are Hypocrites, idol worshippers cowering behind America, the Hubal of the age. His sword jabs simultaneously at the United States and the governments allied with it. His attack was designed to force those governments to choose: You are either with the idol-worshiping enemies of God or you are with the true believers.

The al Qaeda organization grew out of an Islamic religious movement called the Salafiyya—a name derived from al-Salaf al-Salih, "the venerable forefathers," which refers to the generation of the Prophet Muhammad and his companions. Salafis regard the Islam that most Muslims practice today as polluted by idolatry; they seek to reform the religion by emulating the first generation of Muslims, whose pristine society they consider to have best reflected God's wishes for humans. The Salafiyya is not a unified movement, and it expresses itself in many forms, most of which do not approach the extremism of Osama bin Laden or the Taliban. The Wahhabi ideology of the Saudi state, for example, and the religious doctrines of the Muslim Brotherhood in Egypt and a host of voluntary religious organizations around the Islamic world are all Salafi. These diverse movements share the belief that Muslims have deviated from God's plan and that matters can be returned to their proper state by emulating the Prophet.

Like any other major religious figure, Muhammad left behind a legacy that his followers have channeled in different directions. An extremist current in the Salafiyya places great emphasis on jihad, or holy war. Among other things, the Prophet Muhammad fought in mortal combat against idolatry, and some of his followers today choose to accord this aspect of his career primary importance. The devoted members of al Qaeda display an unsettling willingness to martyr themselves because they feel that, like the Prophet, they are locked in a life-or-death struggle with the forces of unbelief that threaten from all sides. They consider themselves an island of true believers surrounded by a sea of iniquity and think the future of religion itself, and therefore the world, depends on them and their battle against idol worship.

In almost every Sunni Muslim country the Salafiyya has spawned Islamist political movements working to compel the state to apply the *shari'a*—that is, Islamic law. Extremist Salafis believe that strict application of the *shari'a* is necessary to ensure that Muslims walk on the path of the Prophet. The more extremist the party, the more insistent and violent the demand that the state must apply the *shari'a* exclusively. In the view of extremist Salafis, the *shari'a* is God's thunderous commandment to Muslims, and failure to adopt it constitutes idolatry. By removing God from the realm of law, a domain that He has clearly claimed for Himself alone, human legislation amounts to worshiping a pagan deity. Thus it was on the basis of failure to apply the *shari'a* that extremists branded Egyptian President Anwar al-Sadat an apostate and then killed him. His assassins came from a group often known as Egyptian Islamic Jihad, the remnants of which have in recent years merged with al Qaeda. In fact, investigators believe that Egyptian Islamic Jihad's leaders, Ayman al-Zawahiri and Muhammad Atef (who was killed in the U.S. air campaign), masterminded the attacks of September 11. In his 1996 "Declaration of War Against the Americans," bin Laden showed that he and his Egyptian associates are cut from the same cloth. Just as Zawahiri and Atef considered the current regime of Hosni Mubarak in Egypt to be a nest of apostates, so bin Laden considered the Saudi monarchy (its Wahhabi doctrines notwithstanding) to have renounced Islam. According to bin Laden, his king adopted "polytheism," which bin Laden defined as the acceptance of "laws fabricated by men ... permitting that which God has forbidden." It is the height of human arrogance and irreligion to "share with God in His sole right of sovereignty and making the law."

Extremist Salafis, therefore, regard modern Western civilization as a font of evil, spreading idolatry around the globe in the form of secularism. Since the United States is the strongest Western nation, the main purveyor of pop culture, and the power most involved in the political and economic affairs of the Islamic world, it receives particularly harsh criticism. Only the apostate Middle Eastern regimes themselves fall under harsher condemnation.

It is worth remembering, in this regard, that the rise of Islam represents a miraculous case of the triumph of human will. With little more than their beliefs to gird them, the Prophet Muhammad and a small number of devoted followers started a movement that brought the most powerful empires of their day crashing to the ground. On September 11, the attackers undoubtedly imagined themselves to be retracing the Prophet's steps. As they boarded the planes with the intention of destroying the Pentagon and the World Trade Center, they recited battle prayers that contained the line "All of their equipment, and gates, and technology will not prevent [you from achieving your aim], nor harm [you] except by God's will." The hijackers' imaginations certainly needed nothing more than this sparse line to remind them that, as they attacked America, they rode right behind Muhammad, who in his day had unleashed forces that, shortly after his death, destroyed the Persian Empire and crippled Byzantium—the two superpowers of the age.

AMERICA, LAND OF THE CRUSADERS

WHEN THINKING ABOUT THE WORLD today and their place in it, the extremist Salafis do not reflect only on the story of the foundation of Islam. They also scour more than a millennium of Islamic history in search of parallels to the present predicament. In his "Declaration of War," for instance, bin Laden states that the stationing of American forces on the soil of the Arabian peninsula constitutes the greatest aggression committed against the Muslims since the death of the Prophet in A.D. 632.

To put this claim in perspective, it is worth remembering that in the last 1,300 years Muslims have suffered a number of significant defeats, including but not limited to the destruction of the Abbasid caliphate by the Mongols, an episode of which bin Laden is well aware. In 1258 the ruthless Mongol leader Hulegu sacked Baghdad, killed the caliph, and massacred hundreds of thousands of inhabitants, stacking their skulls, as legend has it, in a pyramid outside the city walls. Whatever one thinks about U.S. policy toward Iraq, few in America would argue that the use of Saudi bases to enforce the sanctions against Saddam Hussein's regime constitutes a world-historical event on a par with the Mongol invasion of the Middle East. Before September 11, one might have been tempted to pass off as nationalist hyperbole bin Laden's assumption that U.S. policy represents the pinnacle of human evil. Now we know he is deadly serious.

The magnitude of the attacks on New York and Washington make it clear that al Qaeda does indeed believe itself to be fighting a war to save the *umma* from Satan, represented by secular Western culture. Extreme though they may be, these views extend far beyond al Qaeda's immediate followers in Afghanistan. Even a quick glance at the Islamist press in Arabic demonstrates that many Muslims who do not belong to bin Laden's terrorist network consider the United States to be on a moral par with Genghis Khan. Take, for instance, Muhammad Abbas, an Egyptian Islamist who wrote the following in the newspaper Al Shaab on September 21:

> Look! There is the master of democracy whom they have so often sanctified but who causes criminal, barbaric, bloody oppression that abandons the moral standards of even the most savage empires in history. In my last column I listed for readers the five million killed (may God receive them as martyrs) because of the crimes committed by this American civilization that America leads. These five million were killed in the last few decades alone.

Similar feelings led another *Al Shaab* columnist that day, Khalid al-Sharif, to describe the shock and delight that he felt while watching the World Trade Center crumbling:

> Look at that! America, master of the world, is crashing down. Look at that! The Satan who rules the world, east and west, is burning. Look at that! The sponsor of terrorism is itself seared by its fire.

The fanatics of al Qaeda see the world in black and white and advance a particularly narrow view of Islam. This makes them a tiny minority among Muslims. But the basic categories of their thought flow directly from the mainstream of the Salafiyya, a perspective that has enjoyed a wide hearing over the last 50 years. Familiarity thus ensures bin Laden's ideas a sympathetic reception in many quarters.

In Salafi writings, the United States emerges as the senior member of a "Zionist-Crusader alliance" dedicated to subjugating Muslims, killing them, and, most important, destroying Islam. A careful reading reveals that this alliance represents more than just close relations between the United States and Israel today. The international cooperation between Washington and Jerusalem is but one nefarious manifestation of a greater evil of almost cosmic proportions. Thus in his "Declaration of War" bin Laden lists 10 or 12 world hot spots where Muslims have recently died (including Bosnia, Chechnya, and Lebanon) and attributes all of these deaths to a conspiracy led by the United States, even though Americans actually played no role in pulling the trigger. And thus, in another document, "Jihad Against Jews and Crusaders," bin Laden describes U.S. policies toward the Middle East as "a clear declaration of war on God, His messenger, and Muslims."

As strange as it may sound to an American audience, the idea that the United States has taken an oath of enmity toward God has deep roots in the Salafi tradition. It has been around for more than 50 years and has reached a wide public through the works of, among others, Sayyid Qutb, the most important Salafi thinker of the last half-century and a popular author in the Muslim world even today, nearly 40 years after his death. A sample passage taken from his writings in the early 1950s illustrates the point. Addressing the reasons why the Western powers had failed to support Muslims against their enemies in Pakistan, Palestine, and elsewhere, Qutb canvassed a number of common explanations such as Jewish financial influence and British imperial trickery but concluded,

> All of these opinions overlook one vital element in the question … the Crusader spirit that runs in the blood of all Occidentals. It is this that colors all their thinking, which is responsible for their imperialistic fear of the spirit of Islam and for their efforts to crush the strength of Islam. For the instincts and the interests of all Occidentals are bound up together in the crushing of that strength. This is the common factor that links together communist Russia and capitalist America. We do not forget the role of international Zionism in plotting against Islam and in pooling the forces of the Crusader imperialists and communist materialists alike. This is nothing other than a continuation of the role

played by the Jews since the migration of the Prophet to Medina and the rise of the Islamic state.

Sayyid Qutb, Osama bin Laden, and the entire extremist Salafiyya see Western civilization, in all periods and in all guises, as innately hostile to Muslims and to Islam itself. The West and Islam are locked in a prolonged conflict. Islam will eventually triumph, of course, but only after enduring great hardship. Contemporary history, defined as it is by Western domination, constitutes the darkest era in the entire history of Islam.

AMERICA AND THE MONGOL THREAT

WHEN ATTEMPTING TO COME TO GRIPS with the nature of the threat the modern West poses, extremist Salafis fall back on the writings of Ibn Taymiyya for guidance. A towering figure in the history of Islamic thought, he was born in Damascus in the thirteenth century, when Syria stood under the threat of invasion from the Mongols. Modern radicals find him attractive because he too faced the threat of a rival civilization. Ibn Taymiyya the firebrand exhorted his fellow Muslims to fight the Mongol foe, while Ibn Taymiyya the intellectual guided his community through the problems Muslims face when their social order falls under the shadow of non-Muslim power. It is only natural that bin Laden himself looks to such a master in order to legitimate his policies. Using Ibn Taymiyya to target America, however, marks an interesting turning point in the history of the radical Salafiyya.

Bin Laden's "Declaration of War" uses the logic of Ibn Taymiyya to persuade others in the Salafiyya to abandon old tactics for new ones. The first reference to him arises in connection with a discussion of the "Zionist-Crusader alliance," which according to bin Laden has been jailing and killing radical preachers—men such as Sheikh Omar Abdel Rahman, in prison for plotting a series of bombings in New York City following the 1993 bombing of the World Trade Center. Bin Laden argues that the "iniquitous Crusader movement under the leadership of the U.S.A." fears these preachers because they will successfully rally the Islamic community against the West, just as Ibn Taymiyya did against the Mongols in his day. Having identified the United States as a threat to Islam equivalent to the Mongols, bin Laden then discusses what to do about it. Ibn Taymiyya provides the answer: "To fight in the defense of religion and belief is a collective duty; there is no other duty after belief than fighting the enemy who is corrupting the life and the religion." The next most important thing after accepting the word of God, in other words, is fighting for it.

By calling on the *umma* to fight the Americans as if they were the Mongols, bin Laden and his Egyptian lieutenants have taken the extremist Salafiyya down a radically new path. Militants have long identified the West as a pernicious evil on a par with the Mongols, but they have traditionally targeted the internal enemy, the Hypocrites and apostates, rather than Hubal itself. Aware that he is shifting the focus considerably, bin Laden quotes Ibn Taymiyya at length to establish the basic point that "people of Islam should join forces and support each other to get rid of the main infidel," even if that means that the true believers will be forced to fight alongside Muslims of dubious piety. In the grand scheme of things, he argues, God often uses the base motives of impious Muslims as a means of advancing the cause of religion. In effect, bin Laden calls upon his fellow Islamist radicals to postpone the Islamic revolution, to stop fighting Hypocrites and apostates: "An internal war is a great mistake, no matter what reasons there are for it," because discord among Muslims will only serve the United States and its goal of destroying Islam.

The shift of focus from the domestic enemy to the foreign power is all the more striking given the merger of al Qaeda and Egyptian Islamic Jihad. The latter's decision to kill Sadat in 1981 arose directly from the principle that the cause of Islam would be served by targeting lax Muslim leaders rather than by fighting foreigners, and here, too, Ibn Taymiyya provided the key doctrine. In his day Muslims often found themselves living under Mongol rulers who had absorbed Islam in one form or another. Ibn Taymiyya argued that such rulers—who outwardly pretended to be Muslims but who secretly followed non-Islamic, Mongol practices—must be considered infidels. Moreover, he claimed, by having accepted Islam but having also failed to observe key precepts of the religion, they had in effect committed apostasy and thereby written their own death sentences. In general, Islam prohibits fighting fellow Muslims and strongly restricts the right to rebel against the ruler; Ibn Taymiyya's doctrines, therefore, were crucial in the development of a modern Sunni Islamic revolutionary theory.

Egyptian Islamic Jihad views leaders such as Sadat as apostates. Although they may outwardly display signs of piety, they do not actually have Islam in their hearts, as their failure to enforce the *shari'a* proves. This non-Islamic behavior demonstrates that such leaders actually serve the secular West, precisely as an earlier generation of outwardly Muslim rulers had served the Mongols, and as the Hypocrites had served idolatry. Islamic Jihad explained itself back in the mid-1980s in a long, lucid statement titled "The Neglected Duty." Not a political manifesto like bin Laden's tracts, it is a sustained and learned argument that targets the serious believer rather than the angry, malleable crowd. Unlike bin Laden's holy war, moreover, Islamic Jihad's doctrine, though violent, fits clearly in the mainstream of Salafi consciousness, which historically has been concerned much more with the state of the Muslims themselves than with relations between Islam and the outside world. The decision to target America, therefore, raises the question of whether, during the 1990s, Egyptian Islamic Jihad changed its ideology entirely. Did its leaders decide that the foreign enemy was in fact the real enemy? Or was the 1993 bombing in New York tactical rather than strategic?

The answer would seem to be the latter. Bin Laden's "Declaration of War" itself testifies to the tactical nature of his campaign against America. Unlike "The Neglected Duty," which presents a focused argument, the "Declaration of War" meanders from topic to topic, contradicting itself along the way. On the one hand, it calls for unity in the face of external aggression and demands an end to internecine warfare; on the other, it calls in essence for revolution in Saudi Arabia. By presenting a litany of claims against the Saudi ruling family and by discussing the politics of Saudi Arabia at length and in minute detail, bin Laden protests too much: he reveals that he has not, in fact, set aside the internal war among the believers. Moreover, he also reveals that the ideological basis for that internal war has not changed. The members of the Saudi elite, like Sadat, have committed apostasy. Like the Hypocrites of Medina, they serve the forces of irreligion in order to harm the devotees of the Prophet and his message:

> You know more than anybody else about the size, intention, and the danger of the presence of the U.S. military bases in the area. The [Saudi] regime betrayed the *umma* and joined the infidels, assisting them... against the Muslims. It is well known that this is one of the ten "voiders" of Islam, deeds of de-Islamization. By opening the Arabian Peninsula to the crusaders, the regime disobeyed and acted against what has been enjoined by the messenger of God.

Osama bin Laden undoubtedly believes that Americans are Crusader-Zionists, that they threaten his people even more than did the Mongols—in short, that they are the enemies of God Himself. But he also sees them as obstacles to his plans for his native land. The "Declaration of War" provides yet more testimony to the old saw that ultimately all politics is local.

THE FAILURE OF POLITICAL ISLAM

IF THE ATTACKS on the United States represented a change in radical Salafi tactics, then one must wonder what prompted bin Laden and Zawahiri to make that change. The answer is that the attacks were a response to the failure of extremist movements in the Muslim world in recent years, which have generally proved incapable of taking power (Sudan and Afghanistan being the major exceptions). In the last two decades, several violent groups have challenged regimes such as those in Egypt, Syria, and Algeria, but in every case the government has managed to crush, co-opt, or marginalize the radicals. In the words of the "Declaration of War," the Zionist-Crusader alliance moves quickly to contain and abort any "corrective movement" appearing in Islamic countries. Different means and methods are used to achieve their target. Sometimes officials from the Ministry of the Interior, who are also graduates of the colleges of the *shari'a*, are [unleashed] to mislead and confuse the nation and the *umma*... and to circulate false information about the movement, wasting the energy of the nation in discussing minor issues and ignoring the main one that is the unification of people under the divine law of Allah.

Given that in Egypt, Algeria, and elsewhere regimes have resorted to extreme violence to protect themselves, it is striking that bin Laden emphasizes here not the brutality but rather the counterpropaganda designed to divide and rule. Consciously or not, he has put his finger on a serious problem for the extremist Salafis: the limitations of their political and economic theories.

Apart from insisting on the implementation of the *shari'a*, demanding social justice, and turning the *umma* into the only legitimate political community, radical Salafis have precious little to offer in response to the mundane problems that people and governments face in the modern world. Extremist Islam is profoundly effective in mounting a protest movement: it can produce a cadre of activists whose devotion to the cause knows no bounds, it can galvanize people to fight against oppression. But it has serious difficulties when it comes to producing institutions and programs that can command the attention of diverse groups in society over the long haul. Its success relies mainly on the support of true believers, but they tend to fragment in disputes over doctrine, leadership, and agenda.

The limitations of extremist Salafi political theory and its divisive tendencies come to light clearly if one compares the goals of al Qaeda with those of the Palestinian terrorist group Hamas, whose suicide bombers have also been in the headlines recently. The ideology of Hamas also evolved out of the Egyptian extremist Salafiyya milieu, and it shares with al Qaeda a paranoid view of the world: the *umma* and true Islam are threatened with extinction by the spread of Western secularism, the policies of the Crusading West, and oppression by the Zionists. Both Hamas and al Qaeda believe that the faithful must obliterate Israel. But looking more closely at Hamas and its agenda, one can see that it parts company with al Qaeda in many significant ways. This is because Hamas operates in the midst of nationalistic Palestinians, a majority of whom fervently desire, among other things, an end to the Israeli occupation and the establishment of a Palestinian state in part of historic Palestine.

The nationalist outlook of Hamas' public presents the organization with a number of thorny problems. Nationalism, according to the extremist Salafiyya, constitutes *shirk*—that is, polytheism or idolatry. If politics and religion are not distinct categories, as extremist

Salafis argue, then political life must be centered around God and God's law. Sovereignty belongs not to the nation but to God alone, and the only legitimate political community is the *umma*. Pride in one's ethnic group is tolerable only so long as it does not divide the community of believers, who form an indivisible unit thanks to the sovereignty of the *shari'a*. One day, extremist Salafis believe, political boundaries will be erased and all Muslims will live in one polity devoted to God's will. At the moment, however, the priority is not to erase boundaries but to raise up the *shari'a* and abolish secular law. Nationalism is idolatry because it divides the *umma* and replaces a *shari'a*-centered consciousness with ethnic pride.

If Hamas were actually to denounce secular Palestinian nationalists as apostates, however, it would immediately consign itself to political irrelevance. To skirt this problem, the organization has developed an elaborate view of Islamic history that in effect elevates the Palestinian national struggle to a position of paramount importance for the *umma* as a whole. This allows Hamas activists to function in the day-to-day political world as fellow travelers with the nationalists. Thus one of the fascinating aspects of Palestinian extremist Salafiyya is a dog that hasn't barked: in contrast to its sibling movements in neighboring countries, Hamas has refrained from labeling the secular leaders in the Palestinian Authority as apostates. Even at the height of Yasir Arafat's crackdown against Hamas, the movement never openly branded him as an idolater.

Like al Qaeda, Hamas argues that a conspiracy between Zionism and the West has dedicated itself to destroying Islam, but for obvious reasons it magnifies the role of Zionism in the alliance. The Hamas Covenant, for example, sees Zionism as, among other things, a force determining many of the greatest historical developments of the modern period:

> [Zionists] were behind the French Revolution, the communist revolution.... They were behind World War I, when they were able to destroy the Islamic caliphate [i.e., the Ottoman Empire].... They obtained the Balfour Declaration [favoring establishment of a Jewish homeland in Palestine], [and] formed the League of Nations, through which they could rule the world. They were behind World War II, through which they made huge financial gains by trading

in armaments, and paved the way for the establishment of their state. It was they who instigated the replacement of the League of Nations with the United Nations and the Security Council.... There is no war going on anywhere, without [them] having their finger in it.

Do a number of intelligent and educated people actually believe this? Yes, because they must; their self-understanding hinges on it. Since their political struggle must be for the greater good of the *umma* and of Islam as a whole, their enemy must be much more than just one part of the Jewish people with designs on one sliver of Muslim territory. The enemy must be the embodiment of an evil that transcends time and place.

Although the sanctity of Jerusalem works in Hamas' favor, in Islam Jerusalem does not enjoy the status of Mecca and Medina and is only a city, not an entire country. To reconcile its political and religious concerns, therefore, Hamas must inflate the significance of Palestine in Islamic history: "The present Zionist onslaught," the covenant says, "has also been preceded by Crusading raids from the West and other Tatar [Mongol] raids from the East." The references here are to Saladin, the Muslim leader who defeated the Crusaders in Palestine at the battle of Hattin in 1187, and to the Muslim armies that defeated the Mongols at another Palestinian site called Ayn Jalut in 1260. On this basis Hamas argues that Palestine has always been the bulwark against the enemies of Islam; the *umma*, therefore, must rally behind the Palestinians to destroy Israel, which represents the third massive onslaught against the true religion since the death of the Prophet.

Despite the similarities in their perspectives, therefore, al Qaeda and Hamas have quite different agendas. Al Qaeda justifies its political goals on the basis of the holiness of Mecca and Medina and on the claim that the presence of U.S. forces in Arabia constitutes the greatest aggression that the Muslims have ever endured. Hamas sees its own struggle against Israel as the first duty of the *umma*. The two organizations undoubtedly share enough in common to facilitate political cooperation on many issues, but at some point their agendas diverge radically, a divergence that stems from the different priorities inherent in their respective Saudi and Palestinian backgrounds.

The differences between al Qaeda and Hamas demonstrate how local conditions can mold the universal components of Salafi consciousness into distinct world views. They display the creativity of radical Islamists in addressing a practical problem similar to that faced by communists in the early twentieth century: how to build a universal political movement that can nevertheless function effectively at the local level. This explains why, when one looks at the political map of the extremist Salafiyya, one finds a large number of organizations, all of which insist that they stand for the same principles. They do, in fact, all insist on the implementation of the *shari'a*, but the specific social and political forces fueling that insistence differ greatly from place to place. They all march to the beat of God's drummer, but the marchers tend to wander off in different directions.

The new tactic of targeting America is designed to overcome precisely this weakness of political Islam. Bin Laden succeeded in attacking Hubal, the universal enemy: he identified the only target that all of the Salafiyya submovements around the world can claim equally as their own, thereby reflecting and reinforcing the collective belief that the *umma* actually is the political community. He and his colleagues adopted this strategy not from choice but from desperation, a desperation born of the fact that in recent years the extremist Salafis had been defeated politically almost everywhere in the Arab and Muslim world. The new tactic, by tapping into the deepest emotions of the political community, smacks of brilliance, and—much to America's chagrin—will undoubtedly give political Islam a renewed burst of energy.

EXPLAINING THE ECHO

THE DECISION TO TARGET the United States allows al Qaeda to play the role of a radical "Salafi International." It resonates beyond the small community of committed extremists, however, reaching not just moderate Salafis but, in addition, a broad range of disaffected citizens experiencing poverty, oppression, and powerlessness across the Muslim world. This broader resonance of what appears to us as such a wild and hateful message is the dimension of the problem that Americans find most difficult to understand.

One reason for the welcoming echo is the extent to which Salafi political movements, while failing to capture state power, have nevertheless succeeded in capturing much cultural ground in Muslim countries. Many authoritarian regimes (such as Mubarak's Egypt) have cut a deal with the extremists: in return for an end to assassinations, the regime acquiesces in some of the demands regarding implementation of the *shari'a*. In addition, it permits the extremist groups to run networks of social welfare organizations that often deliver services more efficiently than does a state sector riddled with corruption and marred by decay. This powerful cultural presence of the Salafis across the Islamic world means not only that their direct ranks have grown but also that their symbolism is more familiar than ever among a wider public.

But the attack on America also resonates deeply among secular groups in many countries. The immediate response in the secular Arab press, for example, fell broadly into three categories. A minority denounced the attacks forcefully and unconditionally, another minority attributed them to the Israelis or to American extremists like Timothy McVeigh, and a significant majority responded with a version of "Yes, but"—yes, the terrorist attacks against you were wrong, but you must understand that your own policies in the Middle East have for years sown the seeds of this kind of violence.

This rationalization amounts to a political protest against the perceived role of the United States in the Middle East. Arab and Islamic commentators, and a number of prominent analysts of the Middle East in this country, point in particular to U.S. enforcement of the sanctions on Iraq and U.S. support for Israel in its struggle against Palestinian nationalism. Both of these issues certainly cause outrage, and if the United States were to effect the removal of Israeli settlements from the West Bank and alleviate the suffering of the Iraqi people, some of that outrage would certainly subside. But although a change in those policies would dampen some of bin Laden's appeal, it would not solve the problem of the broader anger and despair that he taps, because the sources of those feelings lie beyond the realm of day-to-day diplomacy.

Indeed, secular political discourse in the Islamic world in general and the Arab world in particular bears a striking resemblance to the Salafi interpretation of international affairs, especially insofar as both speak in terms of Western conspiracies. The secular press does not make reference to Crusaders and Mongols but rather to a string of "broken promises" dating back to World War I, when the European powers divided up the Ottoman Empire to suit their own interests. They planted Israel in the midst of the Middle East, so the analysis goes, in order to drive a wedge between Arab states, and the United States continues to support Israel for the same purpose. Bin Laden played to this sentiment in his October 7 statement when he said,

> What the United States tastes today is a very small thing compared to what we have tasted for tens of years. Our nation has been tasting this humiliation and contempt for more than eighty years. Its sons are being killed, its blood is being shed, its holy places are being attacked, and it is not being ruled according to what God has decreed.

For 80 years—that is, since the destruction of the Ottoman Empire—the Arabs and the Muslims have been humiliated. Although they do not share bin Laden's millenarian agenda, when secular commentators point to Palestine and Iraq today they do not see just two difficult political problems; they see what they consider the true intentions of the West unmasked.

Arab commentators often explain, for instance, that Saddam Hussein and Washington are actually allies. They ridicule the notion that the United States tried to depose the dictator. After all, it is said, the first Bush administration had the forces in place to remove the Baath Party and had called on the Iraqi populace to rise up against the tyrant. When the people actually rose, however, the Americans watched from the sidelines as the regime brutally suppressed them. Clearly, therefore, what the United States really wanted was to divide and rule the Arabs in order to secure easy access to Persian Gulf oil—a task that also involves propping up corrupt monarchies in Kuwait and Saudi Arabia. Keeping Saddam on a leash was the easiest way to ensure that Iran could not block the project.

Needless to say, this world view is problematic. Since World War I, Arab societies have been deeply divided among themselves along ethnic, social, religious, and political lines. Regardless of what the dominant Arab discourse regarding broken promises has to say, most of these divisions were not created by the West. The European powers and the United States have sometimes worked to divide the Arabs, sometimes to unify them. Mostly they have pursued their own interests, as have all the other actors involved. Bin Laden is a participant in a profoundly serious civil war over Arab and Muslim identity in the modern world. The United States is also a participant in that war, because whether it realizes it or not, its policies affect the fortunes of the various belligerents. But Washington is not a primary actor, because it is an outsider in cultural affairs and has only a limited ability to define for believers the role of Islam in public life.

The war between extremist Salafis and the broader populations around them is only the tip of the iceberg. The fight over religion among Muslims is but one of a number of deep and enduring regional struggles that originally had nothing to do with the United States and even today involve it only indirectly. Nonetheless, U.S. policies can influence the balance of power among the protagonists in these struggles, sometimes to a considerable degree.

Until the Arab and Muslim worlds create political orders that do not disenfranchise huge segments of their own populations, the civil war will continue and will continue to touch the United States. Washington can play an important role in fostering authentic and inclusive polities, but ultimately Arabs and Muslims more generally must learn to live in peace with one another so as to live comfortably with outsiders. Whether they will do so is anybody's guess.

It is a stark political fact that in the Arab and Muslim worlds today economic globalization and the international balance of power both come with an American face, and neither gives much reason for optimism. Osama bin Laden's rhetoric, dividing the world into two camps—the *umma* versus the United States and puppet regimes—has a deep resonance because on some levels it conforms, if not to reality, then at least to its appearances. This is why, for the first time in modern history, the extremist Salafis have managed to mobilize mass popular opinion.

This development is troubling, but the United States still has some cards to play. Its policies, for instance, on both West Bank settlements and Iraq, are sorely in need of review—but only after bin Laden has been vanquished. These policy changes might help, but the root problem lies deeper. Once al Qaeda has been annihilated without sparking anti-American revolutions in the Islamic world, the United States should adopt a set of policies that ensure that significant numbers of Muslims—not Muslim regimes but Muslims—identify their own interests with those of the United States, so that demagogues like bin Laden cannot aspire to speak in the name of the entire *umma*. In 1991, millions of Iraqis constituted just such a reservoir of potential supporters, yet America turned its back on them. Washington had its reasons, but they were not the kind that can be justified in terms of the American values that we trumpet to the world. Today we are paying a price for that hypocrisy. This is not to say that we caused or deserved the attacks of September 11 in any way. It is to say, however, that we are to some extent responsible for the fact that so few in the Arab and Muslim worlds express vocal and unequivocal support for our cause, even when that cause is often their cause as well.

Since the events of September 11, innumerable articles have appeared in the press discussing America's loss of innocence. To foreigners, this view of Americans as naive bumpkins, a band of Forrest Gumps who just arrived in town, is difficult to fathom. Whether the MTV generation knows it or not, the United States has been deeply involved in other peoples' civil wars for a long time. A generation ago, for example, we supposedly lost our innocence in Vietnam. Back then, Adonis, the poet laureate of the Arab world, meditated on the ambivalence Arabs feel toward America. In the aftermath of the September 11 attacks, his poem seems prophetic:

> *New York, you will find in my land*
> *... the stone of Mecca and the waters of the Tigris.*
> *In spite of all this,*
> *you pant in Palestine and Hanoi.*
> *East and west you contend with people*
> *whose only history is fire.*

These tormented people knew us before we were virgins.

Inside Al-Qaeda's
Hard Drive

Alan Cullison

IN THE AUTUMN OF 2001 I was one of scores of journalists who ventured into northern Afghanistan to write about the U.S.-assisted war against the Taliban. As I crossed the Hindu Kush to cover the fighting for *The Wall Street Journal,* my journey took what looked like a fatal turn: the battered black pickup truck I had rented—which in its better years had been a war wagon for Afghan gunmen—lost its brakes as it headed down a steep mountain path, careened along the edge of a gorge, slammed headlong into the back of a Northern Alliance fuel truck that was creeping down the mountain, and slid to rest on its side in the middle of the road. My bags spilled down the mountainside or were crushed beneath the pickup.

Fortunately, none of the pickup's occupants—a Japanese journalist, two Afghan interpreters, the driver, and a shoeless boy who had been riding on the roof and wiping dust from the windshield—was seriously injured. Only my interpreter, a Russian-speaking Afghan, seemed to be hurt; he clutched his side and said that something had hit him in the ribs. We nursed some cuts and bruises, and climbed aboard a Northern Alliance truck carrying wooden crates of Kalashnikov ammunition.

The wreck might have been just a minor bump in my travels through a land where inhabitants display a whoopsy-daisy attitude toward fatal accidents and killings. But a day later, after bedding down forty miles north of Kabul, I asked my interpreter what had hit him in the ribs. He said it was my computer, which he'd always held in his lap for safekeeping. I got up and removed the computer

This article originally appeared in the September 2004 issue of *The Atlantic Monthly.*

from its black bag, opened its lid, and saw that the screen was smashed. In the coming weeks, living in a fly-infested hut, I scrawled stories by candlelight with a ballpoint pen and read dispatches to my editors over a satellite phone.

That crash became memorable for reasons I never expected. When the Taliban's defenses crumbled, in November of 2001, I joined a handful of malnourished correspondents who rushed into Kabul and filed stories about the city's liberation. We pounced like so many famished crows on the first Western staples we had seen since leaving home: peanut butter, pasteurized milk, and canned vegetables, all of which we found on Chicken Street, Kabul's version of a shopping district. We raided the houses where Arab members of al-Qaeda had been holed up during their stay in Afghanistan, grabbing whatever documents were left in their file cabinets. But unlike most correspondents, I needed to spend some time getting to know Kabul's computer dealers, because I wanted to replace my laptop. It took about an hour to shake hands with all of them.

The regime that had forbidden television and kite-flying as un-Islamic had also taken a dim view of computers. I searched through the bazaars and found Soviet-era radios and television sets, but the electronics dealers had never even seen a computer, and certainly didn't know how to wire one to a satellite phone.

I found my first computer dealer in a drafty storefront office in downtown Kabul, near the city's central park. He worked alone and didn't have a computer in his office, because, he said, he couldn't afford one. He bragged that he was the sole computer consultant for the Afghan national airline, Ariana. This impressed me deeply—until I learned that Ariana had only one computer and only one working airplane.

He told me about another dealer, who ran a computer training school on the second floor of a building overlooking the park. I fumbled my way up a decrepit, unlit stairwell and along a dusty hallway to an office: a long room with a threadbare couch and a desk with a computer on it.

The second dealer told me that he had serviced computers belonging to the Taliban and to Arabs in al-Qaeda. I forgot about my own computer problems and hired him to search for these computers. Eventually he led me to a semiliterate jewelry salesman with wide-set eyes and a penchant for gold chains. This was the man who that December would take $1,100 from me in exchange for two of al-Qaeda's most valuable computers—a 40-gigabyte IBM desktop and a Compaq laptop. He had stolen them from al-Qaeda's central office in Kabul on November 12, the night before the city fell to the Northern Alliance. He wanted the money, he said, so that he could travel to the United States and meet some American girls.

My acquisition of the al-Qaeda computers was unique in the experience of journalists covering radical Islam. In the 1990s the police had seized computers used by al-Qaeda members in Kenya and the Philippines, but journalists and historians learned very little about the contents of those computers; only some information from them was released in U.S. legal proceedings. A much fuller picture would emerge from the computers I obtained in Kabul (especially the IBM desktop), which had been used by al-Qaeda's leadership.

On the night before Kabul fell, Taliban officials were fleeing the city in trucks teetering with their personal effects. The looter who sold me the computers figured that al-Qaeda had fled as well, so he crawled over a brick wall surrounding the house that served as the group's office. Finding nobody inside, he took the two computers, which he had discovered in a room on the building's second floor. On the door of the room, he said, was the name of Muhammad Atef—al-Qaeda's military commander and a key planner of 9/11. Each day, he said, Atef would walk into the office carrying the laptop in its black case. The looter knew he had something good.

So did the U.S. military when it heard what I had bought. The offices of *The Wall Street Journal*, just across from the World Trade Center, had been destroyed on 9/11. Our New York staff, which was working out of a former warehouse in Lower Manhattan, was acutely aware of potential threats; it was carefully screening mail for anthrax. Thinking that the computers might hold information about future attacks, my editors called the U.S. Central Command, which sent three CIA agents to my hotel room in Kabul. They said they needed the computers immediately; I had time to copy only the desktop computer before handing them both over. Atef's laptop was returned to me two months later, by an agent named Bert, at a curbside in Washington, D.C. The CIA said that the drive had been almost empty, but I've always wondered if this was true.

Inside Al-Qaeda's Hard Drive

The desktop computer, it turned out, had been used mostly by Ayman al-Zawahiri, Osama bin Laden's top deputy. It contained nearly a thousand text documents, dating back to 1997. Many were locked with passwords or encrypted. Most were in Arabic, but some were in French, Farsi, English, or Malay, written in an elliptical and evolving system of code words. I worked intensively for more than a year with several translators and with a colleague at *The Wall Street Journal*, Andrew Higgins, interviewing dozens of former jihadis to decipher the context, codes, and intentions of the messages for a series of articles that Higgins and I wrote for the Journal in 2002.

What emerged was an astonishing inside look at the day-to-day world of al-Qaeda, as managed by its top strategic planners—among them bin Laden, al-Zawahiri, Atef, Ramzi bin al-Shibh, and Khalid Sheikh Muhammad, all of whom were intimately involved in the planning of 9/11, and some of whom (bin Laden and al-Zawahiri) are still at large. The documents included budgets, training manuals for recruits, and scouting reports for international attacks, and they shed light on everything from personnel matters and petty bureaucratic sniping to theological discussions and debates about the merits of suicide operations. There were also video files, photographs, scanned documents, and Web pages, many of which, it became clear, were part of the group's increasingly sophisticated efforts to conduct a global Internet-based publicity and recruitment effort.

The jihadis' Kabul office employed a zealous manager—Ayman al-Zawahiri's brother Muhammad, who maintained the computer's files in a meticulous network of folders and subfolders that neatly laid out the group's organizational structure and strategic concerns. (Muhammad's system fell apart after he was arrested in 2000 in Dubai and extradited to Egypt.) The files not only provided critical active intelligence about the group's plans and methods at the time (including the first leads about the shoe bomber Richard Reid, who had yet to attempt his attack) but also, in a fragmentary way, revealed a road map of al-Qaeda's progress toward 9/11. Considered as a whole, the trove of material on the computer represents what is surely the fullest sociological profile of al-Qaeda ever to be made public.

Perhaps one of the most important insights to emerge from the computer is that 9/11 sprang not so much from al-Qaeda's strengths as from its weaknesses. The computer did not reveal any links to Iraq or any other deep-pocketed government; amid the group's penury the members fell to bitter infighting. The blow against the United States was meant to put an end to the internal rivalries, which are manifest in vitriolic memos between Kabul and cells abroad. Al-Qaeda's leaders worried about a military response from the United States, but in such a response they spied opportunity: they had fought the Soviet Union in Afghanistan, and they fondly remembered that war as a galvanizing experience, an event that roused the indifferent of the Arab world to fight and win against a technologically superior Western infidel. The jihadis expected the United States, like the Soviet Union, to be a clumsy opponent. Afghanistan would again become a slowly filling graveyard for the imperial ambitions of a superpower.

Like the early Russian anarchists who wrote some of the most persuasive tracts on the uses of terror, al-Qaeda understood that its attacks would not lead to a quick collapse of the great powers. Rather, its aim was to tempt the powers to strike back in a way that would create sympathy for the terrorists. Al-Qaeda has so far gained little from the ground war in Afghanistan; the conflict in Iraq, closer to the center of the Arab world, is potentially more fruitful. As Arab resentment against the United States spreads, al-Qaeda may look less like a tightly knit terror group and more like a mass movement. And as the group develops synergy in working with other groups branded by the United States as enemies (in Iraq, the Israeli-occupied territories, Kashmir, the Mindanao Peninsula, and Chechnya, to name a few places), one wonders if the United States is indeed playing the role written for it on the computer.

LIFE IN AFGHANISTAN

AL-QAEDA'S LEADERS began decamping to Afghanistan in 1996, after the group was expelled from Sudan. Ayman al-Zawahiri, at the time also the leader of the militant Egyptian group Islamic Jihad, issued a call for other Islamists to follow, and in one letter found on the computer described Afghanistan as a "den of garrisoned lions." But not all Arabs were happy with the move. Afghanistan, racked by more than a decade of civil war and Soviet occupation, struck many as unfit to be the capital of global jihad. Jihadis complained about the food, the bad roads, and the Afghans themselves, who, they said, were uneducated, venal, and not to be trusted.

In April of 1998 a jihadi named Tariq Anwar visited Afghanistan for a meeting of Islamists and wrote back to his colleagues in Yemen about his impressions.

To: Al-Qaeda Members in Yemen
From: Tariq Anwar
Folder: Outgoing Mail—To Yemen
Date: April 1998

I send you my greetings from beyond the swamps to your country, where there is progress and civilization ... You should excuse us for not calling. There are many reasons, the most important of which is the difficulty of calling from this country. We have to go to the city, which involves a number of stages. The first stage involves arranging for a car (as we don't have a car). Of course, we are bound by the time the car is leaving, regardless of the time we want to leave. The second stage involves waiting for the car (we wait for the car, and it may be hours late or arrive before the agreed time). The next stage is the trip itself, when we sit like sardines in a can. Most of the time I have 1/8 of a chair, and the road is very bad. After all this suffering, the last stage is reaching a humble government communication office. Most of the time there is some kind of failure— either the power is off, the lines out of order, or the neighboring country [through which the connection is made] does not reply. Only in rare cases can we make problem-free calls ...

The Arabs' general contempt for the backwardness of Afghanistan was not lost on the Taliban, whose leaders grew annoyed with Osama bin Laden's focus on public relations and the media. Letters found on the computer reveal that relations between the Arabs and the Taliban had grown so tense that many feared the Taliban leader, Mullah Muhammad Omar, would expel the Arabs from the country. A dialogue to resolve the two sides' differences was carried on at the highest levels, as the memo below, from two Syrian operatives, demonstrates. ("Abu Abdullah" is a code name for bin Laden; "Leader of the Faithful" refers to Mullah Omar, in his hoped-for capacity as the head of a new Islamic emirate, based in Afghanistan.)

To: Osama bin Laden
From: Abu Mosab al-Suri and Abu Khalid al-Suri
Via: Ayman al-Zawahiri
Folder: Incoming Mail—From Afghanistan
Date: July 19, 1999

Noble brother Abu Abdullah,
Peace upon you, and God's mercy and blessings.

This message [concerns] the problem between you and the Leader of the Faithful...

The results of this crisis can be felt even here in Kabul and other places. Talk about closing down the camps has spread. Discontent with the Arabs has become clear. Whispers between the Taliban with some of our non-Arab brothers has become customary. In short, our brother Abu Abdullah's latest trouble-making with the Taliban and the Leader of the Faithful jeopardizes the Arabs, and the Arab presence, today in all of Afghanistan, for no good reason. It provides a ripe opportunity for all adversaries, including America, the West, the Jews, Saudi Arabia, Pakistan, the Mas'ud-Dostum alliance, etc., to serve the Arabs a blow that could end up causing their most faithful allies to kick them out... Our brother [bin Laden] will help our enemies reach their goal free of charge! ...

The strangest thing I have heard so far is Abu Abdullah's saying that he wouldn't listen to the Leader of the Faithful when he asked him to stop giving interviews. I think our brother [bin Laden] has caught the disease of screens, flashes, fans, and applause...

The only solution out of this dilemma is what a number of knowledgeable and experienced people have agreed upon...

Abu Abdullah should go to the Leader of the Faithful with some of his brothers and tell them that the Leader of the Faithful was right when he asked you to refrain from interviews, announcements, and media encounters, and that you will help the Taliban as much as you can in their battle, until they achieve control over Afghanistan. ... You should apologize for any inconvenience or pressure you have caused... and commit to the wishes and orders of the Leader of the Faithful on matters that concern his circumstances here...

The Leader of the Faithful, who should be obeyed where he reigns, is Muhammad Omar, not Osama bin Laden. Osama bin Laden and his companions are only guests seeking refuge and have to adhere to the terms laid out by the person who provided it for them. This is legitimate and logical.

The troubled relationship between al-Qaeda and the Taliban hadn't interfered with global plans. Al-Qaeda had developed a growing interest in suicide operations as an offensive weapon against Americans and other enemies around the world. On August 7, 1998, the group simultaneously struck the U.S. embassies in Kenya and Tanzania with car bombs, killing more than 220 people and wounding more than 4,000. Concerned that inflicting such heavy casualties on civilians would tarnish its image even among its supporters, al-Qaeda actively sought religious and legal opinions from Islamic scholars around the world who could help to justify the killing of innocents. The following letter is presumably a typical request for theological guidance.

To: Unknown
From: Unknown
Folder: Outgoing Mail
Date: September 26, 1998

Dear highly respected _____
...I present this to you as your humble brother... concerning the preparation of the lawful study that I am doing on the killing of civilians. This is a very sensitive case—as you know—especially these days...

It is very important that you provide your opinion of this matter, which has been forced upon us as an essential issue in the course and ideology of the Muslim movement...

[Our] questions are:

1. Since you are the representative of the Islamic Jihad group, what is your lawful stand on the killing of civilians, specifically when women and children are included? And please explain the legitimate law concerning those who are deliberately killed.

2. According to your law, how can you justify the killing of innocent victims because of a claim of oppression?

3. What is your stand concerning a group that supports the killing of civilians, including women and children?

With our prayers, wishing you success and stability.

SECRET OPERATIONS

As AL-QAEDA ESTABLISHED ITSELF in Afghanistan in the late 1990s and began managing international operations of ever increasing complexity and audacity, the group focused on ensuring the secrecy of its communications. It discouraged the use of e-mail and the telephone, and recommended faxes and couriers. The electronic files reflect the global nature of the work being done; much of the correspondence was neatly filed by country name. Messages were usually encrypted and often couched in language mimicking that of a multinational corporation; thus Osama bin Laden was sometimes "the contractor," acts of terrorism became "trade," Mullah Omar and the Taliban became "the Omar Brothers Company," the security services of the United States and Great Britain became "foreign competitors," and so on. Especially sensitive messages were encoded with a simple but reliable cryptographic system that had been used by both Allied and Axis powers during World War II—a "one-time pad" system that paired individual letters with randomly assigned numbers and letters and produced messages readable only by those who knew the pairings. The computer's files reveal that in 1998 and 1999, when a number of Islamists connected to al-Qaeda were arrested or compromised abroad, the jihadis in Afghanistan relied heavily on the one-time-pad system. They also devised new code names for people and places.

Letters sent from and to Ayman al-Zawahiri in 1999 contain coded language typical of many files on the computer; they also show the degree to which al-Qaeda operatives abroad were being exposed and detained because of their efforts. In the first of the following two letters much of the code remains mysterious.

To: Yemen Cell Members
From: Ayman al-Zawahiri
Folder: Outgoing Mail—To Yemen
Date: February 1, 1999

... I would like to clarify the following with relation to the birthday [probably an unspecified attack]:

a) Don't think of showering as it may harm your health.

b) We can't make a hotel reservation for you, but they usually don't mind making reservations for guests. Those who wish to make a reservation should go to Quwedar [a famous pastry shop in Cairo].

c) I suggest that each of you takes a recipient to Quwedar to buy sweets, then make the hotel reservation. It is easy. After you check in, walk to Nur. After you attend the birthday go from Quwedar to Bushra St., where you should buy movie tickets to the Za'bolla movie theater.

d) The birthday will be in the third month. How do you want to celebrate it in the seventh? Do you want us to change the boy's birth date? There are guests awaiting the real date to get back to their work.

e) I don't have any gravel [probably ammunition or bomb-making material].

To: Ayman al-Zawahiri
From: Unknown
Folder: Incoming Mail—From Yemen
Date: May 13, 1999

Dear brother Salah al-Din:
... Forty of the contractor's [bin Laden's] friends here were taken by surprise by malaria [arrested] a few days ago, following the telegram they sent, which was similar to Salah al-Din's telegrams [that is, it used the same code]. The majority of them are from here [Yemen], and two are from the contractor's country [Saudi Arabia] ...

We heard that al-Asmar had a sudden illness and went to the hospital [prison]. He will have a session with the doctors [lawyers] early next month to see if he can be treated there, or if he should be sent for treatment in his country [probably Egypt, where jihadis were routinely tortured and hanged] ...

Osman called some days ago. He is fine but in intensive care [being monitored by the police]. When his situation improves he will call. He is considering looking for work with Salah al-Din [in Afghanistan], as opportunities are scarce where he is, but his health condition is the obstacle.

Though troubled by arrests abroad, the jihadis had time and safety for contemplation in Afghanistan. In 1999 al-Zawahiri undertook a top-secret program to develop chemical and biological weapons, a program he and others referred to on the computer as the "Yogurt" project. Though fearsome in its intent, the program had a proposed start-up budget of only $2,000 to $4,000. Fluent in English and French, al-Zawahiri began by studying foreign medical journals and provided summaries in Arabic for Muhammad Atef, including the one that follows.

To: Muhammad Atef
From: Ayman al-Zawahiri
Folder: Outgoing Mail—To Muhammad Atef
Date: April 15, 1999

I have read the majority of the book [an unnamed volume, probably on biological and chemical weapons] ... [It] is undoubtedly useful. It emphasizes a number of important facts, such as:

a) The enemy started thinking about these weapons before WWI. Despite their extreme danger, we only became aware of them when the enemy drew our attention to them by repeatedly expressing concerns that they can be produced simply with easily available materials...

b) The destructive power of these weapons is no less than that of nuclear weapons.

c) A germ attack is often detected days after it occurs, which raises the number of victims.

d) Defense against such weapons is very difficult, particularly if large quantities are used...

I would like to emphasize what we previously discussed—that looking for a specialist is the fastest, safest, and cheapest way [to embark on a biological—and chemical weapons program]. Simultaneously, we should conduct a search on our own... Along these lines, the book guided me to a number of references that I am attaching. Perhaps you can find someone to obtain them...

The letter goes on to cite mid-twentieth-century articles from, among other sources, *Science, The Journal of Immunology,* and *The New England Journal of Medicine,* and lists the names of such books as *Tomorrow's Weapons* (1964), *Peace or Pestilence* (1949), and *Chemical Warfare* (1921).

Al-Zawahiri and Atef appear to have settled on the development of a chemical weapon as the most feasible option available to them. Their exchanges on the computer show that they hired Medhat Mursi al-Sayed, an expert to whom they refer as Abu Khabab, to assist them. They also drew up rudimentary architectural plans for their laboratory and devised a scheme to create a charitable foundation to serve as a front for the operation. According to other sources, Abu Khabab gassed some stray dogs at a testing field in eastern Afghanistan, but there is no indication that al-Qaeda ever developed a chemical weapon it could deploy.

THE BANALITY OF OFFICE LIFE

ALTHOUGH AL-QAEDA has been mythologized as a disciplined and sophisticated foe, united by a deadly commonality of purpose and by the wealth of its leader, internal correspondence on the computer reveals a somewhat different picture. In the years leading up to 9/11 the group was a loose confluence of organizations whose goals did not meld easily, as was seen in both tactical discussions (for example, should they attack Arab governments, America, or Israel?) and day-to-day office operations. At the most basic—that is to say, human—level the work relationships of al-Qaeda's key players were characterized by the same sort of bickering and gossiping and griping about money that one finds in offices everywhere. The following exchange is similar in tone and substance to much of what was found on the computer.

To: Ezzat [real name unknown]
From: Ayman al-Zawahiri
Folder: Outgoing Mail—To Yemen
Date: February 11, 1999

Noble brother Ezzat...
Following are my comments on the summary accounting I received:
... With all due respect, this is not an accounting. It's a summary

accounting. For example, you didn't write any dates, and many of the items are vague.

The analysis of the summary shows the following:

1. You received a total of $22,301. Of course, you didn't mention the period over which this sum was received. Our activities only benefited from a negligible portion of the money. This means that you received and distributed the money as you please...

2. Salaries amounted to $10,085—45 percent of the money. I had told you in my fax... that we've been receiving only half salaries for five months. What is your reaction or response to this?

3. Loans amounted to $2,190. Why did you give out loans? Didn't I give clear orders to Muhammad Saleh to... refer any loan requests to me? We have already had long discussions on this topic.

4. Why have guesthouse expenses amounted to $1,573 when only Yunis is there, and he can be accommodated without the need for a guesthouse?

5. Why did you buy a new fax for $470? Where are the two old faxes? Did you get permission before buying a new fax under such circumstances?

6. Please explain the cell-phone invoice amounting to $756 (2,800 riyals) when you have mentioned communication expenses of $300.

7. Why are you renovating the computer? Have I been informed of this?

8. General expenses you mentioned amounted to $235. Can you explain what you mean? ...

To : Ayman al-Zawahiri
From: Ezzat
Folder: Incoming Mail–From Yemen
Date: February 17, 1999

Kind brother Nur al-Din [al-Zawahiri]:

... We don't have any guesthouses. We have bachelor houses, and the offices are there too. We called it a guesthouse hypothetically, and we don't have any bachelors except Basil and Youssef. And Abd al-Kareem lives at his work place.

If I buy a fax and we have two old ones, that would be wanton or mad.

Communication expenses were $300 before we started using the mobile phone—and all these calls were to discuss the crises of Ashraf and Dawoud and Kareem and Ali and Ali Misarra and Abu Basel and others, in compliance with the orders.

Renovating our computer doesn't mean buying a new one but making sure that adjustments are made to suit Abdullah's [bin Laden's] work. There were many technical problems with the computer. These matters do not need approval.

There are articles for purchase that are difficult to keep track of, so we have put them under the title of general expenses...

The first step for me to implement in taking your advice is to resign from any relationship whatsoever between me and your Emirate. Consider me a political refugee...

THE MERGER

AL-QAEDA'S RELATIONSHIP with the Taliban, though strained at times, grew cozier as the attacks on New York and Washington approached. Mullah Omar was enraged at the U.S. missile strikes on Khost, Afghanistan, in 1998—strikes that were made in retaliation for bin Laden's African-embassy bombings that year. Bin Laden, meanwhile, kept after the Taliban leader with a campaign of flattery. He hailed Mullah Omar as Islam's new caliph (a lofty title not used since the collapse of the Ottoman Empire) and talked of Afghanistan as the kernel of what would become a sprawling and pure Islamic state that would embrace Central Asia and beyond. By 2001, some said, bin Laden had become a confidant of Mullah Omar, helping him to understand the outside world. He encouraged the Taliban leader to destroy the ancient Bamiyan Buddhas and sent him a congratulatory note afterward.

To: Mullah Omar
From: Osama bin Laden
Folder: Publications
Date: April 11, 2001

... I pray to God—after having granted you success in destroying the dead, deaf, and mute false gods—that He will grant you success in destroying the living false gods, the ones that talk and listen. God knows that those [gods] pose more danger to Islam and monotheism than the dead false gods. Among the most important such false gods in our time is the United Nations, which has become a new religion that is worshipped to the exclusion of God. The prophets of this religion are present in the UN General Assembly… The UN imposes all sorts of penalties on all those who contradict its religion. It issues documents and statements that openly contradict Islamic belief, such as the International Declaration for Human Rights, considering all religions are equal, and considering that the destruction of the statues constitutes a crime…

Meanwhile, Ayman al-Zawahiri rallied the support of other jihadis, especially in his militant group Islamic Jihad, which eventually became the largest component of al-Qaeda. Those jihadis from Egypt had been suspicious of him because of his close ties to bin Laden, whom they considered a publicity hound. In the summer of 1999 they ousted al-Zawahiri as the leader of Islamic Jihad and replaced him with a veteran, Tharwat Shehata, who wanted to limit the relationship with bin Laden and concentrate the group's fight against Egypt, not America. But with money scarce and morale low, Shehata soon resigned, and by the spring of 2001 al-Zawahiri had assumed control again. He sent a note to his colleagues in Islamic Jihad proposing a formal merger with bin Laden and al-Qaeda as "a way out of the bottleneck." Borrowing terms from global commerce, he warned of increased market share for "international monopolies"—the CIA and probably also Egyptian intelligence. The merger, he said, could "increase profits"—the publicity and support that terrorism could produce.

To:Unknown
From : Ayman al-Zawahiri
Folder: Letters
Date: May 3, 2001

The following is a summary of our situation: We are trying to return to our previous main activity [probably the merger]. The most important step was starting the school [training camps], the programs of which have been started. We also provided the teachers with means of conducting profitable trade as much as we could. Matters are all promising, except for the unfriendliness of two teachers, despite what we have provided for them. We are patient.

To: Osama bin Laden
From: Azmiray al-Maarek
Folder: Deleted File [Recovered]
Date: November 4, 2001

Sheikh Osama,
God protect you, and grant you highest rewards for me and for the Islamic nation. I would have liked to pray in Jerusalem but I may precede you in going where the permanent heaven is. Please be pious and firm. Here is a group of my poems. I wrote the poem "Going to God" after you gave me the good news [about being selected for a suicide operation]. Please read all these poems, particularly the last one, in public. I hope you will fulfill this wish after I die in the battle against the enemies of religion. Be hopeful. This religion will certainly be victorious. You are one of the symbols through the hands of whom God will grant us victory. You are the guardian of the Muslim nation. Nobody in our time has cared more about it. I have left my will with the brothers in Kandahar. My numbers are in the will, so please give my mother the good news. Please ask all the brothers to forgive me after my death.

God reward you for me. If I am a martyr I will ask God's forgiveness for you. I hope for God's mercy. An hour of patience is the key to heaven.

I hope that God joins us in heaven.

Your son,

Azmiray al-Maarek

"GOING TO GOD"

I am going to God, mother
I am going to live in His mercy
My feet will lead [guide] me
God willing, to His orders and right path.
Don't be sad, sing and ululate.

God has chosen me
As a man, for I have lived every day
As a man that bought his religion and sold his whims.
Mother of my son, be hopeful and patient.
We will meet in heaven.
I will die for my nation to live.
I will be alive in heaven.
Just one push on the trigger and I'm over,
Thus disfiguring the face of the enemies.
May the faces of those who don't fear God be disfigured,
The faces of those who don't defend Him.
May the cowards never sleep.
It is shameful what is happening in Jerusalem.
Get up, coward, as a man,
And perform glorious acts. Don't fear.
Father, forgive my sins,
And feel proud of the son you'll meet in heaven.
For the principle we lived for
I will die so that you may live by it, father.

To: His wife [unnamed]
From: Azmiray al-Maarek
Folder: Deleted File [Recovered]
Date: November 6, 2001

Mother of Ibrahim,
By the time you receive this will, I will be in the craws of birds,
God willing, after having performed a martyrdom operation
against the country of infidelity. This operation, God willing,
will turn the tide for Islam and Muslims. My darling, and
mother of my son, be pious and patient. I have preceded you
to a place the inhabitants of which don't suffer. Follow me
there through obedience to God... Know that my death is
martyrdom, my imprisonment hermitage, my exile tourism in
God's land. I would like to meet you in heaven, so please help
me by waking up at night to pray, fasting during the day, and
staying away from temptation. God is my witness that I am
satisfied with you. Any woman who dies after having obtained

her husband's satisfaction is worthy of heaven. I ask God to grant you heaven. God is my witness that all your deeds were good. You were the best wife, friend, and companion. God bless you. Prayers be upon the Prophet Muhammad, all his family, and his companions.

Your husband,
Father of Ibrahim,
Azmiray al-Maarek

As you know, the situation below in the village [probably Egypt] has become bad for traders [jihadis]. Our Upper Egyptian relatives have left the market, and we are suffering from international monopolies. Conflicts take place between us for trivial reasons, due to the scarcity of resources. We are also dispersed over various cities. However, God had mercy on us when the Omar Brothers Company [the Taliban] here opened the market for traders and provided them with an opportunity to reorganize, may God reward them. Among the benefits of residence here is that traders from all over gather in one place under one company, which increases familiarity and coopera-tion among them, particularly between us and the Abdullah Contracting Company [bin Laden and his associates]. The lat-est result of this cooperation is... the offer they gave. Follow-ing is a summary of the offer:

Encourage commercial activities [jihad] in the village to face foreign investors; stimulate publicity; then agree on joint work to unify trade in our area. Close relations allowed for an open dialogue to solve our problems. Colleagues here believe that this is an excellent opportunity to encourage sales in general, and in the village in particular. They are keen on the success of the project. They are also hopeful that this may be a way out of the bottleneck to transfer our activities to the stage of multi-nationals and joint profit. We are negotiating the details with both sides...

Al-Zawahiri's proposal set off a storm of protest from some mem-bers of Islamic Jihad, who—again—favored focusing on the struggle against the Egyptian government. They accused al-Zawahiri of leading their group in dangerous directions.

Alan Cullison

To: Ayman al-Zawahiri
From: Unknown
Folder: Letters
Date: Summer, 2001

Dear brother Abdullah al-Dayem [another name for al-Zawahiri]:
... I disagree completely with the issue of sales and profits. These
are not profits. They are rather a farce of compound losses. I believe
that going on in this is a dead end, as if we were fighting ghosts or
windmills. Enough of pouring musk on barren land.

I don't believe that we need to give indications of how this un-
planned path will fail. All we need to do is to estimate the company's assets since the beginning of this last phase, then take inventory of what remains. Count the number of laborers in your
farms [probably cells] at the mother's area [probably Egypt], then
see if anyone has stayed. Consider any of the many projects where
you enthusiastically participated. Did any of them succeed, other
than the Badr external greenhouses, which enjoyed limited success?

All indicators point out that the place and time are not suitable
for this type of agriculture. Cotton may not be planted in Siberia,
just as apples cannot be planted in hot areas. I'm sure you are aware
that wheat is planted in winter and cotton in summer. After all our
efforts we haven't seen any crops in winter or summer.

This type of agriculture is ridiculous. It's as if we were throwing
good seeds onto barren land.

In previous experiments where the circumstances and seeds were
better we made major losses. Now everything has deteriorated. Ask
those with experience in agriculture and history.

Despite the protests of certain Islamic Jihad members, a
merger with al-Qaeda had been cemented in the spring of 2001,
and in June the new group issued "Statement No. 1"—a press release of sorts, found on the computer, that warned the "Zionist
and Christian coalition" that "they will soon roast in the same
flame they now play with." The following month someone sat
down at the computer and composed a short message, titled "The
Solution," which trumpeted "martyrdom operations" as the key
to the battle against the West. On August 23 another operative
tapped out a report on a target-spotting mission in Egypt and
Israel that had been carried out by Richard Reid—the British

national who would later try to blow up a Paris-to-Miami airline flight with a bomb packed in one of his high-top sneakers. And on that same day in August the following plan for sending an agent on a target-spotting mission to the U.S.-Canadian border region was typed into the computer.

To: Real name unknown
From: Unknown
Folder: Hamza
Date: August 23, 2001

Special file for our brother Abu Bakr al-Albani ["the Albanian"] on the nature of his mission.

First, the mission: Gather information on:

1. Information on American soldiers who frequent nightclubs in the America-Canada border areas

2. The Israeli embassy, consulate, and cultural center in Canada

3. If it is possible to enter America and gather information on American soldier checkpoints, or on the American army in the border areas inside America

4. Information on the possibility of obtaining explosive devices inside Canada…

I have given to our brother $1,500 for travel expenses in Canada and America, and also the cost of the ticket for the trip back to us after four months, God willing.

AFTER 9/11

THE FIRST EVIDENCE OF WORK on the computer following 9/11 comes just days after the attacks, in the form of a promotional video called "The Big Job"—a montage of television footage of the attacks and their chaotic aftermath, all set to rousing victory music. The office was surely busier than it had ever been before, and soon many members of al-Qaeda's inner circle were competing for time on the computer. Ramzi bin al-Shibh, the senior Yemeni operative who coordinated with Khalid Sheikh Muhammad in masterminding the attacks, used the computer to work on a hasty and unfinished ideological justification for the operation, which he titled "The Truth About the New Crusade: A Ruling on the Killing of Women and Children of the Non-Believers," excerpts of which follow:

> Concerning the operations of the blessed Tuesday [9/11] ... they are legally legitimate, because they are committed against a country at war with us, and the people in that country are combatants. Someone might say that it is the innocent, the elderly, the women, and the children who are victims, so how can these operations be legitimate according to sharia? And we say that the sanctity of women, children, and the elderly is not absolute. There are special cases... Muslims may respond in kind if infidels have targeted women and children and elderly Muslims, [or if] they are being invaded, [or if] the non-combatants are helping with the fight, whether in action, word, or any other type of assistance, [or if they] need to attack with heavy weapons, which do not differentiate between combatants and non-combatants...
>
> Now that we know that the operations were permissible from the Islamic point of view, we must answer or respond to those who prohibit the operations from the point of view of benefits or harms...
>
> There are benefits... The operations have brought about the largest economic crisis that America has ever known. Material losses amount to one trillion dollars. America has lost about two thousand economic brains as a result of the operations. The stock exchange dropped drastically, and American consumer spending deteriorated. The dollar has dropped, the airlines have been crippled, the American globalization system, which was going to spoil the world, is gone...
>
> Because of Saddam and the Baath Party, America punished a whole population. Thus its bombs and its embargo killed millions of Iraqi Muslims. And because of Osama bin Laden, America surrounded Afghans and bombed them, causing the death of tens of thousands of Muslims... God said to assault whoever assaults you, in a like manner... In killing Americans who are ordinarily off limits, Muslims should not exceed four million non-combatants, or render more than ten million of them homeless. We should avoid this, to make sure the penalty [that we are inflicting] is no more than reciprocal. God knows what is best.

Osama bin Laden himself was composing letters on the computer just weeks before the fall of Kabul. In them he defiantly addressed the American people with a statement of al-Qaeda's goals, which he then went on to spell out at much greater length for Mullah Omar, in the spirit of a powerful, high-level political adviser offering advice to a head of state.

To: The American People
From: Osama bin Laden
Folder: Publications
Date: October 3, 2001

What takes place in America today was caused by the flagrant inter-ference on the part of successive American governments into others' business. These governments imposed regimes that contradict the faith, values, and lifestyles of the people. This is the truth that the American government is trying to conceal from the American people.

Our current battle is against the Jews. Our faith tells us we shall defeat them, God willing. However, Muslims find that the Ameri-cans stand as a protective shield and strong supporter, both finan-cially and morally. The desert storm that blew over New York and Washington should, in our view, have blown over Tel Aviv. The American position obliged Muslims to force the Americans out of the arena first to enable them to focus on their Jewish enemy. Why are the Americans fighting a battle on behalf of the Jews? Why do they sacrifice their sons and interests for them?

To: Mullah Omar
From: Osama bin Laden
Folder: Deleted File (Recovered)
Date: October 3, 2001

Highly esteemed Leader of the Faithful,
    Mullah Muhammad Omar, Mujahid,
    May God preserve him…
    1. We treasure your message, which confirms your generous, heroic position in defending Islam and in standing up to the symbols of infidelity of this time.
    2. I would like to emphasize the major impact of your statements

on the Islamic world. Nothing harms America more than receiving your strong response to its positions and statements. Thus it is very important that the Emirate respond to every threat or demand from America… with demands that America put an end to its support of Israel, and that U.S. forces withdraw from Saudi Arabia. Such responses nullify the effect of the American media on people's morale.

Newspapers mentioned that a recent survey showed that seven out of every ten Americans suffer psychological problems following the attacks on New York and Washington.

Although you have already made strong declarations, we ask you to increase them to equal the opponent's media campaign in quantity and force.

Their threat to invade Afghanistan should be countered by a threat on your part that America will not be able to dream of security until Muslims experience it as reality in Palestine and Afghanistan.

3. Keep in mind that America is currently facing two contradictory problems:

    a) If it refrains from responding to jihad operations, its prestige will collapse, thus forcing it to withdraw its troops abroad and restrict itself to U.S. internal affairs. This will transform it from a major power to a third-rate power, similar to Russia.

    b) On the other hand, a campaign against Afghanistan will impose great long-term economic burdens, leading to further economic collapse, which will force America, God willing, to resort to the former Soviet Union's only option: withdrawal from Afghanistan, disintegration, and contraction.

Thus our plan in the face of this campaign should focus on the following:

• Serving a blow to the American economy, which will lead to:

    a) Further weakening of the American economy.

    b) Shaking the confidence in the American economy.

This will lead investors to refrain from investing in America or participating in American companies, thus accelerating the fall of the American economy.

• Conduct a media campaign to fight the enemy's publicity. The campaign should focus on the following important points:

a) Attempt to cause a rift between the American people and their government, by demonstrating the following to the Americans:

- That the U.S. government will lead them into further losses of money and lives.
- That the government is sacrificing the people to serve the interests of the rich, particularly the Jews.
- That the government is leading them to the war front to protect Israel and its security.
- America should withdraw from the current battle between Muslims and Jews.

This plan aims to create pressure from the American people on their government to stop its campaign against Afghanistan, on the grounds that the campaign will cause major losses to the American people.

- Imply that the campaign against Afghanistan will be responded to with revenge blows against America.

I believe that we can issue, with your permission, a number of speeches that we expect will have the greatest impact, God willing, on the American, Pakistani, Arab, and Muslim people.

Finally, I would like to emphasize how much we appreciate the fact that you are our Emir. I would like to express our great appreciation of your historical stands in the service of Islam and in the defense of the Prophet's tradition. We ask God to accept and reward such stands.

We ask God to grant the Muslim Afghani nation, under your leadership, victory over the American infidels, just as he singled this nation out with the honor of defeating the Communist infidels.

We ask God to lead you to the good of both this life and the afterlife.

Peace upon you and God's mercy and blessings.

Your brother,
Osama Bin Muhammad Bin Laden

Why Do They Hate Us?

Fareed Zakaria

TO THE QUESTION "Why do the terrorists hate us?" Americans could be pardoned for answering, "Why should we care?" The immediate reaction to the murder of 5,000 innocents is anger, not analysis. Yet anger will not be enough to get us through what is sure to be a long struggle. For that we will need answers. The ones we have heard so far have been comforting but familiar. We stand for freedom and they hate it. We are rich and they envy us. We are strong and they resent this. All of which is true. But there are billions of poor and weak and oppressed people around the world. They don't turn planes into bombs. They don't blow themselves up to kill thousands of civilians. If envy were the cause of terrorism, Beverly Hills, Fifth Avenue and Mayfair would have become morgues long ago. There is something stronger at work here than deprivation and jealousy. Something that can move men to kill but also to die.

Osama bin Laden has an answer—religion. For him and his followers, this is a holy war between Islam and the Western world. Most Muslims disagree. Every Islamic country in the world has condemned the attacks of September. 11. To many, bin Laden belongs to a long line of extremists who have invoked religion to justify mass murder and spur men to suicide. The words "thug," "zealot" and "assassin" all come from ancient terror cults—Hindu, Jewish and Muslim, respectively—that believed they were doing the work of God. The terrorist's mind is its own place, and like Milton's Satan, can make a hell of heaven, a heaven of hell. Whether it is the Unabomber, Aum Shinrikyo or Baruch Goldstein (who killed scores

This article originally appeared in the October 15, 2001, issue of *Newsweek*. ©2001 by Newsweek Inc.

of unarmed Muslims in Hebron), terrorists are almost always misfits who place their own twisted morality above mankind's.

ADMIRATION FOR BIN LADEN

BUT BIN LADEN and his followers are not an isolated cult like Aum Shinrikyo or the Branch Davidians or demented loners like Timothy McVeigh and the Unabomber. They come out of a culture that reinforces their hostility, distrust and hatred of the West—and of America in particular. This culture does not condone terrorism but fuels the fanaticism that is at its heart. To say that al Qaeda is a fringe group may be reassuring, but it is false. Read the Arab press in the aftermath of the attacks and you will detect a not-so-hidden admiration for bin Laden. Or consider this from the Pakistani newspaper *The Nation*: "September 11 was not mindless terrorism for terrorism's sake. It was reaction and revenge, even retribution." Why else is America's response to the terror attacks so deeply constrained by fears of an "Islamic backlash" on the streets? Pakistan will dare not allow Washington the use of its bases. Saudi Arabia trembles at the thought of having to help us publicly. Egypt pleads that our strikes be as limited as possible. The problem is not that Osama bin Laden believes that this is a religious war against America. It's that millions of people across the Islamic world seem to agree.

This awkward reality has led some in the West to dust off old essays and older prejudices predicting a "clash of civilizations" between the West and Islam. The historian Paul Johnson has argued that Islam is intrinsically an intolerant and violent religion. Other scholars have disagreed, pointing out that Islam condemns the slaughter of innocents and prohibits suicide. Nothing will be solved by searching for "true Islam" or quoting the Quran. The Quran is a vast, vague book, filled with poetry and contradictions (much like the Bible). You can find in it condemnations of war and incitements to struggle, beautiful expressions of tolerance and stern strictures against unbelievers. Quotations from it usually tell us more about the person who selected the passages than about Islam. Every religion is compatible with the best and the worst of humankind. Through its long history, Christianity has supported inquisitions and anti-Semitism, but also human rights and social welfare.

Searching the history books is also of limited value. From the Crusades of the 11th century to the Turkish expansion of the 15th century to the colonial era in the early 20th century, Islam and the West have often battled militarily. This tension has existed for hundreds of years, during which there have been many periods of peace and even harmony. Until the 1950s, for example, Jews and Christians lived peaceably under Muslim rule. In fact, Bernard Lewis, the preeminent historian of Islam, has argued that for much of history religious minorities did better under Muslim rulers than they did under Christian ones. All that has changed in the past few decades. So surely the relevant question we must ask is, Why are we in a particularly difficult phase right now? What has gone wrong in the world of Islam that explains not the conquest of Constantinople in 1453 or the siege of Vienna of 1683 but September 11, 2001?

Let us first peer inside that vast Islamic world. Many of the largest Muslim countries in the world show little of this anti-American rage. The biggest, Indonesia, had, until the recent Asian economic crisis, been diligently following Washington's advice on economics, with impressive results. The second and third most populous Muslim countries, Pakistan and Bangladesh, have mixed Islam and modernity with some success. While both countries are impoverished, both have voted a woman into power as prime minister, before most Western countries have done so. Next is Turkey, the sixth largest Muslim country in the world, a flawed but functioning secular democracy and a close ally of the West (being a member of NATO).

Only when you get to the Middle East do you see in lurid colors all the dysfunctions that people conjure up when they think of Islam today. In Iran, Egypt, Syria, Iraq, Jordan, the occupied territories and the Persian Gulf, the resurgence of Islamic fundamentalism is virulent, and a raw anti-Americanism seems to be everywhere. This is the land of suicide bombers, flag-burners and fiery mullahs. As we strike Afghanistan it is worth remembering that not a single Afghan has been tied to a terrorist attack against the United States. Afghanistan is the campground from which an Arab army is battling America.

But even the Arab rage at America is relatively recent. In the 1950s and 1960s it seemed unimaginable that the United States and the Arab world would end up locked in a cultural clash. Egypt's most powerful journalist, Mohamed Heikal, described the mood at the time: "The whole picture of the United States... was a glamorous one. Britain and France were fading, hated empires. The Soviet Union was 5,000 miles away and the ideology of communism was anathema to the Muslim religion. But America had emerged from World War II richer, more powerful and more appealing than ever." I first traveled to the Middle East in the early 1970s, and even then the image of America was of a glistening, approachable modernity: fast cars, Hilton hotels and Coca-Cola. Something happened in these lands. To understand the roots of anti-American rage in the Middle East, we need to plumb not the past 300 years of history but the past 30.

CHAPTER I: THE RULERS

IT IS DIFFICULT to conjure up the excitement in the Arab world in the late 1950s as Gamal Abdel Nasser consolidated power in Egypt. For decades Arabs had been ruled by colonial governors and decadent kings. Now they were achieving their dreams of independence, and Nasser was their new savior, a modern man for the postwar era. He was born under British rule, in Alexandria, a cosmopolitan city that was more Mediterranean than Arab. His formative years were spent in the Army, the most Westernized segment of the society. With his tailored suits and fashionable dark glasses, he cut an energetic figure on the world stage. "The Lion of Egypt," he spoke for all the Arab world.

Nasser believed that Arab politics needed to be fired by modern ideas like self-determination, socialism and Arab unity. And before oil money turned the Gulf states into golden geese, Egypt was the undisputed leader of the Middle East. So Nasser's vision became the region's. Every regime, from the Baathists in Syria and Iraq to the conservative monarchies of the Gulf, spoke in similar terms and tones. It wasn't that they were just aping Nasser. The Middle East desperately wanted to become modern. It failed. For all their energy these regimes chose bad ideas and implemented them in worse ways. Socialism produced bureaucracy and stagnation. Rather than adjusting to the failures of central planning, the economies never really moved on. The republics calcified into dictatorships. Third World "nonalignment" became pro-Soviet propaganda. Arab unity cracked and crumbled as countries discovered their own national interests and opportunities. Worst of all, Israel humiliated the Arabs in the wars of 1967 and 1973. When Saddam Hussein invaded Kuwait in 1990, he destroyed the last remnants of the Arab idea.

Egypt's Quiet Nightmare

Look at Egypt today. The promise of Nasserism has turned into a quiet nightmare. The government is efficient in only one area: squashing dissent and strangling civil society. In the past 30 years Egypt's economy has sputtered along while its population has doubled. Unemployment is at 25 percent, and 90 percent of those searching for jobs hold college diplomas. Once the heart of Arab intellectual life, the country produces just 375 books every year (compared with Israel's 4,000). For all the angry protests to foreigners, Egyptians know all this.

Shockingly, Egypt has fared better than its Arab neighbors. Syria has become one of the world's most oppressive police states, a country where 25,000 people can be rounded up and killed by the regime with no consequences. (This in a land whose capital, Damascus, is the oldest continuously inhabited city in the world.) In 30 years Iraq has gone from being among the most modern and secular of Arab countries—with women working, artists thriving, journalists writing—into a squalid playpen for Saddam Hussein's megalomania. Lebanon, a diverse, cosmopolitan society with a capital, Beirut, that was once called the Paris of the East, has become a hellhole of war and terror. In an almost unthinkable reversal of a global pattern, almost every Arab country today is less free than it was 30 years ago. There are few countries in the world of which one can say that.

We think of Africa's dictators as rapacious, but those in the Middle East can be just as greedy. And when contrasted with the success of Israel, Arab failures are even more humiliating. For all its flaws, out of the same desert Israel has created a functioning democracy, a modern society with an increasingly high-technology economy and thriving artistic and cultural life. Israel now has a per capita GDP that equals that of many Western countries.

If poverty produced failure in most of Arabia, wealth produced failure in the rest of it. The rise of oil power in the 1970s gave a second wind to Arab hopes. Where Nasserism failed, petroleum would succeed. But it didn't. All that the rise of oil prices has done over three decades is to produce a new class of rich, superficially Western gulf Arabs, who travel the globe in luxury and are despised by the rest of the Arab world. Look at any cartoons of Gulf sheiks in Egyptian, Jordanian or Syrian newspapers. They are portrayed in the most insulting, almost racist manner: as corpulent, corrupt and weak. Most Americans think that Arabs should be grateful for our role in the Gulf War, for we saved Kuwait and Saudi Arabia. Most Arabs think that we saved the Kuwaiti and Saudi *royal families*. Big difference.

Wealth's Negative Effects
The money that the gulf sheiks have frittered away is on a scale that is almost impossible to believe. Just one example: a favored prince of Saudi Arabia, at the age of 25, built a palace in Riyadh for $300 million and, as an additional bounty, was given a $1 billion commission on the kingdom's telephone contract with AT&T. Far from producing political progress, wealth has actually had some negative effects. It has enriched and empowered the gulf governments so that, like their Arab brethren, they, too, have become more repressive over time. The Bedouin societies they once ruled have become gilded cages, filled with frustrated, bitter and discontented young men—some of whom now live in Afghanistan and work with Osama bin Laden. (Bin Laden and some of his aides come from privileged backgrounds in Saudi Arabia.)

By the late 1980s, while the rest of the world was watching old regimes from Moscow to Prague to Seoul to Johannesburg crack, the Arabs were stuck with their aging dictators and corrupt kings. Regimes that might have seemed promising in the 1960s were now exposed as tired, corrupt kleptocracies, deeply unpopular and thoroughly illegitimate. One has to add that many of them are close American allies.

CHAPTER II: FAILED IDEAS

HOW DOES A REGION that once yearned for modernity reject it so dramatically?

About a decade ago, in a casual conversation with an elderly Arab intellectual, I expressed my frustration that governments in the Middle East had been unable to liberalize their economies and societies in the way that the East Asians had done. "Look at Singapore, Hong Kong and Seoul," I said, pointing to their extraordinary economic achievements.

The man, a gentle, charming scholar, straightened up and replied sharply, "Look at them. They have simply aped the West. Their cities are cheap copies of Houston and Dallas. That may be all right for fishing villages. But we are heirs to one of the great civilizations of the world. We cannot become slums of the West."

This disillusionment with the West is at the heart of the Arab problem. It makes economic advance impossible and political progress fraught with difficulty. Modernization is now taken to mean, inevitably, uncontrollably, Westernization and, even worse, Americanization. This fear has paralyzed Arab civilization. In some ways the Arab world seems less ready to confront the age of globalization than even Africa, despite the devastation that continent has suffered from AIDS and economic and political dysfunction. At least the Africans want to adapt to the new global economy. The Arab world has not yet taken that first step.

Past or Future?

The question is how a region that once yearned for modernity could reject it so dramatically. In the Middle Ages the Arabs studied Aristotle (when he was long forgotten in the West) and invented algebra. In the 19th century, when the West set ashore in Arab lands, in the form of Napoleon's conquest of Egypt, the locals were fascinated by this powerful civilization. In fact, as the historian Albert Hourani has documented, the 19th century saw European-inspired liberal political and social thought flourish in the Middle East.

The colonial era of the late 19th and early 20th centuries raised hopes of British friendship that were to be disappointed, but still Arab elites remained fascinated with the West. Future kings and generals attended Victoria College in Alexandria, learning the speech and manners of British gentlemen. Many then went on to Oxford, Cambridge and Sandhurst—a tradition that is still maintained by Jordan's royal family, though now they go to Hotchkiss or Lawrenceville. After World War I, a new liberal age flickered briefly in the Arab world, as ideas about opening up politics and society gained currency in places like Egypt, Lebanon, Iraq and Syria. But since they were part of a world of kings and aristocrats, these ideas died with those old regimes. The new ones, however, turned out to be just as Western.

Nasser thought his ideas for Egypt and the Arab world were modern. They were also Western. His "national charter" of 1962 reads as if it were written by left-wing intellectuals in Paris or London. (Like many Third World leaders of the time, Nasser was a devoted reader of France's *Le Monde* and Britain's *New Statesman*.) Even his most passionately held project, Pan-Arabism, was European. It was a version of the nationalism that had united Italy and Germany in the 1870s—that those who spoke one language should be one nation.

One Failure After Another

America thinks of modernity as all good—and it has been almost all good for America. But for the Arab world, modernity has been one failure after another. Each path followed—socialism, secularism, nationalism—has turned into a dead end. While other countries adjusted to their failures, Arab regimes got stuck in their ways. And those that reformed economically could not bring themselves to ease up politically. The Shah of Iran, the Middle Eastern ruler who tried to move his country into the modern era fastest, reaped the most violent reaction in the Iranian revolution of 1979. But even the shah's modernization—compared, for example, with the East Asian approach of hard work, investment and thrift—was an attempt to buy modernization with oil wealth.

It turns out that modernization takes more than strongmen and oil money. Importing foreign stuff—Cadillacs, Gulfstreams and McDonald's—is easy. Importing the inner stuffings of modern society—a free market, political parties, accountability and the rule of law—is difficult and dangerous. The Gulf states, for example, have gotten modernization lite, with the goods and even the workers imported from abroad. Nothing was homegrown; nothing is even now. As for politics, the Gulf governments offered their people a bargain: we will bribe you with wealth, but in return let us stay in power. It was the inverse slogan of the American revolution—no taxation, but no representation either.

Fareed Zakaria

The new age of globalization has hit the Arab world in a very strange way. Its societies are open enough to be disrupted by modernity, but not so open that they can ride the wave. They see the television shows, the fast foods and the fizzy drinks. But they don't see genuine liberalization in the society, with increased opportunities and greater openness. Globalization in the Arab world is the critic's caricature of globalization—a slew of Western products and billboards with little else. For some in their societies it means more things to buy. For the regimes it is an unsettling, dangerous phenomenon. As a result, the people they rule can look at globalization but for the most part not touch it.

Unstoppable Globalization
America stands at the center of this world of globalization. It seems unstoppable. If you close the borders, America comes in through the mail. If you censor the mail, it appears in the fast food and faded jeans. If you ban the products, it seeps in through satellite television. Americans are so comfortable with global capitalism and consumer culture that we cannot fathom just how revolutionary these forces are.

Disoriented young men, with one foot in the old world and another in the new, now look for a purer, simpler alternative. Fundamentalism searches for such people everywhere; it, too, has been globalized. One can now find men in Indonesia who regard the Palestinian cause as their own. (Twenty years ago an Indonesian Muslim would barely have known where Palestine was.) Often they learned about this path away from the West while they were in the West. As did Mohamed Atta, the Hamburg-educated engineer who drove the first plane into the World Trade Center.

The Arab world has a problem with its Attas in more than one sense. Globalization has caught it at a bad demographic moment. Arab societies are going through a massive youth bulge, with more than half of most countries' populations under the age of 25. Young men, often better educated than their parents, leave their traditional villages to find work. They arrive in noisy, crowded cities like Cairo, Beirut and Damascus or go to work in the oil states. (Almost 10 percent of Egypt's working population worked in the Gulf at one point.) In their new world they see great disparities of wealth and the disorienting effects of modernity; most unsettlingly, they see women, unveiled and in public places, taking buses, eating in cafes and working alongside them.

A huge influx of restless young men in any country is bad news. When accompanied by even small economic and social change, it usually produces a new politics of protest. In the past, societies in these circumstances have fallen prey to a search for revolutionary solutions. (France went through a youth bulge just before the French Revolution, as did Iran before its 1979 revolution.) In the case of the Arab world, this revolution has taken the form of an Islamic resurgence.

CHAPTER III: ENTER RELIGION

The Origins of "Islamic Fundamentalism"

NASSER WAS A REASONABLY devout Muslim, but he had no interest in mixing religion with politics. It struck him as moving backward. This became apparent to the small Islamic parties that supported Nasser's rise to power. The most important one, the Muslim Brotherhood, began opposing him vigorously, often violently. Nasser cracked down on it in 1954, imprisoning more than a thousand of its leaders and executing six. One of those jailed, Sayyid Qutub, a frail man with a fiery pen, wrote a book in prison called "Signposts on the Road," which in some ways marks the beginnings of modern political Islam or what is often called "Islamic fundamentalism."

In his book, Qutub condemned Nasser as an impious Muslim and his regime as un-Islamic. Indeed, he went on, almost every modern Arab regime was similarly flawed. Qutub envisioned a better, more virtuous polity that was based on strict Islamic principles, a core goal of orthodox Muslims since the 1880s. As the regimes of the Middle East grew more distant and oppressive and hollow in the decades following Nasser, fundamentalism's appeal grew. It flourished because the Muslim Brotherhood and organizations like it at least tried to give people a sense of meaning and purpose in a changing world, something no leader in the Middle East tried to do.

In his seminal work, "The Arab Predicament," Fouad Ajami explains, "The fundamentalist call has resonance because it invited men to participate ... [in] contrast to a political culture that reduces citizens to spectators and asks them to leave things to their rulers.

At a time when the future is uncertain, it connects them to a tradition that reduces bewilderment." Fundamentalism gave Arabs who were dissatisfied with their lot a powerful language of opposition.

Few Pathways for Dissent

On that score, Islam had little competition. The Arab world is a political desert with no real political parties, no free press, few pathways for dissent. As a result, the mosque turned into the place to discuss politics. And fundamentalist organizations have done more than talk. From the Muslim Brotherhood to Hamas to Hizbullah, they actively provide social services, medical assistance, counseling and temporary housing. For those who treasure civil society, it is disturbing to see that in the Middle East these illiberal groups *are* civil society.

I asked Sheri Berman, a scholar at Princeton who studies the rise of fascist parties in Europe, whether she saw any parallels. "Fascists were often very effective at providing social services," she pointed out. "When the state or political parties fail to provide a sense of legitimacy or purpose or basic services, other organizations have often been able to step into the void. In Islamic countries there is a ready-made source of legitimacy in the religion. So it's not surprising that this is the foundation on which these groups have flourished. The particular form—Islamic fundamentalism—is specific to this region, but the basic dynamic is similar to the rise of Nazism, fascism and even populism in the United States."

Islamic fundamentalism got a tremendous boost in 1979 when Ayatollah Ruhollah Khomeini toppled the Shah of Iran. The Iranian revolution demonstrated that a powerful ruler could be taken on by groups within society. It also revealed how in a broken society even seemingly benign forces of progress—education and technology—can add to the turmoil. Until the 1970s most Muslims in the Middle East were illiterate and lived in villages and towns. They practiced a kind of street-Islam that had adapted itself to the local culture. Pluralistic and tolerant, these people often worshiped saints, went to shrines, sang religious hymns and cherished religious art, all technically disallowed in Islam. (This was particularly true in Iran.) By the 1970s, however, people had begun moving out of the villages and their religious experience was not rooted in a specific place. At the same time they were learning to read and they discovered that a new Islam was being preached by the fundamentalists, an abstract faith not rooted in historical experience but literal, puritanical and by the book. It was Islam of the High Church as opposed to Islam of the village fair.

Against 'Westoxification'

In Iran, Ayatollah Khomeini used a powerful technology—the audiocassette. His sermons were distributed throughout the country and became the vehicle of opposition to the shah's repressive regime. But Khomeini was not alone in using the language of Islam as a political tool. Intellectuals, disillusioned by the half-baked or overrapid modernization that was throwing their world into turmoil, were writing books against "Westoxification" and calling the modern Iranian man—half Western, half Eastern—rootless. Fashionable intellectuals, often writing from the comfort of London or Paris, would critique American secularism and consumerism and endorse an Islamic alternative. As theories like these spread across the Arab world, they appealed not to the poorest of the poor, for whom Westernization was magical (it meant food and medicine). They appealed to the half-educated hordes entering the cities of the Middle East or seeking education and jobs in the West.

The fact that Islam is a highly egalitarian religion for the most part has also proved an empowering call for people who felt powerless. At the same time it means that no Muslim really has the authority to question whether someone who claims to be a proper Muslim is one. The fundamentalists, from Sayyid Qutub on, have jumped into that void. They ask whether people are "good Muslims." It is a question that has terrified the Muslim world. And here we come to the failure not simply of governments but intellectual and social elites. Moderate Muslims are loath to criticize or debunk the fanaticism of the fundamentalists. Like the moderates in Northern Ireland, they are scared of what would happen to them if they speak their mind.

The biggest Devil's bargain has been made by the moderate monarchies of the Persian Gulf, particularly Saudi Arabia. The Saudi regime has played a dangerous game. It deflects attention from its shoddy record at home by funding religious schools (*madrasas*) and centers that spread a rigid, puritanical brand of

Islam—Wahhabism. In the past 30 years Saudi-funded schools have churned out tens of thousands of half-educated, fanatical Muslims who view the modern world and non-Muslims with great suspicion. America in this world view is almost always evil.

Allied with Fundamentalism

This exported fundamentalism has in turn infected not just other Arab societies but countries outside the Arab world, like Pakistan. During the 11-year reign of Gen. Zia ul-Haq, the dictator decided that as he squashed political dissent he needed allies. He found them in the fundamentalists. With the aid of Saudi financiers and functionaries, he set up scores of *madrasas* throughout the country. They bought him temporary legitimacy but have eroded the social fabric of Pakistan.

If there is one great cause of the rise of Islamic fundamentalism, it is the total failure of political institutions in the Arab world. Muslim elites have averted their eyes from this reality. Conferences at Islamic centers would still rather discuss "Islam and the Environment" than examine the dysfunctions of the current regimes. But as the moderate majority looks the other way, Islam is being taken over by a small poisonous element, people who advocate cruel attitudes toward women, education, the economy and modern life in general. I have seen this happen in India, where I grew up. The rich, colorful, pluralistic and easygoing Islam of my youth has turned into a dour, puritanical faith, policed by petty theocrats and religious commissars. The next section deals with what the United States can do to help the Islamic world. But if Muslims do not take it upon themselves to stop their religion from falling prey to medievalists, nothing any outsider can do will save them.

CHAPTER IV: WHAT TO DO

AMERICA'S greatest sins toward the Arab world are sins of omission. If almost any Arab were to have read this essay so far, he would have objected vigorously by now. "It is all very well to talk about the failures of the Arab world," he would say, "but what about the failures of the West? You speak of long-term decline, but our problems are with specific, cruel American policies." For most Arabs, relations with the United States have been filled with disappointment.

Why Do They Hate Us?

While the Arab world has long felt betrayed by Europe's colonial powers, its disillusionment with America begins most importantly with the creation of Israel in 1948. As the Arabs see it, at a time when colonies were winning independence from the West, here was a state largely composed of foreign people being imposed on a region with Western backing. The anger deepened in the wake of America's support for Israel during the wars of 1967 and 1973, and ever since in its relations with the Palestinians. The daily exposure to Israel's iron-fisted rule over the occupied territories has turned this into the great cause of the Arab—and indeed the broader Islamic—world. Elsewhere, they look at American policy in the region as cynically geared to America's oil interests, supporting thugs and tyrants without any hesitation. Finally, the bombing and isolation of Iraq have become fodder for daily attacks on the United States. While many in the Arab world do not like Saddam Hussein, they believe that the United States has chosen a particularly inhuman method of fighting him—a method that is starving an entire nation.

There is substance to some of these charges, and certainly from the point of view of an Arab, American actions are never going to seem entirely fair. Like any country, America has its interests. In my view, America's greatest sins toward the Arab world are sins of omission. We have neglected to press any regime there to open up its society. This neglect turned deadly in the case of Afghanistan. Walking away from that fractured country after 1989 resulted in the rise of bin Laden and the Taliban. This is not the gravest error a great power can make, but it is a common American one. As F. Scott Fitzgerald explained of his characters in "The Great Gatsby," "They were careless people, Tom and Daisy—they smashed things up and creatures and then retreated back into their money, or their vast carelessness ... and let other people clean up the mess." America has not been venal in the Arab world. But it has been careless.

Explaining Arab Rage

Yet carelessness is not enough to explain Arab rage. After all, if concern for the Palestinians is at the heart of the problem, why have their Arab brethren done nothing for them? (They cannot resettle in any Arab nation but Jordan, and the aid they receive from the

Gulf states is minuscule.) Israel treats its 1 million Arabs as second-class citizens, a disgrace on its democracy. And yet the tragedy of the Arab world is that Israel accords them more political rights and dignities than most Arab nations give to their own people. Why is the focus of Arab anger on Israel and not those regimes?

The disproportionate feelings of grievance directed at America have to be placed in the overall context of the sense of humiliation, decline and despair that sweeps the Arab world. After all, the Chinese vigorously disagree with most of America's foreign policy and have fought wars with U.S. proxies. African states feel the same sense of disappointment and unfairness. But they do not work it into a rage against America. Arabs, however, feel that they are under siege from the modern world and that the United States symbolizes this world. Thus every action America takes gets magnified a thousandfold. And even when we do not act, the rumors of our gigantic powers and nefarious deeds still spread. Most Americans would not believe how common the rumor is throughout the Arab world that either the CIA or Israel's Mossad blew up the World Trade Center to justify attacks on Arabs and Muslims. This is the culture from which the suicide bombers have come.

America must now devise a strategy to deal with this form of religious terrorism. As is now widely understood, this will be a long war, with many fronts and battles small and large. Our strategy must be divided along three lines: military, political and cultural. On the military front—by which I mean war, covert operations and other forms of coercion—the goal is simple: the total destruction of al Qaeda. Even if we never understand all the causes of apocalyptic terror, we must do battle against it. Every person who plans and helps in a terrorist operation must understand that he will be tracked and punished. Their operations will be disrupted, their finances drained, their hideouts destroyed. There will be associated costs to pursuing such a strategy, but they will all fade if we succeed. Nothing else matters on the military front.

The New New World Order

The political strategy is more complex and more ambitious. At the broadest level, we now have a chance to reorder the international system around this pressing new danger. The degree of cooperation from around the world has been unprecedented. We should not look on this trend suspiciously. Most governments feel threatened by the rise of subnational forces like al Qaeda. Even some that have clearly supported terrorism in the past, like Iran, seem interested in re-entering the world community and reforming their ways.

We can define a strategy for the post–Cold War era that addresses America's principal national-security need and yet is sustained by a broad international consensus. To do this we will have to give up some Cold War reflexes, such as an allergy to multi-lateralism, and stop insisting that China is about to rival us militarily or that Russia is likely to re-emerge as a new military threat. (For 10 years now, our defense forces have been aligned for everything but the real danger we face. This will inevitably change.)

The purpose of an international coalition is practical and strategic. Given the nature of this war, we will need the constant cooperation of other governments—to make arrests, shut down safe houses, close bank accounts and share intelligence. Alliance politics has become a matter of high national security. But there is a broader imperative. The United States dominates the world in a way that inevitably arouses envy or anger or opposition. That comes with the power, but we still need to get things done. If we can mask our power in—sorry, work with—institutions like the United Nations Security Council, U.S. might will be easier for much of the world to bear. Bush's father understood this, which is why he ensured that the United Nations sanctioned the Gulf War. The point here is to succeed, and international legitimacy can help us do that.

Now we get to Israel. It is obviously one of the central and most charged problems in the region. But it is a problem to which we cannot offer the Arab world support for its solution—the extinction of the state. We cannot in any way weaken our commitment to the existence and health of Israel. Similarly, we cannot abandon our policy of containing Saddam Hussein. He is building weapons of mass destruction.

Broken Policy in Iraq

However, we should not pursue mistaken policies simply out of spite. Our policy toward Saddam is broken. We have no inspectors in Iraq, the sanctions are—for whatever reason—starving Iraqis, and he continues to build chemical and biological weapons. There is a way to reorient our policy to focus our pressure on Saddam and not his people, contain him militarily but not harm common Iraqis economically. Colin Powell has been trying to do this; he should be given leeway to try again. In time we will have to address the broader question of what to do about Saddam, a question that, unfortunately, does not have an easy answer. (Occupying Iraq, even if we could do it, does not seem a good idea in this climate.)

On Israel we should make a clear distinction between its right to exist and its occupation of the West Bank and Gaza. On the first we should be as unyielding as ever; on the second we should continue trying to construct a final deal along the lines that Bill Clinton and Ehud Barak outlined. I suggest that we do this less because it will lower the temperature in the Arab world—who knows if it will?—than because it's the right thing to do. Israel cannot remain a democracy and continue to occupy and militarily rule 3 million people against their wishes. It's bad for Israel, bad for the Palestinians and bad for the United States.

But policy changes, large or small, are not at the heart of the struggle we face. The third, vital component to this battle is a cultural strategy. The United States must help Islam enter the modern world. It sounds like an impossible challenge, and it certainly is not one we would have chosen. But America—indeed the whole world—faces a dire security threat that will not be resolved unless we can stop the political, economic and cultural collapse that lies at the roots of Arab rage. During the Cold War the West employed myriad ideological strategies to discredit the appeal of communism, make democracy seem attractive and promote open societies. We will have to do something on that scale to win this cultural struggle.

Fresh Thinking in the Arab World
First, we have to help moderate Arab states, but on the condition that they embrace moderation. For too long regimes like Saudi Arabia's have engaged in a deadly dance with religious extremism. Even Egypt, which has always denounced fundamentalism, allows its controlled media to rant crazily about America and Israel. (That way they don't rant about the dictatorship they live under.) But more broadly, we must persuade Arab moderates to make the case to their

people that Islam is compatible with modern society, that it does allow women to work, that it encourages education and that it has welcomed people of other faiths and creeds. Some of this they will do—September 11 has been a wake-up call for many. The Saudi regime denounced and broke its ties to the Taliban (a regime that it used to glorify as representing pure Islam). The Egyptian press is now making the case for military action. The United States and the West should do their own work as well. We can fund moderate Muslim groups and scholars and broadcast fresh thinking across the Arab world, all aimed at breaking the power of the fundamentalists.

Obviously we will have to help construct a new political order in Afghanistan after we have deposed the Taliban regime. But beyond that we have to press the nations of the Arab world—and others, like Pakistan, where the virus of fundamentalism has spread—to reform, open up and gain legitimacy. We need to do business with these regimes; yet, just as we did with South Korea and Taiwan during the Cold War, we can ally with these dictatorships and still push them toward reform. For those who argue that we should not engage in nation-building, I would say foreign policy is not theology. I have myself been skeptical of nation-building in places where our interests were unclear and it seemed unlikely that we would stay the course. In this case, stable political development is the key to reducing our single greatest security threat. We have no option but to get back into the nation-building business.

It sounds like a daunting challenge, but there are many good signs. Al Qaeda is not more powerful than the combined force of many determined governments. The world is indeed uniting around American leadership, and perhaps we will see the emergence, for a while, of a new global community and consensus, which could bring progress in many other areas of international life. Perhaps most important, Islamic fundamentalism still does not speak to the majority of the Muslim people. In Pakistan, fundamentalist parties have yet to get more than 10 percent of the vote. In Iran, having experienced the brutal puritanism of the mullahs, people are yearning for normalcy. In Egypt, for all the repression, the fundamentalists are a potent force but so far not dominant. If the West can help Islam enter modernity in dignity and peace, it will have done more than achieved security. It will have changed the world.

Terror, Islam, and Democracy

Ladan Boroumand and Roya Boroumand

"Why?" That is the question that people in the West have been asking ever since the terrible events of September 11. What are the attitudes, beliefs, and motives of the terrorists and the movement from which they sprang? What makes young men from Muslim countries willing, even eager, to turn themselves into suicide bombers? How did these men come to harbor such violent hatred of the West, and especially of the United States? What are the roots—moral, intellectual, political, and spiritual—of the murderous fanaticism we witnessed that day?

As Western experts and commentators have wrestled with these questions, their intellectual disarray and bafflement in the face of radical Islamist (notice we do not say "Islamic") terrorism have become painfully clear. This is worrisome, for however necessary an armed response might seem in the near term, it is undeniable that a successful long-term strategy for battling Islamism and its terrorists will require a clearer understanding of who these foes are, what they think, and how they understand their own motives. For terrorism is first and foremost an ideological and moral challenge to liberal democracy. The sooner the defenders of democracy realize this and grasp its implications, the sooner democracy can prepare itself to win the long-simmering war of ideas and values that exploded into full fury last September 11. The puzzlement of liberal democracies in the face of Islamist terrorism seems odd. After all, since 1793, when the word "terror" first came into use in its modern political

This article originally appeared in the Spring 2002 issue of the *Journal of Democracy*. ©2002 by the National Endowment for Democracy and The Johns Hopkins University Press.

sense with the so-called Terror of the French Revolution, nearly every country in the West has had some experience with a terrorist movement or regime. Why then does such a phenomenon, which no less than liberal democracy itself is a product of the modern age, appear in this instance so opaque to Western analysts?

Islamist terror first burst onto the world scene with the 1979 Iranian Revolution and the seizure of the U.S. embassy in Tehran in November of that year. Since then, Islamism has spread, and the ideological and political tools that have helped to curb terrorism throughout much of the West have proven mostly ineffective at stopping it. Its presence is global, and its influence is felt not only in the lands of the vast Islamic crescent that extends from Morocco and Nigeria in the west to Malaysia and Mindanao in the east but also in many corners of Europe, India, the former Soviet world, the Americas, and even parts of western China.

Before the Iranian Revolution, terrorism was typically seen as a straightforward outgrowth of modern ideologies. Islamist terrorists, however, claim to fight on theological grounds: A few verses from the Koran and a few references to the *sunna* ("deeds of the Prophet") put an Islamic seal on each operation. The whole ideological fabric appears to be woven from appeals to tradition, ethnicity, and historical grievances both old and new, along with a powerful set of religious-sounding references to "infidels," "idolaters," "crusaders," "martyrs," "holy wars," "sacred soil," "enemies of Islam," "the party of God," and "the great Satan."

But this religious vocabulary hides violent Islamism's true nature as a modern totalitarian challenge to both traditional Islam and modern democracy. If terrorism is truly as close to the core of Islamic belief as both the Islamists and many of their enemies claim, why does international Islamist terrorism date only to 1979? This question finds a powerful echo in the statements of the many eminent Islamic scholars and theologians who have consistently condemned the actions of the Islamist networks.

This is not to say that Islamic jurisprudence and philosophy propound a democratic vision of society or easily accommodate the principles of democracy and human rights. But it does expose the fraudulence of the terrorists' references to Islamic precepts. There is in the history of Islam no precedent for the utterly unrestrained violence of al-Qaeda or the Hezbollah. Even the Shi'ite Ismaili sect known as the Assassins, though it used men who were ready to die to murder its enemies, never descended to anything like the random mass slaughter in which the Hezbollah, Osama bin Laden, and his minions glory.[1] To kill oneself while wantonly murdering women, children, and people of all religions and descriptions—let us not forget that Muslims too worked at the World Trade Center—has nothing to do with Islam, and one does not have to be a learned theologian to see this. The truth is that contemporary Islamist terror is an eminently modern practice thoroughly at odds with Islamic traditions and ethics. [2]

A striking illustration of the tension between Islam and terrorism was offered by an exchange that took place between two Muslims in the French courtroom where Fouad Ali Saleh was being tried for his role in a wave of bombings that shook Paris in 1985–86. One of his victims, a man badly burned in one of these attacks, said to Saleh: "I am a practicing Muslim....Did God tell you to bomb babies and pregnant women?" Saleh responded, "You are an Algerian. Remember what [the French] did to your fathers."[3] Challenged regarding the religious grounds of his actions, the terrorist replied not with Koranic verses but with secular nationalist grievances.

The record of Saleh's trial makes fascinating reading. He was a Sunni Muslim, originally from Tunisia, who spent the early 1980s "studying" at Qom, the Shi'ite theological center in Iran. He received weapons training in Libya and Algeria, and got his explosives from the pro-Iranian militants of Hezbollah. In his defense, he invoked not only the Koran and the Ayatollah Khomeini but also Joan of Arc—who is, among other things, a heroine of the French far right—as an example of someone who "defended her country against the aggressor." After this he read out long passages from *Revolt Against the Modern World* by Julius Evola (1898-1974), an Italian author often cited by European extreme rightists. This strange ideological brew suggests the importance of exploring the intellectual roots of Islamist terrorism.[4]

THE GENEALOGY OF ISLAMISM

THE IDEA OF A "PAN-ISLAMIC"[5] movement appeared in the late nineteenth and early twentieth centuries concomitantly with the rapid transformation of traditional Muslim polities into nation-states. The man who did more than any other to lend an Islamic cast to totalitarian ideology was an Egyptian schoolteacher named Hassan al-Banna (1906–49). Banna was not a theologian by training. Deeply influenced by Egyptian nationalism, he founded the Muslim Brotherhood in 1928 with the express goal of counteracting Western influences.[6]

By the late 1930s, Nazi Germany had established contacts with revolutionary junior officers in the Egyptian army, including many who were close to the Muslim Brothers. Before long the Brothers, who had begun by pursuing charitable, associational, and cultural activities, also had a youth wing, a creed of unconditional loyalty to the leader, and a paramilitary organization whose slogan "action, obedience, silence" echoed the "believe, obey, fight" motto of the Italian Fascists. Banna's ideas were at odds with those of the traditional *ulema* (theologians), and he warned his followers as early as 1943 to expect "the severest opposition" from the traditional religious establishment.[7]

From the Fascists—and behind them, from the European tradition of putatively "transformative" or "purifying" revolutionary violence that began with the Jacobins—Banna also borrowed the idea of heroic death as a political art form. Although few in the West may remember it today, it is difficult to overstate the degree to which the aestheticization of death, the glorification of armed force, the worship of martyrdom, and faith in "the propaganda of the deed" shaped the antiliberal ethos of both the far right and elements of the far left earlier in the twentieth century. Following Banna, today's Islamist militants embrace a terrorist cult of martyrdom that has more to do with Georges Sorel's *Réflexions sur la violence* than with anything in either Sunni or Shi'ite Islam.[8] After the Allied victory in World War II, Banna's assassination in early 1949, and the Egyptian Revolution of 1952–54, the Muslim Brothers found themselves facing the hostility of a secularizing military government and sharp ideological competition from Egyptian communists. Sayyid Qutb (1906–66), the Brothers' chief spokesman and also their liaison with the communists, framed an ideological response that would lay the groundwork for the Islamism of today.

Qutb was a follower not only of Banna but of the Pakistani writer and activist Sayyid Abu'l-A'la Mawdudi (1903–79), who in 1941 founded the Jamaat-e-Islami-e-Pakistan (Pakistan Islamic Assembly), which remains an important political force in Pakistan, though it cannot claim notable electoral support.9 Mawdudi's rejection of nationalism, which he had earlier embraced, led to his interest in the political role of Islam. He denounced all nationalism, labeling it as *kufr* (unbelief). Using Marxist terminology, he advocated a struggle by an Islamic "revolutionary vanguard" against both the West and traditional Islam, attaching the adjectives "Islamic" to such distinctively Western terms as "revolution," "state," and "ideology." Though strongly opposed by the Muslim religious authorities, his ideas influenced a whole generation of "modern" Islamists.

Like both of his preceptors, Qutb lacked traditional theological training. A graduate of the state teacher's college, in 1948 he went to study education in the United States. Once an Egyptian nationalist, he joined the Muslim Brothers soon after returning home in 1950. Qutb's brand of Islamism was informed by his knowledge of both the Marxist and fascist critiques of modern capitalism and representative democracy.10 He called for a monolithic state ruled by a single party of Islamic rebirth. Like Mawdudi and various Western totalitarians, he identified his own society (in his case, contemporary Muslim polities) as among the enemies that a virtuous, ideologically self-conscious, vanguard minority would have to fight by any means necessary, including violent revolution, so that a new and perfectly just society might arise. His ideal society was a classless one where the "selfish individual" of liberal democracies would be banished and the "exploitation of man by man" would be abolished. God alone would govern it through the implementation of Islamic law *(shari'a)*. This was Leninism in Islamist dress.

When the authoritarian regime of President Gamel Abdel Nasser suppressed the Muslim Brothers in 1954 (it would eventually get around to hanging Qutb in 1966), many went into exile in Algeria, Saudi Arabia,11 Iraq, Syria, and Morocco. From there, they spread their revolutionary Islamist ideas—including the organizational and ideological tools borrowed from European totalitarianism—by means of a network that reached into numerous religious schools and universities. Most young Islamist cadres today are the direct intellectual and spiritual heirs of the Qutbist wing of the Muslim Brotherhood.

THE IRANIAN CONNECTION

BANNA AND THE BROTHERHOOD advocated the creation of a solidarity network that would reach across the various schools of Islam. [12] Perhaps in part because of this ecumenism, we can detect the Brothers' influence as early as 1945 in Iran, the homeland of most of the world's Shi'ites.

Returning home from Iraq that year, a young Iranian cleric named Navab Safavi started a terrorist group that assassinated a number of secular Iranian intellectuals and politicians. In 1953, Safavi visited Egypt at the Brothers' invitation and presumably met with Qutb. Although Safavi's group was crushed and he was executed after a failed attempt on the life of the prime minister in 1955, several of its former members would become prominent among those who lined up with the Ayatollah Khomeini (1900–89) to mastermind the Islamic Revolution of 1979.

Khomeini himself first took a political stand in 1962, joining other ayatollahs to oppose the shah's plans for land reform and female suffrage. At this point, Khomeini was not a revolutionary but a traditionalist alarmed by modernization and anxious to defend the privileges of his clerical caste. When his followers staged an urban uprising in June 1963, he was arrested and subsequently exiled, first to Turkey, then to Iraq. The turning point came in 1970, when Khomeini, still in Iraq, became one of the very few Shi'ite religious authorities to switch from traditionalism to totalitarianism. Much like Mawdudi, [13] he called for a revolution to create an Islamic state, and inspired by Qutb, he condemned all non-theocratic regimes as idolatrous. His followers in Iran were active in Islamist cultural associations that spread, among others, the ideas of Qutb and Mawdudi. Qutb's ideology was used by Khomeini's students to recapture for the Islamist movement a whole generation influenced by the world's predominant revolutionary culture—Marxism-Leninism.

Khomeini became a major figure in the history of Islamist terrorism because he was the first truly eminent religious figure to lend it his authority. For despite all its influence on the young, Islamism before the Iranian Revolution was a marginal heterodoxy. Qutb and Mawdudi were theological dabblers whom Sunni scholars had refuted and dismissed. Even the Muslim Brothers had officially rejected Qutb's ideas. As an established clerical scholar, Khomeini gave modern Islamist totalitarianism a religious respectability that it had sorely lacked.

Once in power, the onetime opponent of land reform and women's suffrage became a "progressivist," launching a massive program of nationalization and expropriation and recruiting women for campaigns of revolutionary propaganda and mobilization. The Leninist characteristics of his rule—his policy of terror, his revolutionary tribunals and militias, his administrative purges, his cultural revolution, and his accommodating attitude toward the USSR—alienated the majority of his fellow clerics but also gained him the active support of the Moscow-aligned Iranian Communist Party, which from 1979 to 1983 put itself at the service of the new theocracy.

Khomeini's revolution was not an exclusively Shi'ite phenomenon. Not accidentally, one of the first foreign visitors who showed up to congratulate him was the Sunni Islamist Mawdudi; before long, Qutb's face was on an Iranian postage stamp. Khomeini's successor, Ali Khamenei, translated Qutb into Persian.[14] Khomeini's own interest in creating an "Islamist International"—it would later be known by the hijacked Koranic term Hezbollah ("party of God")—was apparent as early as August 1979.

THE ISLAMIST "COMINTERN"

As these ties suggest, Islamism is a self-consciously pan-Muslim phenomenon. It is a waste of time and effort to try to distinguish Islamist terror groups from one another according to their alleged differences along a series of traditional religious, ethnic, or political divides (Shi'ite versus Sunni, Persian versus Arab, and so on). The reason is simple: *In the eyes of the Islamist groups themselves, their common effort to strike at the West while seizing control of the Muslim world is immeasurably more important than whatever might be seen as "dividing" them from one another.*

The Lebanese-based, Iranian-supported Hezbollah is a case in point. Its Iranian founder was a hardcore Khomeini aide who drew his inspiration from a young Egyptian Islamist—an engineer by training, not a theologian—who was the first to politicize what had been a purely religious term. A closer look at the organization reveals the strong influence of Marxism-Leninism on the ideology of its founders and leadership. The group's current leader, Mohammad Hosein Fadlallah, influenced by Marx's and Nietzsche's theories on violence, [15] has openly advocated terrorist methods and tactical alliances with leftist organizations. [16] Hezbollah is a successful creation of the Islamist "Comintern." "We must," says Sheikh Fadlallah, "swear allegiance to the leader of the [Iranian] revolution and to the revolutionaries as to God himself," because "this revolution is the will of God." [17] One indication of the extent of this allegiance is the fact that all the negotiations over the fate of the hostages held in Lebanon ended up being carried out by Tehran. Similarly, the head of Iran's Revolutionary Guards boasted about having sponsored the attack against French and American peacekeeping forces in Lebanon. [18] Hezbollah's chief military planner, Imad Mughaniyyah, is an Arab who operates from Iran. Western intelligence agencies suspect that Hezbollah has been working with bin Laden on international operations since the early 1990s. [19] Hezbollah's terrorist network in Lebanon contains both Shi'ite and Sunni groups, and there is also a Saudi Arabian wing that was involved in the Khobar Towers bombing, which killed 19 U.S. troops in 1996.

Also inspired by the Iranian Revolution was the independent Sunni terrorist network that later became the basis of al-Qaeda. The Tehran regime began forming propaganda organs to sway opinion among Sunni religious authorities as early as 1982. [20] Among the supranational institutions created was the World Congress of Friday Sermons Imams, which at one time had a presence in no fewer than 40 countries. The overarching goal of these efforts has been to mobilize the "Islam of the people" against the "reactionary Islam of the establishment." [21] For a variety of reasons this network has remained loosely organized, but all of its branches spring from and are fed by the same ideological taproot.

The influence of Iran's Islamist revolution was also cited by the members of Egyptian Islamic Jihad who gunned down President Anwar Sadat in October 1981. Their theoretician was an engineer, Abdessalam Faraj, who was also fond of quoting Qutb to justify terror. [22] The conspirators—including the junior army officers who did the actual shooting—were inspired by the Iranian model, and expected the death of Sadat to trigger a mass uprising that would replay in Cairo the same sort of events which had taken place two years earlier in Tehran[23] (where the Iranian authorities would subsequently name a street after Sadat's killer). Among those imprisoned in connection with the plot was a Cairo physician named Ayman al-Zawahiri. He became Egyptian Islamic Jihad's leader after serving his three-year prison term, met bin Laden in 1985, and then joined him in Sudan in the early 1990s. Zawahiri, who would become al-Qaeda's top operational planner, is reported to have said publicly that Osama is "the new Che Guevara." [24]

The Islamization of the Palestinian question is also partly due to Khomeini's influence on the Palestinian branch of Islamic Jihad. Its founder was another physician, this one named Fathi Shqaqi. His 1979 encomium *Khomeini: The Islamic Alternative* was dedicated to both the Iranian ruler and Hassan al-Banna ("the two men of this century"). The first press run of 10,000 sold out in a few days. [25] Shqaqi, who was of course a Sunni, had nonetheless traveled to Tehran to share the Friday sermon podium with Ali Khameini, denouncing the Mideast peace process and accusing Yasser Arafat of treason. [26]

DISTORTING ISLAM'S HISTORY AND TEACHINGS

As these examples show, such distinctions as may exist among these terrorist groups are overshadowed by their readiness to coalesce and collaborate according to a common set of ideological beliefs. These beliefs are properly called "Islamist" rather than "Islamic" because they are actually in conflict with Islam—a conflict that we must not allow to be obscured by the terrorists' habit of commandeering Islamic religious terminology and injecting it with their own distorted content. One illustration is the Islamists' interpretation of the *hijra*—Mohammed's journey, in September 622 c.e., from Mecca to Medina to found the first fully realized and autonomous Islamic community *(umma)*. Despite a wealth of historical and doctrinal evidence to the contrary, half-educated Islamists insist on portraying this journey as a revolutionary rupture with existing society that licenses their desire to excommunicate contemporary Muslim societies in favor of their own radically utopian vision.

The Islamic Republic of Iran also rests on heterodoxy, in this case Khomeini's novel and even idiosyncratic theory of the absolute power of the single, supreme Islamic jurisprudent *(faqih)*. It was not a coincidence that one of the first uprisings against Khomeini's regime took place under the inspiration of a leading ayatollah, Shariat Madari.[27] Officials of the regime have admitted that most Iranian clerics have always taken a wary view of Khomeinism. It is important to realize that the religious references which Khomeini used to justify his rule were literally the same as those invoked a century earlier by an eminent ayatollah who was arguing for the legitimacy of parliamentarism and popular sovereignty on Islamic grounds.[28] Koranic verses lend themselves to many different and even contradictory interpretations. It is thus to something other than Islamic religious sources that we must look if we want to understand Islamism and the war that it wages on its own society, a war in which international terrorism is only one front.

In a brief article on bin Laden's 1998 declaration of *jihad* against the United States, Bernard Lewis showed brilliantly how bin Laden travestied matters not only of fact (for instance, by labeling the invited U.S. military presence in Saudi Arabia a "crusader" invasion) but also of Islamic doctrine, by calling for the indiscriminate butchery of any and all U.S. citizens, wherever they can be found in the world. Reminding his readers that Islamic law *(shari'a)* holds *jihad* to be nothing but a regular war and subject to the rules that limit such conflicts, Lewis concluded, "At no point do the basic texts of Islam enjoin terrorism and murder. At no point do they even consider the random slaughter of uninvolved bystanders."[29]

What gives force to the terrorist notion of *jihad* invented by the Iranians and later embraced by bin Laden is not its Koranic roots—there are none—but rather the brute success of terrorist acts. Bin Laden has spoken with particular admiration of the Iranian-sponsored suicide truck bombing that killed 241 U.S. Marines and others in Beirut on 23 October 1983, precipitating the U.S. withdrawal from Lebanon.[30] Bin Laden was also not the first to think of setting up training camps for international terrorists—the Tehran authorities were there before him.[31]

A Friday sermon given in 1989 by one of these authorities, Ali-Akbar Hashemi Rafsanjani, then president of the Islamic Parliament, reveals better than any other the logic of Islamist terrorism. Attacking the existence of Israel as another front in the pervasive war of unbelief *(kufr)* against Islam, Rafsanjani added:

> If for each Palestinian killed today in Palestine five Americans, English, or French were executed, they would not commit such acts anymore....[T]here are Americans everywhere in the world....[They] protect Israel. Does their blood have any value? Scare them outside Palestine, so that they don't feel safe....There are a hundred thousand Palestinians in a country. They are educated, and they work....[T]he factories that serve the enemies of Palestine function thanks to the work of the Palestinians. Blow up the factory. Where you work, you can take action....Let them call you terrorists....They [the "imperialism of information and propaganda"] commit crimes and call it human rights. We call it the defense of rights and of an oppressed people....They will say the president of the Parliament officially incites to terror....[L]et them say it.[32]

There is no reference here to religion; Rafsanjani's appeal is purely political. The West's offense he calls human rights; against it he urges Muslims to wield terror as the best weapon for defending the rights of an oppressed people. Rafsanjani, moreover, proudly commends "terror" by name, using the English word and not a Persian or Arabic equivalent. Thus he employs the very term that Lenin had borrowed from *la Terreur* of the French Revolution. The line from the guillotine and the Cheka to the suicide bomber is clear.

With this in mind, let us look for a moment at the French Revolution, where the modern concept of political terror was invented, to find the explanation that the Islamic tradition cannot give. When it announced its policy of terror in September 1793, the "virtuous minority" which then ran the revolutionary government of France was declaring war on its own society. At the heart of this war was a clash between two understandings of "the people" in whose name this government claimed to rule. One was a group of 25 million actually existing individuals, each endowed with inherent rights. The other was an essentially ideological construct, an abstraction, an indivisible and mystical body, its power absolute. The Terror of the French Revolution was neither a mistake nor an unfortunate accident; it was meant to purify this mystical body of what the terrorist elite regarded as corrupting influences, among which they numbered the notion that individual human beings had unalienable rights. 33

The spokesmen of the Islamist revolution echo the terrorists of Jacobin France. The denigration of human rights marks the spot where the internal war on Muslim society meets the terrorist war against the West. Suffice it to hear bin Laden's comments on the destruction of the World Trade Center: "Those awesome symbolic towers that speak of liberty, human rights, and humanity have been destroyed. They have gone up in smoke."34 Every Islamist terror campaign against Westerners during the last 20 years has had as its cognate an Islamist effort to tyrannize over a Muslim population somewhere in the world. Think of the ordeal to which the Taliban and al-Qaeda subjected the people of Aghanistan, or of what ordinary Algerians suffered during the savage Islamist civil wars of the 1990s. Or think of the state terror that daily labors to strangle any hope for recognition of human rights in Iran. To explore fully this correlation between terror against the West and tyranny against Muslims would take a separate essay. Yet we can get an idea of its nature by considering the first instance of Islamist terrorism against the United States, the 1979 hostage-taking in Tehran.

HOLDING DEMOCRACY HOSTAGE TO TERROR

AS THEY RELEASED the hostages in January 1981, the Tehran authorities crowed over their victory, which Prime Minster Mohammad Ali Rajai called "the greatest political gain in the social history of the world" and an act that "had forced the greatest satanic power to its knees." At first glance this claim might seem foolish, for the United States had said no to the revolutionary government's demands to hand over the shah and unfreeze Iranian assets. But a closer look shows that the Iranian Islamists had in fact scored a big political and ideological victory over both the United States and their domestic opponents, and thus had ample cause for jubilation.

The seizure of the U.S. embassy took place at a time when Khomeini and his allies had not yet consolidated their tyrannical regime. An Assembly of Experts was drafting the constitution of the

Islamic Republic. Opposition was gaining strength daily in religious as well as in moderate secular circles. The Marxist-Leninist left, angered by a ban on its press, was growing restive. Open rebellions were breaking out in sensitive border regions populated by ethnic Kurds and Azeris. By sending in its cadres of radical students to take over the U.S. embassy and hold its staff hostage, the regime cut through the Gordian knot of these challenges at a single blow and even put itself in a position to ram through its widely criticized Constitution. Rafsanjani's assessment of what the act meant is instructive:

> In the first months of the revolution, the Washington White House decided in favor of a coup d'état in Iran. The idea was to infiltrate Iranian groups and launch a movement to annihilate the revolution. But the occupation of the embassy and the people's assault against the U.S.A. neutralized this plan, pushing the U.S. into a defensive stand. [35]

One could describe this version of the facts as a parody: The U.S. government in 1979 clearly had neither the will nor the ability to stage a coup against the Islamic Republic. But totalitarians typically speak an esoteric language of their own devising. Those who administered the Terror in revolutionary France painted some of their country's best-known republicans with the label "monarchist" before sending them off to be guillotined. The Bolsheviks called striking workers and the sailors of Kronstadt "bandits" and "counterrevolutionaries" before slaughtering them. In 1979, promoting human rights was a prominent aspect of how the United States described its foreign policy. By Rafsanjani's logic, therefore, any Iranian group that spoke of human rights was thereby revealing itself as a tool of the United States.

And indeed, as muddled negotiations over the hostages dragged on, the administration of President Jimmy Carter dropped any talk of supporting democracy in Iran [36]—the very cause for which Carter had taken the risk of ending U.S. support for the shah. Meanwhile, the revolutionary regime began using the Stalinist tactic of claiming that anyone who spoke in favor of a more representative government was really a U.S. agent. [37] With the hostage crisis, the Islamist regime was able to make anti-Americanism such a leading theme that Iranian Marxists rallied to its support, while Moscow extended its tacit protection to the new theocracy.

After the failure of the U.S. military's "Desert One" rescue attempt on 25 April 1980 and eight more months of negotiations, the United States at last succeeded in obtaining the release of the hostages. To do so, it had to agree to recognize the legitimacy of the Iranian revolutionary regime, and it had to promise not to file any complaints against Iran before international authorities, despite the gross violations of human rights and international law that had occurred. Though these concessions may have appeared necessary at the time, in retrospect we can see that they emboldened the Islamists to sink to new levels of hatred and contempt for the West and its talk of human rights. For had not the revolutionary students and clerics in Tehran forced the Great Satan to abandon its principles and brought it to its knees?

The terrorists accurately assessed the extent of their victory and drew conclusions from it. They used terror to achieve their goal, and upon the continued use of terror their survival depends. "[America] is on the defensive. If tomorrow it feels safe, then it will think to implement its imperialistic projects."[38] Among these projects are human rights, which a representative of the Islamic Republic denounced before the UN Human Rights Committee as an "imperialist myth."[39]

From the taking of the hostages in Tehran in 1979 until the terrorist attacks of last September, Western policy makers too often implicitly downgraded the claims of justice and shirked their duty both to their own citizens and to the cause of human rights by refusing to pursue the terrorists with any real determination. Considerations of "pragmatism" and "prudence" were put forward to justify a sellout of justice which, in one of the cruelest ironies revealed by the harsh light of September 11, proved not to have been prudent at all.

Since the impunity granted to the hostage-takers of Tehran, terrorist outrages have increased both in frequency and in scale. In addition to all the questions raised about security measures, intelligence failures, accountability in foreign-policy decision making, and the like, the atrocity of September 11 also forces citizens of democratic countries to ask themselves how strongly they are committed to democratic values. Their enemies may believe in a chimera, but it is one for which they have shown themselves all too ready to die. In the mirror of the terrorists' sacrifice, the citizens of the free world are called to examine their consciences; they must reevaluate the nature of their loyalty to fragile and imperfect democracy. In particular, the strongly solidaristic networks that the Islamist totalitarians have created should make citizens in democratic societies ask how much they and their governments have done to help pro-democracy activists who have been persecuted for years in Iran, in Algeria, in Afghanistan, in Sudan, and elsewhere. Unarmed, they stand on the front lines of the struggle against terror and tyranny, and they deserve support. Here is a moral, political, and even philosophical challenge upon which the minds and hearts of the West should focus.

WHITHER THE MUSLIM WORLD?

ISLAMIST TERROR POSES a different but no less grave problem for those of us (including the authors of this essay) who come from Islamic countries, and it carries a special challenge for Muslim intellectuals. Public opinion in the Muslim world has largely—if perhaps too quietly—condemned the massacres of September 11. In Iran, young people poured spontaneously into the streets, braving arrest and police violence in order to hold candlelight vigils for the victims. But there were also outbursts of celebration in some Muslim countries, and sizeable anti-American demonstrations in Pakistan. Perhaps more disturbing still have been the persistent and widespread rumors going around Muslim societies that somehow an Israeli conspiracy was behind the attack. The force and pervasiveness of this rumor are symptoms of a collective flight from an uncontrollable reality. It is true that the Palestinian question is a painful and complicated one that requires an equitable solution. But it is equally true that reaching for foreign conspiracies has become an easy way of evading responsibility for too many of us from Muslim countries.

For the last several centuries, the Islamic world has been undergoing a traumatizing encounter with the West. Since this encounter began, our history has been a story of irreversible modernization, but also of utter domination on the one side, and humiliation and resentment on the other. To Muslim minds the West and its ways have become a powerful myth—evil, impenetrable, and incomprehensible. Whatever the Western world's unfairness toward Muslims, it remains true that Western scholars have at least made the effort to learn about and understand the Islamic world. But sadly, the great and brilliant works of the West's "Orientalists" have found no echo in a Muslim school of "Occidentalism."

We have been lacking the ability or the will to open up to others. We have opted for an easy solution, that of disguising in the clothes of Islam imported Western intellectual categories and concepts. In doing so we have not only failed to grasp the opportunity to understand the West, we have also lost the keys to our own culture. Otherwise, how could a degenerate Leninism aspire today to pass itself off as the true expression of a great monotheistic religion? The Islamists see themselves as bold warriors against modernity and the West, but in fact it is they who have imported and then dressed up in Islamic-sounding verbiage some of the most dubious ideas that ever came out of the modern West, ideas which now—after much death and suffering—the West itself has generally rejected. Had we not become so alien to our own cultural heritage, our theologians and intellectuals might have done a better job of exposing the antinomy between what the Islamists say and what Islam actually teaches. They might have more effectively undercut the terrorists' claim to be the exclusive and immediate representatives of God on earth, even while they preach a doctrine that does nothing but restore human sacrifice, as if God had never sent the angel to stop Abraham from slaying his son.

Our incapacity to apprehend reality lies at the root of our paranoia. If we were to take a clear and careful look at the West, we would see that it draws its strength from its capacity for introspection and its intransigent self-criticism. We would know that Western culture has never stopped calling on us, on the figure of the stranger, to help it understand itself and fight its vices. When it could not find the other, it invented it: Thomas More imagined a faraway island called Utopia to mirror the social problems of his time; Michel de Montaigne couched his criticisms of French politics in the form of a conversation with an Indian chief from Brazil; and Montesquieu invented letters from a Persian tourist to denounce the vices of Europe.

Had we had our own eminent experts on Western civilization, we might know that the West is a diverse, plural, and complex entity. Its political culture has produced horrors but also institutions that protect human dignity. One of these horrors was the imperialism imposed on Muslim and other lands, but even that did as much harm to the Europeans themselves as it did to us, as anyone familiar with the casualty figures from the First World War will know. Our experts might have helped us understand that Qutb and Khomeini's denunciations of human rights were remarkably similar to Pope Pius VI's denunciation of the French Declaration of the Rights of Man of 1789. We might have grasped that, not long ago, Westerners faced the same obstacles that we face today on the road to democracy. Citizens in the West fought for their freedoms; in this fight they lost neither their souls nor their religion. We too must roll up our sleeves to fight for freedom, remembering that we are first and foremost free and responsible human beings whom God has endowed with dignity.

Endnotes

1. Bernard Lewis, *The Assassins: A Radical Sect in Islam* (New York: Oxford University Press, 1987), 133–34.

2. On the heterodoxy of the Islamists' references to Muslim jurisprudent Ibn Taymiyya (1263–1328), see Olivier Carré, *Mystique et politique: Lecture révolutionnaire du Coran par Sayyid Qutb, Fr'ere musulman radical* (Paris: Cerf, 1984), 16–17. On Ibn Taymiyya's theology and life, see Henri Laoust, *Pluralisme dans l'Islam* (Paris: Librairie Orientaliste Paul Geuthner, 1983).

3. This account of the Saleh case is based on reports in *Le Monde* (Paris), 8 and 10 April 1992.

4. For an overview of the career of Islamist terror networks, see Xavier Raufer, *La Nebuleuse: Le terrorisme du Moyen-Orient* (Paris: Fayard, 1987); Roland Jacquard, *Au nom d'Oussama Ben Laden: Dossier secret sur le terroriste le plus recherché du monde* (Paris: Jean Picollec, 2001); Yossef Bodansky, *Bin Laden: The Man Who Declared War on America* (Rocklin, Calif.: Prima, 1999); Gilles Kepel, *Jihad: Expansion et déclin de l'islamisme* (Paris: Gallimard, 2000); and Yonah Alexander and Michael S. Swetnam, *Usama Bin Laden's al-Qaida: Profile of a Terrorist Network* (New York: Transnational Publishers, 2001).

5. To confront Western colonialism, Muslim intellectuals and religious scholars such as Sayyid Jamal al-Din 'al-Afghani of Iran and Muhammad Abduh of Egypt concluded that a reformation and a new interpretation of Islam were needed in Muslim societies. The reforms that they advocated were aimed at reconciling Islam and modernity. They sought to promote individual freedom, social justice, and political liberalism. After the First World War, however, this movement was succeeded by one that was hostile to political liberalism. On Afghani, see Nikki K. Keddie, *An Islamic Response to Imperialism: Political and Religious Writings of Sayyid Jamal al-Din 'al-Afghani* (Berkeley: University of California Press, 1983). On Abduh, see Yvonne Haddad, "Muhammad Abduh: Pioneer of Islamic Reform," in Ali Rahnema, ed., *Pioneers of Islamic Revival* (London: Zed, 1994), 31–63.

6. This section draws on David Dean Commins, "Hassan al-Banna (1906–49)," in Ali Rahnema, ed., *Pioneers of Islamic Revival*, 146–47; as well as Richard P. Mitchell, *The Society of the Muslim Brothers* (London: Oxford University Press, 1969). See also Gilles Kepel, *Muslim Extremism in Egypt* (Berkeley: University of California Press, 1993).

7. Richard P. Mitchell, *The Society of the Muslim Brothers*, 29.

8. The widespread but mistaken impression that a Shi'ite cult of martyrdom serves as a religious inspiration for suicide attacks is one of the illusions about themselves that the terrorists skillfully cultivate. It is true that Shi'ites revere Hussein (d. 680 C.E.), the third Imam and a grandson of the Prophet, as a holy martyr. Yet Shi'ite teaching also enjoins the avoidance of martyrdom, even recommending *taqieh* ("hiding one's faith") as a way of saving one's life from murderous persecutors. Moreover, Sunnis are not noted for devotion to Hussein, and yet when it comes to suicide attacks, there is little difference between the Sunnis of al-Qaeda and the mostly Shi'ite cadres of Hezbollah. There are striking similarities between the Islamist justification for violence and martyrdom and the discourse of German and Italian Marxist terrorists from the 1970s. On this subject see Philippe Raynaud, "Les origines intellectuelles du terrorisme," in François Furet et al., eds., *Terrorisme et démocratie* (Paris: Fayard, 1985), 65ff.

9. On Mawdudi, see Seyyed Vali Reza Nasr, *The Vanguard of the Islamic Revolution: The Jama'at-i Islami of Pakistan* (Berkeley: University of California Press, 1994); and Seyyed Vali Reza Nasr, *Mawdudi and the Making of Islamic Revivalism* (New York: Oxford University Press, 1996).

10. Olivier Carré, *Mystique et politique*, 206–7.

11. Muhammad Qutb, Sayyid Qutb's brother, was among the Muslim Brothers who were welcomed in Saudi Arabia. He was allowed to supervise the publication and distribution of his brother's works, and became ideologically influential in his own right: The official justification for the Saudi penal code uses his definition of secular and liberal societies as a "new era of ignorance." Exiled Muslim Brothers became influential in Saudi Arabia. Wahabism, the intolerant and fanatical brand of Islam that prevails in Saudi Arabia, was not in its origins a modern totalitarian ideology, but it provides fertile ground for the dissemination of terrorist ideology and facilitates the attraction of young Saudis to terrorist groups. See Olivier Carré, *L'utopie islamique dans l'Orient arabe* (Paris: Presses de la Fondation Nationale des Sciences politiques, 1991), 112–14; and Gilles Kepel, *Jihad*, 72–75.

12. Banna's followers recalled that he often said, "Each of the four schools [of Islam] is respectable," and urged, "Let us cooperate in those things on which we can agree and be lenient in those on which we cannot." Richard P. Mitchell, *The Society of the Muslim Brothers*, 217.

13. Mawdudi, *The Process of Islamic Revolution* (Lahore, 1955).

14. See Baqer Moin, *Khomeini: Life of the Ayatollah* (London: I.B. Tauris, 1999), 246.

15. Cited in Olivier Carré, *L'utopie islamique dans l'Orient arabe*, 197.

16. Cited in Olivier Carré, *L'utopie islamique dans l'Orient arabe*, 231–32.

17. Olivier Carré, *L'utopie islamique dans l'Orient arabe*, 232.

18. The then-head of the Iranian Revolutionary Guards, Mohsen Rafiqdoust, said that "both the TNT and the ideology which in one blast sent to hell 400 officers, NCOs, and soldiers at the Marine headquarters have been provided by Iran." *Resalat* (Tehran), 20 July 1987.

19. On 22 March 1998, the *Times of London* reported that bin Laden and the Iranian Revolutionary Guards had signed a pact the previous February 16 to consolidate their operations in Albania and Kosovo. Roland Jacquard adds that in September 1999, the Turkish intelligence services learned of an Islamist group financed by bin Laden in the Iranian city of Tabriz. See Roland Jacquard, *Au nom d'Oussama Ben Laden*, 287-88.

20. The first conference on the unification of Islamist movements was organized under Iranian auspices in January 1982. See the speeches of Khamenei and Mohammad Khatami (who is now the elected president of the Islamic Republic) in *Etela'at* (Tehran), 9 January 1982.

21. Xavier Rauffer, *La Nebuleuse*, 175.

22. Charles Tripp, "Sayyid Qutb: The Political Vision," in Ali Rahnema, ed., *Pioneers of Islamic Revival*, 178–79.

23. Gilles Kepel, *Jihad*, 122–23.

24. Roland Jacquard, *Au nom d'Oussama Ben Laden*, 76.

25. Gilles Kepel, *Jihad*, 187 and 579.

26. As reported in *Jomhouri-e Islami* (Tehran), 5 March 1994 (14 esfand 1372), 14 and 2.

27. Reported in the daily *Khalq-e Mosalman*, 4 and 9 December 1979.

28. M.H. Naïni, *Tanbih al-Omma va Tanzih al-mella*, 5th ed. (Tehran, 1979), 75–85.

29. Bernard Lewis, "License to Kill: Usama bin Ladin's Declaration of Jihad," *Foreign Affairs* 77 (November–December 1998): 19. Bin Laden's declaration of *jihad* mentions Ibn Taymiyya's authority and yet clearly contradicts the latter's ideas on *jihad*. Ibn Taymiyya explicitly forbids the murder of civilians and submits jihad to strict rules and regulations. See Henri Laoust, *Le traité de droit public d'Ibn Taimiya* (annotated translation of *Siyasa shar'iya)* (Beirut, 1948), 122–35.

30. See "Declaration of war against the Americans occupying the land of the two holy places: A Message from Usama Bin Muhammad bin Laden unto his Muslim Brethren all over the world generally and in the Arab Peninsula specifically" (23 August 1996), in Yonah Alexander and Michael S. Swetnam, *Usama Bin Laden's al-Qaida,* 13.

31. In 1989, the vice-president of Parliament, Hojatol-Eslam Karoubi, proposed the creation of training camps for the "anti-imperialist struggle in the region." Quoted in the daily *Jomhouri-e Eslami* (Tehran), 7 May 1989, 9.

32. *Jomhouri-e Eslami* (Tehran), 7 May 1989, 11.

33. In this connection, it is worth noting that after the end of the Terror, the Declaration of the Rights of Man and the Citizen was not officially restored to constitutional status in France until 1946.

34. Howard Kurtz, "Interview Sheds Light on Bin Laden's Views," *Washington Post,* 7 February 2002, A12. Bin Laden gave this interview to Tayseer Alouni of the Arabic-language satellite television network al-Jazeera in October 2001.

35. Ali-Akbar Hashemi Rafsanjani, *Enqelabe va defa'e Moqadass* (Revolution and its sacred defense) (Tehran: Press of the Foundation of 15 Khordad, 1989), 63–64.

36. Russell Leigh Moses, *Freeing the Hostages: Reexamining U.S.-Iranian Negotiations and Soviet Policy, 1979–1981* (Pittsburgh: University of Pittsburgh Press, 1996), 174–75.

37. In an interview that ran in the Tehran daily *Jomhouri-e Eslami* on 4 November 1981 to mark the second anniversary of the embassy seizure, student-radical leader Musavi Khoeiniha remarked that the neutralization of Iranian liberals and democrats was the hostage-taking's most important result.

38. Ali-Akbar Hashemi Rafsanjani, *Enqelabe va defa'e Moqadass,* 64.

39. *Amnesty International Newsletter,* September 1982. The representative was Hadi Khosroshahi, another translator of Sayyid Qutb.

Left, Right, and Beyond

The Changing Face of Terror

Walter Laqueur

OVER THE CENTURIES, terrorism has appeared in many guises. It is not an ideology or a political doctrine, but rather a method—the substate application of violence or the threat of violence to sow panic and bring about political change. Although it has rarely been absent from history, it has been more common in some ages and some civilizations than in others.

Those who try to understand terrorism in terms of the causes particular terrorists happen to support are bound to be baffled by the frequent and often extreme changes that have taken place in terrorists' political orientation over the years. Throughout the nineteenth and early twentieth centuries, terrorism came predominantly from the left, from anarchists and social revolutionaries, as well from nationalist separatists (as in Ireland). But during the interwar years, the main perpetrators of terrorism were on the extreme right and frequently had fascist sympathies.

Little or no terrorism erupted during World War II or its immediate aftermath, although there was a great deal of guerrilla warfare, which is something quite different. Then, in the late 1960s and 1970s, came a sudden upsurge of left-wing terrorism in Europe, Latin America, and elsewhere. This sudden resurgence had an unfortunate impact on terrorism studies, a field that emerged at about the same time. The news media, along with some in the academy, tended to take the slogans of contemporary terrorists at face value while

This article originally appeared in *How Did This Happen: Terrorism and the New War,* edited by James F. Hoge Jr. and Gideon Rose (New York: PublicAffairs, 2001). Reprinted by permission.

ignoring terrorism's lengthy history. This led them to see terrorism as a new and unprecedented phenomenon, something that was essentially a response to injustice. If political, social, and economic justice could be achieved, the argument ran, there would be no terrorism, and so the way to deal with it was to address its "root causes": the grievances, stresses, and frustrations that lay behind the violence. Seen in this light, terrorists were fanatical believers driven to despair by intolerable conditions. They were poor and oppressed, or at least on the side of the poor and oppressed, and their inspiration was deeply ideological.

Left-wing terrorism also had a certain influence at this time on nationalist terrorism. The doctrine and the slogans of organizations such as the Basque separatist group ETA, sections of the Irish Republican Army, and the various Popular Fronts for the Liberation of Palestine clearly showed the impact of Marxism-Leninism. Subsequent events, however, would reveal that this ideological patina was merely a reflection of the zeitgeist, did not go very deep or last long, and hardly affected the staunch nationalism at these movements' cores.

Left-wing terrorism lasted for about a decade and then petered out or was suppressed, in Germany and Italy, Uruguay and Argentina—and in the United States. It was followed by a wave of terrorism that came from the extreme right, including attacks on refugees in various European countries and the rise of neofascist groups in Italy and elsewhere. Left-wing terrorist cells did not totally disappear, but they were no longer in the front rank.

Those who had sympathized with what they thought were the justified grievances behind terrorism found themselves in a quandary. The most devastating act of terrorism in American history before the attacks of September 11, for example, was carried out in 1995 in Oklahoma City. No one could deny that Timothy McVeigh had deeply felt grievances, but they were hardly the type with which people on the left wanted to sympathize. They were the grievances of *The Turner Diaries*, of America taken over by foreigners and degenerates, of the holy duty of all patriots to cleanse the country in a river of blood—in short, the worldview of a virulent form of fascism.

McVeigh was not unique, moreover. Similar descriptions could apply to the murderers of Anwar al-Sadat, Yitzhak Rabin, and Mohandas Gandhi. Their assassins belonged to fanatical nationalist and right-wing undergrounds firmly convinced that they were doing their patriotic duty by liquidating traitors. These terrorists could hardly be said to be engaging in "revolutionary violence," nor could poverty, oppression, or free-floating rage help to explain the torching of asylum-seekers' homes in Germany or the unspeakable atrocities perpetrated by Islamist terrorists in Algeria, where they were fighting not colonial rulers but their own compatriots.

THE NEW VULNERABILITY

OVER THE LAST TWO DECADES, changes in targets, weapons, and motives combined to make terrorists more dangerous than ever before. As the result of technical progress, developed societies became more vulnerable to attack. (So have the megacities of the developing world, for that matter, but the political repercussions of that vulnerability may take longer to unfold.) Traditional terrorist weapons such as explosives, meanwhile, became more lethal and efficient, and the technology and skills needed to make weapons of mass destruction diffused throughout the world. At the same time, there was also an upsurge of religious fundamentalism in many parts of the globe, and at the margins of this movement radical groups appeared that were prepared to engage in terrorist attacks.

This trend toward increased vulnerability was occurring even before the Internet sped it along. Until the middle of the nineteenth century, a group of people who wanted to kill their enemies had to go quite literally from house to house in order to locate and assassinate their victims. Whole cities could not be paralyzed until after the introduction of power plants, centralized water supplies, and other technical developments resulting in the centralization of services. It is true that even in the 1840s some philosophers of the bomb had already foreseen weapons of mass destruction. Karl Heinzen, a fiery if somewhat unbalanced German revolutionary, envisaged the use of poison gas, not to mention ballistic missiles. But at the time this was no more than terrorist science fiction. He and his followers did not pursue this course of action, and Heinzen went on to a more peaceable career as an editor of German-language newspapers in Louisville, Kentucky, and then Boston.

Many considered the invention of dynamite by Alfred Nobel several decades later to be a turning point in the history of terrorism. But the early bombs were still heavy, bulky, and dangerous to construct, and only with the miniaturization of explosives in the twentieth century did it become possible to launch terrorist bomb attacks on a large scale. Similarly, with the invention of the airplane, another dimension of terrorist attacks materialized, and even before World War I Russian revolutionaries were considering airplanes' terrorist potential, while Irish radicals were contemplating the submarine in similar terms. Both ideas were premature, however, and it would take decades for these fantasies to become realistic possibilities.

Traditional terrorists, whether left-wing, right-wing, or nationalist-separatist, were not greatly drawn to these opportunities for greater destruction. One reason was scruples. A hundred years ago, terrorists often would desist from an attack if their victim happened to be accompanied by family members or if there was a danger that innocents would be killed. Terrorism has become far more brutal and indiscriminate since then, and the terrorists of the second half of the twentieth century managed to persuade themselves that there were no innocents and that indiscriminate murder was permissible if it served the political aim. But even they tended to hesitate before carrying out true mass murder, partly because of the risk of a backlash against their cause, and partly because such actions were alien to their traditions and would repel their own supporters. They hated their enemies, but they had not been totally blinded by their hate. For the radical religious practitioners of the new terrorism, however, murder and destruction on an unprecedented scale did not pose much of a problem.

THE NEW TERRORISTS

RECENT YEARS HAVE WITNESSED a growth of radical groups on the fringe of several religions. No one has yet fully determined why such processes should take place. In the Muslim world this development may have been connected with the declining attraction of other radical ideologies such as fascism and communism. But the trend was not limited to Islam. It could be found, for example, among certain millenarian Christian sects. As the century drew to a close, these latter groups caused security officers in various places to worry about attacks in conjunction with the turn of the new millennium. Much to the officers' relief, such attacks did not materialize. But the fear had not been unjustified, for it is only one step from believing that the world is deeply corrupt and sinful, and that only massive destruction in a final battle between good and evil will bring about redemption, to deciding to take an active hand in catalyzing the process. Among small extremist Jewish groups in Israel, in fact, could be found the same belief in a final battle between the forces of good and evil (Gog and Magog),and some even thought that acts such as the destruction of the Muslim shrines on the Temple Mount would give history a little push.

Radical religious groups have been particularly strong and particularly prone to turn violent in the Muslim world. Scanning the present world map of terrorism shows that Muslim states or Muslim minorities are involved in almost 90 percent of all substate terrorist conflicts, from the Philippines to the Middle East, from Nigeria to the Balkans. This has not always been the case, nor is there reason to believe that it will always remain so, but about the present state of affairs there can be no two opinions. Other, non-Muslim terrorist groups are continuing the struggles in which they have been engaged, such as those in Ireland, in the Basque country, in Greece, and in Sri Lanka. But these terrorists are relatively small, localized, and unimportant in comparison with the terrorism of radical Islamist groups.

How to explain this upsurge of terrorist violence? It has been argued that wherever Muslims live they have been the subject of oppression and persecution and that terrorism is the natural response to such conditions. This might have been a persuasive explanation prior to World War I, or even World War II, when only a handful of independent Islamic states existed. There are still a few Muslim minorities in the world that have not yet achieved autonomy or independence, but this is true for many non-Muslim minorities as well. Since 1948, many dozens of Muslim states have come into being and the great majority of Muslims now live in states of their own; if there is oppression, it is mainly by their own kind.

Can the frequency of violence be explained as the result of a "clash of civilizations"? No, because the bloodiest conflicts have occurred not between Muslim groups or states and the West but within the Muslim world itself. This holds true for both interstate conflicts (such as the Iran-Iraq War and the Iraqi invasion of Kuwait) as well as intrastate conflict (such as the terrorism of the Algerian Islamists against their fellow citizens, as a result of which some 70,000 people are believed to have been killed). It applies also to the persecution of the Kurds, as well as to the civil war in Afghanistan. It applies to the many assassination attempts, successful and unsuccessful, against Arab and Muslim leaders.

This pattern of events has led to speculation about the possibility of some particularly aggressive element in Islam that inspires terrorism, and it is not difficult to point to various historical examples, such as the notorious sect of the Assassins. Yet although there was Muslim terrorism in the age of imperialism in both India and Egypt, these instances were rare, terrorism was never in the mainstream, and the inspiration was probably more nationalistic than religious.

The recent rise of Islamist radicalism can more usefully be explained as the result of the decline of other political doctrines and the emergence of an intellectual and spiritual vacuum waiting to be filled. Here the adoption of Islamist doctrine by once-Marxist Arab intellectuals is most illuminating. During the 1990s, Horst Mahler, a former leading member and ideologist of the Baader-Meinhof Gang, Germany's left-wing terrorist group, became a spokesperson for extreme right-wing views. There were many Mahlers in the Middle East. This change in the zeitgeist led to a rejection of the Western way of life and Western values, a revolt against modernity in general, and, in extreme cases, a call for *jihad,* or holy war.

Similar trends were by no means wholly unknown to Western civilization. The concept of a crusade, after all, is not Islamic: Christianity has also carried out holy wars. European fascism was also a revolt against the West, the Enlightenment, and humanism, and illuminating parallels can be discovered by comparing certain European fascist movements (for instance, those in Romania and the early Falange in Spain) with the radical Islamists. The Romanian and Spanish fascist movements were mystical and religious in inspiration, in contrast to Nazi Germany and fascist Italy, and their attitudes toward martyrdom and death were similar to that of the radical Islamists. But in Europe the idea of crusades went out fashion many centuries ago and the clerical-fascist cult has also disappeared, whereas in the Muslim world the concept of *jihad* has had a revival. In other places the general trend has beentoward multiculturalism and the coexistence of religions, but this has not been the case in the contemporary Muslim world.

IDEAS AND POLITICS

STILL, THE CONNECTION between this radical fundamentalist revival and terrorism is not as straightforward as it might appear. Islamist fundamentalism comes in a variety of forms and is often quietist. Saudi Arabia finances Islamist activities in scores of countries, benefiting mosques and cultural institutions that serve as recruiting ground for the terrorists, but the Saudis do not allow any such activities within their own country. One of the guiding lights of modern Islamist radicalism, the Egyptian dissident Sayyid Qutb, argued that existing Arab regimes should be overthrown first because only then would a *jihad* be successful. Some of Qutb's disciples continued the struggle in the spirit of their master, but other militants established a different order of priorities, directing their attacks at the unbelievers of the West instead.

Furthermore, it is unclear whether the upsurge of terrorism can be explained mainly, let alone exclusively, by the history of ideas. In all probability it has as much to do with Muslims' feelings of frustration with their own countries' recent track records, compared to both West and East. These non-Muslim regions have made considerable economic progress, whereas the countries of the Middle East have generally stagnated or shown negative growth. This stagnation has resulted in growing poverty and unemployment, increased numbers of educated young people who have not found jobs in their professions, and growing resentment against those who have been more successful. It has also produced a wish to blame foreigners for the misery—self-criticism being too painful and too dangerous.

The frustration also stems from the lack of progress in much of the Muslim world toward anything resembling democratic institutions.

The demand for political democracy may not be overwhelming: according to public-opinion polls only about 10 percent of respondents favor a political system of this kind. But little freedom exists even on the local level, and even Arab critics have conceded the lamentable state of affairs on the cultural and intellectual scene. More important yet, militarily these societies have not been able to assert themselves (witness the repeated defeat of Pakistan by India, the victories of Israel over its Arab neighbors). All these frustrations have created a climate that acts as a breeding ground for terrorist activities. To what extent the prevailing ideology that developed in response to this unhappy state of affairs is radical Islamist, nationalist, or a mixture of the two may be difficult to establish, and generalizations are impossible because the situation varies from place to place and from time to time. But what is common is the feeling that the misery must have been caused by an outside enemy, and hence a resentment and a hate not felt in countries that have made progress.

KNOW THINE ENEMY

THE NEW TERRORISM is a fanaticism that expresses itself in, among other things, suicide bombing and the willingness to cause indiscriminate slaughter. In contrast to widespread belief, however, suicide bombing is not a recent phenomenon. On the contrary, until fairly recently terrorism was more or less synonymous with a suicide mission. The main weapon of the attack was the dagger, and unless the victim could be found alone and defenseless, the *sicarii* of Jewish history and the Assassins of Muslim history were unlikely to return from their missions. This was true even for much of the nineteenth century, as the makeshift bombs of the anarchists and the Russian revolutionaries were so unstable that they had to be thrown from a short distance (that is, if they did not explode first in the hands of the attacker). Those who went on an attack of this kind were fully aware of the risk, and many of them wrote farewell letters to their friends and families. Only with the advent of more sophisticated weapons in the twentieth century and the growing conviction among terrorists that it was permissible to kill the innocent did terrorism become less risky.

Even in our age, suicide bombing has by no means been limited to terrorists in Islamic countries. It has been a favorite form of attack by the Liberation Tigers of Tamil Eelam in Sri Lanka, members of which have carried out some 180 such attacks over the years in their country and in India. (The former Indian prime minister Rajiv Gandhi was one of their victims.) In Sri Lanka, the total number of Tamils—who are not Muslim and are not religiously motivated—is only a few million, and their per capita rate of suicide terrorists is thus far higher than that among either Muslims or Arabs. And suicide bombing has occurred, albeit on a smaller scale, in many terrorist movements during the last decade.

Muslim suicide bombers have tended to be young and deeply indoctrinated, led to believe that it is their duty to make the ultimate sacrifice for their group, country, or religion and that a far more enjoyable form of existence awaits them in the hereafter. But the world has also experienced many secular terrorist bombers who had no paradise awaiting them, such as the 4,000 young Japanese who volunteered for kamikaze actions at the end of World War II and the members of elite German SS units asked to undertake suicide missions when the Nazi war effort was approaching final defeat.

It is easier to trace the psychological and cultural sources of terrorist suicide missions than to trace the phenomenon of fanaticism that plays such a central role in the new terrorism. Fanaticism has existed in every civilization and at almost all times, but it has not necessarily expressed itself in terrorist action. At present, fanaticism can be found far more often in certain societies and cultures than in others, and psychiatry has not been of much help in explaining this phenomenon. Psychiatrists have shied away from confronting this subject, doubting whether it was part of their discipline; criminologists have been reluctant to discuss evil, for even if it is real it is a theological concept rather than a social science one. Madness, especially paranoia, plays a role in contemporary terrorism. Not all paranoiacs are terrorists, but all terrorists believe in conspiracies by powerful, hostile forces and suffer from some form of delusion and persecution mania.

Although a disturbed childhood and other forms of deprivation can explain the mind-set of some violent criminals, this profile by no means fits most serial murderers. Similarly, it is a hopeless exercise to try to explain terrorists, individually or collectively, wholly in social categories such as national or social oppression, messianic belief, or protest against injustice. In the bloodiest terrorist campaigns the element of crime and madness plays an important role, even if many are reluctant to acknowledge it.

WHAT COMES NEXT

SOME TERRORIST CAMPAIGNS have lasted longer than others, but all have come sooner or later to an end, and the present one will be no exception. Radical Islamist groups are in the forefront of terrorism today, but this is unlikely to remain the case forever. It is precisely in those countries where the population has been exposed to fundamentalist regimes or violence, such as Afghanistan, Iran, or Algeria, that enthusiasm for violent action is least prevalent. The candidates for terrorism have come mainly from *madrassas* (Islamic schools) in Pakistan or similar institutions in Europe. It is futile to speculate from where the terrorists of the future will emerge. Terrorism can appear on the extreme fringe of almost any ideology or cult. As weapons of mass destruction will give unprecedented power to small groups of individuals, and as there is no accounting for the mental sanity of a handful of people, the element of madness will probably play an even greater role in the future than is does at present or has in the past.

Are weapons of mass destruction likely to be used soon, and if so by whom? This depends, in part, on the success of the present operations against those responsible for the attacks of September 11 and those responsible for the anthrax mailings. If the operations succeed, terrorist movements—although not all individuals or small groups, whose behavior is unpredictable—will think twice before using nuclear, biological, or chemical weapons in a major way. The recent attacks, moreover, have shown that even conventional weapons can have devastating results if used creatively. Still, we know that the use of weapons of mass destruction has been contemplated by certain radical terrorist groups, and that the barrier to using biological weapons has been broken, and so preparations for such eventualities are imperative. Today's world has no Clausewitz or Machiavelli to serve as our guide to terrorism and counterterrorism. But certain basic observations can be made based on past experience and common sense. No society can protect all its members from terrorist attack, but all societies can reduce the risk by taking the offensive, by keeping terrorists on the run rather than concentrating on defense alone. Terrorism in previous periods of history was little more than a nuisance, but as a result of the technological and other trends mentioned above, the danger is now much greater. In past ages, state and society could face terrorists with some equanimity. If one plane was hijacked, all others continued to fly; if one bank was robbed, all others continued to function; if one politician was killed, others were only too willing to take his place. But in an age of weapons of mass destruction this is no longer the case; even one attack can be overwhelmingly devastating.

It is difficult to imagine a world without terrorism in the foreseeable future, for it would imply a world without conflict and tension. There will always be groups, small and not so small, with grievances against other groups and an inclination toward violence. Some of these grievances will be justified and will also be open to a political solution. Others will be justified but may collide with the equally justified claims of another group. And still others may simply be beyond rational discourse and any known approach of conflict resolution.

Even with all that is going on today, therefore, it would be a mistake to focus only on the present threat. Movements inspired by religious and radical fanaticism do not last forever. Past experience shows that the original fanaticism tends to peter out, whether because of internal quarrels, external setbacks, or the rise of a new generation with different priorities. The main future danger to civilization, in other words, could well come from different quarters than those that generated the present one. But this does not offer much comfort, because even if the political and religious orientation of terrorists changes, the capacity to inflict unacceptable damage will not. For this reason, one must conclude that the world is now entering a new phase in its history, more dangerous than any before.

II
The War

Counterterrorism Before 9/11

National Policy Coordination

9/11 Commission Staff Statement No. 8

THE STRUCTURE OF POLICYMAKING

COUNTERTERRORISM ISSUES had not been a high priority during the administration of George H. W. Bush. When the Clinton administration took office in 1993, terrorism issues were handled in a small directorate of the NSC staff for "International Programs," commonly referred to as "drugs and thugs." Terrorist attacks early in the new administration, particularly the 1993 attempt to blow up the World Trade Center, quickly changed this perspective. The first World Trade Center attack also spotlighted the problem of how or whether the NSC could bridge the divide between foreign policy and traditionally domestic issues such as criminal justice. That attack, handled by the FBI as a matter for domestic law enforcement, had been carried out by a mixture of American citizens, resident aliens, and foreign nationals with ties overseas.

President Clinton concluded that the National Security Act of 1947 allowed the NSC to consider issues of domestic security arising from a foreign threat. The President later issued a formal directive on counterterrorism policy. This was Presidential Decision Directive 39, signed in June 1995 after at least a year of interagency consultation and coordination. That directive characterized terrorism as a national security concern as well as a matter for law enforcement. It also articulated a "lead agency" approach to counterterrorism policy. It had four main program areas: reducing vulnerabilities, deterring terrorism, responding to terrorism, and preventing terrorists from acquiring weapons of mass destruction. In each area responsibilities were assigned to the departments and agencies of the government.

These efforts were to be coordinated by a subordinate NSC committee called the CSG. During the Clinton administration these initials stood for "Counterterrorism and Security Group." This committee was chaired by an NSC staff member, Richard Clarke. The CSG was the place where domestic security agencies, such as the FBI, regularly met alongside representatives from the traditional national security agencies.

Since 1989 each administration has organized its top NSC advisory bodies in three layers. At the top is the National Security Council, the formal statutory body whose meetings are chaired by the president. Beneath it is the Principals Committee, with cabinet-level representatives from agencies. The Principals Committee is usually chaired by the national security adviser. Next is the Deputies Committee, where the deputy agency heads meet under the chairmanship of the deputy national security adviser. Lower-ranking officials meet in many other working groups or coordinating committees, reporting to the deputies and, through them, to the principals. The CSG was one of these committees.

This ordinary committee system is often adjusted in a crisis. Because of the sensitivity of the intelligence and the military options being considered, President Clinton created a "Small Group" in which a select set of principals would frequently meet without aides to discuss Khobar Towers or Usama Bin Ladin. The participants would usually be National Security Adviser Samuel Berger, DCI George Tenet, Secretary of State Madeleine Albright, Defense Secretary William Cohen, Joint Chiefs of Staff Chairman Hugh Shelton, Deputy National Security Adviser James Steinberg, White House Chief of Staff John Podesta, Richard Clarke, and Vice President Gore's national security adviser, Leon Fuerth. Attorney General Janet Reno and FBI Director Louis Freeh would sometimes participate.

National Security Adviser Berger told us that he designed the Small Group process to keep the highly-sensitive information closely held. There were few paper records. One tradeoff in such a system was that other senior officials in agencies around the government sometimes had little knowledge about what was being decided in this group, other than what they could obtain from the principals or Clarke. This sometimes led to misunderstandings and friction.

PRESIDENTIAL DECISION DIRECTIVE 62
AND THE NATIONAL COORDINATOR

IN EARLY 1998, the Clinton administration prepared a new presidential directive on counterterrorism. Its goals were to strengthen the "lead agency" approach in ten program areas, reemphasize the importance President Clinton attached to unconventional threats at home and abroad, and strengthen interagency coordination. The draft directive would strengthen Clarke's role by creating the position of a national coordinator for counterterrorism who would be a full member of the Principals Committee or Deputies Committee for meetings on these topics.

The duties of the national coordinator were debated in the preparation of this directive. Prior episodes, including Iran-Contra in the 1980s, had underscored the problems of operations run by White House or NSC staff whose legal authorities are derived solely from the president and are therefore outside of the usual process of congressional confirmation, budgeting, or oversight. Responding to such concerns, the May 1998 directive, Presidential Decision Directive 62, provided that the coordinator would not direct operations, that the CSG would ordinarily report to the Deputies Committee, and that the new structure would not change the established budget process.

Nevertheless, as it evolved during the Clinton administration, the CSG effectively reported directly to principals, and with the principals often meeting only in the restricted Small Group.

This process could be very effective in overseeing fast-developing but sensitive operations, moving issues quickly to the highest levels, and keeping secrets. However, since the Deputies and other sub-cabinet officials were not members of the CSG, this process created a challenge for integrating counterterrorism issues into the broader agenda of these agencies and the U.S. government.

Clarke was a controversial figure. A career civil servant, he drew wide praise as someone who called early and consistent attention to the seriousness of the terrorism danger. A skilled operator of the levers of government, he energetically worked the system to address vulnerabilities and combat terrorists. Some colleagues have described his working style as abrasive. Some officials told us that Clarke had sometimes misled them about presidential decisions or interfered in their chain of command. National Security Adviser Berger told us that several of his colleagues had wanted Clarke fired. But Berger's net assessment was that Clarke fulfilled an important role in pushing the interagency process to fight Bin Ladin. As Berger put it, "I wanted a pile driver."

Clarke often set the agenda and laid out the options, but he did not help run any of the executive departments of the government. Final decision-making responsibility resided with others.

CHANGING STRATEGY AGAINST BIN LADIN AND HIS NETWORK

PRESIDENT CLINTON often discussed terrorism publicly as the dark side of globalization. He was particularly and vocally concerned about the danger of terrorists acquiring weapons of mass destruction, especially biological weapons. He tended to receive his intelligence in written briefings rather than personally from the DCI, and he frequently would pass back questions to follow up on items related to Bin Ladin or other terrorist threats. National Security Adviser Berger and others told us that the East Africa embassy bombings of August 1998 were a watershed event in the level of attention given to the Bin Ladin threat. Before August 1998, several officials told us their attention on terrorism was focused more on Iranian-sponsored groups, such as Hizbollah.

After the August 1998 military strikes against Afghanistan and Sudan, Clarke turned his attention to a government-wide strategy for destroying the Bin Ladin threat. His proposed strategy was Political-Military Plan Delenda, circulated among CSG and Small Group participants in late August and September 1998. As mentioned yesterday, the term "Delenda" is from the Latin "to destroy," evoking the famous Roman vow to erase rival Carthage. The plan's goal was to immediately eliminate any significant threat to Americans from the "Usama Bin Ladin network," to prevent further attacks, and prevent the group from acquiring weapons of mass destruction. The strategy sought to combine four main approaches:

• Diplomacy to eliminate the sanctuary in Afghanistan and bring terrorists to justice;

• Covert action to disrupt terrorist cells and prevent attacks. The highest priority was to target the enemy in Afghanistan;

• Financial measures, beginning with the just-adopted executive order to freeze the funds of Bin Ladin-related businesses; and

• Military action to attack targets as they were developed. This would be an ongoing campaign, not a series of responses or retaliations to particular provocations.

This strategy was not formally adopted, and Cabinet-level participants in the Small Group have little or no recollection of it, at least as a formal policy document. The principals decided against the rolling military campaign described in the plan. However, Clarke continued to use the other components of the Delenda plan to guide his efforts.

The momentum from the August 1998 attacks and the initial policy responses to it carried forward into 1999....

In June 1999, National Security Adviser Berger and Clarke summarized for President Clinton what had been accomplished against Bin Ladin. An active program to disrupt al Qaeda cells around the world was underway and recording some successes. The efforts to track Bin Ladin's finances with help from Saudi Arabia and the United Arab Emirates had not yet been successful. The U.S. government was pressing Pakistan and the Emirates to cut off support for the Taliban. Covert action efforts in Afghanistan had not borne fruit. Proposals to intervene against the Taliban by helping the Northern Alliance had been deferred. The intelligence needed for missile attacks to kill Bin Ladin was too thin, and this situation was not likely to change.

Berger and Clarke said it was a "virtual certainty" that there would be more attacks on American facilities. They were also worried about Bin Ladin's possible acquisition of weapons of mass destruction, a subject on which they had recently received some fragmentary but disturbing intelligence. The quality of that intelligence was unlikely to improve, his advisers reported.

Given this overall picture, they returned to the idea they had discussed in the fall of 1998, of a preemptive strike on terrorist camps such as the one reportedly involved in WMD work. Alternatively, they wrote, the government could retaliate after the next attack, but the camps might then be emptied. The Small Group met to consider some of these ideas on JUNE 24, 1999.

From some notes, it appears the Group discussed military strikes against al Qaeda infrastructure, but rejected this approach for reasons including the relatively slight impact of strikes balanced against the potentially counterproductive results.

The NSC staff kept looking for new options or ideas. Later in 1999, for example, the new leadership team at the CIA's Counterterrorist Center produced a plan for increased intelligence collection and relationships with other potential partners for clandestine or covert action against Bin Ladin. Berger and Clarke made sure that these efforts received both attention and authorizations to proceed.

THE MILLENNIUM ALERTS

As 1999 DREW to a close, Jordanian intelligence discovered an al Qaeda-connected plot to attack tourists gathering in Jordan for Millennium events. Intelligence revealed links to suspected terrorists who might be in the United States. Meanwhile a Customs agent caught Ahmed Ressam, an Algerian jihadist, trying to cross with explosives from Canada into the United States.

Both staff and principals were seized with this threat. The CSG met constantly, frequently getting the assistance of principals to spur particular actions. These actions included pressuring Pakistan to turn over particular suspects and issuing an extraordinary number of domestic surveillance warrants for investigations in the United States. National Security Adviser Berger said that principals convened on a nearly daily basis in the White House Situation Room for almost a month. The principals communicated their own sense of urgency throughout their agencies.

By all accounts, the Millennium period was also a high point in the troubled relationship with the FBI. Before 9/11, the FBI did not ordinarily produce intelligence reports. Records of the FBI's intelligence work usually consisted of only the reports of interviews with witnesses or memoranda requesting the initiation or expansion of an investigation. The senior FBI headquarters official for counterterrorism, Dale Watson, was a member of the CSG, and Clarke had good personal relations with him and FBI agents handling al Qaeda–related investigations. But the NSC staff told us that the FBI rarely shared information about its domestic investigations. The Millennium alert period was an exception. After the Millennium surge subsided, National Security Adviser Berger and his deputy, James Steinberg, complained that, despite regular meetings with Attorney General Reno and FBI Director Freeh, the FBI withheld terrorism data on the grounds that it was inappropriate to share information related to pending investigations being presented to a grand jury.

In a January 2000 note to Berger, Clarke reported that the CSG drew two main conclusions from the Millennium crisis. First, it had concluded that U.S.-led disruption efforts "have not put too much of a dent" into Bin Ladin's network abroad. Second, it feared that "sleeper cells" or other links to foreign terrorist groups had taken root in the United States. Berger then led a formal Millennium after-action review next steps, culminating in a meeting of the full Principals Committee on March 10.

The principals endorsed a four-part agenda to strengthen the U.S. government's counterterrorism efforts:

• Increase disruption efforts. This would require more resources for CIA operations, to assist friendly governments, and build a stronger capacity for direct action;

• Strengthen enforcement of laws restricting the activity of foreign terrorist organizations in the United States;

• Prevent foreign terrorists from entering the United States by strengthening immigration laws and the capacity of the Immigration and Naturalization Service; and

• Improve the security of the U.S.-Canadian border.

Some particular program ideas, like expanding the number of Joint Terrorism Task Forces across the United States, were adopted. Others, like a centralized translation unit for domestic intercepts, were not. In its January hearing, the Commission reviewed the progress of efforts on border and immigration issues.

Prodded to do more by President Clinton, the NSC staff pursued other initiatives in the spring of 2000. The NSC staff pushed for better technical intelligence collection, working closely with Assistant DCI for Collection Charles Allen and Vice Admiral Scott Fry of the Joint Staff. ... This effort spurred use of the Predator reconnaissance aircraft in Afghanistan later in 2000 and produced other innovative ideas. A draft presidential directive on terrorist fundraising apparently did not win approval.

COORDINATING A COUNTERTERRORISM BUDGET

OVERALL U.S. GOVERNMENT spending connected to counter-terrorism grew rapidly during the late 1990s. Congress appropriated billions of additional dollars in supplemental appropriations for improvements like building more secure embassies, managing the consequences of a WMD attack, and protecting military forces.

Clarke and others remained frustrated, however, at the CIA's spending on counterterrorism. They complained that baseline spending at headquarters on Bin Ladin efforts or on operational efforts overseas remained nearly level. The CIA funded an expanded level of activity on a temporary basis with supplemental appropriations, but baseline spending requests, and thus core staffing, remained flat. The CIA told us that Clarke kept promising more budget support, but could never deliver.

The Clinton administration began proposing significant in-creases in the overall national intelligence budget in January 2000, for Fiscal Year 2001. Until that time, at least, CIA officials have told us that their main effort had been to rebuild the Agency's operating capabilities after what they said had been years of cuts and re-trenchment. They believed counterterrorism efforts were relatively well off compared with the needs elsewhere.

In 2000 the budget situation in CIA's counterterrorism effort be-came critical. The strain on resources from the alert period had nearly exhausted available funds for the current fiscal year.

Among counterterrorism officials, frustration with funding levels was growing. In August 1999, the senior Defense Department partic-ipant in the CSG noted that it seemed to him the CIA was "under-funding critical programs" in the covert action budget for countering terrorism. On top of these concerns, the Millennium after-action review recommended significantly more spending. National Security Adviser Berger and DCI Tenet, along with their respective staffs, discussed where the money could be found, on the order of $50–100 million. Working with senior officials in the White House Office of Management and Budget (OMB), Clarke had devised an innovative process to develop and analyze a counterterrorism budget picture across the government. Spending for the CIA, however, was handled under different procedures over which Clarke had less influence.

The White House initially preferred that the CIA find the money from within its existing funds. The CIA insisted that its other programs were vital too, and that the administration should seek another supplemental appropriation from Congress. The CIA's argument ultimately prevailed, and Congress adopted a supplemental appropriation.

On August 1, 2000, Clarke outlined for Berger a few key goals he hoped the administration could accomplish before it left office: to significantly erode al Qaeda's leadership and infrastructure; to gain the still-pending supplemental appropriations for the counterterrorism effort; and to advance the Predator program.

In August, Clarke urged that the CSG and the Principals Committee be ready for emergency meetings to decide whether to fire cruise missiles if Bin Ladin were spotted by the Predator. Berger noted to Clarke, though, that before considering any action he would need more than a verified location; he would also need data on a pattern of movements to provide some assurance that Bin Ladin would stay in place.

In September, Clarke wrote that the drones were providing "truly astonishing" imagery, including a "very high probability" of a Bin Ladin sighting. Clarke was also more upbeat about progress with disruptions of al Qaeda cells elsewhere. Berger wrote back praising Clarke's and the CSG's performance while observing that this was no time for complacency: "Unfortunately the light at the end of the tunnel is another tunnel."

THE ATTACK ON THE U.S.S. *Cole*

THE U.S.S. *Cole* was attacked on October 12 in Yemen. By November 11, Berger and Clarke reported to the President that, while the investigation was continuing, it was becoming increasingly clear that al Qaeda planned and directed the bombing. In an update two weeks later, the President was informed that FBI and CIA investigations had not reached a formal conclusion, but Berger and Clarke expected the investigations would soon conclude that the attack had been carried out by a large cell headed by members of al Qaeda and that most of those involved were trained at Bin Ladin–operated camps in Afghanistan. So far, Bin Ladin had not been tied personally to the attacks, but there were reasons to suspect he was involved. In discussing possible responses, Berger stated that inherent in them was the "unproven assumption" that al Qaeda was responsible for the attack.

Berger told us he wanted a more definitive judgment from the DCI before using force. By December 21, the CIA's "preliminary judgment" for principals was that, while al Qaeda appeared to have supported the attack, the CIA still had no definitive answer on the "crucial question" of outside direction of the attack. Clarke added to us that while both the State Department and the Pentagon had reservations about retaliation, the issue never came to a head because the FBI and the CIA had not provided a definitive conclusion about responsibility.

The *Cole* attack prompted renewed consideration of what could be done. Clarke told us that Berger upbraided DCI Tenet so sharply after the *Cole* attack—repeatedly demanding to know why the United States had to put up with such attacks—that it led Tenet to walk out of a Principals Committee meeting. …Berger obtained a fresh briefing on military options from General Shelton.

In December 2000, the CIA developed initiatives based on the assumption that policy and money were no longer constraints. The result was the "Blue Sky memo," which we discussed earlier today. This was forwarded to the NSC staff.

As the Clinton administration drew to a close, the NSC counterterrorism staff developed another strategy paper, the first such comprehensive effort since the Delenda plan of 1998. The resulting paper, a "Strategy for Eliminating the Threat from the Jihadist Networks of al Qida: Status and Prospects," reviewed the threat, the record to date, incorporated the CIA's new ideas from the "Blue Sky" memo, and posed several near-term policy choices. The goal was to "roll back" al Qaeda over a period of three to five years, reducing it eventually to a "rump group" like other formerly feared but now largely defunct terrorist organizations of the 1980s. "Continued anti–al Qida operations at the current level will prevent some attacks," Clarke and his staff wrote, "but will not seriously attrit their ability to plan and conduct attacks."

THE BUSH ADMINISTRATION

THE BUSH ADMINISTRATION decided to retain Clarke and his core counterterrorism staff. National Security Adviser Rice knew Clarke from prior government experience. She was aware he was controversial, but she and Hadley thought they needed an experienced crisis manager in place during the first part of the administration. Working with Clarke, Rice and her deputy, Stephen Hadley, concentrated Clarke's responsibilities on terrorism issues, and planned to spin off some of his office's responsibilities—for cybersecurity, international crime, and consequence management—to other parts of the NSC staff. Clarke in particular wished to elevate the attention being given to the cybersecurity problem. On May 8, President Bush asked Vice President Cheney to chair an effort looking at preparations for managing a WMD attack and problems of national preparedness. It was just getting underway when the 9/11 attack occurred.

Rice and Hadley decided that Clarke's CSG should report to the Deputies Committee, chaired by Hadley, rather than bringing its issues directly to the principals. Clarke would still attend Principals Committee meetings on terrorism, but without the central role he had played in the Clinton-era Small Group. Hadley told us that subordinating the CSG to the Deputies would help resolve counterterrorism issues in a broader context. Clarke protested the change, arguing that it would slow decision-making. Clarke told us that he considered this move a demotion to being a staffer rather than being a de facto principal on terrorism. On operational matters, however, Clarke could and did go directly to Rice.

Clarke and his staff said that the new team, having been out of government for at least eight years, had a learning curve to understand al Qaeda and the new transnational terrorist threat. During the transition, Clarke briefed Secretary of State–designate Powell,

Rice, and Hadley on al Qaeda, including a mention of "sleeper cells" in many countries, including the United States. Clarke gave a similar briefing to Vice President Cheney in the early days of the administration. Berger said he told Rice during the transition that she would spend more time on terrorism and al Qaeda than on any other issue. Although Clarke briefed President Bush on cyber-security issues before 9/11, he never briefed or met with President Bush on counterterrorism, which was a significant contrast from the relationship he had enjoyed with President Clinton. Rice pointed out to us that President Bush received his counterterrorism briefings directly from DCI Tenet, who began personally providing intelligence updates at the White House each morning.

Asked by Hadley to offer major initiatives, on January 25, 2001, Clarke forwarded his December 2000 strategy paper, and a copy of his 1998 Delenda plan, to the new national security adviser, Condoleezza Rice. Clarke laid out a proposed agenda for urgent action by the new administration:

• Approval of covert assistance to the Northern Alliance and others.

• Significantly increased funding to pay for this and other CIA activity in preparation of the administration's first budget, for Fiscal Year 2002.

• Choosing a standard of evidence for attributing responsibility for the U.S.S. *Cole* and deciding on a response.

• Going forward with new Predator reconnaissance missions in the spring and preparation of an armed version of the aircraft.

• More work on terrorist fundraising.

Clarke asked on several occasions for early Principals Committee meetings on these issues and was frustrated that no early meeting was scheduled. He wanted principals to accept that al Qaeda was a "first order threat" and not a routine problem being exaggerated by "chicken little" alarmists. No Principals Committee meetings on al Qaeda were held until September 4, 2001. Rice and Hadley said this was because the Deputies Committee needed to work through the many issues related to new policy on al Qaeda. The Principals Committee did meet frequently before 9/11 on other subjects, Rice told us, including Russia, the Persian Gulf, and the Middle East peace process.

Rice and Hadley told us that although the Clinton administration had worked very hard on the al Qaeda problem, its policies on al Qaeda "had run out of gas," as Hadley put it. On March 7, Hadley convened an informal meeting of some of his counterparts from other agencies to discuss al Qaeda. After reviewing the background on the issues, Clarke pressed for immediate decisions on covert assistance to the Northern Alliance and others, as well as for Predator reconnaissance missions. Development of a new presidential directive on terrorism was also discussed.

The proposal for aid to the Northern Alliance was moved into this policy review. ...In April, the deputies decided not to approve new aid to the Northern Alliance, pending decisions about a broader aid program that would include other opposition groups in Afghanistan.

The administration took action on the intelligence budget for Fiscal Year 2002. It proposed a 27 percent increase in CIA counterterrorism spending.

On the issue of the *Cole*, the Bush administration received essentially the same "preliminary judgment" that had been briefed to the Clinton administration in December. Clarke consistently pressed officials to adopt some standard of evidence that would permit a response. He recommended on January 25 that the United States adopt the approach of responding at a time, place, and manner of its choosing, "and not be forced into a knee-jerk response." Rice agreed with the time, place, and manner point. Hadley added that the discussion of retaliation was less about the evidence and more about what to do. Rice and Hadley told us they did not want to launch cruise missiles in a "tit-for-tat" strike as in 1998, which they considered ineffectual. According to Rice, President Bush had the same reaction: don't do something weak. There was no formal decision not to retaliate. Hadley told us the new administration's response to the *Cole* would take the form of a more aggressive strategy on al Qaeda.

...Additional policy direction on terrorist fundraising was incorporated in the planned presidential directive.

As spring turned to summer, Clarke was impatient for decisions on aid to the Northern Alliance and on the Predator program, issues managed by Hadley and the Deputies Committee. Clarke and others perceived the process as slow. Clarke argued that the policy on Afghanistan and Pakistan did not need to be settled before moving ahead against al Qaeda. Hadley emphasized to us the time needed to get new officials confirmed and in place. He told us that they moved the process along as fast as they could. The Deputies Committee met seven times from April to September 10 on issues related to al Qaeda, Afghanistan, and Pakistan.

Rice recalled that in May 2001, as threats of possible terrorist attacks came up again and again in DCI Tenet's morning discussions with President Bush, the President expressed impatience with "swatting flies" and pushed his advisers to do more. Rice and Tenet met at the end of May, along with their counterterrorism advisers, to discuss what Rice at the time called "taking the offensive" against al Qaeda. This led to a discussion about how to break the back of Bin Ladin's organization. Within the NSC staff, Clarke was asked to put together a broad policy to eliminate al Qaeda, to be codified in the presidential directive. The Deputies Committee discussed complementary policies that would be adopted on Afghanistan and Pakistan as well.

Clarke and his staff regarded the new approach as essentially similar to the proposal they had developed in December 2000 and had put forward to the new administration in January 2001. Clarke's staff produced a draft presidential directive on al Qaeda. Hadley circulated it to his counterparts in early June as "an admittedly ambitious program."

The draft had the goal of eliminating the al Qaeda network as a threat over a multi-year period. It had headings such as "No Sanctuaries" and "No Financial Support." The draft committed the administration to providing sufficient funds to support this program in its budgets from Fiscal Year 2002 to Fiscal Year 2006. Specific annexes dealt with activities to be undertaken by the CIA and planning to be done by the Defense Department.

From April through July, alarming threat reports were pouring in. Clarke and the CSG were consumed with coordinating defensive reactions. In late June, Clarke wrote Rice that the threat reporting had reached a crescendo. Security was stepped up for the G-8 summit in Genoa, including air-defense measures. U.S. embassies were temporarily closed. Units of the Fifth Fleet were redeployed from usual locations in the Persian Gulf. Administration officials, including

Vice President Cheney, Secretary Powell, and DCI Tenet, contacted foreign officials to urge them to take needed defensive steps.

On July 2, the FBI issued a national threat advisory. Rice recalls asking Clarke on July 5 to bring additional law enforcement and domestic agencies into the CSG threat discussions. That afternoon, officials from a number of these agencies met at the White House, following up with alerts of their own, including FBI and FAA warnings. The next day, the CIA told CSG participants that al Qaeda members "believe the upcoming attack will be a 'spectacular,' qualitatively different from anything they have done to date." On July 27 Clarke reported to Rice and Hadley that the spike in intelligence indicating a near-term attack appeared to have ceased, but he urged them to keep readiness high; intelligence indicated that an attack had been postponed for a few months.

In early August, the CIA prepared an article for the president's daily intelligence brief on whether or how terrorists might attack the United States. Neither the White House nor the CSG received specific, credible information about any threatened attacks in the United States. Neither Clarke nor the CSG were informed about the August 2001 investigations that produced the discovery of suspected al Qaeda operatives in the United States. Nor did the group learn about the arrest or FBI investigation of Zacarias Moussaoui in Minnesota.

Arguments about flying the Predator continued. Rice and Hadley, contrary to Clarke's advice, acceded to the CIA view that reconnaissance flights should be held off until the armed version was ready. Hadley sent a July 11 memo to his counterparts at the CIA and the Defense Department directing them to have Predators capable of being armed ready to deploy no later than September 1.

At the beginning of August Rice and Hadley again reviewed the draft presidential directive on al Qaeda. Rice commented that it was "very good," and principals needed to discuss it briefly, just for closure, before it was submitted to President Bush. This meeting was scheduled for September 4.

The directive envisioned an expanded covert action program against al Qaeda, including significantly increased funding and more support for the Northern Alliance, anti-Taliban Pashtuns, and other groups. But the authorities for this program had not yet been approved, and the funding to get this program underway still had not been found. Although the administration had proposed a larger covert action budget for fiscal year 2002, the Congress had not yet appropriated the money and the fiscal year had not begun. The planned covert action program would need funds going well beyond what had already been budgeted for the current fiscal year, including the supplemental passed at the end of 2000. This budget problem was not resolved before 9/11.

The policy streams converged at a meeting of the Principals Committee, the Administration's first such meeting on al Qaeda issues, on September 4. Before this meeting, Clarke wrote to Rice summarizing many of his frustrations. He urged policymakers to imagine a day after a terrorist attack, with hundreds of Americans dead at home and abroad, and ask themselves what they could have done earlier. He criticized the military for what he called its unwillingness to retaliate for the *Cole* attack or strike Afghan camps. He accused senior CIA officials of trying to block the Predator program. He warned that unless adequate funding was found for the planned effort, the directive would be a hollow shell. He feared, apparently referring to President Bush's earlier comment, that Washington might be left with a modest effort to swat flies, relying on foreign governments while waiting for the big attack.

Rice chaired the meeting of principals. They apparently approved the draft directive. ...They agreed that the armed Predator capability was needed, leaving open issues related to command and control. DCI Tenet was also pressed to reconsider his opposition to starting immediately with reconnaissance flights and, after the meeting, Tenet agreed to proceed with such flights.

Various follow-up activities began in the following days, including discussions between Rice and Tenet, Hadley's September 10 directive to Tenet to develop expanded covert action authorities, and, that same day, further Deputies Committee consideration of policy toward Afghanistan and Pakistan. Then came the attacks on September 11.

Address to a Joint Session of Congress and the American People

September 20, 2001

George W. Bush

Mr. Speaker, Mr. President Pro Tempore members of Congress, and fellow Americans:

In the normal course of events, Presidents come to this chamber to report on the state of the Union. Tonight, no such report is needed. It has already been delivered by the American people.

We have seen it in the courage of passengers, who rushed terrorists to save others on the ground—passengers like an exceptional man named Todd Beamer. And would you please help me to welcome his wife, Lisa Beamer, here tonight.

We have seen the state of our Union in the endurance of rescuers, working past exhaustion. We have seen the unfurling of flags, the lighting of candles, the giving of blood, the saying of prayers—in English, Hebrew, and Arabic. We have seen the decency of a loving and giving people who have made the grief of strangers their own.

My fellow citizens, for the last nine days, the entire world has seen for itself the state of our Union—and it is strong.

Tonight we are a country awakened to danger and called to defend freedom. Our grief has turned to anger, and anger to resolution. Whether we bring our enemies to justice, or bring justice to our enemies, justice will be done.

I thank the Congress for its leadership at such an important time. All of America was touched on the evening of the tragedy to see Republicans and Democrats joined together on the steps of this

Capitol, singing "God Bless America." And you did more than sing; you acted, by delivering $40 billion to rebuild our communities and meet the needs of our military.

Speaker Hastert, Minority Leader Gephardt, Majority Leader Daschle and Senator Lott, I thank you for your friendship, for your leadership and for your service to our country.

And on behalf of the American people, I thank the world for its outpouring of support. America will never forget the sounds of our National Anthem playing at Buckingham Palace, on the streets of Paris, and at Berlin's Brandenburg Gate.

We will not forget South Korean children gathering to pray outside our embassy in Seoul, or the prayers of sympathy offered at a mosque in Cairo. We will not forget moments of silence and days of mourning in Australia and Africa and Latin America.

Nor will we forget the citizens of 80 other nations who died with our own: dozens of Pakistanis; more than 130 Israelis; more than 250 citizens of India; men and women from El Salvador, Iran, Mexico and Japan; and hundreds of British citizens. America has no truer friend than Great Britain. Once again, we are joined together in a great cause—so honored the British Prime Minister has crossed an ocean to show his unity of purpose with America. Thank you for coming, friend.

On September the 11th, enemies of freedom committed an act of war against our country. Americans have known wars—but for the past 136 years, they have been wars on foreign soil, except for one Sunday in 1941. Americans have known the casualties of war—but not at the center of a great city on a peaceful morning. Americans have known surprise attacks—but never before on thousands of civilians. All of this was brought upon us in a single day—and night fell on a different world, a world where freedom itself is under attack.

Americans have many questions tonight. Americans are asking: Who attacked our country? The evidence we have gathered all points to a collection of loosely affiliated terrorist organizations known as al Qaeda. They are the same murderers indicted for bombing American embassies in Tanzania and Kenya, and responsible for bombing the USS *Cole*.

Al Qaeda is to terror what the mafia is to crime. But its goal is not making money; its goal is remaking the world—and imposing its radical beliefs on people everywhere.

The terrorists practice a fringe form of Islamic extremism that has been rejected by Muslim scholars and the vast majority of Muslim clerics—a fringe movement that perverts the peaceful teachings of Islam. The terrorists' directive commands them to kill Christians and Jews, to kill all Americans, and make no distinction among military and civilians, including women and children.

This group and its leader—a person named Osama bin Laden—are linked to many other organizations in different countries, including the Egyptian Islamic Jihad and the Islamic Movement of Uzbekistan. There are thousands of these terrorists in more than 60 countries. They are recruited from their own nations and neighborhoods and brought to camps in places like Afghanistan, where they are trained in the tactics of terror. They are sent back to their homes or sent to hide in countries around the world to plot evil and destruction.

The leadership of al Qaeda has great influence in Afghanistan and supports the Taliban regime in controlling most of that country. In Afghanistan, we see al Qaeda's vision for the world.

Afghanistan's people have been brutalized—many are starving and many have fled. Women are not allowed to attend school. You can be jailed for owning a television. Religion can be practiced only as their leaders dictate. A man can be jailed in Afghanistan if his beard is not long enough.

The United States respects the people of Afghanistan—after all, we are currently its largest source of humanitarian aid—but we condemn the Taliban regime. It is not only repressing its own people, it is threatening people everywhere by sponsoring and sheltering and supplying terrorists. By aiding and abetting murder, the Taliban regime is committing murder.

And tonight, the United States of America makes the following demands on the Taliban: Deliver to United States authorities all the leaders of al Qaeda who hide in your land. Release all foreign nationals, including American citizens, you have unjustly imprisoned. Protect foreign journalists, diplomats and aid workers in your country. Close immediately and permanently every terrorist training camp in Afghanistan, and hand over every terrorist, and every person in their support structure, to appropriate authorities. Give the United States full access to terrorist training camps, so we can make sure they are no longer operating.

These demands are not open to negotiation or discussion. The Taliban must act, and act immediately. They will hand over the terrorists, or they will share in their fate.

I also want to speak tonight directly to Muslims throughout the world. We respect your faith. It's practiced freely by many millions of Americans, and by millions more in countries that America counts as friends. Its teachings are good and peaceful, and those who commit evil in the name of Allah blaspheme the name of Allah. The terrorists are traitors to their own faith, trying, in effect, to hijack Islam itself. The enemy of America is not our many Muslim friends; it is not our many Arab friends. Our enemy is a radical network of terrorists, and every government that supports them.

Our war on terror begins with al Qaeda, but it does not end there. It will not end until every terrorist group of global reach has been found, stopped and defeated.

Americans are asking, why do they hate us? They hate what we see right here in this chamber—a democratically elected government. Their leaders are self-appointed. They hate our freedoms— our freedom of religion, our freedom of speech, our freedom to vote and assemble and disagree with each other.

They want to overthrow existing governments in many Muslim countries, such as Egypt, Saudi Arabia, and Jordan. They want to drive Israel out of the Middle East. They want to drive Christians and Jews out of vast regions of Asia and Africa.

These terrorists kill not merely to end lives, but to disrupt and end a way of life. With every atrocity, they hope that America grows fearful, retreating from the world and forsaking our friends. They stand against us, because we stand in their way.

We are not deceived by their pretenses to piety. We have seen their kind before. They are the heirs of all the murderous ideologies of the 20th century. By sacrificing human life to serve their radical visions—by abandoning every value except the will to power—they follow in the path of fascism, and Nazism, and totalitarianism. And they will follow that path all the way, to where it ends: in history's unmarked grave of discarded lies.

Americans are asking: How will we fight and win this war? We will direct every resource at our command—every means of diplomacy, every tool of intelligence, every instrument of law enforcement, every financial influence, and every necessary weapon of war—to the disruption and to the defeat of the global terror network.

This war will not be like the war against Iraq a decade ago, with a decisive liberation of territory and a swift conclusion. It will not look like the air war above Kosovo two years ago, where no ground troops were used and not a single American was lost in combat.

Our response involves far more than instant retaliation and isolated strikes. Americans should not expect one battle, but a lengthy campaign, unlike any other we have ever seen. It may include dramatic strikes, visible on TV, and covert operations, secret even in success. We will starve terrorists of funding, turn them one against another, drive them from place to place, until there is no refuge or no rest. And we will pursue nations that provide aid or safe haven to terrorism. Every nation, in every region, now has a decision to make. Either you are with us, or you are with the terrorists. From this day forward, any nation that continues to harbor or support terrorism will be regarded by the United States as a hostile regime.

Our nation has been put on notice: We are not immune from attack. We will take defensive measures against terrorism to protect Americans. Today, dozens of federal departments and agencies, as well as state and local governments, have responsibilities affecting homeland security. These efforts must be coordinated at the highest level. So tonight I announce the creation of a Cabinet-level position reporting directly to me—the Office of Homeland Security.

And tonight I also announce a distinguished American to lead this effort, to strengthen American security: a military veteran, an effective governor, a true patriot, a trusted friend—Pennsylvania's Tom Ridge. He will lead, oversee and coordinate a comprehensive national strategy to safeguard our country against terrorism, and respond to any attacks that may come.

These measures are essential. But the only way to defeat terrorism as a threat to our way of life is to stop it, eliminate it, and destroy it where it grows.

Many will be involved in this effort, from FBI agents to intelligence operatives to the reservists we have called to active duty. All deserve our thanks, and all have our prayers. And tonight, a few miles from the damaged Pentagon, I have a message for our military: Be ready. I've called the Armed Forces to alert, and there is a reason. The hour is coming when America will act, and you will make us proud.

This is not, however, just America's fight. And what is at stake is not just America's freedom. This is the world's fight. This is civilization's fight. This is the fight of all who believe in progress and pluralism, tolerance and freedom.

We ask every nation to join us. We will ask, and we will need, the help of police forces, intelligence services, and banking systems around the world. The United States is grateful that many nations and many international organizations have already responded—with sympathy and with support. Nations from Latin America, to Asia, to Africa, to Europe, to the Islamic world. Perhaps the NATO Charter reflects best the attitude of the world: An attack on one is an attack on all.

The civilized world is rallying to America's side. They understand that if this terror goes unpunished, their own cities, their own citizens may be next. Terror, unanswered, can not only bring down buildings, it can threaten the stability of legitimate governments. And you know what—we're not going to allow it.

Americans are asking: What is expected of us? I ask you to live your lives, and hug your children. I know many citizens have fears tonight, and I ask you to be calm and resolute, even in the face of a continuing threat.

I ask you to uphold the values of America, and remember why so many have come here. We are in a fight for our principles, and our first responsibility is to live by them. No one should be singled out for unfair treatment or unkind words because of their ethnic background or religious faith.

I ask you to continue to support the victims of this tragedy with your contributions. Those who want to give can go to a central source of information, libertyunites.org, to find the names of groups providing direct help in New York, Pennsylvania, and Virginia.

The thousands of FBI agents who are now at work in this investigation may need your cooperation, and I ask you to give it.

I ask for your patience, with the delays and inconveniences that may accompany tighter security; and for your patience in what will be a long struggle.

I ask your continued participation and confidence in the American economy. Terrorists attacked a symbol of American prosperity. They did not touch its source. America is successful because of the hard work, and creativity, and enterprise of our people. These were the true strengths of our economy before September 11th, and they are our strengths today.

And, finally, please continue praying for the victims of terror and their families, for those in uniform, and for our great country. Prayer has comforted us in sorrow, and will help strengthen us for the journey ahead.

Tonight I thank my fellow Americans for what you have already done and for what you will do. And ladies and gentlemen of the Congress, I thank you, their representatives, for what you have already done and for what we will do together.

Tonight, we face new and sudden national challenges. We will come together to improve air safety, to dramatically expand the number of air marshals on domestic flights, and take new measures to prevent hijacking. We will come together to promote stability and keep our airlines flying, with direct assistance during this emergency.

We will come together to give law enforcement the additional tools it needs to track down terror here at home. We will come together to strengthen our intelligence capabilities to know the plans of terrorists before they act, and find them before they strike.

We will come together to take active steps that strengthen America's economy, and put our people back to work.

Tonight we welcome two leaders who embody the extraordinary spirit of all New Yorkers: Governor George Pataki, and Mayor Rudolph Giuliani. As a symbol of America's resolve, my administration will work with Congress, and these two leaders, to show the world that we will rebuild New York City.

After all that has just passed—all the lives taken, and all the possibilities and hopes that died with them—it is natural to wonder if America's future is one of fear. Some speak of an age of terror. I know there are struggles ahead, and dangers to face. But this country will define our times, not be defined by them. As long as the United States of America is determined and strong, this will not be an age of terror; this will be an age of liberty, here and across the world.

Great harm has been done to us. We have suffered great loss. And in our grief and anger we have found our mission and our moment. Freedom and fear are at war. The advance of human freedom—the great achievement of our time, and the great hope of every time—now depends on us. Our nation—this generation—will lift a dark threat of violence from our people and our future. We will rally the world to this cause by our efforts, by our courage. We will not tire, we will not falter, and we will not fail.

It is my hope that in the months and years ahead, life will return almost to normal. We'll go back to our lives and routines, and that is good. Even grief recedes with time and grace. But our resolve must not pass. Each of us will remember what happened that day, and to whom it happened. We'll remember the moment the news came—where we were and what we were doing. Some will remember an image of a fire, or a story of rescue. Some will carry memories of a face and a voice gone forever.

And I will carry this: It is the police shield of a man named George Howard, who died at the World Trade Center trying to save others. It was given to me by his mom, Arlene, as a proud memorial to her son. This is my reminder of lives that ended, and a task that does not end.

I will not forget this wound to our country or those who inflicted it. I will not yield; I will not rest; I will not relent in waging this struggle for freedom and security for the American people.

The course of this conflict is not known, yet its outcome is certain. Freedom and fear, justice and cruelty, have always been at war, and we know that God is not neutral between them.

Fellow citizens, we'll meet violence with patient justice—assured of the rightness of our cause, and confident of the victories to come. In all that lies before us, may God grant us wisdom, and may He watch over the United States of America.

Thank you.

A Flawed Masterpiece

Michael E. O'Hanlon

ASSESSING THE AFGHAN CAMPAIGN

THROUGHOUT most of the twentieth century, the U.S. armed forces were seen as an overmuscled giant, able to win wars through brute strength but often lacking in daring and cleverness. This basic strategy worked during the two world wars, making the United States relatively tough to challenge. But it failed in Vietnam, produced mediocre results in Korea, and worked in the Persian Gulf War largely because the terrain was ideally suited to American strengths.

What a difference a new century makes. Operation Enduring Freedom has been, for the most part, a masterpiece of military creativity and finesse. Secretary of Defense Donald Rumsfeld, U.S. Central Command (CENTCOM) head General Tommy Franks, and Director of Central Intelligence George Tenet devised a plan for using limited but well-chosen types of American power in conjunction with the Afghan opposition to defeat the Taliban and al Qaeda. Secretary of State Colin Powell helped persuade Pakistan to sever its ties with the Taliban, work with Afghanistan's Northern Alliance, provide the bases and overflight rights needed by U.S. forces, and contribute to the general war effort. Besides pushing his national security team to develop an innovative and decisive warfighting strategy, President George W. Bush rallied the American people behind the war effort and established a close relationship with Russian President Vladimir Putin, making it far easier for the United States to work militarily in Central Asia. The U.S. effort to overthrow the Taliban deprived al Qaeda of its sanctuary within Afghanistan and left its surviving leaders running for their lives.[1]

This article originally appeared in the May/June 2002 issue of *Foreign Affairs*.

A Flawed Masterpiece

At their peak, the U.S. forces involved in the war effort numbered no more than 60,000 (about half of which were in the Persian Gulf), and Western allies added no more than 15,000. But the U.S.-led military campaign has hardly been small in scale. By the end of January, the United States had flown about 25,000 sorties in the air campaign and dropped 18,000 bombs, including 10,000 precision munitions. The number of U.S. sorties exceeded the number of U.S. sorties flown in the 1999 Kosovo war, and the United States dropped more smart bombs on Afghanistan than NATO dropped on Serbia in 1999. In fact, the total number of precision munitions expended in Afghanistan amounted to more than half the number used in Operation Desert Storm. (In addition, more than 3,000 U.S. and French bombs were dropped on surviving enemy forces in March during Operation Anaconda, in which some 1,500 Western forces and 2,000 Afghans launched a major offensive against about 1,000 enemy troops in the mountainous region of eastern Afghanistan.)

If the U.S. strategy has had many virtues, however, it has also had flaws. Most important, it has apparently failed to achieve a key war goal: capturing or killing Osama bin Laden and other top enemy leaders. Such hunts are inherently difficult, but the prospects for success in this case were reduced considerably by U.S. reliance on Pakistani forces and Afghan militias for sealing off enemy escape routes and conducting cave-to-cave searches during critical periods. If most al Qaeda leaders stay at large, the United States and other countries will remain more vulnerable to terrorism than they would be otherwise—perhaps significantly so.

But on balance, Operation Enduring Freedom has been very impressive. It may wind up being more notable in the annals of American military history than anything since Douglas MacArthur's invasion at Inchon in Korea half a century ago. Even Norman Schwarzkopf's famous "left hook" around Iraqi forces in Operation Desert Storm was less bold; had it been detected, U.S. airpower still could have protected coalition flanks, and American forces could have outrun Iraqi troops toward most objectives on the ground. By contrast, Operation Enduring Freedom's impressive outcome was far from preordained. Too much American force (e.g., a protracted and punishing strategic air campaign or an outright ground invasion) risked uniting Afghan tribes and militias to fight the outside power, angering the Arab world, destabilizing

Pakistan, and spawning more terrorists. Too little force, or the wrong kind of force, risked outright military failure and a worsening of Afghanistan's humanitarian crisis—especially given the limited capabilities of the small militias that made up the anti-Taliban coalition.

ZEROING IN

BEGINNING ON OCTOBER 7, Afghans, Americans, and coalition partners cooperated to produce a remarkable military victory in Afghanistan. The winning elements included 15,000 Northern Alliance fighters (primarily from the Tajik and Uzbek ethnic groups), 100 combat sorties a day by U.S. planes, 300–500 Western special operations forces and intelligence operatives, a few thousand Western ground forces, and thousands of Pashtun soldiers in southern Afghanistan who came over to the winning side in November. Together they defeated the Taliban forces, estimated at 50,000 to 60,000 strong, as well as a few thousand al Qaeda fighters.

Various Western countries, particularly several NATO allies and Australia, played important roles as well. A formal NATO role in the war was neither necessary nor desirable, given the location of the conflict and the need for a supple and secretive military strategy. Still, NATO allies stood squarely by America's side, invoking the alliance's Article V mutual-defense clause after September 11, and demonstrated that commitment by sending five AWACS aircraft to help patrol U.S. airspace. Forces from the United Kingdom, Australia, France, and Canada appear to have frequently contributed to the effort in Afghanistan; forces from Denmark, Norway, and Germany also participated in Operation Anaconda in March. Allied aircraft flew a total of some 3,000 sorties on relief, reconnaissance, and other missions. As noted, France dropped bombs during Operation Anaconda, and the United Kingdom fired several cruise missiles on the first day of battle as well. Numerous countries, including the Netherlands, Italy, and Japan, deployed ships to the Arabian Sea. The cooperation continues today, as major Western allies constitute the backbone of the unauthorized stability force in Kabul.

The short war has had several phases. The first began on October 7 and lasted a month; the second ran through November and

saw the Taliban lose control of the country; the third was characterized by intensive bombing of suspected al Qaeda strongholds in
the Tora Bora mountain and cave complex in December; the fourth
began with the inauguration of Hamid Karzai as interim prime
minister and continues to date.

During the first part of the war, Taliban forces lost their large
physical assets such as radar, aircraft, and command-and-control
systems, but they hung on to power in most regions. Most al Qaeda
training camps and headquarters were also destroyed. Although
Taliban forces did not quickly collapse, they were increasingly isolated
in pockets near the major cities. Cut off from each other physically,
they were unable to resupply or reinforce very well and had problems
communicating effectively.

In the first week of the war, U.S. aircraft averaged only 25 combat
sorties a day, but they soon upped that total to around 100. (Some
70 Tomahawk cruise missiles were fired in the early going; a total
of about 100 had been used by December.) The United States
comparably increased the number of airlift, refueling, and other
support missions. U.S. air strikes by B-52 and B-1 bombers operating out of Diego Garcia typically involved six sorties a day; other
land-based aircraft, primarily F-15ES and AC-130 gunships from
Oman, flew about as much. Planes from the three U.S. aircraft
carriers based in the Arabian Sea provided the rest of the combat
punch. Reconnaissance and refueling flights originated from the
Persian Gulf region and Diego Garcia. Some air support and relief missions also came from, or flew over, Central Asia, where
U.S. Army soldiers from the Tenth Mountain Division helped
protect airfields.

Most air attacks occurred around Afghanistan's perimeter, because
the rugged central highlands were not a major operating area for the
Taliban or al Qaeda. By the middle of October, most fixed assets
worth striking had already been hit, so combat sorties turned to
targeting Taliban and al Qaeda forces in the field. Aircraft continued
to fly at an altitude of at least 10,000 feet, because the Pentagon was
fearful of antiaircraft artillery, Soviet SA-7 and SA-13 portable antiaircraft missiles, and some 200-300 Stinger antiaircraft missiles
presumed to be in Taliban or al Qaeda possession. But most precision-

guided weapons are equally effective regardless of their altitude of origin, provided that good targeting information is available—as it was in this case, thanks to U.S. troops on the ground.

The first month of the war produced only limited results and had many defense and strategic analysts worried about the basic course of the campaign. Some of those critics began, rather intemperately and unrealistically, to call for a ground invasion; others opposed an invasion but thought that a substantial intensification of efforts would prove necessary.

In phase two, beginning in early November, that intensification occurred. But it was due not so much to an increased number of airplanes as to an increase in their effectiveness. By then, 80 percent of U.S. combat sorties could be devoted to directly supporting opposition forces in the field; by late November, the tally was 90 percent. In addition, the deployment of more unmanned aerial vehicles and Joint Surveillance and Target Attack Radar System (JSTARS) aircraft to the region helped the United States maintain continuous reconnaissance of enemy forces in many places. Most important, the number of U.S. special operations forces and CIA teams working with various opposition elements increased greatly. In mid-October, only three special operations "A teams," each consisting of a dozen personnel, were in Afghanistan; in mid-November, the tally was 10; by December 8, it was 17. This change meant the United States could increasingly call in supplies for the opposition, help it with tactics, and designate Taliban and al Qaeda targets for U.S. air strikes using global positioning system (GPS) technology and laser range finders. The Marine Corps also began to provide logistical support for these teams as the war advanced.

As a result, enemy forces collapsed in northern cities such as Mazar-i-Sharif and Taloqan over the weekend of November 9–11. Taliban fighters ran for their lives, provoking their leader, Mullah Muhammad Omar, to broadcast a demand that his troops stop "behaving like chickens." Kabul fell soon afterward. By November 16, Pentagon officials were estimating that the Taliban controlled less than one-third of the country, in contrast to 85 percent just a week before. Reports also suggested that Muhammad Atef, a key al Qaeda operative, was killed by U.S. bombs in mid-November. Kunduz, the last northern stronghold of enemy forces where several thousand Taliban and al Qaeda troops apparently remained, fell on November 24–25.

In late November, more than 1,000 U.S. marines of the 15th and 26th Marine Expeditionary Units established a base about 60 miles southwest of Kandahar, which the Taliban continued to hold. They deployed there directly from ships in the Arabian Sea, leapfrogging over Pakistani territory at night (to minimize political difficulties for the government of President Pervez Musharraf) and flying 400 miles inland to what became known as Camp Rhino. Their subsequent resupply needs were largely met using Pakistani bases. Once deployed, they began to interdict some road traffic and carry out support missions for special operations forces.

Meanwhile, Pashtun tribes had begun to oppose the Taliban openly. By November, they were accepting the help of U.S. special forces, who had previously been active principally in the north of the country. Two groups in particular—one led by Hamid Karzai, the other by another tribal leader, Gul Agha Shirzai—closed in on Kandahar. Mullah Omar offered to surrender in early December but in the end fled with most of his fighters, leaving the city open by December 8–9. Pockets of Taliban and al Qaeda resistance, each with hundreds of fighters or more, remained in areas near Mazar-i-Sharif, Kabul, Kandahar, and possibly elsewhere, but the Taliban no longer held cities or major transportation routes.

Why this part of the campaign achieved such a rapid and radical victory remains unclear. Taliban forces presumably could have held out longer if they had hunkered down in the cities and put weapons near mosques, hospitals, and homes, making their arsenal hard to attack from the air. Opposition fighters were too few to defeat them in street-to-street fighting in most places, and starving out the Taliban would have required the unthinkable tactic of starving local civilian populations as well.

Most likely, the Taliban got caught in positions outside major cities that they could neither easily escape nor defend. Once the Afghan opposition began to engage the enemy seriously in November and Taliban forces returned fire, they revealed their positions to American special operations personnel who could call in devastating air strikes. Sometimes they were tricked into revealing their locations over the radio. Even trench lines were poor defenses against 2-ton bombs delivered within 10 to 15 meters of their targets. Just what Taliban fighters could have done differently, once stranded in that open terrain, is unclear. They might have been better advised either to go on the offensive or to try to escape back into urban settings under cover of night or poor weather, although many U.S. reconnaissance assets work well under such conditions. But both approaches would have been difficult and dangerous, especially for a relatively unsophisticated military force such as the Taliban.

The third main phase of the war began in early December. By this time, U.S. intelligence had finally pinpointed much of al Qaeda's strength near Jalalabad, in eastern Afghanistan. In particular, al Qaeda forces, including Osama bin Laden, were supposedly holed up in the mountain redoubts of Tora Bora. Traveling with perhaps 1,000 to 2,000 foreign fighters, most of them fellow Arabs, bin Laden could not easily evade detection from curious eyes even if he might elude U.S. overhead reconnaissance. Thus, once Afghan opposition fighters, together with CIA and special operations forces, were deployed in the vicinity, U.S. air strikes against the caves could become quite effective. By mid-December, the fight for Tora Bora was over. Most significant cave openings were destroyed and virtually all signs of live al Qaeda fighters disappeared. Sporadic bombing continued in the area, and it was not until mid-January that a major al Qaeda training base, Zawar Kili, was destroyed. But most bombing ended by late 2001.

So why did bin Laden and other top al Qaeda leaders apparently get away? The United States relied too much on Pakistan and its Afghan allies to close off possible escape routes from the Tora Bora region. It is not clear that these allies had the same incentives as the United States to conduct the effort with dogged persistence. Moreover, the mission was inherently difficult. By mid-December, the Pentagon felt considerably less sure than it had been of the likely whereabouts of bin Laden, even though it suspected that he and most of his top lieutenants were still alive.

Although estimates remain rough, Taliban losses in the war were considerable. According to *New York Times* correspondent Nicholas Kristof, as many as 8,000 to 12,000 were killed—roughly 20 percent of the Taliban's initial fighting capability. Assuming conservatively at least two wounded for every person killed, Taliban losses could have represented half their initial fighting strength, a point at which most armies have traditionally started to crumble. Another 7,000 or more were taken prisoner. Kristof's tally also suggests that Afghan civilian casualties totaled only about 1,000, a mercifully low number despite several wrongly targeted U.S. bombings and raids during the war. Although a couple of those U.S. mistakes probably should have been prevented, they do not change the basic conclusion that the war caused relatively modest harm to innocents.

U.S. forces had lost about 30 personnel by the middle of March: about a dozen on the battlefield (8 during Operation Anaconda) and the rest in and around Afghanistan through accidents. Most were Marine Corps and Army troops, but other personnel were lost as well, including a CIA operative. The casualty total was 50 percent greater than those of the invasions of Grenada and Haiti in the 1980s but less than the number of troops killed in Somalia in 1992–93.

FOLLOW THE LEADER

On the whole, Operation Enduring Freedom has been masterful in both design and execution. Using specially equipped CIA teams and special operations forces in tandem with precision-strike aircraft allowed for accurate and effective bombing of Taliban and al Qaeda positions. U.S. personnel also contributed immensely to helping the Northern Alliance tactically and logistically. By early November, the strategy had produced mass Taliban retreats in the north of the country; it had probably caused many Taliban casualties as well.

More notably, the U.S. effort helped quickly galvanize Pashtun forces to organize and fight effectively against the Taliban in the south, which many analysts had considered a highly risky proposition and CENTCOM had itself considered far from certain. Had these Pashtun forces decided that they feared the Northern Alliance and the United States more than the Taliban, Afghanistan might have become effectively partitioned, with al Qaeda taking refuge exclusively in the south and the war effort rendered largely futile. Convincing these Pashtun to change sides and fight against the Taliban required just the right mix of diplomacy, military momentum and finesse, and battlefield assistance from CIA and special operations teams.

Yet despite the overall accomplishments, mistakes were made. The Pentagon's handling of the al Qaeda and Taliban detainees at Guantanamo Bay, Cuba, was one of them. Whether these men should have been designated as prisoners of war can be debated. Neither group fought for a recognized government, and al Qaeda fighters satisfied virtually none of the standard criteria associated with soldiers. The Bush administration's decision not to designate the detainees as POWs is thus understandable, particularly since it did not want to be forced to repatriate them once hostilities in Afghanistan ended. But it probably would have been wiser to accord the detainees POW rights initially, until a military tribunal could determine them ineligible for POW status, as the Geneva Conventions stipulate.

The POW issue aside, the administration's initial reluctance to guarantee the basic protections of the Geneva Conventions to Taliban soldiers and its continued refusal to apply them to al Qaeda were unwise. These decisions fostered the impression that the detainees were not being treated humanely. This perception was wrong, but it became prevalent. Rumsfeld had to go on the defensive after photos circulated around the world showing shackled prisoners kneeling before their open-air cells; Joint Chiefs of Staff Chairman General Richard Myers talked somewhat hyperbolically about how the detainees might gnaw through hydraulic cables on airplanes if not forcibly restrained; and some Pentagon officials even suggested that the detainees did not necessarily deserve Geneva treatment, given the crimes of al Qaeda on September 11. But Rumsfeld's comments came too late, and America's image in the Arab world in particular took another hit.

The big U.S. mistake, however, concerned the hunt for top al Qaeda leaders. If Osama bin Laden, Ayman al-Zawahiri, Abu Zubaydah, and other top al Qaeda officials are found to have survived, the war will have failed to achieve a top objective. Rather than relying on Afghan and Pakistani forces to do the job in December near Tora Bora, Rumsfeld and Franks should have tried to prevent al Qaeda fighters from fleeing into Pakistan by deploying American forces on or near the border. U.S. troops should also have been used in the pursuit of Mullah

Omar and remnants of the Taliban, even though this mission was less important than the one against al Qaeda leaders.

Admittedly, there were good reasons not to put many Americans in Afghanistan. First, Washington feared a possible anti-American backlash, as Rumsfeld made clear in public comments. Complicating matters, the United States would have had a hard time getting many tens of thousands of troops into Afghanistan, since no neighboring country except Pakistan would have been a viable staging base—and Pakistan was not willing to play that role.

But even though Rumsfeld's reasoning was correct in general, it was wrong for Tora Bora. Putting several thousand U.S. forces in that mountainous, inland region would have been difficult and dangerous. Yet given the enormity of the stakes in this war, it would have been appropriate. Indeed, CENTCOM made preparations for doing so. But in the end, partly because of logistical challenges but perhaps partly because of the Pentagon's aversion to casualties, the idea was dropped. It is supremely ironic that a tough-on-defense Republican administration fighting for vital national security interests appeared almost as reluctant to risk American lives in combat as the Clinton administration had been in humanitarian missions—at least until Operation Anaconda, when it may have been largely too late.

Furthermore, local U.S. allies were just not up to the job in Tora Bora. Pakistan deployed about 4,000 regular army forces along the border itself. But they were not always fully committed to the mission, and there were too few well-equipped troops to prevent al Qaeda and Taliban fighters from outflanking them, as many hundreds of enemy personnel appear to have done. Afghan opposition forces were also less than fully committed, and they were not very proficient in fighting at night.

What would have been needed for the United States to perform this mission? To close off the 100 to 150 escape routes along the 25-mile stretch of the Afghan-Pakistani border closest to Tora Bora would have required perhaps 1,000 to 3,000 American troops. Deploying such a force from the United States would have required several hundred airlift flights, followed by ferrying the troops and supplies to frontline positions via helicopter. According to CENTCOM, a new airfield might have had to be created, largely for delivering fuel. Such an operation would have taken a week or more. But two

Marine Corps units with more than 1,000 personnel were already in the country in December and were somewhat idle at that time. If redeployed to Tora Bora, they could have helped prevent al Qaeda's escape themselves. They also could have been reinforced over subsequent days and weeks by Army light forces or more marines, who could have closed off possible escape routes into the interior of Afghanistan. Such an effort would not have assured success, but the odds would have favored the United States.

How much does it matter if bin Laden, al-Zawahiri, and their cohorts go free? Even with its top leaders presumably alive, al Qaeda is weaker without its Afghan sanctuary. It has lost training bases, secure meeting sites, weapons production and storage facilities, and protection from the host-country government. But as terrorism expert Paul Pillar has pointed out, the history of violent organizations with charismatic leaders, such as the Shining Path in Peru and the Kurdistan Workers' Party (PKK) in Turkey, suggests that they are far stronger with their leaders than without them. The imprisonment of Abimael Guzman in 1992 and Abdullah Ocalan in 1999 did much to hurt those organizations, just as the 1995 assassination of Fathi Shikaki of the Palestinian Islamic Jihad weakened that group significantly. Some groups may survive the loss of an important leader or become more violent as a result—for example, Hamas flourished after the Israelis killed "the Engineer" Yahya Ayyash in 1996. But even they may have a hard time coming up with new tactics and concepts of operations after such a loss.

If bin Laden, al-Zawahiri, and other top al Qaeda leaders continue to evade capture, they may have to spend the rest of their lives on the run. And their access to finances may be sharply curtailed. But they could still inspire followers and design future terrorist attacks. If successful, their escape would be a major setback ...

Endnote

1. Bob Woodward and Dan Balz, "At Camp David, Advise and Dissent," *The Washington Post,* January 31, 2002, p. A1; Bill Keller, "The World According to Powell," *The New York Times Magazine,* November 25, 2001, pp. 61–62.

The Jihadist
Threat to Pakistan

Stephen Philip Cohen

IN PAKISTAN, radical Islamic groups seek revolutionary changes in the Pakistani political and social order, support violence to achieve those changes, and may be actively involved in violence and terrorism across Pakistan's frontiers, but their attempts to infiltrate the government of Pakistan have proven feeble and easily countered thus far. On the street, radical Islamists do not—at least not yet— have significant influence in the Punjab, Pakistan's largest and most important province. With little mass support in this deeply Islamic yet still moderate country, radical Islamists have not been able to successfully conduct an Islamic coup to seize the levers of government, and they stand little chance of doing so within the next five years. Beyond that, however, Pakistan's future is uncertain.

The political dominance and institutional integrity of the Pakistani army remains the chief reason for the marginality of radical Islamic groups. Although the army has a long history of using radical and violent Islamists for political purposes, it has little interest in supporting their larger agenda of turning Pakistan into a more comprehensively Islamic state. Pakistan's political, institutional, economic, and social decay will have to accelerate before radical groups emerge as an independent political force.

Unless steps are taken now to rebuild a moderate Pakistan, however, the rise of radical Islamists as a significant political force could be one of several unpalatable futures for this increasingly chaotic, nuclear-

This article originally appeared in the Summer 2003 issue of *The Washington Quarterly*. ©2003 by the Center for Strategic and International Studies (CSIS) and the Massachusetts Institute of Technology.

armed state. Pakistan's educational system must be reconstructed; its economy requires massive overhaul; and the generals' obsession with adventurist and ultimately debilitating foreign policy goals must be curbed. Otherwise, radical Islamists will see their power grow, possibly in conjunction with new separatist movements and an increase in state authoritarianism. The dangers of Islamic radicalism in Pakistan in the short run have been exaggerated, but within a decade, that country could truly become one of the world's most dangerous states.

THE SCENE AND SCOPE OF THE THREAT

RADICAL ISLAM certainly has found a home in Pakistan. Radical parties are profuse, and terrorism is an oft-employed tactic. Yet, the historically complex role of Islam in the state; the diverse, specific goals of Islamic parties as well as their limited capacities to build wider support and pose formidable threats; and the inherently disorganized nature of terrorist activity, let alone the state's interests in maintaining at least some of that activity, collectively limit the threat they actually pose to Pakistan's governing establishment.

An Islamic State or the State of Islam?

The chief objective of the Pakistan movement was to create a Muslim-majority state in South Asia—a homeland for India's Muslims. Little attention was paid to what this state would look like, exactly, or just how "Islamic" it would be; Pakistanis still debate vigorously how fully their state should reflect Islamic law, the Koran, and earlier models of Muslim states. Both the individual, Muhammad Ali Jinnah, and the organization, the Muslim League, that wrested Pakistan from the chaos of partition in 1947 were secular. Inclined toward electoral politics and the rule of law, they propelled Pakistan's politics in the direction of moderate constitutionalism, even in light of an inability to agree on a constitution. Of the new state's more avowedly Islamic groups and political parties, the most important was a carryover from undivided India, the Jama'at-i-Islami (JI),[1] which had been unenthusiastic about the creation of a state that would divide India's Muslim population.

Early on, Pakistan's predominately secular leaders tried to express its Islamic nature in the form of an Objectives Resolution that the Constituent Assembly passed in 1949. Over the years, a number of Islamic provisions—some of them of doubtful authenticity—were embedded into law. For example, the president of Pakistan must be Muslim; the Ahmediyya sect, which claims that Muhammad was not the last prophet, was declared to be non-Muslim; there was a flirtation with a ban on interest; and, for a number of years, businesses had to close on Friday. In general, however, Pakistan has not gone very far down the Islamic road. Islamic law, or *shari'a*, does not yet govern the state or the personal lives of Pakistanis, although parts of the *shari'a*, such as a ban on alcohol, have become law, though even this ban is often privately ignored by Pakistanis.

The notion of an Islamic state is widely accepted in Pakistan, but the country cannot agree on which elements of Islam should dominate. All Pakistanis value their state's role in various international Islamic organizations and favor support for oppressed Muslims elsewhere, particularly in Palestine, Bosnia, and Kashmir. Most middle-class and urban Pakistanis, especially the Mohajirs—Urdu-speaking Pakistanis originally from what is now India—believe that Pakistan should be a modern but Islamic state, with the Islamic part confined to just a few spheres of public life.

Pakistan's Islamic Parties: Profuse But Divided

The Islamist parties have never been politically successful, and until recently, no single Islamic political party captured more than 5 percent of the national vote. In the October 2002 election, Muttahida Majlis-e-Amal (MMA), an alliance of six Islamic parties, polled 11 percent of the vote, which the electoral system translated into 53 seats in the National Assembly (17 percent of the total), giving the MMA control over the government in the Northwest Frontier Province (NWFP), partnership in a coalition government in Balochistan, and the status of leading opposition party at the federal level.

Pakistan's current leading Islamic organizations range from moderate to militant. Reflecting the hallowed Islamic traditions of piety and charity, there are numerous apolitical missionary, spiritual, and social groups, the most important of which is the Tablighi Jama'at.[2] Theoretically, the Tablighi could serve as a recruitment base for more radical groups or could spin off a more militant faction operating under the cover of a widely respected Tablighi member. There is some hint that this group has been infiltrated by violent sectarian groups as a way of avoiding detection by law enforcement agencies.

In organizational integrity, appeal to Pakistan's elite, and street power in the Punjab, the most influential Islamic group in Pakistan is the JI—a powerful force in many urban areas and, reflecting its middle-class and sophisticated ideology, historically strong in Pakistan's universities, where its student wing, the Islami Jamiat-i-Tulabah, has become a formidable street force. The JI favors a return to a strict parliamentary system with reduced presidential powers as a way of trimming the power of Pakistan's entrenched political-military establishment and, unlike most of its MMA coalition partners, favors women's education and social reform (the JI leader's daughter was elected to the National Assembly). The JI is a vocal supporter of Kashmiri militants, whom it regards as freedom fighters, but did not support the more radical Taliban. Finally, the JI is nonsectarian and stays clear of the bloody violence that has plagued Pakistan for the last 20 years.

This sectarianism, encouraged by some *ulema* (Islamic clerics) is dominated by violent Sunni groups, which pose a grave threat to law and order. Armed groups supported by Pakistan's Shi'as, who constitute about 12 percent of the population, have also emerged. Today, sectarian violence rages throughout Pakistan, notably in Karachi, where professionals (especially Shi'a doctors) have been routinely targeted for assassination, leading to the mass departure of highly trained medical personnel from Karachi and, in most cases, from Pakistan itself. Numerous sectarian battles have broken out among Sunnis, with pitched battles between Barelvis and Deobandis, often for control over Karachi's mosques.[3]

The largest Islamic sects with the greatest control over religious schools are the Deobandis, who control an estimated 65 percent of Pakistan's *madaris* and are among the most militant in their demands for the Pakistani state to become truly Islamic—as they would define it. Deobandi groups were in the forefront of the movement to declare the Ahmediyya to be non-Muslims and are behind much of the nation's anti-Shi'a sectarian violence. The larger Deobandi sect includes the Jamiat-e-Ulema-e-Islam (JUI),4 which is associated with the Harkat-ul-Mujahideen (HUM), a terrorist organization operating in Kashmir and the first Pakistani group to be put on the U.S. list of terrorist organizations. HUM's chief ideologue, Maulana Masood Azhar, is also the founder of another organization, Jaish-e-Muhammad (JeM). These, along with other Pakistani militant groups—Sipah-e-Shahaba Pakistan (SSP) and Lashkar-e-Jhangvi Pakistan (LJP), both Deobandi sects—have been active in Kashmir and parts of India.

The notorious Lashkar-e-Taiba (LeT), also on the U.S. list of terrorist organizations, has been implicated in a number of terrorist acts in India and is closely linked by doctrine and possibly financial support to Saudi Arabia. LeT and related groups have had a stunning increase in membership since the 1980s, directly traceable to increased private Saudi support for their *madaris*, where 15 percent of the students are thought to be foreigners; recently, there has been an upsurge in new students.5 Although LeT was and may still be active in India, informed sources indicate that it has not been involved in Pakistan's sectarian violence.

The last 15 years reveal that, despite some overlap among them, the rapidly proliferating sectarian and religious groups have very different objectives. The JI is focused primarily on Pakistan and seeks to restore civilian rule, although it has strong positions on Kashmir and India. Most of the violent, sectarian Sunni and Shi'a groups are Pakistan-centric, while a number of militant outfits were active in Afghanistan and/or Kashmir and retain an interest in each. The JUI, for example, has a strong Pashtun ethnic component as well as close ties to the Taliban. The Punjab-based LJP, with past operations in Afghanistan, India, and Kashmir, also has ties to the Taliban.

Although Islamist groups in Pakistan share a general identification with the Islamic world, an opposition to India's policies in Kashmir, a concern with Palestine, and a deep suspicion of the United States, none of them has a fully developed global agenda. This situation could change as anti-Americanism grows in Pakistan and in the Pakistani diaspora as a result of the U.S. war in Iraq and the Pakistani government's support for U.S. antiterrorist operations. Support for groups such as Al Qaeda has thus far been limited, but recent reports indicate that JI functionaries provided several fugitive Al Qaeda leaders with safe houses and, of course, the more radical Islamic parties were allied with Al Qaeda in their support of the Taliban in Afghanistan. If sympathy with Al Qaeda's ideas and similar ideologies should spread to Pakistan's politically moderate, educated classes, the country is likely to see new recruits for globally oriented, radical Islamic causes emerge.

The case of Omar Saeed Sheikh helps to convey how Islam has served as a unifying and mobilizing force for those with only a superficial understanding of the religion yet a deep perception of injustice. Born into a prosperous British-Pakistani family in the United Kingdom and educated at an elite college in Lahore and at the London School of Economics, Sheikh was apparently affected deeply by perceived injustices to Muslims in Bosnia and Kashmir as well as the Middle East.[6] Upon his return to South Asia, Sheikh participated in the kidnapping of foreign tourists in India and eventually the kidnapping and murder of Daniel Pearl in Pakistan. Does his career represent a trend among the Pakistani elite and the Pakistan diaspora? Great Britain, the United States, and other Western countries may not produce large numbers of radical Muslims, but they could yield a few dedicated cadres. The September 11 hijackers were drawn from the same strata of angry, professional, and Westernized Muslims. These groups are all the more worrisome for the threats they may pose to Western societies because of their ability to function within them, but thus far, these groups have had little systemic consequences for Pakistan.

Terrorism: Threatening Stability More Than the State

Pakistani terrorist groups supported or tolerated by the state operate within their own country, in Indian-administered parts of Kashmir, and in India itself. Many would like to reestablish a foothold in Afghanistan, perhaps with the assistance of the same Pakistani intelligence officers who once supported their operations on behalf of the Taliban government. The literature on terrorism frequently draws a comparison between acts of terrorism and the theater, positing that terrorists play to an audience. In South Asia, terrorism is geared toward at least three different audiences.

The immediate audience is the enemy, the target of violence. Hurting the enemy can be a cathartic act. This notion particularly applies to sectarian terrorists operating within Pakistan, who regard their mission as holy and the enemy to be worse than unbelievers: they are apostates. Although President Pervez Musharraf has made the suppression of sectarian violence a top priority, he has been unable to stem attacks on Christian churches and Western, especially U.S., facilities; there have been several reported attempts on his life. Pakistani terrorists are proving increasingly dangerous because they are using suicide squads—a new development. In the case of Kashmir, the goal is to provoke the Indian government into retaliatory measures that decrease its own legitimacy and make the terrorist/ freedom fighter the defender of Kashmiris. In practice, these activities have degenerated into random acts of terrorism, often against the Kashmiris themselves.

Suicide and terrorist attacks originating in Pakistan are also prominent in India, with grave implications for regional stability. Assaults on several important Hindu temples in Gujarat and the Indian parliament building in New Delhi as well as an attack on the families of Indian soldiers in Kashmir all contributed to a major military buildup in 2002. A dedicated, radical Islamic faction might try to use such attacks in 2003 to trigger a more serious conflict between India and Pakistan in an attempt to precipitate a harsh Indian response against Pakistan across the Line of Control, the internationally recognized boundary. From the perspective of many Islamic radicals, this outcome would, at a minimum, demonstrate the incompetence of the hated regime of General Musharraf or ultimately serve as the catalyst for an apocalyptic conflict between Islamabad and New Delhi.

The second target, the bystander, constitutes the largest audience. The goal of the terrorist is to use an extreme act to change the way in which the audience sees a new reality. As in the case of violence in literature and films, the level of horror has to increase over time to attract the attention of bystanders, who have their own mechanisms for coping with the awful. In Pakistan, the most important bystanders include the army—terrorists believe it is important not to alienate the military—the largely secular political community, and members of nonradical Islamic groups and parties. For this audience, acts of terrorism can demonstrate that violence is morally and practically superior to parliamentary methods for achieving important and shared objectives and that the groups that practice terrorism are legitimately pursuing objectives shared by a wide swath of Pakistanis. Terrorist acts may not lead to political power, but they might make the government more tolerant of these groups and less inclined to clamp down on them.

The final audience is comprised of the potential pool of recruits to the cause. Suicide plays an especially important role for this audience because the act helps to undo the moral damage caused by the obvious targeting of innocents. The death of a few martyrs who are on the side of good can compensate for the death of many innocents who happen to be on the side of evil. In addition, the message of the terrorist is that "small is beautiful" and a few dedicated cadres can take on and defeat the much larger enemy; therefore, the cause is not hopeless and is worth supporting, even with one's life. In Pakistan, the potential supporters of terrorism include the large pool of unemployed college students and graduates; the threat here lies in the fact that the numbers of such supporters will grow steadily if the economy remains stagnant and population growth continues out of control.

A Mixed Lot

In sum, Pakistan's Islamic extremists are a mixed lot. Some are criminals wrapped in the mantle of divine justice; some have modest Pakistani-related objectives; and others are seized with sectarian hatred. The radical groups' theological origins inherently divide them, and although most are Deobandis, some are not, including the extremely violent Shi'a groups. Nevertheless, all these groups tend to splinter in ways reminiscent of the extreme Right and Left in other parts of the world, and a burning sense of injustice may motivate a few foreign-born radicals to join them.

These groups expend their energy on ordinary Pakistani citizens or on one another; or they direct their efforts—usually with government assistance—toward India and, until recently, Afghanistan. Some radical Islamic groups are linked to more mainstream political movements or serve as the fighting or terrorist arm of such movements.

Moreover, Pakistan's radical groups disagree with one another in their diagnosis of the country's political, economic, and social problems. In the NWFP and northern Baluchistan, radical Islamic groups are becoming the vehicle for Pashtun dissent and anger, displacing the region's traditional Pashtun political party. Most radical Islamists hold deeply anti-U.S. sentiments, parting company with the more centrist JI, which acknowledges that Pakistan has benefited from its ties to the United States and must maintain some links to the world's sole superpower if the country is to emerge as a state that is both modern and Islamic.

A few groups are, in fact, delusional and believe that terrorism can bring down the American empire. Even more believe that selected acts of terror will demonstrate the artificiality of India as a state and that India's Muslims are seething with discontent and must be liberated from Hindu oppression through jihad. Some radical groups prefer to direct their anger toward the Pakistani state and call for the immediate establishment of the *shari'a* as official, comprehensive state law, with Pakistan returning to a purer form of Islam and purging itself of corrupt Western and Hindu cultural trappings.

Where they have come to power, however, especially in the NWFP, the radical and centrist Islamists seem to have reached the understanding that, although rhetoric will continue to be inflammatory, the actual imposition of Islamic law and the more extreme parts of the MMA manifesto will continue to be held in abeyance. These groups know that the imposition of more radical measures would not only be unpopular in the NWFP but also might lead to the dismissal of the provincial government by the army-dominated government in Islamabad. Although they have grown in importance over the last year, Islamist groups do not dominate Pakistani society; they have not proven all that effective in pursuing their main goals; and they remain under the careful watch of the central government.

RADICALISM'S REAL EFFECT ON THE STATE

RADICAL ISLAMIST GROUPS in Pakistan can be most accurately and collectively defined, as noted earlier, as those that seek major changes in the Pakistani political and social order and support violence to achieve those changes. Paradoxically, it has almost always been the state, especially the Pakistani army, that has allowed most radical Islamic groups to function on a wider stage—equipping and training them when necessary and providing overall political and strategic guidance for their activities. Arguably, therefore, in Pakistan, radical groups have been more of a tool of the state than a serious threat to it.

The Pakistani government's record in dealing with such radical groups is almost as mixed as the motives of the groups themselves. The government banned JeM and LeT in January 2002 under U.S. pressure, but the disbanding or banning of such radical groups usually means a name change or the temporary suspension of operations. Bans have had no impact on either the membership or the leadership of these groups, nor have they stopped the Pakistani government from using them for its own purposes. For example, the Nawaz Sharif government sought the LeT's help in countering the sectarian Deobandi groups, while the Musharraf government continues to look the other way as radical groups head to Kashmir and India, where they have increased their operations since Musharraf's pledge to Washington to constrain them. Until the Pakistani government demonstrates the will and the capacity to carry out these pledges, it will not be radical Islamic groups that threaten the basic stability of Pakistan but the state organs that encourage them.

Exploited by the State

The state first exploited radical and violent Islamic groups in 1970–1971 in East Pakistan, when the Pakistani army called on right-wing Islamic militants, notably the student wing of the JI, to terrorize, torture, and murder Bengali intellectuals, politicians, and other supporters of the Bangladesh movement. Although Pakistan was confronted with an Indian-supported separatist movement, the brutal crackdown was counterproductive, and it weakened Islamabad's international position. Many of these militants were not Bengalis; they were drawn from the Bihari community of East Pakistan. Thus began a long and sordid history of the use of Islamic terror squads by the Pakistani state and its intelligence services to intimidate opponents of the regime; ethnic separatists; elements of moderate political parties; and, when necessary, other violent groups.

Pakistan's lurch toward Islamic extremism continued under Zulfiqar Ali Bhutto from 1971 onward. Bhutto cynically promoted Islamization as a cover for his own autocratic tendencies, but he was deposed by the pious General Zia ul-Haq in 1977. Zia (unlike Bhutto) was an extremely devout Muslim whose views were close to the JI. Zia was the first army chief openly to praise and support Islamic groups. He developed political ties with, and then later abandoned, the JI; in 1981 he provided massive arms and economic support for some of the most noxious and radical yet militarily effective Islamic groups in Afghanistan in the war to oust the Soviets from the country. Many of these groups had ties to counterparts in Pakistan, and most were based in the Pakistani city of Peshawar where, as in other parts of the NWFP, they developed ties to Arab and other Islamic volunteers in the jihad.[7]

In the late 1980s, Pakistan's dominant intelligence service, the Inter-Services Intelligence (ISI) Directorate, began training Kashmiri dissidents, many of whom had fled to Pakistan after the rigged Kashmir election in 1989. ISI facilitated the Kashmiri operations undertaken by various Pakistani-based radical Islamic groups from 1989 onward; a few years later, under the direction of Benazir Bhutto, some of these groups were encouraged to support the Taliban, which Islamabad saw as a way to end Afghanistan's chaos and, at the same time, install a pro-Pakistani government in Kabul. The army also intervened from time to time to end sectarian disputes among radical Islamists within Pakistan, especially when they threatened to spread to the army, which has always prided itself as being above religious fanaticism. The problem persists today, as Musharraf has declared yet another crackdown on sectarianism, yet the situation remains inevitable so long as the state continues to—sporadically and to its own ends—support these groups.

Challenging The State

Within a few years of the Soviet withdrawal from Afghanistan in 1989–1990, U.S. policy toward Pakistan hardened, and a separatist uprising broke out in the Indian-administered portions of the state of Jammu and Kashmir. These events emboldened a few radical Islamists, convinced that Pakistan was ripe for an Islamic coup, to launch one in September 1995.

The goal was to establish a strict Islamic order in Pakistan and carry the jihad more vigorously to India (and, via the Taliban, to Central Asia). The coup was a failure, even if the coup-makers actually shared some of the policy goals of the government, which implemented in the late 1980s a "forward policy" in Afghanistan and Kashmir to extend Pakistan's influence to Central Asia and weaken India's hold on the disputed province.

More typically, Pakistan army officers are guided by professional military norms, not religious ones. They wish to keep the army free of sectarianism (especially Sunni-Shi'a disputes) and do not want to see the army turned into a vehicle of religious propagation. Above all, there is a powerful incentive to follow channels and to work the system in the army because dissident and maverick officers are unlikely to reap the rewards of promotion or of plush government jobs upon retirement. The coup-makers were going against a trend, as the army was purged of ideologically motivated officers two years earlier when army chief Asif Nawaz Janjua implemented a plan to sidetrack the "bearded" ones, the more devout and blatantly pious officers. Speculatively, that purge may have sent many of these individuals into the ISI or out of the army, where they linked up with some of the radical Islamic groups that were then being cultivated for tasks in Afghanistan and Kashmir.

There is no evidence that the army is currently seething with Islamic radicalism, that an Islamic cabal is in a position to seize power in a coup, or that the lower ranks of the officer corps are any more "Islamic" than would be expected in a society that has seen the steady rise of Islamic sentiments. A recent visit to the Pakistan Military Academy, discussions with its directors and some cadets, and many conversations with active and retired Pakistani army officers all indicate little change from earlier years, which is not to say that the tenor and outlook of the officer corps remain unchanged as one generation succeeds another.

The reaction of Musharraf's generation of army officers against Zia's Islamic zealotry in no way represents a rejection of the more limited strategy of using radical Islamic groups as instruments of Pakistani foreign policy, especially against India. The dispute over Kashmir, like Pakistan's relations with Afghanistan, is viewed as a domestic matter whose resolution is vital to Pakistan's society and security. Manipulating Islamic radicals, however, may have consequences for Pakistan's civil society—a subject that has generated considerable debate in Pakistan.

FACTORS TO CONSIDER

THE RESULTS OF the 2002 Pakistani elections and continued tension between India and Pakistan in Kashmir, especially in light of the two nations' demonstrated nuclear capabilities, have understandably attracted a great deal of attention to Pakistan's radical *madaris* and Islamist terrorism. Yet, the reality is that most Pakistanis remain moderates while the largely nonradical army retains the preeminent political position. Longer-term trends in the nation, however, particularly those that have resulted and can continue to result from Islamic terrorist campaigns abroad, and often encouraged by the state, are more troubling for their potential to give rise to stronger radical Islamism in Pakistan.

Radical Groups Don't Make a Radical State

Although most of Pakistan's Muslims are devout, they are not particularly radical. Moreover, Pakistani politics historically have been dominated by ethnic, linguistic, and economic issues, not by religion. The power of religious parties derived from state patronage. From Zia's time onward, religious parties have been used by political leaders to balance the secular and more influential Pakistan

Muslim League and Pakistan People's Party; thus, religious parties primarily derived the minimal power they currently have from state patronage. Despite their recent achievement of coming to power in one province and sharing it in another, there is reason to doubt that they will soon acquire the street power needed to threaten any military regime or democratically elected government or that they will have enough votes to win a free election at the national level.[8]

In other states, Islamic parties and radical movements often become the only outlet for anger and resentment on the part of ethnic or linguistic sub-groups. In Pakistan, however, the two major centrist political parties, the Muslim League and the Pakistan People's Party, have tried to articulate a wide range of views and positions; and during the decade of democracy from 1988 to 1999, a two-party system evolved. Where these parties have failed spectacularly has been in addressing corruption, gaining the confidence of the military, and dealing with the grievances of some of Pakistan's less-populous provinces, notably Sindh, Balochistan, and the NWFP. Sindhis and Baluchis have not turned to Islam, although they have at times turned to terrorism; the rise of Islamic parties in the NWFP and Balochistan may be a sign that Islam is now the vehicle for Pashtun subnationalism.

Pakistan remains ethnically, culturally, and regionally a pluralistic state, but these divisions do not correspond with the splits among its Islamic sects. In 1971, Islam was unable to keep the state together in the face of a Bengali separatist movement, and it is not likely to be a unifying factor in the future. When paired with ethnic or regional grievance, however, religion can be a potentially powerful negative force, further weakening Pakistan if the rise of religious extremism drives out its most educated and talented citizens, further isolating the country internationally. Whereas some Saudis may welcome the rise of Sunni Islamic radicalism, China, India, and the West would regard such a development in Pakistan as threatening, as would Shi'a Iran.

The Army's Preeminence

Although Pakistan still lacks a strong national identity and Islam—especially radical Islam—is not likely to provide one, the Pakistani state is nevertheless strong, and the army remains its core.9 Unless Pakistan is defeated in a war or undergoes an internal split of unprecedented magnitude—and neither scenario is likely—the army will retain its professional and organizational integrity and will prevent any radical Islamic group's rise to power in its own right, although the army may continue to use them in its own interests.

In grasping the unique role of the army in Pakistan, the perceptions by the Pakistani security community, and by the army in particular, are of special importance. Pakistan is a paranoid state that has enemies. The strategic elite do not want to see their country become a West Bangladesh—a state denuded of its military power and politically as well as economically subordinated to a hegemonic India. Although radical groups share this assessment, Pakistan's establishment only partially shares these groups' solutions: Islamic purification of Pakistan, dependence on the Islamic world for security assistance and friendship, and a calculated use of Islamic radicalism to extend Pakistan's influence. The Pakistani establishment subscribes to the latter prescription, but not to the point where the country would provoke a war with India or allow Islamic radicals to acquire significant power within Pakistan itself.

A series of assassinations of senior army officials would only confirm the army's institutional view that it remains Pakistan's last bastion and that civilians of all stripes are not qualified to govern Pakistan effectively. This assessment applies to radical Islamists as much as to moderate Pakistanis. Nevertheless, the army's disdain for civilians—radicals and moderates alike—will not prevent the army and its intelligence services from continuing to manipulate them for domestic and foreign policy purposes. Pakistan's history shows that the army cannot run Pakistan effectively by itself but that the army is also unwilling to entrust civilians completely with the job. Although this state of affairs makes it likely that Pakistan will not progress, it also ensures that Pakistan will not soon become a radical state.

The only scenario involving the army that could bring radical Islamists to a position of influence would be the army leadership's decision to don the cloak of radical Islam, which would be unlikely in the near future because the current army leaders are openly critical of Zia's experiments in this realm. Should the quasi-secular Musharraf be disgraced and the state thus lose its capacity to govern, however, one option might be a pseudocoalition of radical Islamists and the military. Still, at this point, such a coalition seems extremely unlikely.

Blowback

As Pakistan's ISI supported hard-line Islamists in their self-proclaimed jihad against India and the war against the Soviet Union in Afghanistan—characterized as a religious struggle with U.S. support—consequences for Pakistan's domestic stability were inevitable. The blowback effect of events in Afghanistan and Kashmir is self-evident. Liberal and professional Pakistanis are deeply concerned about the rise in sectarian violence, guns, and disorder, whereas radical Islamic groups praise these operations as true jihads. Furthermore, at least one credible newspaper report indicates that foreign intelligence services have infiltrated disaffected Islamic radicals and that some of the violence directed against Christians and foreigners indicates that the Pakistan government has lost control over some sections of its carefully cultivated horde of Islamic extremists.[10]

Social Economic and Demographic Trends

Pakistan remains dominated by a secular establishment, presiding over the slow decay of the state and the idea of Pakistan. Formed in the 1950s in the Ayub Khan era, the establishment—an oligarchy consisting of less than one thousand military, political, bureaucratic, business, and media elites—can perpetuate itself but seems unable to take the steps required to transform Pakistan into a modern state.

Pakistan's educational and demographic trends, its enfeebled institutions, and its near-flat economy could produce a situation where even the army would be unable to stem the growth of radical Islamic groups and might even be captured by them. This is a long-term prospect, however, probably more than five to eight years away. Nevertheless, the trends should be monitored closely and should shape U.S. policy, especially if the global war on terrorism moves in a direction that causes Pakistan again to lose its strategic importance for the United States, which could happen if key Al Qaeda leaders who had taken refuge in Pakistan were caught or if Afghanistan were to achieve a greater degree of stability. Ironically, although it is in Pakistan's interests to deliver the occasional Al Qaeda or Taliban leader to U.S. authorities, once the stock is exhausted, there will be less incentive for Washington to continue its large aid program to Pakistan.

One key warning sign of Pakistan's breakdown would be migration patterns. If Pakistan is seen as a land of no hope, more and more of its elite will send their children abroad for education and will follow them as expatriates. The number of Pakistanis emigrating to the United States provides impressive evidence for this assessment. The large number of children of the elite who have chosen to stay in Pakistan, however, even taking an active role in politics, is also impressive. If this generation becomes radicalized, who will be left to hold the center together? If not reversed, these trends pose the greatest chances for radicalization down the line; there is ample anecdotal evidence that Pakistan's young, Westernized elites are growing increasingly disenchanted with the West and more attracted to what they see as the honesty and moral clarity of the Islamists.[11]

DEMONIZATION OF PAKISTANIS

MOST REVOLUTIONS are fueled by a burning sense of injustice. Some revolutions take the path to parliamentarianism, as did those led by India's Mahatma Gandhi and Pakistan's Jinnah, but others lead to dictatorship or totalitarian rule. Typically, revolutions are led by individuals who were subjected to discrimination and radicalized. Several recent incidents point to a worrisome trend that might accelerate the growth of a similar kind of movement in Pakistan.

Upper-class, educated Pakistanis, including those living abroad, are now subject to some harassment; and the communities' sense of beleaguerment, always present, is ballooning. Pakistan's original promise seems to have been betrayed by both the generals and the politicians; only the Islamic parties hold a pure and untainted vision of the future. Pakistan has also lost many of its foreign friends, and those that remain—China and Saudi Arabia—cannot be expected to encourage democratic solutions to Pakistan's problems. If the process continues, it will only be a matter of time before a sizable percentage of these Pakistani citizens come to share the belief held by all extremist Pakistani Muslims that there is, indeed, a conflict of civilizations between Islam and the West, or at least between Pakistani Muslims and U.S. citizens and their allies, including the Pakistani government itself.

IMPLICATIONS FOR THE UNITED STATES

ROBERT KAPLAN concluded his reviews of two recent books on Pakistan by asserting that the U.S. government's best bet in Pakistan is Musharraf. Kaplan quotes General Anthony C. Zinni's claim that the U.S. interest in Musharraf is not so much his personal qualities but the likelihood that "what would come after him would be a disaster."[12] This conclusion is false: if Musharraf stepped down or was removed, he would be replaced by a colleague or peer who is unlikely to be enthusiastic about radical Islam. Musharraf's successor would be replaced in turn by still another general with a similar semisecular outlook. The army may use Islamic extremists and may not be able to reconstruct and build a normal Pakistani society, but for the foreseeable future, it is most capable of blocking anyone else from coming to power.

Though the potential for a radical leader to emerge anytime soon is not a legitimate concern and the radical Islamic threat to Pakistan generally has in fact been exaggerated, what should the United States be watching? The following list provides a summary of those developments worthy of consideration by U.S. policymakers in determining U.S. concerns in Pakistan.

• *Long-term national decay.* The long-term decay of Pakistan may not unite radical Islamists, but it would provide them with a larger recruitment base and more resources by increasing the ranks of the frustrated, the angry, and the educated underemployed.

• *Popular frustration with Musharraf and the United States.* A second Zia might not be attractive to the current generation of army officers, but a later generation—frustrated with Musharraf's secularism, somewhat more Islamized, and even more adamantly opposed to the United States—could move in this direction, allowing an eventual successor's successor to don the Islamic cloak.

• *Reactions to U.S. presence in Afghanistan.* The war in Afghanistan was a major reason for the MMA's success in Balochistan and the NWFP; a continuing U.S. presence just next door, without tangible positive results for the Afghan people, will further intensify Pakistani grievances and fuel their discontent with any government that supports Washington.

• *Political repression.* Blocking secular and ethnic channels of expression by a fresh ban on political activities would open the door wider for radical Islamists, who are capable of using informal channels for their operations, especially via the *madaris*.

• *Pashtun nationalism aligning with radical Islamism.* If this movement were to link up with a revived radical Islamic faction in Afghanistan, such as the Taliban or Gulbuddin Hekmatyar's group, both the regime in Kabul and the integrity of Pakistan could be threatened.

• *Ongoing conflict with India.* Another conflict with India could strengthen the hand of some Pakistani radical Islamists, who believe there is a civilizational war between Islam and the unholy alliance of the Christian and Jewish West and Hindu India. If Islamabad were unable to protect Pakistan from Indian pressure, the army just might move in an Islamic direction; however, a general war is a more likely outcome.

COPING STRATEGIES FOR THE NEXT FIVE YEARS

PAKISTAN HAS A LONG-STANDING, if frequently abused, tradition of parliamentary democracy. Democracy in Pakistan is feeble in comparison to that of its neighbor India and always will be problematic. The best strategy available for the United States to prevent the emergence of a radical Islamic movement in Pakistan, however, is to insist that the Pakistan government allow the moderate, secular political parties, such as Bhutto's Pakistan People's Party and Sharif's Muslim League, to function freely, as well as to be tougher on those Islamist groups, parties, and leaders that have practiced and preached violence within Pakistan and across its borders in India and Afghanistan. The

United States should also seek dialogue with those Islamist parties, such as the JI, which seek power through parliamentary means.

Ironically, the chief obstacle to the emergence of a functioning democracy in Pakistan is the army, which is also the principal barrier to Pakistan's movement toward political extremism. The generals cannot govern Pakistan, but they will not let anyone else govern it. The army is not Islamized, although its officers and men reflect the generally devout quality of Pakistanis, and under present circumstances, the army is immune to the lure of an alliance with radical Islam.

The army derives its legitimacy from its claim to be the one institution that best understands the threats to Pakistan. Officers boast that only they have the education, the discipline, and the resources to accomplish vital national objectives, including defending Pakistan against Indian aggression, ensuring domestic law and order, and establishing boundaries beyond which the political parties may not roam. The present arrangement could be overturned if the army itself were to lose its integrity through military defeat, internal professional and personal rivalries, or the meddling of politicians. Although the likelihood of the army allying with Islamic forces in the foreseeable future is slim, in the long run, Pakistan's reasonably stable system could be gradually transformed.

U.S. policy must deal not only with the tactical problem of retaining Musharraf's support but also with problems that will arise several years from now after Musharraf is gone. The global war on terrorism— a response to the direct threat from Al Qaeda—is not likely to last more than a few more years in South Asia, but radical Islamic movements in Pakistan are now putting down roots. Ultimately, the residual power of radical Islamists can be further attenuated by a strategy that incorporates:

• *Encouraging the further revival of democracy in Pakistan.* Public and private support would give the moderate Islamic groups a chance to compete against the traditional, moderate political parties and give those traditional moderate parties time to develop real political organizations. In the process, support for radical Islamists will be seen to be quite limited, except in unusual cases such as the NWFP.

• *Real dialogue between India and Pakistan.* The United States must actively go beyond mere lip service to promote a peace process between the two countries that seeks the well-being of the Kashmiri people—not merely the legal status of Kashmir—as its primary motivation. This support would have several important consequences: (1) it would address a major cause taken up by the radical Islamists and many moderate Pakistanis; (2) it could be the basis for an effective ban on the external operations of radical Islamists; (3) it would make the army less central to Pakistan's future; and (4) it would also be in India's interest in the long run. Starting and sustaining such a process should be one of the major goals of U.S. policy in South Asia.

• *Vigilance in Afghanistan.* The process of nation and state building in Afghanistan must continue and must be seen as continuing with the support of the United States and the international community at large.

• *Improving the benefits of U.S. aid for the Pakistani people.* Pakistan must have tangible evidence that its government's tilt in favor of the United States brings significant benefits to the Pakistani people, especially in improved education. Most aid is invisible to the average Pakistani, who cares little about debt relief or balance of payment problems. A massive educational airlift that would train Pakistani educators, officials, and others, on the other hand, would demonstrate for the Pakistani people that the United States has an interest in Pakistani well-being as well as in maintaining Musharraf's support in the war on terrorism. Despite Washington's current plans for a very modest educational program, cases of maltreatment of visiting Pakistani scholars and journalists in the United States have already offset this potential benefit.

For the United States, Pakistan is both part of the problem and part of the solution. Pakistan is an ally in the war against terrorism yet, at the same time, a potential base of Islamic radicalism—if not on this administration's watch, then on the next. Washington has no option but to work with Pakistan in the short run, cajoling Islamabad to stop its support of radical Islamic groups that have operated in Afghanistan, India, and other countries. The U.S. government must also address the deeper causes of Pakistan's malaise, however, lest the country become the kind of nuclear-armed monster state that its critics already think it is.

Endnotes

1. For an authoritative account of the Jama'at-i-Islami, see Seyyed Vali Reza Nasr, *The Vanguard of the Islamic Revolution: The Jama'at-i-Islami of Pakistan* (London: I. B. Taurus, 1994).

2. For a history of this group, see Yoginder Sikand, *The Origins and Development of the Tablighi-Jama'at (1920–2000): A Cross-Country Comparative Study* (Hyderabad, India: Orient Longman, 2002). See also Khaled Ahmed, "The Grand Tableeghi Congregation," *Friday Times,* November 7, 2002.

3. For a reasonably accurate Indian account of these groups, see "Pakistan Terrorist Groups," http://www.satp.org/satporgtp/countries/pakistan/terroristoutfits/index.html (accessed April 15, 2003). The site is maintained by the Institute of Conflict Management, whose leading member, K. P. S. Gill, was responsible for the strategy that eventually defeated the Khalistan movement in India's Punjabi state.

4. Mandavi Mehta and Teresita C. Schaffer, "Islam in Pakistan: Unity and Contradictions," Project on Pakistan's Future and U.S. Policy Options, Center for Strategic and International Studies, Washington, D.C., October 7, 2002.

5. Peter W. Singer, "Pakistan's Madrassahs: Ensuring a System of Education, Not Jihad," *Analysis Paper* # 14 (Washington, D.C.: Brookings Institution, November 2001).

6. For a revealing account of Omar's transformation by a former school friend, see Mohamed Ahmed Khan, "A Pakistani Gora in Lahore," *Herald* (Karachi), August 2002.

7. See Stephen Philip Cohen, *The Pakistan Army,* 2d ed. (Oxford and New York: Oxford University Press, 1998), postscript; see also Hasan Askari Rizvi, "Islam and the Military," in *Military, State and Society in Pakistan* (London: Macmillan, 2000), p. 245.

8. See International Crisis Group, "Pakistan: The Dangers of Conventional Wisdom," www.intl-crisis-group.org/projects/showreport.cfm?reportid=578 (accessed April 15, 2003).

9. For a discussion of Pakistan as a state versus its identity as a nation, see Stephen Philip Cohen, "The Nation and the State of Pakistan," *The Washington Quarterly* 25, no. 3 (Summer 2002): 109–122.

10. Wajahat Sajjad [pseud.], "RAW Penetrates Disgruntled Jihadi Groups," *Friday Times,* October 11–17, 2002.

11. John Lancaster, "Secular Pakistanis, Upset by War, Turn to Religious Parties," *The Washington Post,* April 4, 2003.

12. Robert Kaplan, "A Nuclear Yugoslavia," reviews of *Pakistan: In the Shadow of Jihad and Afghanistan,* by Mary Anne Weaver, and *Pakistan: Eye of the Storm,* by Owen Bennett Jones, *The New York Times Book Review,* November 3, 2002, p. 13.

Saudi Arabia and the War on Terrorism

F. Gregory Gause III

THE STARTING POINT for an effective approach toward Saudi Arabia in the war on terrorism is an accurate diagnosis of just what role the country has played in the growth of al Qaeda and Sunni Muslim extremism. Exaggeration of that role has become so common in the United States that it threatens to destroy a relationship that, though troubled, is essential to American national interests in the Middle East, in the fight against terrorism, and in the world oil market.

The next step is a realistic policy prescription that deals with the problems emanating from Saudi Arabia. The policy prescription must emphasize those areas where tangible progress can be made and must avoid, to the greatest extent possible, unintended consequences that would damage American interests.

DIAGNOSIS

AN ACCURATE UNDERSTANDING of Wahhabism is the crucial first step in diagnosing the Saudi role in the global war on terrorism. This is not simply a semantic issue or an arcane exegesis of Islamic texts. Many in the United States contend that Wahhabism is itself the root of Sunni Muslim violence and terrorism.[1] In their appendix to the Congressional Joint Committee report on the September 11 attacks, Senators Jon Kyl and Pat Roberts refer to Wahhabism as "a radical,

This article originally appeared in *A Practical Guide to Winning the War on Terrorism* (edited by Adam Garfinkle), and has been reprinted with the permission of the publisher, Hoover Institution Press. ©2004 by the Board of Trustees of the Leland Stanford Junior University.

anti-American variant of Islam."[2] Senators Kyl and Charles Schumer later wrote that Wahhabism "seeks our society's destruction."[3]

If this were true, then we would have no choice but to treat Saudi Arabia as we treated the Taliban regime in Afghanistan, because Saudi Arabia is certainly a Wahhabi state. However, these views misunderstand both Wahhabism itself and its centrality in the growth of violent Sunni Muslim extremist groups.

The puritanical version of Islam preached by Muhammad ibn Abd al-Wahhab in central Arabia in the eighteenth century, which served as the animating ideology for the Al-Saud family's efforts to build a state in Arabia, is not very attractive to most outside observers. It is literalist in its desire to replicate the milieu of the Prophet Muhammad in every possible way. It is extremely intolerant of other interpretations of Islam, particularly Shiism. It is wary and suspicious of non-Muslims. Its views on the role of women in society run counter to international norms, to say the least. It is also hostile to the canons of modern science, with some Saudi clerics holding, to this day, that the world is flat and at the center of the solar system.

But none of this is new. Wahhabism has been the official interpretation of Islam in the Saudi domain since the founding of the modern state at the outset of the twentieth century. It has not been a barrier to a very close Saudi-American relationship over the past decades. The phenomenon of anti-American terror in the Sunni Muslim community is much more recent. If this terror were grounded solely in Wahhabism, it should have manifested itself much earlier and should have prevented the historically close Saudi-American relationship.

Wahhabism, as it has developed in Saudi Arabia, is a state ideology, not a revolutionary creed. As retrograde as it might be on social issues, Wahhabism's official arbiters counsel loyalty to the ruler, not revolution. They accord the ruler wide latitude to conduct foreign affairs. Leading Wahhabi scholars and clerics, for example, publicly gave their seal of approval to both the invitation of American forces to Saudi Arabia in 1990 and the use of Saudi Arabia as a base for the 1991 attack on Iraq. They have vehemently rejected the bin Ladenist logic of violence, condemning the attacks of September 11, the bombings in Riyadh in May and November 2003, and the surge of terrorist violence thereafter. Even Wahhabi clerics deeply critical of American policy in the Middle East and of the Saudi-American relationship have spoken out against bin Laden and the violence that he and his followers have perpetrated.[4]

One reason that many have equated "bin Ladenism" with Wahhabism is that bin Laden himself claims to follow the "true" Wahhabi line. He calls for the overthrow of the Saudi regime and condemns the official clerics for deviating from that line. But allowing bin Laden to define Wahhabism is like allowing the militia movement in the United States to define what it means to be a patriotic American. We should not be taken in by such claims.

Violent anti-American Sunni extremism, personified by bin Laden, is the product of a much more contemporary and complicated set of ideological trends and political experiences. Wahhabism is a part of that mix, but only a part. The crucible of the development of bin Ladenism was the jihad against the Soviet Union in Afghanistan in the 1980s. Among the Arab volunteers there, the retrograde social views and theological intolerance of Saudi Wahhabism came to be blended with the revolutionary political doctrines developed in the 1960s by Muslim Brotherhood thinkers, particularly in Egypt. It is no accident that bin Laden's chief lieutenant in al Qaeda is an Egyptian, Ayman al-Zawahiri, who was prominent in the violent fringes of Egyptian Islamist movements of the 1970s and 1980s. This ideological mélange was filtered through the jihad's success, which was taken as no less than a divine sanction for the political message that developed out of it. Imbued with this confidence, the "Arab Afghans" returned to continue the jihad against their "insufficiently Muslim" governments in Algeria, Egypt, Jordan, and, to a lesser extent, Saudi Arabia. It is only with their failure to remake the politics of the region that, in the mid-1990s, bin Laden began to focus his jihad explicitly against the United States.

Meanwhile, the success in Afghanistan brought a new luster to the concept of jihad in Saudi Arabia (and many other Muslim countries). The Saudi government had encouraged public support for the Afghan jihad (as had the American government). Jihad became a more prominent part of many Saudis' understanding of Islam. Muslims were also "oppressed," as Saudis saw it, by non-Muslims in places like Bosnia, Kashmir, Chechnya, and the West Bank and Gaza. If jihad worked in Afghanistan to free a Muslim population from non-Muslim rule, why should it not work in these other places?

Some of these causes received more official support in Saudi Arabia than others. Bosnian and Palestinian Muslims received much largesse. Saudi diplomatic relations with Russia and India, however, put limits on official support for the Chechen and Kashmiri jihads. But it is undeniable that the Saudi government not only did not oppose the developing jihadist subculture in the country but in some ways encouraged it.

Here is the true intersection in the 1990s between the bin Ladenist movement and Saudi Arabia. Bin Laden himself had been expelled from the country and stripped of his citizenship in 1994. His movement in the country seemed to be rolled up in the mid-1990s, after large-scale arrests. But al Qaeda was active in these other jihadi movements and, in time, was able to make common cause with, or take over, Saudi-funded organizations active in these causes.5

It is this intersection that highlights the most important role of Saudi Arabia in the spread of Sunni Islamist extremism. Saudi funding sources, developed during the Afghan jihad and maintained through the 1990s, either wittingly or unwittingly came to support al Qaeda and groups like it. The new prominence of jihad in Saudi Arabia came to be transmitted through Saudi-supported Islamic international organizations (like the Islamic Conference Organization) and nongovernmental organizations (like the World Muslim League and the World Assembly of Muslim Youth) to the rest of the Muslim world. The spread of the jihadist subculture clearly facilitated al Qaeda recruitment and created an atmosphere in which sympathy for al Qaeda could grow. Saudi recruitment channels for jihadis at home, developed in the 1980s to send young Saudis to Afghanistan and continuing in the 1990s to other areas, came to be exploited by al Qaeda to recruit Saudis directly into the organization.

Funding, ideological legitimation, and recruitment are the areas where Saudi Arabia played a key role in developing Sunni Muslim extremism. But that is a far cry from claiming that the Saudi government itself, directly and wittingly, boosted bin Laden and his views. It is even a farther cry from the theories that the Al-Saud were behind September 11, theories on a par with those holding the CIA or the Israeli Mossad responsible for those atrocities. The reality is challenge enough; no good purpose is served by marketing error and delusion.

PRESCRIPTION

FUNDING, IDEOLOGICAL LEGITIMATION, and recruitment are precisely the areas that American foreign policy should target in its policy toward Saudi Arabia in the war on terrorism. In all of these areas, the United States is today dealing with a Saudi government that is usually, though not always, willing to cooperate. The level of cooperation has varied, in part because not all elements of the Saudi regime have been equally committed to that cooperation.

A number of factors contribute to that reluctance, including tensions over the direction of American Middle East policy in general and very clear differences between the two countries regarding the definition of terrorism as it relates to the Arab-Israeli conflict. However, the key to Saudi reluctance is the domestic political costs of confronting a movement that had considerable sympathy within Saudi Arabia for many of its goals if not its tactics. Being against Islam is not a winning position in Saudi politics. The fact that any cooperation with the United States would be seen by many as bowing to American pressure, when (from the late 1990s) the United States has been profoundly unpopular in Saudi Arabia, has furnished further disincentive.

However, the attacks on the United States on September 11, 2001, and on the housing compounds in Riyadh on May 12 and November 9, 2003, led to new levels of seriousness on the part of the Saudi authorities in addressing the problem of Sunni extremism that they had, however unwittingly, helped to create. These events brought home to the Saudi leadership, more quickly to some than to others, the threat posed by Sunni Muslim extremism to the domestic stability of their own regime.

On the funding issue, American pressure and the Saudi realization of the seriousness of the threat have led to important steps by

Riyadh to exercise more control over Saudi-supported charities and to monitor financial transactions from the kingdom. During 2002, the Saudi government took several steps in this direction, including requiring Foreign Ministry approval of any charitable project undertaken outside the country, ordering audits of Saudi charities, and establishing new oversight bodies in the government to monitor charities.[6] After the May 2003 bombings Riyadh moved to close ten of the foreign offices of the al-Haramain Foundation, frequently cited as a conduit of funds for extremist groups, after earlier closing the foundation's offices in Bosnia and Somalia.[7]

The task for American foreign policy is to hold the Saudi government's feet to the fire on this issue, pushing it to follow up on its own declared policy. The Bush administration has been doing so, dispatching in August 2003 a team of senior counterterrorist officials to press the Saudis.[8] Just a few weeks later, the Saudi cabinet adopted new regulations against money laundering, and the Saudi government allowed the IRS and FBI to establish a permanent liaison office in Riyadh to coordinate with Saudi counterparts.[9] A practical step in this direction would be to press the Saudis to actually create the Saudi Higher Authority for Relief and Charity Work, a step that had been announced but not implemented, to serve as the oversight body for all charitable organizations and associations offering services outside the country.[10]

In December 2003, Saudi sources at the embassy in Washington revealed that the Saudi government intends to stop providing diplomatic status for Islamic clerics and educators preaching and teaching overseas. These sources also claimed an intent to "shut down the Islamic affairs section in every embassy."[11] If this actually occurs, it will be a significant step and a major signal of change in Saudi policy.

While many in Washington remain skeptical of the Saudi commitment in this area, some appear to have become too complacent. It still makes sense to pressure Riyadh to demonstrate its good intentions rather than to assume they either will or will not follow through on recent initiatives. If further cooperation is not forthcoming, the United States should not hesitate to "name and shame" Saudi individuals and organizations involved in the deliberate financing of al Qaeda and affiliate groups.

Saudi Arabia and the War on Terrorism

One area of particular sensitivity in the issue of funding is Saudi support, official and private, for Hamas, the Palestinian Islamist group officially designated as a terrorist organization by the United States. There is no question that Saudi money goes to Hamas organizations and projects.[12] Pushing the Saudis to end as much of that support as they can would be valuable, but the negative consequences of making the Hamas issue a very high-profile public part of Saudi-American relations are considerable. In terms of Saudi public opinion, equating al Qaeda and Hamas does not delegitimate the latter; it legitimates the former. Better for Washington to separate the al Qaeda issue from the Hamas issue by pushing publicly and privately for absolute cooperation on the former and keeping the latter in the realm of private diplomacy, at least while al Qaeda remains America's foremost priority.

On legitimation, Washington has a less public role to play than on funding. The U.S. government will not be successful in telling Muslims what Islam is, and it should not try to do so. Here, the key is to press the Saudis to use their considerable ideological resources, both at home and in the Muslim world in general, to place bin Laden, his actions, and his interpretation of Islam outside the pale of acceptable Muslim discourse. This requires the Saudis to confront head-on the jihadist subculture that they indirectly nurtured during the past two decades.

As in the funding area, the Saudis have recently demonstrated a willingness to take on this task. In late May 2003, after the bombings in Riyadh, the Saudi Ministry of Islamic Affairs announced the removal of 353 religious officials from their positions (because they lacked the "qualifications" to work in mosques) and the requirement that 1,357 religious officials undergo further training.[13] Immediately after September 11, leading Saudi religious officials condemned the attacks and, since then, have consistently and publicly rejected bin Laden's interpretation of jihad. A recent example was the statement of the Higher Council of Ulama in August 2003, reaffirming that violent attacks on innocents "are criminal acts . . . not jihad in the path of God." The council called on the Saudi authorities to bring before the courts any scholar who issues a *fatwa* ("religious judgment") approving of such acts.[14] Continuing efforts by the Saudis in this direction, not only at home but also through the Islamic intergovernmental and nongovernmental organizations that they fund, are essential.

On recruitment, the Saudis need to police much more stringently the networks of al Qaeda members and sympathizers that have developed within the kingdom itself. For too long, even after September 11, Riyadh refused to face up to this issue. Just days before the May 2003 bombing, the country's chief security official, Interior Minister Prince Na'if, termed the al Qaeda presence in the country as "weak and almost nonexistent."[15] Since the bombing, Saudi security forces have been much more aggressive in efforts to root out al Qaeda. In the aftermath of the May and November 2003 bombings, more than six hundred Saudis were arrested. There have been a number of shootouts between Saudi police and suspected al Qaeda sympathizers, with tens killed on each side, and Saudi security services have discovered a number of substantial arms caches.[16] The United States should urge the Saudis to make a special effort to prevent infiltration by al Qaeda sympathizers and other Islamist militants across the long and largely unguarded Saudi-Iraqi border.

The Saudis could do more on all of these issues, and the United States should monitor Saudi government actions carefully. There is also the larger issue, beyond the scope of this essay, of the consequences of Wahhabi proselytizing in the Muslim world. Even if the official Saudi interpretation of Islam is not, in and of itself, the wellspring of anti-American terror, its retrograde views on social tolerance, gender issues, and democracy place it at variance with American goals throughout the Muslim world, including in the United States itself. Helping other Muslim countries promote more tolerant and inclusive interpretations of Islam should be part of the American foreign policy agenda, to the extent that Washington can help on these issues. But on the specific issue of anti-American terrorism, there is a clear willingness, more pronounced since the May 2003 bombings, on the part of the Saudi government to cooperate with Washington. That is a basis upon which to build.

DO NO HARM

THE UNITED STATES should avoid superficially appealing policies toward Saudi Arabia that will redound to our disadvantage. In particular, Washington should suppress its natural tendency to believe that more democracy will make things better in foreign countries.

Democratic elections in Saudi Arabia would reflect the very strong anti-Americanism now prevalent in the country. A Gallup poll, conducted in late January-early February 2002, reported that 64 percent of Saudi respondents viewed the United States either very unfavorably or most unfavorably. Majorities in the poll associated America with the adjectives "conceited, ruthless and arrogant." Fewer than 10 percent saw the United States as either friendly or trustworthy.[17] A Zogby International poll, conducted in March 2002, reported similar results. Only 30 percent of the Saudis polled supported American-led efforts to fight terrorism, while 57 percent opposed them.[18] A subsequent Zogby poll, conducted in July 2003, found that 70 percent of the Saudis polled had an unfavorable impression of the United States, with only 24 percent having a favorable impression.[19] An elected Saudi legislature, for example, would put pressure on the Saudi government to cooperate less, not more, with the United States in the war on terrorism and on general Middle East issues.

Saudi anti-Americanism is not an immutable fact. It reflects the tensions in the relationship since September 11, the negative reactions to American attacks on Afghanistan and Iraq, and the collapse of the Arab-Israeli peace process. But it can change with time, as regional realities change. However, a push for democracy in Saudi Arabia now would not serve American interests. President Bush cannot take back what he said at the National Endowment for Democracy on November 6, 2003, but he can selectively implement his vision. And he should. Cautious steps from the Saudis themselves to broaden the scope of political participation in their society, such as the October 2003 announcement of plans for municipal elections to fill half the seats of the proposed municipal councils, should be welcomed. Washington should not push for countrywide elections to national institutions, such as the Consultative Council (an appointed body).

The United States must also avoid the temptation to simply throw up its hands and declare the Saudis an enemy. This impulse is based on a faulty reading of the role of Wahhabism and Saudi Arabia in the development of Sunni Islamist extremism, as discussed earlier. Beyond that, the temptation seems to be an emotionally satisfying thought for many who see Wahhabism, the monarchy, the treatment of women, the Saudi stance on Arab-Israeli issues, and various other elements of Saudi society and governance as so antithetical to American principles that our country should have no truck with the House of Saud. As in so many things in life, however, what temporarily satisfies our emotional needs would not be good for us in the long run.

Those who urge such a policy fail the basic test of practical politics: They offer no alternative to the Saudi-American relationship.[20] They are extremely fuzzy on what Washington should do the day after it declares Saudi Arabia an enemy. Military invasion and occupation of the oil fields? Given how difficult and expensive U.S. occupation of Iraq has become, this cannot be a serious option. Those who advocate "regime change" in Riyadh, through greater democracy or direct U.S. action, can offer no assurances that a new regime would be any friendlier to the United States, harder on Islamist extremists, or more in tune with global human rights norms than the incumbents.

The plain fact is that not only do the rulers of Riyadh sit on 25 percent of all the world's known conventional oil reserves, but they also control the Muslim holy cities of Mecca and Medina, the focal point of faith for 1.4 billion Muslims in the world. Surely having a government there that, despite its problems, responds to American pressures on oil questions and the war on terrorism is better for American interests than the leap into the dark that military occupation or regime change would represent. Looking around the region, it is better than several other easily imaginable alternatives as well.

Endnotes

1. The first and most influential post–September 11 book to make this claim is Stephen Schwartz, *The Two Faces of Islam: The House of Sa'ud from Tradition to Terror* (New York: Doubleday, 2002).

2. "Additional Views—Senator Jon Kyl, Senator Pat Roberts," http://news.findlaw.com/hdocs/docs/911rpt/addviewsmem.pdf, p. 20.

3. Jon Kyl and Charles Schumer, "Saudi Arabia's Teachers of Terror," *The Washington Post*, August 18, 2003.

4. See F. Gregory Gause III, "Be Careful What You Wish For: The Future of U.S.-Saudi Relations," *World Policy Journal* 49, no. 1 (Spring 2002).

Saudi Arabia and the War on Terrorism

5. There are persistent charges that members of the Saudi ruling family either directly or indirectly cut a deal with bin Laden, at minimum promising not to impede his fundraising and recruiting in Saudi Arabia, perhaps even supporting him financially, in exchange for al Qaeda refraining from targeting Saudi Arabia. The major published source to raise this charge is Gerald Posner, *Why America Slept: The Failure to Prevent 9/11* (New York: Random House, 2003). Nothing in the public record supports this charge. The car bomb attack on the American training mission to the Saudi National Guard in Riyadh in November 1995, which killed seven and wounded sixty, was perpetrated by Saudis who, before their execution, publicly identified bin Laden as their inspiration. However, it is impossible to disprove the charge as well. In the past, Saudi leaders have attempted to buy off foreign opponents, and the ruling family is large enough that it is possible that some prince or group of princes took it upon themselves to explore this option. The most that can be said with certainty is that, if there ever were such an agreement, it did not work very well for the Al-Saud.

6. *Al-Hayat*, March 21, 2002, 1, 6; John Mintz, "Saudis Deny Dragging Feet on Terrorism," *The Washington Post*, December 4, 2002.

7. John Mintz, "Wahhabi Strain of Islam Faulted," *The Washington Post*, June 27, 2003.

8. Susan Schmidt, "U.S. Officials Press Saudis on Aiding Terror," *The Washington Post*, August 6, 2003.

9. "Cabinet OK's Anti-Money Laundering legislation," *Arab News*, August 19, 2003; "U.S. and Saudis Join in Anti-Terror Effort," *The New York Times*, August 26, 2003.

10. As of late May 2003, the body had yet to be established, according to the Saudi response to questions posed by the Counter-Terrorism Committee of the UN Security Council. The reference to the body is on page 11 of the response, Counter-Terrorism Committee document S/2003/583.

11. See Susan Schmidt and Caryle Murphy, "U.S. Revokes Visa of Cleric at Saudi Embassy," *The Washington Post*, December 7, 2003.

12. Adil al-Jubeir, foreign affairs adviser to Crown Prince Abdallah, has admitted as much. David R. Sands, "Kingdom Moves Against Terrorism," *The Washington Times*, June 13, 2003. See also Matthew Levitt, "Who Pays for Palestinian Terror?" *The Weekly Standard*, August 25, 2003.

13. *Al-Hayat*, May 28, 2003, 1, 6.

14. *Al-Hayat*, August 17, 2003, 1, 6.

15. Glenn Kessler and Alan Sipress, "Western Targets Bombed in Riyadh," *The Washington Post*, May 13, 2003.

16. Neil MacFarquhar, "Al Qaeda Blamed in Deadly Attack on Saudi Homes," *The New York Times*, November 10, 2003.

17. Richard Burkholder, "The U.S. and the West—Through Saudi Eyes," *Gallup Tuesday Briefing*, August 6, 2002.

18. "The 10 Nation 'Impressions of America' Poll Report," Zogby International, August 7, 2002.

19. www.zogby.com/news/ReadNews.dbm?ID=025.

20. Argued in Adam Garfinkle, "Weak Realpolitik: The Vicissitudes of Saudi Bashing," *The National Interest*, no. 67 (Spring 2002).

Is Southeast Asia
the Second Front?

John Gershman

PHASE 1.5

IN LATE JANUARY 2002, the Bush administration sent 660 U.S. troops to the Philippines, deploying them in the south of the archipelago to assist in hostage rescue and counterinsurgency operations. The move was widely heralded as the opening of a second front in Washington's war on terrorism. And that perception was understandable: after all, the deployment followed hard on the heels of the arrests of dozens of alleged al Qaeda operatives in Singapore, Malaysia, and the Philippines. With the Taliban in Afghanistan having been routed, Southeast Asia—home to radical Islamist groups such as the Jemaah Islamiah (JI), Abu Sayyaf, and the Kumpulan Mujahideen Malaysia (KMM)—was starting to seem like the new home base for the terrorist movement that had brought down the World Trade Center.

Whether or not this is actually the case, September 11 and its aftermath have already transformed U.S. relations with many Southeast Asian nations. America's previously chilly interactions with Muslim-majority Malaysia have thawed considerably; Prime Minister Mahathir bin Mohamad has won plaudits from Washington for supporting the U.S. war on terrorism. Indonesia, meanwhile, has come in for heavy American criticism for failing to be similarly cooperative and crack down on its own extremists (although the United States has softened its tone on this issue in recent months). At the same time, many U.S. policymakers are now looking to overturn congressional restrictions on aid to Indonesia's military, once spurned

---

This article originally appeared in the July/August 2002 issue of *Foreign Affairs*.

for its human rights abuses, as a way to bolster the state's capacity to fight terrorism. And little more than a decade after the Philippine Senate refused to renew leases on U.S. bases in that country—prompting Washington to slash its aid to Manila—the American military is now returning in force. Indeed, the Philippines has not occupied such a prominent place in U.S. foreign policy since the end of the Cold War.

The intensifying U.S. involvement in Southeast Asia reflects the somewhat hysterical tone adopted by many recent policy and press reports about the strength and scope of the terrorist threat there. In February, a secret FBI report called Malaysia a "primary operational launch pad" for the September 11 attacks—a charge that has since been dismissed as exaggerated by Western intelligence sources. Even the FBI itself has backpedaled from the claim. Meanwhile, some U.S. analysts have described Abu Sayyaf, the rebel group now fighting the government in the southern Philippine islands around Mindanao and known for kidnapping Westerners, as similar to the Taliban—despite the fact that Abu Sayyaf operates in a limited area, lacks a major organized base, and has no coherent political agenda. And *The National Review* and analysts at the Heritage Foundation have already declared Indonesia the next Afghanistan.

Such overheated rhetoric is a mistake. Looking at Southeast Asia through the lens of Afghanistan will lead U.S. policymakers to the wrong conclusions and the wrong policy. The analogy will cause Washington to overestimate the threat of al Qaeda links to groups in the area and will push it into an over-militarized response to the problems that do exist—a response that will be at best ineffective and at worst counterproductive. Even if al Qaeda operatives in Southeast Asia are neutralized and Abu Sayyaf is crushed, the underlying conditions that facilitated the emergence of these movements—namely, weak states unable to enforce basic law and order, and the economic marginalization and political subordination of large segments of their populations—will continue to exist. If Washington really wants to make a lasting contribution to peace and security in the area, it should work to address these basic flaws and not just beef up its military contributions or law enforcement operations.

John Gershman

AT FIRST GLANCE, Southeast Asia does indeed seem like a good candidate for the second front in the U.S. campaign. After all, the region is home to the world's most populous Muslim-majority country, Indonesia, as well as two other mostly Muslim states, Malaysia and Brunei. In addition, Singapore, the Philippines, and Thailand all have significant Muslim minorities, and decades-old Islamist rebellions still simmer in the latter two countries. Furthermore, political Islam, in both violent and nonviolent forms, has been on the rise in Indonesia since former President Suharto's fall in 1998. Since the mid-1990s, a number of dramatic terrorist attacks have been planned in the region, including attacks on the pope, President Bill Clinton, and commercial jets. These plans were frustrated only by happenstance. All these factors together, combined with the recent arrests of alleged al Qaeda operatives in Southeast Asia, seem to form a strong prima facie case for bringing the fight against terrorism there.

There are, however, several significant reasons why the threat posed by radical Islam in Southeast Asia is not nearly as great as it might at first seem. First, there is no risk in the region of state-sponsored terrorism against U.S. interests. Second, the profound ethnic and religious diversity (including in the practice of Islam) that characterizes the area militates against the establishment of a fundamentalist hegemony by any one group. Third, all the major Southeast Asian countries are more or less democratic. Dissent is generally tolerated, making radical Islam less attractive as a broader vehicle for opposition to the government (a role it played under Suharto's repressive regime in Indonesia). Finally, the only terror groups in the region that have demonstrated a capacity for large-scale attacks—the JI and the KMM—are made up of the well-educated middle classes. Their members are globalization's beneficiaries, not its victims, and these organizations have not managed to build a constituency among the masses of the poor. Both the JI and the KMM have small memberships and only limited ties to more broad-based Islamist groups. The two organizations therefore remain a challenge primarily for law enforcement, not the military.

Is Southeast Asia the Second Front?

At least some in the Bush administration seem to recognize this distinction, and a debate is now being waged in Washington between those who favor a law enforcement approach and those who want to strengthen ties with militaries in the region. Both positions, however, fail to examine the broader economic and political conditions that have facilitated the emergence of extremist political Islam in the first place.

Washington's current framing of Southeast Asia as the second front in the war on terrorism, in fact, presents four distinct problems. First, it conflates different forms of political Islam. Second, it fails to recognize that the emergence of terrorist groups was caused by weak states, inadequate cooperation between countries in the region, and a number of social problems, including anemic economies, unequal patterns of development, and fragile democratic institutions. Third, the U.S. approach relies too much on cooperation with militaries that are unaccountable (especially in the Philippines and Indonesia) and commit human rights violations with impunity. And finally, the current U.S. campaign also risks legitimizing a broader crackdown on dissent by Southeast Asian leaders eager to do away with inconvenient opposition figures.

FACES OF THE ENEMY

Washington's tendency to lump together the various Islamist groups in Southeast Asia has elided crucial distinctions between what are actually very different organizations. The groups fall into several distinct categories: Islamic revivalist movements that focus on cultural and spiritual renewal, political parties, armed and unarmed organizations fighting for autonomy or secession for Muslim areas, radical Islamist paramilitary groups, and transnational terrorist cells and networks. But the differences between them have been obscured by the Bush administration's rhetoric, which has emphasized that countries are "either with us or against us" in the war on terrorism. Such a simplistic paradigm ignores the fact that many Islamic organizations genuinely oppose al Qaeda (and similar extremist groups) yet also disapprove of the U.S. military campaign in Afghanistan and other Bush administration policies, especially its Middle East strategy.

Most Islamic groups in Southeast Asia are in fact nonviolent. The largest and most influential are either political parties or revivalist organizations. The latter have surfaced periodically throughout history in the region, typically in response to economic or political crises. One such group is the Nahdlatul Ulama (NU), Indonesia's—and the world's—largest Islamic organization, with 30 million followers. The NU espouses "traditional" Muslim values, but "traditional" in this context means a fairly tolerant and pluralistic approach to the observance and practice of Islam. Indeed, the NU recently agreed to help combat the extremism of some Islamist groups and has supported efforts to crack down on violence.

In Indonesia, the rise of political Islam, in contrast, can be linked to the collapse of Suharto's regime, the nation's continuing economic crisis, and the fragility of local democracy. Political organizations representing modernist Muslims were banned from the 1950s to the 1980s, and many of their leaders were imprisoned. Although such groups have since become a major political force, more extremist forms of Islamism remain at the fringes—despite the increase in their popularity in the aftermath of the Asian financial crisis. And the popularity of even moderate Muslim groups should not be overstated. Only a quarter of the parties that contested the 1999 elections advocated creating an Islamic government in Indonesia. These parties received about 16 percent of the vote, whereas secular parties polled over 60 percent and moderate Islamic parties received 20 percent. By contrast, in Indonesia's previous free and fair election, in 1955, more than 40 percent of the vote went to parties pushing for an Islamic state in one form or another. Today, on the other hand, as Australian analyst Greg Fealy has noted, "Islamic parties [in Indonesia] are more divided than at any time in history since 1945."

Islamist political parties are also prominent in Malaysia. Indeed, in 1999, the Pan-Malaysian Islamic Party won its greatest-ever victory at the polls, capturing 27 parliamentary seats (out of a total of 193) and gaining control of 2 of Malaysia's 14 states. But this vote was as much about Mahathir's repression of reform as it was about a popular commitment to political Islam.

Is Southeast Asia the Second Front?

NONE OF THIS, of course, is meant to deny that violent Islamist terrorist groups do exist in Southeast Asia. The organization that has come to be referred to as the JI, for example, is a small group that advocates the creation through force of an Islamic state from southern Thailand through the lower part of the Philippines. When and where the JI originated remains murky. A generally accepted version credits Abdullah Achmad Sungkar and Abu Bakar Bashir as being two of its key founders, but the exact date of that founding remains uncertain. Some reports mention the existence in Indonesia of a group called the Jemaah Islamiah as far back as 1976, and Indonesian court documents from the 1980s also refer to the organization. Most intelligence and recent press reports, however, date the JI's founding to the 1990s, presenting it as a creation of al Qaeda operatives.

Bashir is believed to have taken over the leadership of JI upon Sungkar's death. Bashir returned to Indonesia after the fall of Suharto and now runs the religious boarding school that he and Sungkar cofounded in 1971; he also heads the pan-Islamist Mujahideen Council of Indonesia. Other alleged leaders of the JI include Hambali, also known as Nurjaman Riduan Isamuddin, who is thought to be Bashir's lieutenant and is wanted by Indonesian police for his role in a series of bombings in Indonesia on Christmas Eve 2000 and also by Malaysian police for alleged links to terrorist groups; Mohammad Iqbal Rahman, who has been detained under Malaysia's Internal Security Act since June 2001; and Fathur Rahman al Ghozi, accused of organizing a series of bombings in Manila in December 2000 and recently sentenced to 12 years in prison by a Philippine court for possession of explosives.

Members of both the JI and the KMM tend to be middle-class professionals and include graduates of both Asian and Western universities. They count among their ranks businessmen such as Yazid Sufaat, a biochemistry graduate of a California university who, in October 2000, hosted two of the September 11 hijackers and Zacarias Moussaoui (alleged to be the 20th conspirator). It was this meeting that led some experts to identify Malaysia as a launching pad for terrorist attacks; Hambali is currently the subject of an international manhunt.

Bashir and other alleged members of the JI got their start as part of an Islamist opposition to Suharto's rule in Indonesia in the 1970s and 1980s. Bashir was arrested in 1978 and accused of agitating for an Islamic state, a crime under Indonesia's now-repealed subversion law. He relocated to Malaysia after serving half of a nine-year prison term; once there, he settled with his friend, Sungkar, who had been jailed in Indonesia on the same charges.

In addition to these violent Islamist groups, Southeast Asia is also home to various militant organizations for which Islam is an important element of their identity—but only as it relates to demands for autonomy or secession, not as an end in and of itself. This category includes several organizations operating in southern Thailand, the Moro National Liberation Front and Moro Islamic Liberation Front in the Philippines, and the Free Aceh Movement in Indonesia. These groups, unlike the JI or the KMM, engage in community-level organization, enjoy mass membership bases, have genuine political agendas, and (with exceptions) generally limit their violence to military targets. A significant number of groups in Aceh and the southern Philippines also work for self-determination through nonviolent means.

The final category to consider is radical Islamist paramilitary groups that blur the edges between criminal gangs and militias. This type includes Abu Sayyaf in the Philippines and Laskar Jihad in Indonesia, which represent a particular kind of Southeast Asian outfit that mixes politics with criminal activities such as extortion and racketeering. Such groups have been found on both sides of the independence battle in Mindanao since the late 1960s and have been employed by the government to fight Moro and communist insurgents in the Philippines. Known as *preman* (literally, free men) in Indonesia, the gangs have also played an important role in politics in that country, where they were used to massacre suspected communists in 1965–66 and as anti-independence paramilitaries in East Timor in the 1990s.

The *preman* (and similar groups elsewhere), however, should not be viewed as creations of the military; rather, they represent alliances of convenience between criminals and segments of the political and military elites. The Islamic Defenders Front (known by its Bahasa

Indonesia acronym, FPI), for example, was established in Indonesia in 1998 with the assistance of several high-ranking military officers. And it was the FPI that led some of the small but noisy anti-American demonstrations after the September 11 attacks. The similar Laskar Jihad, meanwhile, may have an ideological affinity with the Taliban, with whom Laskar's leader, Jafar Umar Thalib, has publicly aligned himself. But there is no clear evidence that this connection has translated into actual cooperation with al Qaeda, although there has been some contact between the two groups, and Jafar has tried to distance himself from Osama bin Laden. Nevertheless, Jafar was arrested in early May on charges of insulting Indonesia's president and vice president and for inciting an attack on a Christian village in the Moluccas in April.

ROOTS

WHAT WASHINGTON SHOULD KEEP in mind about all of these organizations is that, although their details vary, they are all symptoms of the same diseases: problems in the local economy, the weakness of states in the region, and the fragility of democratic institutions and regional intergovernmental organizations.

The JI and the KMM have proved especially good at exploiting such ills. Unlike nationally based radical Islamist groups such as Laskar Jihad, the JI and the KMM are more like international criminal corporations. They have only weak ties to the broader Islamist movements in the region or to political and military officials. But they make up for these shortcomings in several ways that make them more threatening than other groups. Like transnational corporations, the JI and the KMM use modern communication technologies to plan and coordinate their actions. They also exploit the weaknesses of local governments, the porousness of borders, and the absence of international cooperation, all of which make it easy to move around money and people.

Malaysia, for example, requires no visas for citizens of other Muslim countries, and the Philippines has notoriously lax immigration controls. As of February 1, 2002, the Philippines and Indonesia had both been named by the international Financial Action Task Force on Money Laundering as noncooperative in efforts to fight that crime. Thailand passed its first anti-money laundering law only in 1999, and the Philippines passed its version in 2001; Indonesia, meanwhile, has yet to enact any such legislation, although it is working on some now with help from the Asian Development Bank.

Besides money laundering and illegal transfers, other kinds of crime also remain rampant in the area. Acts of piracy in Southeast Asia increased significantly after the end of the Cold War, which reduced the presence of warships in the area, and again after the economic crisis of mid-1997, which sent locals scrambling for alternative sources of income. Although the number of attacks in 2001 was down from the previous year, it remained higher than in 1999. Indonesian waters, in fact, are now the most dangerous in the world. More than half of the 335 pirate attacks worldwide in 2001 occurred in Asia, and data from the International Maritime Bureau show that 91 such attacks occurred in Indonesian waters alone—the highest incidence of piracy anywhere. Attacks in the first quarter of 2002 exceeded those of last year. Pirates have even begun to share their loot with local coastal communities, thus earning themselves some protection from the authorities.

Of course, although poverty may be the source of crimes such as piracy, it is not a sufficient explanation for groups like the JI, with its middle-class leadership. Like the Laskar Jihad and the Abu Sayyaf, however, the JI has successfully exploited the relative failure of the Indonesian and Philippine states to meet basic needs of the people. Laskar recruits its soldiers from the unemployed, urban male population and pays stipends to their families during their service. In both Thailand and the Philippines, Muslim regions have the worst poverty, income inequality, infant and maternal mortality rates, and literacy levels—all of which have also made recruitment easier. In the Philippines, the government granted autonomy in the late 1980s to parts of Mindanao (where Abu Sayyaf operates), in an attempt to address the grinding poverty, political subordination, and anti-Muslim discrimination that have contributed to more than two decades of war. But a combination of factors—including Manila's failure to provide the autonomous government with adequate resources or address massive inequalities in access to land and natural resources, as well as corruption and incompetence on the part of the local administration—have frustrated expectations. Public services remain rare or nonexistent, feeding public anger.

SEND TRAINERS, GUNS AND MONEY?

AFTER SEPTEMBER 11, Washington's first inclination was to respond to the Islamist threat in Southeast Asia militarily—hence the significant increases in military aid to the Philippines in late 2001 and the subsequent deployment of U.S. troops. Since then, U.S. Deputy Secretary of Defense Paul Wolfowitz (a former ambassador to Indonesia) has declared that the U.S. approach to the region will henceforth come through law enforcement, not more troops. And indeed, Robert Mueller, the FBI director, has already made a trip to the region. But Wolfowitz's promise sits uneasily with statements by his boss, Defense Secretary Donald Rumsfeld, that the United States hopes to quickly resume military ties with the Indonesian military, or with the fact that Admiral Dennis Blair, until recently the commander in chief of the U.S. Pacific Command, has had a higher profile in the region than any State Department personnel.

A further U.S. military response would be misguided, for several reasons. If Southeast Asia poses a security threat, it is not a military one (although Washington should improve its force protection, embassy security, intelligence sharing, and police cooperation in the region). Greater U.S. military assistance will not help matters in general and could well make local conditions much worse, by strengthening local armed forces that have committed serious human rights abuses and remain impervious to effective civilian control.

In the Philippines, for example, the military's campaign against Abu Sayyaf and other Moro organizations had displaced 150,000 people by the end of November 2001, and there have been allegations of widespread human rights violations on the island of Basilan and elsewhere. Indonesian military abuses in East Timor and other areas, meanwhile, are infamous. Further strengthening these armed forces could weaken already fragile civilian institutions, undermining still-young local democracies. An increase in repression could also enhance the appeal of radical Islam.

It is also important to recognize that although relationships between local military and political officials and groups like Abu Sayyaf and Laskar Jihad are often opaque, it is clear that they do not correspond to the conventional picture of a unified military fighting a terrorist foe. Elements of the Indonesian armed forces have trained and in some cases encouraged Islamist terror groups to engage in paramilitary actions, worsening communal conflicts. Indeed, Laskar Jihad's fighters have played such a role in the Moluccas, central Sulawesi, and West Papua (formerly known as Irian Jaya). In the case of the Moluccas, Laskar Jihad was able to import combatants from Java without any government opposition, despite the fact that President Abdurrahman Wahid and other officials had appealed to the security forces to stop them.

The Philippines presents even more dramatic evidence of official collusion. On June 2, 2001, the Philippine army had the chance to wipe out virtually the entire leadership of the Abu Sayyaf faction based in Basilan. After a 12-hour standoff, however, in which the Islamists were pinned down by tanks, helicopters, and 3,000 soldiers at a walled hospital and church compound, the army pulled its troops away from the rear of the building. The rebels duly escaped, along with most of their captives. But before they fled, three of their hostages walked free, including a construction magnate and his girlfriend. Numerous accounts suggest that the businessman bought his freedom for 25 million pesos ($500,000), which Abu Sayyaf then split with the local government and military officials who let the rebels escape. The Philippine Senate has held an inquiry into these allegations, but the results have yet to be released. The military's own investigation cleared army officials of any wrongdoing.

For much of the Cold War, the United States maintained close ties with the armed forces in the region. Washington ended its military relationship with Jakarta in 1999, however, in response to the army's complicity in post-referendum massacres in East Timor. Links have since been restored, but the United States still maintains an embargo on sales of combat equipment, restrictions that the Indonesians are eager to see lifted.

The conventional argument in favor of renewed military aid to Indonesia is that increased American engagement will better enable the United States to promote a democratic model of military professionalism. But if U.S. engagement with the Indonesian military is so conducive to professionalism, why did it not have that impact during the three decades of the Suharto regime? As the International Crisis Group noted in a July 2001 report, "the bilateral military relationship has not been effective to date in producing an Indonesian military that meets the standards of a modern, professional force under civilian control or promoting long-term stability in Indonesia." And there remains no reason to think it would be so now.

A better way to improve security and help fight terrorism across Southeast Asia would be to strengthen the civilian police forces in these countries. Doing so would both enhance the state apparatus best equipped to meet the nature of the threat and provide a counterbalance to the military. The police were formally separated from military control in the Philippines in the mid-1990s and in Indonesia in 2001. Today it is not uncommon for firefights to break out between military and police units in both countries, often over who will benefit from lucrative racketeering and smuggling operations. This suggests that improving the police will not be easy. But doing so would strengthen the legal and juridical infrastructure, enhancing democracy and the rule of law.

The final danger of a military-oriented approach, or even a law enforcement approach that fails to take democracy into account, is that such operations could give governments in the region an opportunity to repress political opponents of all stripes. Already there are signs that this is occurring: the Indonesian military, for example, has cracked down on separatists who have nothing to do with al Qaeda. And arrests in Malaysia under the Internal Security Act (ISA) have focused on political opponents of Mahathir and pro-reform activists as well as suspected terrorists. The ISA (and similar legislation in Singapore) allows for indefinite detention without trial, and its indiscriminate use has prompted criticism from a range of civic organizations and the government-appointed Human Rights Commission. The Bush administration, however— now a new friend of Mahathir—has refused to voice any concern over the ISA's use or the broader crackdown.

John Gershman

FIGHT THE POWER

IN THE END, a limited role does exist for small increases in American training and military assistance to the countries of Southeast Asia. But such efforts should focus on the coast guard and naval capacities of those countries. And any increases in military assistance must have significant human rights conditions attached.

A more nuanced and effective U.S. approach to the problem of criminal Islamist groups in Southeast Asia should involve several additional elements, however. Washington should back civilian-controlled efforts to crack down on terrorist cells as part of a broader effort to combat piracy, money laundering, and other crimes that reflect weak state regulation and poor regional cooperation. These efforts would be both more politically viable and ultimately more effective than increased U.S. military involvement alone, because they would be less politically sensitive and because they already have natural constituencies within these countries. These potential allies include civic organizations concerned about the connections between money laundering, political corruption, and capital flight—as well as terrorism.

The United States should also support efforts to strengthen fragile democratic institutions such as domestic human rights mechanisms. Linking U.S. policy too closely to the militaries in Indonesia and the Philippines would strengthen the least accountable institutions of these states, which are guilty of major human rights violations. Until Washington sees signs that these militaries have been brought under effective civilian and legal control, it should not increase military aid to any appreciable degree.

In addition, Washington should back efforts to improve local government in both Indonesia and the Philippines, which would give a boost to recent decentralization and autonomy initiatives and might weaken support for rebel groups. Aid should be funneled through the Asia Foundation (a nonprofit group, largely funded by the U.S. government, that supports nongovernmental organizations), which has managed, despite dwindling budgets since the end of the Cold War, to support watchdogs that help promote accountability and openness in government.

And then there is the fight against poverty. Poverty alone cannot explain the existence of transnational terrorist networks such as the JI. Poverty and inequality have, however, contributed to popular discontent and thus helped such groups as Laskar Jihad and Abu Sayyaf. Long-standing economic grievances have also created support for secessionist groups in southern Thailand, Indonesia, and the Philippines. Because Southeast Asia has still not recovered from the 1997 financial crisis, the Bush administration should support economic policies that promote broad-based growth, even if these policies diverge from the wholesale liberalization typically advocated by Washington. Targeted foreign aid can also play a limited role in poverty reduction in the worst-off regions and help support social safety nets. An even more valuable step would be to reconsider U.S. policies that have been an obstacle to expanding growth, such as opposition to debt reduction. Despite three successive reschedulings of its debt since the 1997 crisis, Indonesia will spend 40 percent of its budget this coming year on debt service. This is not the basis for creating a dynamic economy. Convincing the U.S. Congress to reduce this debt will not be easy, but enlightened American self-interest makes it an urgent task.

Finally, the United States should commit to regional efforts to improve economic, political, and social conditions. Successive U.S. administrations have offered little support for regional initiatives under the auspices of the Association of Southeast Asian Nations; indeed, the United States has not acted as a partner with countries in the region since the end of the Cold War. Now that Washington has rediscovered Southeast Asia as the source of a perceived security threat, however, the partnership should be recreated in a way that addresses issues of mutual concern. Such a partnership should focus not just on countering existing terrorist networks but also on strengthening regional coordination to attack the roots of violent Islamism.

Promoting Democracy and Fighting Terror

Thomas Carothers

SPILT PERSONALITY

WHEN GEORGE W. BUSH took office two years ago, few observers expected that promoting democracy around the world would become a major issue in his presidency. During the 2000 presidential campaign Bush and his advisers had made it clear that they favored great-power realism over idealistic notions such as nation building or democracy promotion. And as expected, the incoming Bush team quickly busied itself with casting aside many policies closely associated with President Bill Clinton. Some analysts feared democracy promotion would also get the ax. But September 11 fundamentally altered this picture. Whether, where, and how the United States should promote democracy around the world have become central questions in U.S. policy debates with regard to a host of countries including Egypt, Iran, Iraq, Kyrgyzstan, Pakistan, Russia, Saudi Arabia, Uzbekistan, and many others.

Although the war on terrorism has greatly raised the profile of democracy as a policy matter, it has hardly clarified the issue. The United States faces two contradictory imperatives: on the one hand, the fight against al Qaeda tempts Washington to put aside its democratic scruples and seek closer ties with autocracies throughout the Middle East and Asia. On the other hand, U.S. officials and policy experts have increasingly come to believe that it is precisely the lack of democracy in many of these countries that helps breed Islamic extremism.

Resolving this tension will be no easy task. So far, Bush and his foreign policy team have shown an incipient, albeit unsurprising,

---

This article originally appeared in the January/February 2003 issue of *Foreign Affairs*.

case of split personality: "Bush the realist" actively cultivates warm relations with "friendly tyrants" in many parts of the world, while "Bush the neo-Reaganite" makes ringing calls for a vigorous new democracy campaign in the Middle East. How the administration resolves this uncomfortable dualism is central not only to the future of the war on terrorism but also to the shape and character of Bush's foreign policy as a whole.

FRIENDS IN LOW PLACES

IT IS ON and around the front lines of the campaign against al Qaeda that the tensions between America's pressing new security concerns and its democracy interests are most strongly felt. The most glaring case is Pakistan. The cold shoulder that Washington turned toward General Pervez Musharraf after he seized power in 1999 has been replaced by a bear hug. In recognition of the Pakistani leader's critical supporting role in the war on terrorism, the Bush administration has showered Musharraf with praise and attention, waived various economic sanctions, assembled a handsome aid package that exceeded $600 million in 2002, and restarted U.S.-Pakistan military cooperation.

Bush officials insist that they combine their embrace with frequent private messages to Musharraf about the importance of returning to democracy. But during the past year the Pakistani president has steadily consolidated his authoritarian grip, a process punctuated by a clumsy referendum last spring and a sweeping series of anti-democratic constitutional amendments in the summer. Bush and his aides have reacted only halfheartedly to this process, publicly repeating tepid calls for democracy but exerting no real pressure.

This soft line is a mistake and should be revised, yet the complexities of the situation must also be acknowledged. Pakistan's cooperation in the campaign against al Qaeda is not a nice extra— it is vital. In addition, a return to democracy in Pakistan is not simply a matter of getting an authoritarian leader to step aside. The two main civilian political parties have failed the country several times, and during the 1990s discredited themselves in many Pakistanis' eyes with patterns of corruption, ineffectiveness, and authoritarian behavior. Democratization will require a profound, multifaceted process of change in which Pakistan's military will have to not only give up formal leadership of the country but pull out of politics altogether. Meanwhile, the civilian politicians will have to remake themselves thoroughly and dedicate themselves to rebuilding public confidence in the political system. Rather than erring on the side of deference to Musharraf, Washington should articulate such a long-term vision for Pakistan and pressure all relevant actors there to work toward it.

Central Asia, meanwhile, presents a mosaic of dilemmas relating to the tradeoff between democracy and security in U.S. foreign policy. The U.S. need for military bases and other forms of security cooperation in the region has moved Washington much closer to the autocratic leaders of Uzbekistan, Kazakhstan, and Kyrgyzstan. Even Saparmurat Niyazov, the totalitarian megalomaniac running Turkmenistan, received a friendly visit from Defense Secretary Donald Rumsfeld in April 2002. At the same time, U.S. officials are pushing for reform in the region, emphasizing to their local counterparts that this is a once-in-a-lifetime opportunity for the region's states to obtain significant outside support for the full set of economic, political, and social reforms necessary to join the modern world.

Surprisingly, it is in Uzbekistan, one of the region's harshest dictatorships, where this dual approach may pay at least modest dividends. President Islam Karimov has undoubtedly received a boost at home from the new diplomatic attention, economic aid, and military partnership with the United States. Yet for the first time since Uzbekistan became independent, U.S. officials are also meeting regularly with a wide range of Uzbek officials and conveying strongly worded messages about the need for change. And there are signs of nascent political and economic reforms, albeit small, tentative ones. Karimov is still very much a dictator with little understanding of or interest in either democracy or market economics. But he also seems to realize that some positive moves are necessary to ensure his own political future and that the increased external support post–September 11 is a real opportunity.

Unfortunately, in Kazakhstan the U.S. approach appears less promising. President Nursultan Nazarbayev displays no interest in meeting the United States even partway. Instead, he is using the new context to tighten his dictatorial hold on the country and is openly spurning U.S. reform efforts. Given Kazakhstan's sizable oil and gas reserves, and Nazarbayev's cooperation on both security and economic measures, he appears to have calculated correctly that the Bush administration is unlikely to step up its mild pressure for reform. If the United States is serious about trying to steer Kazakhstan away from potentially disastrous authoritarian decay, however, Washington will have to become more forceful.

Kyrgyzstan is a more ambiguous but still discouraging case. President Askar Akayev is less dictatorial than Karimov or Nazarbayev but has also slid toward authoritarianism in recent years. The Bush administration has made some effort to steer him away from this unfortunate path. But it has not taken full advantage of the Kyrgyz elite's obvious eagerness for a close security relationship with the United States to push hard on key issues such as freeing political prisoners or curbing corruption.

Running throughout all of the new U.S. security relationships in South and Central Asia is an institutional divide that weakens the administration's ability to balance security and democracy. The State Department has shown some real commitment to raising human rights and democracy issues with these countries. The Pentagon, on the other hand, often focuses more on the immediate goal of securing military access or cooperation and less on the politics of the relevant host government. Given the importance that foreign leaders place on the U.S. military, they may sometimes assume that friendly words from the Pentagon mean they can ignore other messages they are receiving. Ensuring a consistent U.S. front on democracy and human rights, therefore, is a prerequisite for a coherent approach.

Afghanistan is perhaps the most telling example of this challenge. The initial post–September 11 action by the United States in that country was of course not a downgrading of democracy concerns but a sudden step forward, through the ouster of the fundamentalist Taliban regime. But the conduct of U.S. military operations there has since undermined the administration's promises of a lasting, deep commitment to democratic reconstruction. The Pentagon initially relied on Afghan warlords as proxy fighters against al Qaeda, arming them and thus helping them consolidate their regional power. This assistance helped entrench the centrifugal politics that threaten Afghanistan's weak new government. Ironically, the strategy seems also to have been a partial military miscalculation, leading to the escape of a significant number of al Qaeda fighters at Tora Bora.

At the same time, administration opposition to the use of either U.S. or UN peacekeeping troops outside of Kabul, and significant shortfalls in the delivery of promised aid, make it impossible for the Karzai government to guarantee security, gain meaningful control beyond the capital, or achieve legitimacy by delivering peace to its citizens. Ethnic rivalries, the opium trade, and newly empowered local strongmen make a return to state failure and civil war a very real possibility. Despite the insistence of many U.S. officials in the immediate aftermath of September 11 on the connection between failed states and vital U.S. security interests, the Bush team's aversion to nation building has not really changed.

No easy solutions to Afghanistan's profound political problems are in sight. At a minimum, however, the administration must strengthen its commitment to making reconstruction work. This means not only delivering more fully on aid, but exerting real pressure on regional power brokers to accept the Kabul government's authority and working harder to establish an Afghan national army. No matter how pressing are the other fronts of the war against al Qaeda (such as the increasingly worrisome situation in northern Pakistan), the United States must fulfill the responsibilities for reconstruction that came with its invasion of Afghanistan.

RIPPLE EFFECTS

THE TENSIONS POSED by the war on terrorism for U.S. support of democracy abroad have quickly spread out beyond the immediate front lines. Southeast Asia is one affected region. Indonesia has become an important theater in the U.S. antiterrorist campaign, because of U.S. fears that al Qaeda leaders are taking refuge there and that the country's numerous Islamist groups are connecting with extremist networks. The White House continues to support Indonesia's shaky, somewhat democratic government. But in a setback on human rights policy, the administration has proposed restarting aid to the Indonesian military. That aid was progressively reduced during the 1990s in response to the Indonesian forces' atrocious human rights record and was finally terminated in 1999, when Indonesian troops participated in massacres in East Timor. Administration officials have downplayed this decision to renew military aid, stressing that most of the proposed $50 million package is directed at the police rather than the military. But the willingness of the U.S. government to enter into a partnership with a security force that just a few years ago was involved in a horrendous campaign of slaughter and destruction against civilians sends a powerful negative message throughout the region and beyond. Some officials argue that the new training programs will give U.S. military personnel a chance to instruct their Indonesian counterparts in human rights. But U.S. officials repeatedly made the same argument in defense of these programs in previous decades, right up to when the Indonesian military committed the human rights abuses that sank the relationship.

Malaysia's leader, Prime Minister Mahathir Mohamad, is another beneficiary of a changed U.S. foreign policy. Mahathir has made himself useful to Washington by arresting Islamic militants, sharing intelligence, and cooperating in other ways with an antiterrorist campaign that neatly dovetails with his authoritarian domestic agenda. And in response, Washington's previous critical stance toward the Malaysian leader—highlighted in Vice President Al Gore's much-publicized call for *reformasi* during his visit to Kuala Lumpur in 1998—has been reversed. Top U.S. officials now laud Mahathir as "a force for regional stability" and "a model of economic development that has demonstrated tolerance," and President Bush praised him at an amicable joint press conference after Mahathir's visit to the White House in May 2002.

An emphasis on democracy and human rights is also in question in U.S. policy toward Russia and China. Russia's new role as a U.S. ally in the war on terrorism has progressed less smoothly than some initially hoped, with significant continuing differences over Iraq, Iran, Georgia, and other places. Nevertheless, President Bush regards President Vladimir Putin very favorably and has not pressed the

Russian leader about his shortcomings on democracy and human rights, such as in Chechnya or with regard to maintaining a free press. Somewhat similarly, the Chinese government has been able to leverage the new security context to solidify a much friendlier U.S.-China relationship than seemed likely in the early months of 2001, when the Bush administration appeared to view China as threat number one.

In both cases, however, the change is more of degree than kind. Bush's surprisingly personal and warm embrace of Putin started before September 11, with Bush getting "a sense of [Putin's] soul" during their meeting in Slovenia in June 2001. And at no time prior to September 11, whether under Bush or Clinton before him, was the Russian government subjected to any significant U.S. government criticism for Chechnya or any of its other democratic flaws. With respect to China, it is true that September 11 did block movement toward a new hard-line policy from Washington that some administration hawks may have wanted. But the current relatively positive state of relations, with mild U.S. pressure on human rights greatly outweighed by an ample, mutually beneficial economic relationship, is not especially different from the overall pattern of the past decade or more.

One can look even further afield and identify possible slippage in U.S. democracy policies resulting from the war on terrorism, such as insufficient attention to the growing crisis of democracy in South America or inadequate pressure on oil-rich Nigeria's flailing president, Olusegun Obasanjo, to turn around his increasingly poor governance of Africa's most populous nation. Ironically, and also sadly, however, the greatest source of negative ripple effects has come from the administration's pursuit of the war on terrorism at home. The heightened terrorist threat has inevitably put pressure on U.S. civil liberties. But the administration failed to strike the right balance early on, unnecessarily abridging or abusing rights through the large-scale detention of immigrants, closed deportation hearings, and the declaration of some U.S. citizens as "enemy combatants" with no right to counsel or even to contest the designation. The Justice Department's harsh approach sent a powerful negative signal around the world, emboldening governments as diverse as those of Belarus, Cuba, and India to curtail domestic liberties, supposedly in aid of their own struggles against terrorism. In the United States, an independent judiciary and powerful Congress ensure that the appropriate balance between security and rights is gradually being achieved. In many countries, however, the rule of law is weak and copycat restrictions on rights resound much more harmfully.

REAGAN REBORN?

WHEREAS "BUSH THE REALIST" holds sway on most fronts in the war on terrorism, a neo-Reaganite Bush may be emerging in the Middle East. In the initial period after September 11, the administration turned to its traditional autocratic allies in the Arab world, especially Egypt and Saudi Arabia, for help against al Qaeda. This move did not sacrifice any U.S. commitment to democracy; for decades, the United States had already suppressed any such concerns in the region, valuing autocratic stability for the sake of various economic and security interests. Over the course of the last year, however, a growing chorus of voices within and around the administration has begun questioning the value of America's "friendly tyrants" in the Middle East. These individuals highlight the fact that whereas the autocratic allies once seemed to be effective bulwarks against Islamic extremism, the national origins of the September 11 attackers make clear that these nations are in fact breeders, and in the case of Saudi Arabia, financiers, of extremism. Invoking what they believe to be the true spirit of President Ronald Reagan's foreign policy, they call for a change toward promoting freedom in U.S. Middle East policy. The core idea of the new approach is to undercut the roots of Islamic extremism by getting serious about promoting democracy in the Arab world, not just in a slow, gradual way, but with fervor and force.

President Bush is clearly attracted by this idea. Last summer his declarations on the Middle East shifted noticeably in tone and content, setting out a vision of democratic change there. According to this vision, the United States will first promote democracy in the Palestinian territories by linking U.S. support for a Palestinian state with the achievement of new, more democratic Palestinian leadership.

Second, the United States will effect regime change in Iraq and help transform that country into a democracy. The establishment of two successful models of Arab democracy will have a powerful demonstration effect, "inspiring reforms throughout the Muslim world," as Bush declared at the United Nations in September. As the policies toward Iraq and Palestine unfold, the administration may also step up pressure on recalcitrant autocratic allies and give greater support to those Arab states undertaking at least some political reforms, such as some of the smaller Persian Gulf states. The decision last August to postpone a possible aid increase to Egypt as a response to the Egyptian government's continued persecution of human rights activist Saad Eddin Ibrahim was a small step in this direction.

It is not yet clear how sharply Bush will shift U.S. Middle East policy toward promoting democracy. Certainly it is time to change the long-standing practice of reflexively relying on and actually bolstering autocracy in the Arab world. But the expansive vision of a sudden, U.S.-led democratization of the Middle East rests on questionable assumptions. To start with, the appealing idea that by toppling Saddam Hussein the United States can transform Iraq into a democratic model for the region is dangerously misleading. The United States can certainly oust the Iraqi leader and install a less repressive and more pro-Western regime. This would not be the same, however, as creating democracy in Iraq.

The experience of other countries where in recent decades the United States has forcibly removed dictatorial regimes—Grenada, Panama, Haiti, and most recently Afghanistan—indicates that post-invasion political life usually takes on the approximate character of the political life that existed in the country before the ousted regime came to power. After the 1982 U.S. military intervention in Grenada, for example, that country was able to recover the tradition of moderate pluralism it had enjoyed before the 1979 takeover by Maurice Bishop and his gang. Haiti, after the 1994 U.S. invasion, has unfortunately slipped back into many of the pathologies that marked its political life before the military junta took over in 1991. Iraqi politics prior to Saddam Hussein were violent, divisive, and oppressive. And the underlying conditions in Iraq—not just the lack of significant previous experience with pluralism but also sharp ethnic and religious differences and an oil-dependent economy—will inevitably make democratization there very slow and difficult. Even under the most optimistic scenarios, the United States would have to commit itself to a massive, expensive, demanding, and long-lasting reconstruction effort. The administration's inadequate commitment to Afghanistan's reconstruction undercuts assurances by administration officials that they will stay the course in a post-Saddam Iraq.

Furthermore, the notion that regime change in Iraq, combined with democratic progress in the Palestinian territories, would produce domino democratization around the region is far-fetched. A U.S. invasion of Iraq would likely trigger a surge in the already prevalent anti-Americanism in the Middle East, strengthening the hand of hard-line Islamist groups and provoking many Arab governments to tighten their grip, rather than experiment more boldly with political liberalization. Throughout the region, the underlying economic, political, and social conditions are unfavorable for a wave of democratic breakthroughs. This does not mean the Arab world will never democratize. But it does mean that democracy will be decades in the making and entail a great deal of uncertainty, reversal, and turmoil. The United States can and should actively support such democratic change through an expanded, sharpened set of democracy aid programs and real pressure and support for reforms. But as experience in other parts of the world has repeatedly demonstrated, the future of the region will be determined primarily by its own inhabitants.

Aggressive democracy promotion in the Arab world is a new article of faith among neoconservatives inside and outside the administration. However, it combines both the strengths and the dangers typical of neo-Reaganite policy as applied to any region. Perhaps the most important strength is the high importance attached to the president's using his bully pulpit to articulate a democratic vision and to attach his personal prestige to the democracy-building endeavor.

But two dangers are also manifest. One is the instrumentalization of prodemocracy policies—wrapping security goals in the language of democracy promotion and then confusing democracy promotion with the search for particular political outcomes that enhance those security goals. This was often a problem with the Reagan administration's attempts to spread democracy in the 1980s. To take just one example, for the presidential elections in El Salvador in 1984, the Reagan administration labored mightily to establish the technical structures necessary for a credible election. The administration then covertly funneled large amounts of money to the campaign of its preferred candidate, José Napoléon Duarte, to make sure he won the race. This same tension between democracy as an end versus a means has surfaced in the administration's press for democracy in the Palestinian territories. Bush has urged Palestinians to reform, especially through elections, yet at the same time administration officials have made clear that certain outcomes, such as the reelection of Yasir Arafat, are unacceptable to the United States. A postinvasion process of installing a new "democratic" regime in Iraq would likely exhibit similar contradictions between stated principle and political reality.

The administration demonstrated worrisome signs of the same tendency last April during the short-lived coup against Venezuela's problematic populist president, Hugo Chávez. Washington appeared willing or even eager to accept a coup against the leader of an oil-rich state who is despised by many in the U.S. government for his anti-American posturing and dubious economic and political policies. But given that it came in a region that has started to work together to oppose coups, and that other regional governments condemned Chavez's ouster, the administration's approach undermined the United States' credibility as a supporter of democracy. If democracy promotion is reduced to an instrumental strategy for producing political outcomes favorable to U.S. interests, the value and legitimacy of the concept will be lost.

The second danger is overestimating America's ability to export democracy. U.S. neoconservatives habitually overstate the effect of America's role in the global wave of democratic openings that occurred in the 1980s and early 1990s. For example, they often argue that the Reagan administration brought democracy to Latin America through its forceful anticommunism in the 1980s. Yet the most significant democratization that occurred in Argentina, Brazil, and various other parts of South America took place in the early 1980s, when Reagan was still trying to embrace the fading right-wing dictators that Jimmy Carter had shunned on human rights grounds. Excessive optimism about U.S. ability to remake the Middle East, a region far from ripe for a wave of democratization, is therefore a recipe for trouble—especially given the administration's proven disinclination to commit itself deeply to the nation building that inevitably follows serious political disruption.

A FINE BALANCE

THE CLASHING IMPERATIVES of the war on terrorism with respect to U.S. democracy promotion have led to a split presidential personality and contradictory policies—decreasing interest in democracy in some countries and suddenly increasing interest in one region, the Middle East. The decreases are widespread and probably still multiplying, given the expanding character of the antiterrorism campaign. Yet they are not fatal to the overall role of the United States as a force for democracy in the world. Some of them are relatively minor modifications of policies that for years imperfectly fused already conflicting security and political concerns. And in at least some countries where it has decided warmer relations with autocrats are necessary, the Bush administration is trying to balance new security ties with proreform pressures.

More broadly, in many countries outside the direct ambit of the war on terrorism, the Bush administration is trying to bolster fledgling democratic governments and pressure nondemocratic leaders for change, as have the past several U.S. administrations. Sometimes diplomatic pressure is used, as with Belarus, Zimbabwe, and Burma. In other cases, Washington relies on less visible means such as economic and political support as well as extensive democracy aid programs, as with many countries in sub-Saharan Africa, southeastern Europe, the former Soviet Union, Central America, and elsewhere. Quietly and steadily during the last 20 years, democracy promotion has become institutionalized in the U.S. foreign policy and foreign aid bureaucracies. Although not an automatically overriding priority, it is almost always one part of the foreign policy picture. Partly to address "the roots of terrorism," moreover, the administration has also proposed a very large new aid fund, the $5 billion

Millennium Challenge Account. By signaling that good governance should be a core criterion for disbursing aid from this fund, President Bush has positioned it as a potentially major tool for bolstering democracies in the developing world.

Although the new tradeoffs prompted by the war on terrorism are unfortunate, and in some cases overdone, the fact that U.S. democracy concerns are limited by security needs is hardly a shocking new problem. Democracy promotion has indeed become gradually entrenched in U.S. policy, but both during and after the Cold War it has been limited and often greatly weakened by other U.S. interests. President Clinton made liberal use of pro-democracy rhetoric and did support democracy in many places, but throughout his presidency, U.S. security and economic interests—whether in China, Egypt, Jordan, Kazakhstan, Saudi Arabia, Vietnam, or various other countries—frequently trumped an interest in democracy. The same was true in the George H.W. Bush administration and certainly also under Ronald Reagan, whose outspoken support for freedom in the communist world was accompanied by close U.S. relations with various authoritarian regimes useful to the United States, such as those led by Suharto in Indonesia, Mobutu Sese Seko in Zaire, the generals of Nigeria, and the Institutional Revolutionary Party of Mexico.

George W. Bush is thus scarcely the first U.S. president to evidence a split personality on democracy promotion. But the suddenness and prominence of his condition, as a result of the war on terrorism, makes it especially costly. It is simply hard for most Arabs, or many other people around the world, to take seriously the president's eloquent vision of a democratic Middle East when he or his top aides casually brush away the authoritarian maneuverings of Musharraf in Pakistan, offer warm words of support for Nazarbayev in Kazakhstan, or praise Mahathir in Malaysia. The war on terrorism has laid bare the deeper fault line that has lurked below the surface of George W. Bush's foreign policy from the day he took office— the struggle between the realist philosophy of his father and the competing pull of neo-Reaganism.

There is no magic solution to this division, which is rooted in a decades-old struggle for the foreign policy soul of the Republican

Party and will undoubtedly persist in various forms throughout this administration and beyond. For an effective democracy-promotion strategy, however, the Bush team must labor harder to limit the tradeoffs caused by the new security imperatives and also not go overboard with the grandiose idea of trying to unleash a democratic tsunami in the Middle East. This means, for example, engaging more deeply in Pakistan to urge military leaders and civilian politicians to work toward a common vision of democratic renovation, adding teeth to the reform messages being delivered to Central Asia's autocrats, ensuring that the Pentagon reinforces proreform messages to new U.S. security partners, not cutting Putin slack on his democratic deficits, going easy on the praise for newly friendly tyrants, more effectively balancing civil rights and security at home, and openly criticizing other governments that abuse the U.S. example. In the Middle East, it means developing a serious, well-funded effort to promote democracy that reflects the difficult political realities of the region but does not fall back on an underlying acceptance of only cosmetic changes. This will entail exerting sustained pressure on autocratic Arab allies to take concrete steps to open up political space and undertake real institutional reforms, bolstering democracy aid programs in the region, and finding ways to engage moderate Islamist groups and encourage Arab states to bring them into political reform processes.

Such an approach is defined by incremental gains, long-term commitment, and willingness to keep the post-September 11 security imperatives in perspective. As such it has neither the hard-edged appeal of old-style realism nor the tantalizing promise of the neo-conservative visions. Yet in the long run it is the best way to ensure that the war on terrorism complements rather than contradicts worldwide democracy and that the strengthening of democracy abroad is a fundamental element of U.S. foreign policy in the years ahead.

Democracy Promotion

Explaining the Bush Administration's Position

Paula J. Dobriansky

THE CORE OF U.S. FOREIGN POLICY

THOMAS CAROTHERS'S article "Promoting Democracy and Fighting Terror" (January/February 2003, see page 248) critiques the Bush administration's democracy promotion record and offers some broad recommendations on how best to integrate human rights causes into American foreign policy. The author's long-term involvement in democracy-related activities and his passion about this subject are commendable, but both his analysis and his policy prescriptions are unpersuasive.

Carothers alleges that, driven by imperatives related to the war on terrorism, the administration has come to cooperate with a number of authoritarian regimes and turned a blind eye to various antidemocratic practices carried out by these newfound allies. This claim is incorrect. The administration's September 2002 National Security Strategy, which lays out our post–September 11 strategic vision, prominently features democracy promotion. The strategy describes it as a core part of our overall national security doctrine and commits us to help other countries realize their full potential:

In pursuit of our goals, our first imperative is to clarify what we stand for: the United States must defend liberty and justice because these principles are right and true for all people everywhere.... America

---

This exchange originally appeared in the May/June 2003 issue of *Foreign Affairs*.

must stand firmly for the nonnegotiable demands of human dignity: the rule of law; limits on the absolute power of the state; free speech; freedom of worship; equal justice; respect for women; religious and ethnic tolerance; and respect for private property.

It is also a matter of record that this administration, whenever it encounters evidence of serious human rights violations or antidemocratic practices in specific countries, has raised a voice of opposition to such violations and sought to address these problems. This is certainly the case with such countries as Pakistan, Indonesia, and Malaysia, as well as Russia, Uzbekistan, and China. In general, we do this irrespective of the identity of the offender and, when circumstances merit it, criticize even some of our close allies. We manifest our concerns through a variety of channels, including diplomatic dialogue, both public and private, and the State Department's reports on human rights, international religious freedom, and trafficking in persons.

Bilateral efforts aside, a great deal of our multilateral diplomacy, including American engagement at the UN and the Organization of American States, is shaped by the imperatives of human rights and democracy promotion. Although greatly distressed by the selection of Libya to chair the UN Human Rights Commission, the United States intends to remain a driving force at the commission and will challenge this forum to fulfill its mandate to uphold international standards on human rights. We have also worked hand in hand with other democracies to strengthen the Community of Democracies (CD). I led the American delegation to last November's CD meeting in Seoul, where delegates adopted an ambitious plan of action with many specific initiatives designed to enable emerging democracies from different parts of the world to share "best practices" and help each other.

For the Bush administration, democracy promotion is not just a "made in the U.S." venture, but a goal shared with many other countries. We also seek to broaden our partnerships with local and global nongovernmental organizations and international organizations, so that we can work together on democracy promotion, advancement of human rights, and humanitarian relief. In fact, the National Endowment for Democracy, Freedom House, and other organizations have played pivotal roles in the development of a democratic culture and the strengthening of civil society.

Ironically, many of the world's countries, including some of our allies, often chide us not for failing to do enough in the democracy arena, but for trying to do too much, for elevating democratic imperatives above those of trade and diplomatic politesse. Yet we remain committed to doing what is right. President George W. Bush observed in his June 1, 2002, West Point speech, "Some worry that it is somehow undiplomatic or impolite to speak the language of right or wrong. I disagree. Different circumstances require different methods, but not different moralities." When appropriate, we go beyond words and subject persistent human rights violators to economic sanctions and other forms of pressure. I cannot think of any other country that has been as willing as the United States has to use both soft and hard power to promote democracy.

To be sure, some have argued that we should do even more, and specifically that we should withhold military and intelligence cooperation from certain of our allies whose human rights records leave much to be desired. As they see it, we improperly allow realpolitik considerations to trump the human rights imperatives. But this argument is myopic. No responsible U.S. decision-maker can allow our foreign policy to be driven by a single imperative, no matter how important. Thus, our policy toward a given country or region is shaped by a variety of considerations, including security concerns, economic issues, and human rights imperatives. The most difficult task of our statecraft is to strike the right balance among these imperatives and arrive at the policy mix that best advances an entire set of our values and interests. Invariably, it is a nuanced and balanced approach that produces the best results. And invariably, this administration has struck the right balance. For example, in the post– September 11 environment, as we began to engage a number of Central Asian governments whose help we needed to prosecute the war against al Qaeda and the Taliban, we simultaneously intensified our efforts to improve the human rights situation in these countries. By cooperating on intelligence and security issues, we have actually enhanced our leverage on democracy-related matters. Although a great deal more needs to be done, we believe that this integrated approach is working.

Any effort to juxtapose or contrast our efforts to win the war against terrorism and our democracy-promotion strategy is conceptually flawed. Pan-national terrorist groups (such as al Qaeda) and rogue regimes (such as that of the Taliban or of Saddam Hussein) pose grave threats to democratic systems, as do the xenophobic, intolerant ideologies that they espouse. Accordingly, fighting against these forces is both in our national security interest and a key ingredient of democracy promotion. And democracy promotion is the best antidote to terrorism. Significantly, the Seoul Plan of Action, adopted at the 2002 CD meeting, contains a series of actions that democracies can take to counter emerging threats through the promotion of democracy.

Carothers also criticizes what he terms an "instrumentalization" of our democracy promotion. In essence, he complains that, for example, the administration's efforts to promote democracy in a post-Saddam Iraq and, more generally, to advance democracy across the Arab world are somehow tainted because we have other reasons for our actions—e.g., removing the threat that Saddam's arsenal of weapons of mass destruction and his long-standing defiance of the international community pose to the world. Democracy promotion, it seems, should not only trump all other foreign policy imperatives; it should always be the one and only policy driver. This, of course, would immunize human rights offenders and despots who also present security threats—not an outcome that anyone who cares about human rights causes should welcome. More generally, the fact that we are advancing policies that simultaneously promote democracy over the long haul and mitigate the security threats that we face in the near term underscores the extent to which human rights causes have become integrated into our foreign policy. In a very real sense, this is American statecraft at its best.

Despite the enormous demands of the war against terrorism, this administration has found time for and evidenced keen interest in launching several major new democracy-promotion initiatives. Although human rights and democracy causes have a long bipartisan pedigree, it has been the Bush administration that has reordered the country's approach to development assistance so as to reward and encourage "good governance" through a pathbreaking initiative: the Millennium Challenge Account (MCA). In 2003 alone, the administration has requested $1.3 billion for the MCA, which means

15 percent of our foreign assistance will be dedicated to good governance, investment in people, and economic development. In addition to changing our own policy, the leadership and commitment President Bush displayed at the March 2002 Monterrey summit on financing development have convinced many of our allies, international lending and aid-delivery institutions, and the UN to change the ways in which they do business.

The administration has also launched a high-level initiative to improve political, economic, and cultural participation by women and combat discrimination against them. This effort began in Afghanistan, where the Taliban regime practiced what amounted to gender apartheid, and grew into a broad, sustained campaign focused on those governments that deprive women of political and economic opportunity. This strategy is spearheaded by the Office of International Women's Issues at the State Department and has featured participation by the president and the first lady, Secretary of State Colin Powell, presidential adviser Karen Hughes, and numerous other senior administration officials. Our overarching goal is to improve women's access to education and health and ensure that nowhere in the world are women treated as second-class citizens, unable to work, vote, or realize their dreams. We have also launched a Middle East Partnership Initiative that seeks to support political, economic, and educational reform in that region.

Overall, the promotion of democracy is a key foreign policy goal of the Bush administration. This sentiment is reflected in all of our international endeavors and is animated by a mixture of both idealistic and pragmatic impulses. We seek to foster a global society of nations, in which freedom and democracy reign and human aspirations are fully realized.

THOMAS CAROTHERS REPLIES

I AM FRANKLY ASTONISHED that Undersecretary of State Paula Dobriansky attempts to refute the central thesis of my article: that the war on terrorism has impelled the Bush administration to seek friendlier relations with authoritarian regimes in many parts of the world for the sake of their cooperation on security matters. It is simply a fact that since the terrorist attacks of September 11, 2001, the Bush administration has sought closer ties and enhanced security cooperation with a host of authoritarian or semi-authoritarian regimes—in Algeria, Bahrain, China, Egypt, Jordan, Kazakhstan, Kuwait, Malaysia, Pakistan, Qatar, Uzbekistan, Yemen, and even Syria.

Dobriansky claims that the administration always strikes the right balance between democracy and security, and that whenever the administration has encountered antidemocratic practices on the part of its security partners, it has raised a voice of opposition. As I highlighted in my article, in some cases, such as Uzbekistan, the administration has indeed tried to leaven its new security embrace with urgings to do better on human rights and democracy. Even in such situations, however, the overall message of the new relationships—with their friendly, public words of praise during high-level visits, their heightened security cooperation, and, often, their enlarged aid packages—is one of support for undemocratic regimes. Moreover, unfortunately, in some cases the administration has not voiced any substantial objection to overtly antidemocratic practices.

For example, the renewed U.S.-Pakistan relationship developed precisely in a period when President Pervez Musharraf was carrying out a series of antidemocratic actions, including rewriting key parts of the Pakistani constitution to ensure his continued rule. President Bush has repeatedly avoided making any criticisms of these measures. At a press conference last August, he made America's priorities with Pakistan crystal clear when, in response to a direct question about Musharraf's manhandling of the constitution, he said the following: "My reaction about President Musharraf, he's still tight with us on the war against terror, and that's what I appreciate." About the Pakistani leader's abridgment of human rights and democracy, Bush could manage only a tepid statement: "To the extent that our friends promote democracy, it's important. We will continue to work with our friends and allies to promote democracy."

The point of my article was not to excoriate the Bush administration for struggling with the tension between the war on terrorism and democracy promotion. Rather, it was to discuss the problem openly and clearly and to identify where and how the tension can be better mitigated.

Paula J. Dobriansky, Thomas Carothers

Dobriansky's insistence that there is no tension, and her relentless portrait of the United States as a country uniquely devoted to democracy promotion, is part of a pattern of rhetorical overkill by administration officials that weakens rather than strengthens this country's credibility in the eyes of others. People around the world are quite capable of seeing that the United States has close, even intimate relations with many undemocratic regimes for the sake of American security and economic interests, and that, like many other countries, the United States struggles very imperfectly to balance its ideals with the realist imperatives it faces. A more honest acknowledgment of this reality and a considerable toning down of self-congratulatory statements about the United States' unparalleled altruism on the world stage would be a big boost in the long run to a more credible pro-democracy policy.

III
The Home Front

America the Vulnerable

Stephen E. Flynn

THE UNGUARDED HOMELAND

IT IS PAINFUL to recall that, prior to September 11, Washington's singular preoccupation when it came to protecting the U.S. homeland was national missile defense. That urgency about guarding the United States from a potential missile attack now stands in stark contrast to the government's complacency about policing America's transportation networks and land and sea borders. On September 10, just over 300 U.S. Border Patrol agents supported by a single analyst were assigned the job of detecting and intercepting illegal border crossings along the entire vast 4,000-mile land and water border with Canada. Meanwhile, after a decade of budgetary neglect, the U.S. Coast Guard, tasked with maintaining port security and patrolling 95,000 miles of shoreline, was forced to reduce its ranks to the lowest level since 1964 and to cannibalize its decades-old cutters and aircraft for spare parts to keep others operational. While debates over the merits of new missile-intercept technologies made headlines, the fact that America's terrestrial and maritime front doors were wide open did not rate even a brief mention.

Until the World Trade Center towers were reduced to rubble and the Pentagon was slashed open, most Americans, along with their government, were clearly in denial about their exposure to a terrorist attack on their own soil. Oceans to the east and west and friendly continental neighbors to the north and south had always offered a healthy measure of protection. And Americans have generally disapproved of extensive efforts at domestic security. They were willing to staff and bankroll the defense and intelligence communities to contain the Soviet Union and to deal with conflicts "over there," but

This article originally appeared in the January/February 2002 issue of *Foreign Affairs*.

the quid pro quo was supposed to allow civilians at home to enjoy the full extent of their accustomed freedoms.

As Americans now contemplate the road ahead, they need to accept three unpleasant facts. First, there will continue to be anti-American terrorists with global reach for the foreseeable future. Second, these terrorists will have access to the means—including chemical and biological weapons—to carry out catastrophic attacks on U.S. soil. And third, the economic and societal disruption created by both the September 11 attacks and the subsequent anthrax mailings will provide grist for the terrorist mill. Future terrorists bent on challenging U.S. power will draw inspiration from the seeming ease with which the United States can be attacked, and they will be encouraged by the mounting costs to the U.S. economy and the public psyche exacted by the hasty, ham-handed efforts to restore security.

STOPPING THE PENDULUM

THE CAMPAIGN IN AFGHANISTAN has commanded the bulk of the waking moments of the senior leadership at the White House, the Pentagon, and the State Department. But at the end of the day, even if all goes well in this fight, only the terrorists of the moment will have been defeated. Places will always exist for terrorists to hide, especially before they have committed large-scale atrocities, and new adversaries will eventually arise to fill the shoes of those who have perished. As with the war on drugs, "going to the source" is seductive in principle but illusive in practice.

Focusing exclusively on the current terrorist hunt, moreover, takes precious time and political capital away from confronting perhaps the most serious danger emanating from the September 11 attacks: the exposure of the soft underbelly of globalization. The very same system that fueled the glory days of the 1990s—the openness of the U.S. economy to the world, which helped spawn unparalleled growth— also increased America's vulnerability. For years U.S. policymakers, trade negotiators, and business leaders have operated on the naive assumption that there was no downside to building frictionless global networks of international trade and travel. "Facilitation" was the order of the day. Inspectors and agents with responsibility for policing the flows of people and goods passing through those networks were seen as nuisances at best—and at worst, as barriers to competitiveness who should be marginalized, privatized, or eliminated wherever possible.

By the afternoon of September 11, however, the pendulum had swung the other way. The attackers had hijacked four domestic airliners. Federal authorities nevertheless immediately ordered the closing of U.S. airspace to all flights, both foreign and domestic, shut down the nation's major seaports, and slowed truck, car, and pedestrian traffic across the land borders with Canada and Mexico to a trickle. This draconian response reflected an appropriate lack of confidence in the routine measures used for filtering the dangerous from the benign in the cross-border flows of people, cargo, and conveyances. Nineteen men wielding box-cutters ended up accomplishing what no adversary of the world's sole superpower could ever have aspired to: a successful blockade of the U.S. economy.

Luckily, an alternative exists between maintaining trade and travel lanes so open that they practically invite terrorists to do their worst, and turning off the global transportation spigot whenever a terrorist attack occurs or a credible threat of one arises. It is possible to keep global commerce flowing while still putting in place systems that reduce risk. But the first step has to be an acknowledgment that we have been sold a bill of goods by the purveyors of a "less-is-more" approach to managing globalization. Global integration will be sustainable, we now know, only if systems for regulating and policing it keep improving as well.

Governments around the world that share an interest in sustaining the free flow of people, goods, capital, and ideas must be encouraged to develop and enact common preventive and protective measures to facilitate legitimate cross-border movements while stopping illegitimate and dangerous ones. Washington has the leverage necessary to gain support for such a process, since all roads lead to and from U.S. markets. It must now put that leverage to good use. Most of the owners, operators, and users of the global transportation networks are in the private sector, however, and they must also be enlisted in any effort to enhance security and controls. The result will be an imperfect system but one that will do a much better job at controlling the risks and consequences of catastrophic terrorist attacks than do the arrangements prevailing now.

THE SHIPPING NEWS

THE WORLD was understandably shocked by the carnage and the audacity of the September 11 attacks. But the aftermath may have been almost as distressing. Americans who had felt invulnerable discovered that their government had been lax in detecting and intercepting terrorists alighting on U.S. shores. Queasiness about border control and transport-security measures quickly spread to include many of the systems that underpin the U.S. economy and daily life. Suddenly guards were being posted at water reservoirs, power plants, and bridges and tunnels. Maps of oil and gas lines were removed from the Internet. In Boston, a ship carrying liquefied natural gas, an important source of fuel for heating New England homes, was forbidden to enter the harbor because local fire officials feared that, if targeted by a terrorist, it would create a destructive bomb that could lay low much of the city's densely populated waterfront. An attack on a driver by a knife-wielding lunatic on a Florida-bound Greyhound bus led to the immediate cessation of the entire national bus service and the closing of the Port Authority Bus Terminal in New York City. Agricultural crop-dusting planes were grounded out of concern that they could be used to spread chemical or biological agents.

As Americans continue their ad hoc post-September 11 domestic security survey, they will likely be horrified by what they find. The competitiveness of the U.S. economy and the quality of life of the American people rest on critical infrastructure that has become increasingly more concentrated, more interconnected, and more sophisticated. Almost entirely privately owned and operated, the system has very little redundancy. But most of the physical plant, telecommunications, power, water supply, and transportation infrastructure on U.S. territory lies unprotected or is equipped with security sufficient to deter only amateur vandals, thieves, or hackers. For terrorists interested in causing mass disruption, these vulnerable networks present extremely attractive targets.

The problem, however, is not just that the United States offers an almost limitless menu of enticing targets. It is that the existing border-management architecture provides no credible means for denying foreign terrorists and their weapons entry into the United States to get access to these targets. Given the limited staff and tools border inspectors have to accomplish their mission, they face horrific odds. In 2000 alone, 489 million people, 127 million passenger vehicles, 11.6 million maritime containers, 11.5 million trucks, 2.2 million railroad cars, 829,000 planes, and 211,000 vessels passed through U.S. border inspection systems. And the majority of this traffic was concentrated in just a handful of ports and border crossings. One-third of all the trucks that enter the United States annually, for example, traverse just four international bridges between the province of Ontario and the states of Michigan and New York.

The rule of thumb in the border-inspection business is that it takes five inspectors three hours to conduct a thorough physical inspection of a loaded 40-foot container or an 18-wheel truck. Even with the assistance of new high-tech sensors, inspectors have nowhere near the time, space, or personnel to inspect all the cargo arriving. A case in point is the Ambassador Bridge between Detroit, Michigan, and Windsor, Ontario. There, at the world's busiest commercial land-border crossing, nearly 5,000 trucks entered the United States each day in 2000. With only 8 primary inspection lanes and a parking lot that can hold just 90 tractor-trailers at a time for secondary or tertiary inspections, U.S. Customs officers must average no more than two minutes per truck. If they fall behind, the parking lot fills, trucks back up onto the bridge, and the resulting pileup virtually closes the border, generating roadway chaos throughout metropolitan Windsor and Detroit.

The loads these trucks carry are mostly low-risk shipments of auto parts and materials, but a substantial amount of the cross-border cargo with Canada originates overseas. One half of the one million containers arriving in the Port of Montreal each year, for instance, is destined for the northeastern or midwestern United States. In trying to figure out whether these containers might pose a risk, Canadian inspectors have little to go by. The cargo manifest provides only the sketchiest of details about a container's contents and in many cases includes no information about the original sender or the ultimate customer. To get more information, inspectors must engage in the labor-intensive and time-consuming act of tracking down shipping intermediaries, who are often difficult to reach.

Moreover, whether a container arrives in the United States through Canada or directly from Europe or Asia, it is unlikely to be examined when it first arrives on U.S. soil. The U.S. Customs Service inspection system is built around clearing cargo not at its arrival port but at its final destination (confusingly known as the "port of entry," referring to the point at which goods enter the U.S. economy). Chicago, for example, is the nation's fourth-largest port of entry. An importer operating there can count on Customs officers' never reviewing the cargo manifest until after a container has reached the city itself, even though the shipment may have actually entered the United States through Los Angeles, Miami, or the St. Lawrence Seaway. Furthermore, the importer has up to 30 days to transport cargo from its arrival port to its port of entry. At any given time, therefore, U.S. authorities are not in a position to verify the contents or senders of thousands of multi-ton containers traveling on trucks, trains, or barges on U.S. roads, rails, and waterways through America's heartland.

MALIGN NEGLECT

THE REMARKABLE advances in U.S. economic competitiveness over the last decade are rooted in the very openness and efficiency that have permitted people and commerce to flow so readily within and across U.S. borders. Modern businesses have capitalized on improvements in the timeliness and reliability of transport by constructing global assembly lines centered around outsourcing contracts. At the same time, managers have squeezed inventory stocks to reduce overhead costs. Traditionally, companies could ensure their ability to meet customers' demands by relying on internal production or well-stocked shelves. The advent of "just-in-time" delivery systems, however, has lowered the need to carry such insurance and has allowed corporations such as Wal-Mart to become enormously profitable.

Not surprisingly, many private-sector actors have not been fans of the administrative and inspection work of regulatory and enforcement officials charged with overseeing the people, conveyances, and cargo arriving at U.S. borders or moving through global transport networks. The pervasive view among many in the private sector has been that

Stephen E. Flynn

more inspectors mean more inspections, which translates into slower shipments. Accordingly, the growth in the volume and velocity of cross-border trade has generated little political support for a commensurate growth in the staffing, training, and equipping of the agencies responsible for providing security. Instead, those agencies have been starved of personnel, forced to work with obsolete data-management systems, and even, thanks to congressional pressure, subjected to performance sanctions if they disrupt the flow of commerce by making anything more than token random spot-checks.

Even as U.S. trade with Canada climbed from $116.3 billion in 1985 to $409.8 billion in 2000, for example, the number of Customs inspectors assigned to the northern border decreased by roughly one-quarter. Prior to September 11, half of the primary inspection booths at the border crossings in the states of Washington, Montana, North Dakota, Minnesota, Michigan, New York, Vermont, and Maine routinely remained closed because no one was there to staff them. And those inspectors working the booths that were open were evaluated in part by how well they met "facilitation" performance standards designed to reduce waiting times.

The world may be well into the electronic age, but the U.S. Customs Service is still struggling with paper-based systems. For years its proposed Automated Commercial Environment and International Trade Data System projects have run aground on the twin shoals of flat federal budgets and industry disputes over the timing, format, and quantity of commercial data to provide to Customs in advance. It was only in April 2001 that the Customs Service received the seed money to get started on these projects, which it projects will take years to develop and implement. In the interim, inspectors will have to rely on only the bluntest of data-management tools.

If the data-management and data-mining situation is grim for Customs, it is even grimmer for other front-line agencies such as the Coast Guard, the Immigration and Naturalization Service (INS), and the Department of Agriculture, all of whose officers desperately need communication and decision-support tools to carry out their jobs. But even if these agencies did join the information age, they would still face bureaucratic and legal barriers that currently hinder them from talking with one another.

For example, consider the case of a ship with a shadowy record of serving in the darker corners of the maritime trade. Its shipping agent sends notice that it will be importing a type of cargo that does not square with its home port or its recent ports of call. Some of its crew are on an intelligence watch list because they are suspected of having links with radical Islamist organizations. And the ship is scheduled to arrive on the same day as a tanker carrying highly volatile fuel. The U.S. public might reasonably expect that with a shady past, suspect cargo, questionable crew, and clear target of opportunity, such a ship would be identified, stopped, and examined before it could enter U.S. waters. The odds of such an interdiction happening are slightly better now than prior to September 11, but there remain significant structural hurdles to anyone's being able to see all the red flags simultaneously.

The Coast Guard would be likely to know something about the ship itself and about the scheduled arrival of a tanker carrying hazardous cargo. The Customs Service might have some advance cargo manifest information (although if a ship is carrying bulk materials, this information is typically not collected until after the ship gets to its arrival port). The INS should know something about the crew, but its information is likely to arrive in a fax and must be manually entered into its computers by an agent. None of the front-line inspectors in these agencies, meanwhile, is likely to have access to intelligence from the FBI or the CIA. None of them, therefore, would see the whole picture or pass on his or her information to somebody who would. And in today's system, all of the agencies face far more potentially suspect people, cargoes, and ships than they can ever manage to inspect.

THE PRICE OF HOMELAND INSECURITY

GIVEN THE DISGRACEFUL NEGLECT of front-line regulatory and law enforcement agencies, the surprise is not that the attacks of September 11 took place; it is that the United States managed to dodge the catastrophic terrorism bullet for so long. Now that this sad precedent has been set, however, improving the capability to detect and intercept terrorists or the means of terrorism heading for U.S. shores is even more critical than before, for three reasons.

Stephen E. Flynn

First, the absence of a credible capacity to filter illicit cross-border activity will carry a high price tag in a newly security-conscious world. The automotive industry offers a simple example. Just 36 hours after the September 11 attack, DaimlerChrysler announced that it would have to close one of its assembly plants because Canadian supplies were caught in an 18-hour traffic jam at the border. Ford then announced that five of its assembly plants would have to lie idle the following week. The cost of this loss in productivity? Each assembly plant produces on average $1 million worth of cars per hour.

In the future, not only will the risk of another attack be higher but the number of threats and warnings that must be taken seriously will increase dramatically. U.S. policymakers may thus find themselves routinely compelled to order up a transportation quarantine as a preventive measure to protect the homeland. The costs are difficult to calculate, but they are sure to take a toll on international trade and U.S. competitiveness. Companies have made massive capital outlays in technology and infrastructure to leach as much uncertainty and friction as possible from the logistics and transportation networks. Now they may see the expected savings and efficiencies from their investments in just-in-time delivery systems go up in smoke.

The political and diplomatic costs of not getting border management right, meanwhile, will also be painfully high. If U.S. policymakers believe the chances of detecting and intercepting terrorist attacks are small, they may feel compelled to rush into foreign counterterrorist operations that are ill-advised or premature. The price of securing foreign cooperation in these efforts—often some form of diplomatic concession or averted eyes—could prove high in the long run. So restoring a sense that terrorist threats to the United States can be managed, thus giving Washington the breathing room to make considered choices about counterterrorism policy, is important.

Finally, a sense of defeatism about the possibility of stopping terrorism places a heavy burden on domestic policing and civil defense. If the assumption is that terrorists will always be able to slip through the border and set up shop on U.S. soil, then the argument for allowing law enforcement and intelligence agencies to conduct increasingly more intrusive domestic surveillance becomes compelling. Giving up on border management could also lead to the imposition of an extremely costly "security tax" on significant areas of national life.

INTERNATIONAL TRANSPORTATION networks are the arteries that feed global markets by moving commodities, cargo, business travelers, and tourists. Protecting that circulatory system from compromise by terrorists is an imperative unto itself, even if an adversary or a weapon of mass destruction could find an alternative way into U.S. territory. In fact, this task deserves top billing over other, competing defensive measures such as constructing a missile defense system. If a missile were fired at a U.S. city and it could not be intercepted, it could cause horrible destruction and mass casualties. But if a weapon of mass destruction were loaded on a boat, truck, train, or maritime container and set off in a congested seaport, on a bridge during rush hour, or downtown in a major urban center, the results would be even worse. In addition to the local destruction and casualties, such an attack would expose the lack of credible security within the country's transportation networks and bring them to a complete standstill. The first scenario would involve damage caused by the adversary; the second would include both the damage caused by the adversary and the costs associated with a self-applied tourniquet to our global transport lifelines.

Enhancing security for transportation networks, therefore, is partly about preventing terrorists from exploiting those networks and partly about sustaining the continued viability of international commerce. The authorities can accomplish this task by moving from ad hoc controls at the borders of individual countries toward point-of-origin controls, supported by a concentric series of checks at points of transshipment (transfer of the cargo from one conveyance to another) and at points of arrival. This more comprehensive system is particularly important for the United States, where trying to distinguish the illicit from the licit at the border or within ports is like trying to catch minnows at the base of Niagara Falls.

Moving upstream is not as difficult or futuristic a task as it might appear. As a start, the United States and its allies should capitalize on the enormous leverage over global transportation networks that just a few key jurisdictions exercise. The overwhelming majority of trade moves by sea, and at some point during its journey nearly all the ships that carry it must steam into or out of just a handful of global megaports such as Long Beach and Los Angeles, Hong Kong, Singapore, Hamburg, Antwerp, and Rotterdam. If the port authorities and governments responsible for just these seven ports could agree to common standards for security, reporting, and information-sharing for operators, conveyances, and cargo, those standards would become virtually universal overnight. Anyone who chose to not play by those rules would be effectively frozen out of competitive access to the world's major markets.

Megaports could require, for example, that anyone who wants to ship a container through them must have that container loaded in an approved, security-sanitized facility. These facilities would have loading docks secured from unauthorized entry and the loading process monitored by camera. In high-risk areas, the use of cargo and vehicle scanners might be required, with the images stored so that they could be cross-checked with images taken by inspectors at a transshipment or arrival destination.

After loading, containers would have to be fitted with a theft-resistant mechanical seal. The drivers of the trucks that deliver goods to the port would be subjected to mandatory background checks. Jacob Schwartz, a professor of mathematics and computer science at New York University, has suggested that the routes of trucks into ports could be monitored and even controlled by available technology. A microcomputer connected to a transponder and global positioning system (GPS) could be attached to the motor control system of the trucks involved, so that if they strayed out of licensed routes their engines would shut down and the authorities would be automatically notified. The transponder, like those used for the "E-Z Pass" toll-payment system across the northeastern United States, would give authorities the ability to monitor and control each vehicle's movements, and it would be programmed so that tampering with it would result in an automatic alert to the police.

GPS transponders and electronic tags could also be placed on shipping containers so that they could be tracked. A light or temperature sensor installed in the interior of the container could be programmed to set off an alarm if the container were opened illegally at some point during transit. Importers and shippers would be required to make this tracking information available upon request to regulatory or enforcement authorities within the jurisdictions through which their cargo would move or toward which it would be destined.

Manufacturers, importers, shipping companies, and commercial carriers, finally, could agree to provide authorities with advance notice of the details of their shipments, operators, and conveyances. This early notice would give inspectors time to assess the validity of the data, check it against any watch lists they may be maintaining, and provide support to a field inspector deciding what should be targeted for examination.

As with many safety or universal quality-control standards, private trade associations could hold much of the responsibility for monitoring compliance with these security measures. As a condition of joining and maintaining membership within an association, a company would be subjected to a preliminary review of its security measures and would agree to submit to periodic and random spot checks. Without membership, access to ships servicing the megaports, in turn, would be denied.

To confirm the legal identity and purpose of international travelers, off-the-shelf technologies could be readily embraced to move away from easily forgeable paper-based documents such as visas or passports. Governments could embrace universal biometric travel identification cards that would contain electronically scanned fingerprints or retina or iris information. These ATM-style cards would be issued by consulates and passport offices and presented at the originating and connecting points of an individual's international travel itinerary. Airports, rail stations, rental car agencies, and bus terminals could all be required to install and operate card readers for any customers moving across national jurisdictions. Once entered, electronic identity information would be forwarded in real time to the jurisdiction of the final destination. The objective would be to provide authorities with the opportunity to check the identity information against their watch lists. If no red flags appeared, it would not be necessary to conduct a time-consuming and intrusive search. For noncitizens, a country could also require the presentation of these cards for renting cars, flying on domestic flights, or using passenger rail service.

Mandating that data be provided is one thing; effectively managing and mining it so as to make a credible determination of risk is another. Front-line agencies must be brought out of their stovepiped, nineteenth-century record-keeping worlds. To reduce the potential for overload, some existing data collection requirements could be eliminated, consolidated, or accomplished by other methods, such as statistical sampling. The goal should be to create within each national jurisdiction one clearing-house for receiving data about people, cargo, and conveyances. All government users of the data could then collect and analyze what they needed from that pool.

Inspectors and investigators assigned to border-control agencies will continue to play a critical role in the timely detection and interception of anomalies. To be effective, however, a serious effort must be made to improve their pay, staffing numbers, and training, and to push them beyond the border itself into common bilateral or multilateral international inspection zones. Megaports and regional transshipment ports should play host to these zones and allow agents from a number of countries to work side by side. Such an approach would take better advantage of information collected by law enforcement officials at the point of departure, allow transport-related intelligence to get into the security system sooner, and reduce the congestion caused by concentrating all inspections at the final destination. The bilateral inspection zones set up by French and British officials at both ends of the English Channel tunnel could serve as a model.

RETHINKING HOMELAND SECURITY

As the nineteenth-century Prussian military theorist Karl von Clausewitz famously noted, "war is not an independent phenomenon, but the continuation of politics by other means." At its heart, therefore, an appropriate response to the kind of asymmetric warfare that catastrophic terrorism represents must weaken its political value for an adversary. If an attack, even on the scale of those carried out on September 11, fails to translate into any tangible change in U.S. power or policies, then it becomes only a contemptible act of mass murder and high-end vandalism. Of course, a few evil people will still remain willing to commit such crimes. But a terrorist who concludes that the business of America will continue unabated despite an attack on U.S. soil will likely find little value in launching such an attack.

Building a credible system for detecting and intercepting terrorists who seek to exploit or target international transport networks would go a long way toward containing the disruptive potential of a catastrophic terrorist act. A credible system would not necessarily have to be perfect, but it would need to be good enough so that when an attack does occur, the public deems it to be the result of a correctable fault in security rather than an absence of security.

Such a system, however, must extend beyond U.S. borders. Washington must move quickly beyond the Bush administration's initial steps in this area, which seem based on a mission of homeland security seen largely through the prism of civil defense. If America's future safety and prosperity were tied only to infrastructure located on U.S. soil, then a White House Office of Homeland Security dedicated to herding federal, state, and local bureaucratic officials might be appropriate. In fact, however, the United States depends on infrastructure that spans the globe.

Reducing the risk and consequences of attacks directed against the United States, therefore, cannot be accomplished simply by tweaking the roles and capabilities of agencies whose writ runs only to the nation's shores. Better preparedness and coordination of domestic agencies is important and necessary, but it is not sufficient. And the same is true for military and diplomatic campaigns overseas to root out international terrorism at its source. Manhunts carried out by U.S.-led international posses will continue to be an essential weapon in the counterterrorism arsenal. But the more daunting challenge will be to reduce the vulnerability of the systems of transport, energy, information, finance, and labor.

The massive post–September 11 outpouring of public and international support for combating terrorism will inevitably wane. This makes it all the more urgent to begin the painful process of fundamentally reforming border-management practices so that good and bad flows can be distinguished from one another and treated appropriately. Ultimately, getting homeland security right is not about constructing barricades to fend off terrorists. It is, or should be, about identifying and taking the steps necessary to allow the United States to remain an open, prosperous, free, and globally engaged society.

Fixing Intelligence

Richard K. Betts

THE LIMITS OF PREVENTION

As THE DUST from the attacks on the World Trade Center and the Pentagon was still settling, the chants began: The CIA was asleep at the switch! The intelligence system is broken! Reorganize top to bottom! The biggest intelligence system in the world, spending upward of $30 billion a year, could not prevent a group of fanatics from carrying out devastating terrorist attacks. Drastic change must be overdue. The new conventional wisdom was typified by Tim Weiner, writing in *The New York Times* on October 7: "What will the nation's intelligence services have to change to fight this war? The short answer is: almost everything."

Yes and no. A lot must, can, and will be done to shore up U.S. intelligence collection and analysis. Reforms that should have been made long ago will now go through. New ideas will get more attention and good ones will be adopted more readily than in normal times. There is no shortage of proposals and initiatives to shake the system up. There is, however, a shortage of perspective on the limitations that we can expect from improved performance. Some of the changes will substitute new problems for old ones. The only thing worse than business as usual would be naive assumptions about what reform can accomplish.

Paradoxically, the news is worse than the angriest critics think, because the intelligence community has worked much better than they assume. Contrary to the image left by the destruction of September 11, U.S. intelligence and associated services have generally done very well at protecting the country. In the aftermath of a catastrophe, great successes in thwarting previous terrorist attacks are too easily forgotten—successes such as the foiling of plots to

This article originally appeared in the January/February 2002 issue of *Foreign Affairs*.

bomb New York City's Lincoln and Holland tunnels in 1993, to bring down 11 American airliners in Asia in 1995, to mount attacks around the millennium on the West Coast and in Jordan, and to strike U.S. forces in the Middle East in the summer of 2001.

The awful truth is that even the best intelligence systems will have big failures. The terrorists that intelligence must uncover and track are not inert objects; they are living, conniving strategists. They, too, fail frequently and are sometimes caught before they can strike. But once in a while they will inevitably get through. Counterterrorism is a competitive game. Even Barry Bonds could be struck out at times by a minor-league pitcher, but when a strikeout means people die, a batting average of less than 1.000 looks very bad indeed.

It will be some time before the real story of the September 11 intelligence failure is known, and longer still before a reliable public account is available. Rather than recap the rumors and fragmentary evidence of exactly what intelligence did and did not do before September 11, at this point it is more appropriate to focus on the merits of proposals for reform and the larger question about what intelligence agencies can reasonably be expected to accomplish.

SPEND A LOT TO GET A LITTLE

ONE WAY TO IMPROVE intelligence is to raise the overall level of effort by throwing money at the problem. This means accepting additional waste, but that price is paid more easily in wartime than in peacetime. Unfortunately, although there have certainly been misallocations of effort in the past, there are no silver bullets that were left unused before September 11, no crucial area of intelligence that was neglected altogether and that a few well-targeted investments can conquer. There is no evidence, at least in public, that more spending on any particular program would have averted the September 11 attacks. The group that carried them out had formidable operational security, and the most critical deficiencies making their success possible were in airport security and in legal limitations on domestic surveillance. There are nevertheless several areas in which intelligence can be improved, areas in which previous efforts were extensive but spread too thinly or slowed down too much.

Fixing Intelligence

It will take large investments to make even marginal reductions in the probability of future disasters. Marginal improvements, however, can spell the difference between success and failure in some individual cases. If effective intelligence collection increases by only five percent a year, but the critical warning indicator of an attack turns up in that five percent, gaining a little information will yield a lot of protection. Streamlining intelligence operations and collection is a nice idea in principle but risky unless it is clear what is not needed. When threats are numerous and complex, it is easier to know what additional capabilities we want than to know what we can safely cut.

After the Cold War, intelligence resources went down as requirements went up (since the country faced a new set of high-priority issues and regions). At the end of the 1990s there was an uptick in the intelligence budget, but the system was still spread thinner over its targets than it had been when focused on the Soviet Union. Three weeks before September 11, the director of central intelligence (DCI), George Tenet, gave an interview to *Signal* magazine that now seems tragically prescient. He agonized about the prospect of a catastrophic intelligence failure: "Then the country will want to know why we didn't make those investments; why we didn't pay the price; why we didn't develop the capability."

The sluice gates for intelligence spending will open for a while. The challenge is not buying some essential element of capability that was ignored before but helping the system do more of everything and do it better. That will increase the odds that bits and pieces of critical information will be acquired and noticed rather than falling through the sieve.

Another way to improve intelligence is to do better at collecting important information. Here, what can be improved easily will help marginally, whereas what could help more than marginally cannot be improved easily. The National Security Agency (NSA), the National Imagery and Mapping Agency (NIMA), and associated organizations can increase "technical" collection—satellite and aerial reconnaissance, signals intelligence, communications monitoring—by buying more platforms, devices, and personnel to exploit them. But increasing useful human intelligence, which everyone agrees is the most critical ingredient for rooting out secretive terrorist groups, is not done easily or through quick infusions of money.

Technical collection is invaluable and has undoubtedly figured in previous counterterrorist successes in ways that are not publicized. But obtaining this kind of information has been getting harder. For one thing, so much has been revealed over the years about U.S. technical collection capabilities that the targets now understand better what they have to evade. State sponsors of terrorism may know satellite overflight schedules and can schedule accordingly activities that might otherwise be observable. They can use more fiber-optic communications, which are much harder to tap than transmissions over the airwaves. Competent terrorists know not to use cell phones for sensitive messages, and even small groups have access to impressive new encryption technologies.

Human intelligence is key because the essence of the terrorist threat is the capacity to conspire. The best way to intercept attacks is to penetrate the organizations, learn their plans, and identify perpetrators so they can be taken out of action. Better human intelligence means bolstering the CIA'S Directorate of Operations (DO), the main traditional espionage organization of the U.S. government. The DO has been troubled and periodically disrupted ever since the evaporation of the Cold War consensus in the late stage of the Vietnam War provoked more oversight and criticism than spies find congenial. Personnel turnover, tattered esprit, and a growing culture of risk aversion have constrained the DO's effectiveness.

Some of the constraint was a reasonable price to pay to prevent excesses, especially in a post–Cold War world in which the DO was working for the country's interests rather than its survival. After the recent attacks, however, worries about excesses have receded, and measures will be found to make it easier for the clandestine service to operate. One simple reform, for example, would be to implement a recommendation made by the National Commission on Terrorism a year and a half ago: roll back the additional layer of cumbersome procedures instituted in 1995 for gaining approval to employ agents with "unsavory" records—procedures that have had a chilling effect on recruitment of the thugs appropriate for penetrating terrorist units.

Fixing Intelligence

Building up human intelligence networks worldwide is a long-term project. It inevitably spawns concern about waste (many such networks will never produce anything useful), deception (human sources are widely distrusted), and complicity with murderous characters (such as the Guatemalan officer who prompted the 1995 change in recruitment guidelines). These are prices that can be borne politically in the present atmosphere of crisis. If the sense of crisis abates, however, commitment to the long-term project could falter.

More and better spies will help, but no one should expect breakthroughs if we get them. It is close to impossible to penetrate small, disciplined, alien organizations like Osama bin Laden's al Qaeda, and especially hard to find reliable U.S. citizens who have even a remote chance of trying. Thus we usually rely on foreign agents of uncertain reliability. Despite our huge and educated population, the base of Americans on which to draw is small: there are very few genuinely bilingual, bicultural Americans capable of operating like natives in exotic reaches of the Middle East, Central and South Asia, or other places that shelter the bin Ladens of the world.

For similar reasons there have been limitations on our capacity to translate information that does get collected. The need is not just for people who have studied Arabic, Pashto, Urdu, or Farsi, but for those who are truly fluent in those languages, and fluent in obscure dialects of them. Should U.S. intelligence trust recent, poorly educated immigrants for these jobs if they involve highly sensitive intercepts? How much will it matter if there are errors in translation, or willful mistranslations, that cannot be caught because there are no resources to cross-check the translators? Money can certainly help here, by paying more for better translators and, over the long term, promoting educational programs to broaden the base of recruits. For certain critical regions of the world, however, there are simply not enough potential recruits waiting in the wings to respond to a crash program.

SHARPENED ANALYSIS

MONEY CAN BUY additional competent people to analyze collected information more readily than it can buy spies who can pass for members of the Taliban—especially if multiplying job slots are accompanied by enhanced opportunities for career development within intelligence agencies to make long service attractive for analysts. Pumping up the ranks of analysts can make a difference within the relatively short time span of a few years. The U.S. intelligence community has hundreds of analysts, but also hundreds of countries and issues to cover. On many subjects the coverage is now only one analyst deep—and when that one goes on vacation, or quits, the account may be handled out of the back pocket of a specialist on something else. We usually do not know in advance which of the numerous low-priority accounts might turn into the highest priority overnight (for example, Korea before June 1950, or Afghanistan before the Soviet invasion).

Hiring more analysts will be a good use of resources but could turn out to have a low payoff, and perhaps none at all, for much of what they do. Having half a dozen analysts on hand for some small country might be a good thing if that country turns out to be central to the campaign against terrorists, but those analysts need to be in place before we know we need them if they are to hit the ground running in a crisis. In most such cases, moreover, those analysts would serve their whole careers without producing anything that the U.S. government really needs, and no good analyst wants to be buried in an inactive account with peripheral significance.

One option is to make better use of an intelligence analyst reserve corps: people with other jobs who come in to read up on their accounts a couple of days each month to maintain currency, and who can be mobilized if a crisis involving their area erupts. There have been experiments with this system, but apparently without enough satisfaction to institutionalize it more broadly.

Of course, the quantity of analysts is less important than the quality of what they produce. Postmortems of intelligence failures usually reveal that very bright analysts failed to predict the disaster in question, despite their great knowledge of the situation, or that they had warned that an eruption could happen but without any idea of when. In fact, expertise can get in the way of anticipating a radical departure from the norm, because the depth of expert knowledge of why and how things have gone as they have day after day for years naturally inclines the analyst to estimate that developments will continue along the same trajectory. It is always a safer bet to predict that the situation tomorrow will be like it has been for the past dozen years than to say that it will change abruptly. And of course, in the vast majority of cases predictions of continuity are absolutely correct; the trick is to figure out which case will be the exception to a powerful rule.

A standard recommendation for reform—one made regularly by people discovering these problems for the first time—is to encourage "outside the box" analyses that challenge conventional wisdom and consider scenarios that appear low in probability but high in consequence. To some, this sort of intellectual shake-up might well have led the intelligence system, rather than Tom Clancy, to anticipate the kamikaze hijacking tactic of September 11.

All well and good. The problem, however, lies in figuring out what to do with the work this great analysis produces. There are always three dozen equally plausible dangers that are possible but improbable. Why should policymakers focus on any particular one of these hypothetical warnings or pay the costs of taking preventive action against all of them? One answer is to use such analysis to identify potential high-danger scenarios for which low-cost fixes are available. If President Bill Clinton had gotten a paper two years before September 11 that outlined the scenario for what ultimately happened, he probably would not have considered its probability high enough to warrant revolutionizing airport security, given all the obstacles: vested interests, opposition to particular measures, hassles for the traveling public. He might, however, have pushed for measures to allow checking the rosters of flight schools and investigating students who seemed uninterested in takeoffs and landings.

Another problem frequently noted is that the analytical corps has become fully absorbed in current intelligence, leaving no time for long-term research projects that look beyond the horizon. This, too, is something that more resources can solve. But as good a thing as more long-range analysis is, it is uncertain how productive it would be for the war on terrorism. The comparative advantage of the intelligence community over outside analysts is in bringing together secret information with knowledge from open sources. The more far-seeing a project, the less likely secret information is to play a role in the assessment. No one can match the analysts from the CIA, the Defense Intelligence Agency (DIA), or the NSA in estimating bin Laden's next moves, but it is not clear that they have a comparative advantage over Middle East experts in think tanks or universities when it comes to estimating worldwide trends in radical Islamist movements over the next decade. Such long-term research is an area in which better use of outside consultants and improved exploitation of academia could help most.

THE WAR AT HOME

THERE IS A WORLD of difference between collecting intelligence abroad and doing so at home. Abroad, intelligence operations may break the laws of the countries in which they are undertaken. All domestic intelligence operations, however, must conform to U.S. law. The CIA can bribe foreign officials, burglarize offices of foreign political parties, bug defense ministries, tap the phones of diplomats, and do all sorts of things to gather information that the FBI could not do within the United States without getting a warrant from a court. Collection inside the United States is the area where loosened constraints would have done most to avert the September 11 attacks. But it is also the area in which great changes may make Americans fear that the costs exceed the benefits—indeed, that if civil liberties are compromised, "the terrorists will have won."

A Minnesota flight school reportedly alerted authorities a month before September 11 that one of its students, Zacarias Moussaoui, was learning to fly large jets but did not care about learning to take off or land. Moussaoui was arrested on immigration charges, and French intelligence warned U.S. officials that he was an extremist. FBI headquarters nevertheless decided against seeking a warrant for a wiretap or a search, reportedly because of complaints by the chief judge of the Foreign Intelligence Surveillance Court about other applications for wiretaps. After September 11, a search of Moussaoui's computer revealed that he had collected information about crop-dusting aircraft—a potential delivery system for chemical or biological weapons. U.S. officials came to suspect that Moussaoui was supposed to have been the fifth hijacker on United Airlines flight 93, which went down in Pennsylvania.

In hindsight, the hesitation to mount aggressive surveillance and searches in this case—hesitation linked to a highly developed set of legal safeguards rooted in the traditional American reverence for privacy—is exactly the sort of constraint that should have been loosened. High standards for protecting privacy are like strictures against risking collateral damage in combat operations: those norms take precedence more easily when the security interests at stake are not matters of your country's survival, but they become harder to justify when national security is on the line.

There have already been moves to facilitate more extensive clandestine surveillance, and there have been reactions against going too far. There will be substantial loosening of restraint on domestic intelligence collection, but how far it goes depends on the frequency and intensity of future terror attacks inside the United States. If there are no more that seem as serious as September 11, compromises of privacy will be limited. If there are two or three more dramatic attacks, all constraint may be swept away.

It is important to distinguish between two types of constraints on civil liberties. One is political censorship, like the suppression of dissent during World War I. There is no need or justification for this; counterterrorism does not benefit from suppression of free speech. The other type involves compromises of individual privacy, through secret surveillance, monitoring of communications, and searches. This is where pressing up to the constitutional limits offers the biggest payoff for counterterrorist intelligence. It also need not threaten individuals unnecessarily, so long as careful measures are instituted to keep secret the irrelevant but embarrassing information that may inadvertently be acquired as a by-product of monitoring. Similarly, popular but unpersuasive arguments have been advanced against the sort of national identification card common in other democratic countries. The U.S. Constitution does not confer the right to be unidentified to the government.

Even slightly more intrusive information-gathering will be controversial, but if it helps to avert future attacks, it will avert far more draconian blows against civil liberties. Moreover, Americans should remember that many solid, humane democracies—the United Kingdom, France, and others—have far more permissive rules for gathering information on people than the United States has had, and their citizens seem to live with these rules without great unease.

RED TAPE AND ORGANIZATION

IN A BUREAUCRACY, reform means reorganization; reorganization means changing relationships of authority; and that means altering checks and balances. Five days after September 11, Tenet issued a directive that subsequently was leaked to the press. In it he proclaimed the wartime imperative to end business as usual, to cut through *red tape* and "give people the authority to do things they might not ordinarily be allowed to do.... If there is some bureaucratic hurdle, leap it.... We don't have time to have meetings about how to fix problems, just fix them." That refreshing activism will help push through needed changes. Some major reorganization of the intelligence community is inevitable. That was the response to Pearl Harbor, and even before the recent attacks many thought a major shake-up was overdue.

The current crisis presents the opportunity to override entrenched and outdated interests, to crack heads and force the sorts of consolidation and cooperation that have been inhibited by bureaucratic constipation. On balance, reorganization will help—but at a price: mistakes will increase, too. As Herbert Kaufman revealed in his classic 1977 book Red Tape, most administrative obstacles to efficiency do not come from mindless obstructionism. The sluggish procedures that frustrate one set of purposes have usually been instituted to safeguard other valid purposes. Red tape is the warp and woof of checks and balances. More muscular management will help some objectives and hurt others.

The crying need for intelligence reorganization is no recent discovery. It is a perennial lament, amplified every time intelligence stumbles. The community has undergone several major reorganizations and innumerable lesser ones over the past half-century. No one ever stays satisfied with reorganization because it never seems to do the trick—if the trick is to prevent intelligence failure. There is little reason to believe, therefore, that the next reform will do much better than previous ones.

Reorganizations usually prove to be three steps forward and two back, because the intelligence establishment is so vast and complex that the net impact of reshuffling may be indiscernible. After September 11, some observers complained that the intelligence community is too regionally oriented and should be organized more in terms of functional issues. Yet back in the 1980s, when William Casey became President Ronald Reagan's DCI and encountered the functional organization of the CIA's analytical directorate, he experienced the reverse frustration. Rather than deal with functional offices of economic, political, and strategic research, each with regional subunits, he shifted the structure to one of regional units with functional subunits. Perhaps it helped, but there is little evidence that it produced consistent improvement in analytical products. There is just as little evidence that moving back in the other direction will help any more.

What about a better fusion center for intelligence on counter-terrorism, now touted by many as a vital reform? For years the DCI has had a Counter-Terrorism Center (CTC) that brings together assets from the CIA's directorates of operations and intelligence, the FBI, the DIA, the State Department, and other parts of the community. It has been widely criticized, but many believe its deficiencies came from insufficient resources—something reorganization alone will not cure. If the CTC's deficiencies were truly organizational, moreover, there is little reason to believe that a new fusion center would not simply replace those problems with different ones.

Some believe, finally, that the problem is the sheer complexity and bulk of the intelligence community; they call for it to be stream-lined, turned into a leaner and meaner corps. Few such proposals specify what functions can be dispensed with in order to thin out the ranks, however. In truth, bureaucratization is both the U.S. intelligence community's great weakness and its great strength. The weakness is obvious, as in any large bureaucracy: various forms of sclerosis, inertia, pettiness, and paralysis drive out many vibrant people and deaden many who remain. The strength, however, is taken for granted: a coverage of issues that is impressively broad and sometimes deep. Bureaucratization makes it hard to extract the right information efficiently from the globs of it lying around in the system, but in a leaner and meaner system there will never be much lying around.

Some areas can certainly benefit from reorganization. One is the integration of information technologies, management systems, and information sharing. Much has been done within the intelligence community to exploit the potential of information technology in recent years, but it has been such a fast-developing sector of society and the economy in general that constant adaptation may be necessary for some time.

Another area of potential reorganization involves making the DCI's authority commensurate with his or her responsibility. This is a long-standing source of tension, because roughly 80 percent of the intelligence establishment (in terms of functions and resources) has always been located in the Defense Department, where primary lines of authority and loyalty run to the military services and to the secretary of defense. The latest manifestation of this problem was the increased priority given during the 1990s to the mission of support for military operations (SMO)—a priority levied not only on Pentagon intelligence agencies but on the CIA and others as well. Such a move was odd, given that military threats to the United States after the Cold War were lower than at any other time in the existence of the modern intelligence community, while a raft of new foreign policy involvements in various parts of the world were coming to the fore. But the SMO priority was the legacy of the Persian Gulf War and the problems in intelligence support felt by military commanders, combined with the Clinton administration's unwillingness to override strong military preferences.

Matching authority and responsibility is where the test of the most immediate reform initiative—or evidence of its confusion—will come. Early reports on the formation of the Office of Homeland Security indicated that the new director, Tom Ridge, will be responsible for coordinating all of the agencies in the intelligence community. This is odd, because that was precisely the function for which the office of Director of Central Intelligence was created in the National Security Act of 1947. The position of DCI was meant to centralize oversight of the dispersed intelligence activities of the military services, the State Department, and the new Central Intelligence Agency, and to coordinate planning and resource allocation among them.

As the community burgeoned over the years, adding huge organizations such as the NSA, the DIA, NIMA, and others, the DCI remained the official responsible for knitting their functions together. The DCI's ability to do so increased at times, but it was always limited by the authority of the secretary of defense over the Pentagon's intelligence agencies. Indeed, hardly anyone but professionals within the intelligence community understands that there is such a thing as a DCI. Not only the press, but presidents and government officials as well never refer to the DCI by that title; they always speak instead of the "Director of the CIA," as if that person were simply an agency head, forgetting the importance of the larger coordination responsibility.

Is Ridge to become the central coordinating official in practice that the DCI is supposed to be in principle? If so, why will he be better positioned to do the job than the DCI has been in the past? The DCI has always had an office next to the White House as well as at the CIA, and Ridge will have to spend most of his time on matters other than intelligence. A special review by a group under General Brent Scowcroft, the new head of the President's Foreign Intelligence Advisory Board, has reportedly recommended moving several of the big intelligence agencies out of the Defense Department, putting them under the administrative control of the DCI. That would certainly give the DCI more clout to back up the responsibility for coordination. Such a proposal is so revolutionary, however, that its chances of adoption seem slim.

The real problem of DCI's in doing their jobs has generally been that presidents have not cared enough about intelligence to make the DCI one of their top advisers. Assigning coordination responsibility to Ridge may work if the president pays more attention to him than has been paid to the DCI, but otherwise this is the sort of reform that could easily prove to be ephemeral or unworkable— yet advertised as necessary in the short term to proclaim that something significant is being done.

Richard K. Betts

FROM AGE OLD TO NEW AGE SURPRISE

THE ISSUE FOR REFORM is whether any fixes at all can break a depressing historical pattern. After September 11, intelligence officials realized that fragmentary indicators of impending action by bin Laden's network had been recognized by the intelligence system but had not been sufficient to show what or where the action would be. A vague warning was reportedly issued, but not one that was a ringing alarm. This is, sadly, a very common occurrence.

What we know of intelligence in conventional warfare helps explain why powerful intelligence systems are often caught by surprise. The good news from history is that attackers often fail to win the wars that they start with stunning surprises: Germany was defeated after invading the Soviet Union, Japan after Pearl Harbor, North Korea after 1950, Argentina after taking the Falkland Islands, Iraq after swallowing Kuwait. The bad news is that those initial attacks almost always succeed in blindsiding the victims and inflicting terrible losses.

Once a war is underway, it becomes much harder to surprise the victim. The original surprise puts the victim on unambiguous notice. It shears away the many strong reasons that exist in peacetime to estimate that an adversary will not take the risk of attacking. It was easier for Japan to surprise the United States at Pearl Harbor than at Midway. But even in the midst of war, surprise attacks often succeed in doing real damage: recall the Battle of the Bulge or the Tet offensive. For Americans, September 11 was the Pearl Harbor of terrorism. The challenge now is to make the next attacks more like Midway than like Tet.

Surprise attacks often succeed despite the availability of warning indicators. This pattern leads many observers to blame derelict intelligence officials or irresponsible policymakers. The sad truth is that the fault lies more in natural organizational forces, and in the pure intractability of the problem, than in the skills of spies or statesmen.

After surprise attacks, intelligence postmortems usually discover indicators that existed in advance but that were obscured or contradicted by other evidence. Roberta Wohlstetter's classic study of Pearl Harbor identified this as the problem of signals (information hinting at the possibility of enemy attack) getting lost in a crescendo of "noise" (the voluminous clutter of irrelevant information that floods in, or other matters competing for attention). Other causes abound. Some have been partially overcome, such as technical limitations on timely communication, or organizational obstacles to sharing information. Others are deeply rooted in the complexity of threats, the ambiguity of partial warnings, and the ability of plotters to overcome obstacles, manipulate information, and deceive victims.

One reason surprise attacks can succeed is the "boy who cried wolf" problem, in which the very excellence of intelligence collection works against its success. There are often numerous false alarms before an attack, and they dull sensitivity to warnings of the attack that does occur. Sometimes the supposed false alarms were not false at all, but accurate warnings that prompted timely responses by the victim that in turn caused the attacker to cancel and reschedule the assault—thus generating a self-negating prophecy.

Attacks can also come as a surprise because of an overload of incomplete warnings, a particular problem for a superpower with world-spanning involvements. In the spring of 1950, for example, the CIA warned President Harry Truman that the North Koreans could attack at any time, but without indications of whether the attack was certain or when it would happen. "But this did not apply alone to Korea," Truman noted in his memoirs. The same reports also continually warned him of many other places in the world where communist forces had the capability to attack.

Intelligence may correctly warn of an enemy's intention to strike and may even anticipate the timing but still guess wrong about where or how the attack will occur. U.S. intelligence was warning in late November 1941 that a Japanese strike could be imminent but expected it in Southeast Asia. Pearl Harbor seemed an impractical target because it was too shallow for torpedo attacks. That had indeed been true, but shortly before December the Japanese had adjusted their torpedoes so they could run in the shallows. Before September 11, similarly, attacks by al Qaeda were expected, but elsewhere in the world, and not by the technical means of kamikaze hijacking.

The list of common reasons why attacks often come as a surprise goes on and on. The point is that intelligence can rarely be perfect and unambiguous, and there are always good reasons to misinterpret it. Some problems of the past have been fixed by the technically sophisticated system we have now, and some may be reduced by adjustments to the system. But some can never be eliminated, with the result being that future unpleasant surprises are a certainty.

Reorganization may be the proper response to failure, if only because the masters of intelligence do not know how else to improve performance. The underlying cause of mistakes in performance, however, does not lie in the structure and process of the intelligence system. It is intrinsic to the issues and targets with which intelligence has to cope: the crafty opponents who strategize against it, and the alien cultures that are not transparent to American minds.

Reform will happen and, on balance, should help. But for too many policymakers and pundits, reorganization is an alluring but illusory quick fix. Long-term improvements are vaguer and less certain, and they reek of the lamp. But if the United States is going to have markedly better intelligence in parts of the world where few Americans have lived, studied, or understood local mores and aspirations, it is going to have to overcome a cultural disease: thinking that American primacy makes it unnecessary for American education to foster broad and deep expertise on foreign, especially non-Western, societies. The United States is perhaps the only major country in the world where one can be considered well educated yet speak only the native tongue.

The disease has even infected the academic world, which should know better. American political science, for example, has driven area studies out of fashion. Some "good" departments have not a single Middle East specialist on their rosters, and hardly any at all have a specialist on South Asia—a region of more than a billion people, two nuclear-armed countries, and swarms of terrorists. Yet these same departments can afford a plethora of professors who conjure up spare models naively assumed to be of global application.

Reforms that can be undertaken now will make the intelligence community a little better. Making it much better, however, will ultimately require revising educational norms and restoring the prestige of public service. Both are lofty goals and tall orders, involving general changes in society and professions outside government. Even if achieved, moreover, such fundamental reform would not bear fruit until far in the future.

Fixing Intelligence

But this is not a counsel of despair. To say that there is a limit to how high the intelligence batting average will get is not to say that it cannot get significantly better. It does mean, however, that no strategy for a war against terror can bank on prevention. Better intelligence may give us several more big successes like those of the 1990s, but even a .900 average will eventually yield another big failure. That means that equal emphasis must go to measures for civil defense, medical readiness, and "consequence management," in order to blunt the effects of the attacks that do manage to get through. Efforts at prevention and preparation for their failure must go hand in hand.

The Law of War in the War on Terror

Washington's Abuse of Enemy Combatants

Kenneth Roth

WHAT ARE THE BOUNDARIES of the Bush administration's "war on terrorism?" The recent battles fought against the Afghan and Iraqi governments were classic wars between organized military forces. But President George W. Bush has suggested that his campaign against terrorism goes beyond such conflicts; he said on September 29, 2001, "Our war on terror will be much broader than the battlefields and beachheads of the past. The war will be fought wherever terrorists hide, or run, or plan."

This language stretches the meaning of the word "war." If Washington means "war" metaphorically, as when it speaks about a "war" on drugs, the rhetoric would be uncontroversial, a mere hortatory device intended to rally support for an important cause. Bush, however, seems to think of the war on terrorism quite literally—as a real war—and this concept has worrisome implications. The rules that bind governments are much looser during wartime than in times of peace. The Bush administration has used war rhetoric precisely to give itself the extraordinary powers enjoyed by a wartime government to detain or even kill suspects without trial. In the process, the administration may have made it easier for itself to detain or eliminate suspects. But it has also threatened the most basic due process rights.

This article originally appeared in the January/February 2004 issue of *Foreign Affairs*.

The Law of War in the War on Terror

LAW AT PEACE, LAW AT WAR

By literalizing its "war" on terror, the Bush administration has broken down the distinction between what is permissible in times of peace and what can be condoned during a war. In peacetime, governments are bound by strict rules of law enforcement. Police can use lethal force only if necessary to meet an imminent threat of death or serious bodily injury. Once a suspect is detained, he or she must be charged and tried. These requirements—what one can call "law-enforcement rules"—are codified in international human rights law.

In times of war, law-enforcement rules are supplemented by a more permissive set of rules: namely, international humanitarian law, which governs conduct during armed conflict. Under such "war rules," unlike during peacetime, an enemy combatant can be shot without warning (unless he or she is incapacitated, in custody, or trying to surrender), regardless of any imminent threat. If a combatant is captured, he or she can be held in custody until the end of the conflict, without any trial.

These two sets of rules have been well developed over the years, both by tradition and by detailed international conventions. There is little law, however, to explain exactly when one set of rules should apply instead of the other. For example, the Geneva Conventions— the principal codification of war rules—apply to "armed conflict," but the treaties do not define the term. Fortunately, in its commentary on them, the International Committee of the Red Cross (ICRC), the conventions' official custodian, has provided some guidance. One test that the ICRC suggests can help determine whether wartime or peacetime rules apply is to examine the intensity of hostilities in a given situation. The Bush administration, for example, has claimed that al Qaeda is at "war" with the United States because of the magnitude of its attacks on September 11, 2001, its bombings of the U.S. embassies in Kenya and Tanzania, its attack on the U.S.S. *Cole* in Yemen, and the bombing of residential compounds in Saudi Arabia. Each of these attacks was certainly a serious crime warranting prosecution. But technically speaking, was the administration right to claim that they add up to a war? The ICRC's commentary does not provide a clear answer.

In addition to the intensity of hostilities, the ICRC suggests considering factors such as the regularity of armed clashes and the degree to which opposing forces are organized. Whether a conflict is politically motivated also seems to play an unacknowledged role in deciding whether it is a "war" or not. Thus organized crime or drug trafficking, although methodical and bloody, are generally understood to fall under law-enforcement rules, whereas armed rebellions, once sufficiently organized and violent, are usually seen as "wars." The problem with these guidelines, however, is that they were written to address political conflicts rather than global terrorism. Thus they do not make it clear whether al Qaeda should be considered an organized criminal operation (which would not trigger the application of war rules) or a rebellion (which would).

Even in the case of war, another factor in deciding whether law-enforcement or war rules should be applied is the nature of a given suspect's involvement. Such an approach can be useful because war rules treat as combatants only those who are taking an active part in hostilities. Typically, this category includes members of a military who have not laid down their arms as well as others who are fighting or approaching a battle, directing an attack, or defending a position. Under this rule, even civilians who pick up arms and start fighting can be considered combatants and treated accordingly. But this definition is difficult to apply to terrorism, where roles and activities are clandestine and a person's relationship to specific violent acts is often unclear.

HARD CASES

GIVEN THAT SO MUCH CONFUSION exists about whether to apply wartime or law-enforcement rules to a given situation, a better approach would be to make the decision based on its public policy implications. Unfortunately, the Bush administration seems to have ignored such concerns. Consider, for example, the cases of Jose Padilla and Ali Saleh Kahlah al-Marri. Federal officials arrested Padilla, a U.S. citizen, in May 2002 when he arrived from Pakistan at Chicago's O'Hare Airport, allegedly to scout out targets for a radiological ("dirty") bomb. As for al-Marri, a student from Qatar, he was arrested in December 2001 at his home in Peoria, Illinois, for allegedly being a "sleeper" agent: an inactive terrorist who, once activated, would help others launch attacks. President Bush, invoking war rules, has declared both men to be "enemy combatants," allowing the U.S. government to hold them without charge or trial until the end of the war against terrorism—whenever that is.

But should Padilla and al-Marri, even if they have actually done what the government claims, really be considered warriors? Aren't they more like ordinary criminals? A simple thought experiment shows how dangerous are the implications of treating them as combatants. The Bush administration has asserted that the two men planned to wage war against the United States and therefore can be considered de facto soldiers. But if that is the case, then under war rules, the two men could have been shot on sight, regardless of whether they posed any immediate danger to the United States (although they might have been spared under what is known as the doctrine of "military necessity," which holds that lethal force should not be used if an enemy combatant can be neutralized through lesser means). Under the administration's logic, then, Padilla could have been gunned down as he stepped off his plane at O'Hare, and al-Marri as he left his home in Peoria. That, after all, is what it means to be a combatant in time of war.

But the Bush administration has not claimed that either suspect was anywhere near to carrying out his alleged terrorist plan. Neither man, therefore, posed the kind of imminent threat that would justify the use of lethal force under law-enforcement rules. Given this fact, it would have been deeply disturbing if they were shot as enemy soldiers. Of course, the White House has not proposed killing them; instead, it plans to detain the two men indefinitely. But if Padilla and al-Marri should not be considered enemy combatants for the purpose of killing them, they should not be considered enemy combatants for the purpose of detaining them, either.

A similar classification problem, although with a possibly different result, arose in the case of Qaed Salim Sinan al-Harethi. Al-Harethi, who Washington alleges was a senior al Qaeda official, was killed by a drone-fired missile in November 2002 while driving in a remote tribal area of Yemen. Five of his companions, including a U.S. citizen, also died in the attack, which was carried out by the CIA. The Bush administration apparently considered al-Harethi to be an enemy combatant for his alleged involvement in the October 2000 U.S.S. *Cole* bombing. In this instance, the case for applying war rules was stronger than with Padilla or al-Marri (although the Bush administration never bothered to spell it out). Al-Harethi's mere participation in the 2000 attack on the *Cole* would not have made him a combatant in 2002, since he could have subsequently withdrawn from al Qaeda; war rules permit attacking only current combatants, not past ones. And if al-Harethi were a civilian, he could not have legally been attacked unless he was actively engaged in hostilities at the time. But the administration alleged that al-Harethi was a "top bin Laden operative in Yemen," implying that he was in the process of preparing future attacks. If true, this would have made the use of war rules against him more appropriate. And unlike in the cases of Padilla and al-Marri, arresting al-Harethi may not have been an option. The Yemeni government has little control over the tribal area where he was killed; indeed, 18 Yemeni soldiers had reportedly died in an earlier attempt to arrest him.

Although there may have been a reasonable case for applying war rules to al-Harethi, the Bush administration has applied these rules with far less justification in other episodes outside the United States. For example, in October 2001, Washington sought the surrender of six Algerian men in Bosnia. At first, the U.S. government followed law-enforcement rules and secured the men's arrest. But then, after a three-month investigation, Bosnia's Supreme Court ordered the suspects released for lack of evidence. Instead of providing additional evidence, however, Washington simply switched to war rules. It pressured the Bosnian government to hand the men over anyway and whisked them out of the country—not to trial, but to indefinite detention at the U.S. naval base at Guantánamo Bay.

The administration followed a similar pattern in June 2003, when five al Qaeda suspects were detained in Malawi. Malawi's high court ordered local authorities to follow the law and either charge or release the five men, all of whom were foreigners. Ignoring local law, the Bush administration then insisted that the men be handed over to U.S. security forces instead. The five were spirited out of the country to an undisclosed location—not for trial, but for interrogation. The move sparked riots in Malawi. The men were released a month later in Sudan, after questioning by Americans failed to turn up any incriminating evidence.

A BAD EXAMPLE

THESE CASES ARE NOT ANOMALIES. In the last two and a half years, the U.S. government has taken custody of a series of al Qaeda suspects in countries such as Indonesia, Pakistan, and Thailand. In many of these cases, the suspects were not captured on a traditional battlefield. Yet instead of allowing the men to be charged with a crime under local law-enforcement rules, Washington had them treated as combatants and delivered to a U.S. detention facility.

There is something troubling about such a policy. Put simply, using war rules when law-enforcement rules could reasonably be followed is dangerous. Errors, common enough in ordinary criminal investigations, are all the more likely when a government relies on the kind of murky intelligence that drives many terrorist investigations. If law-enforcement rules are used, a mistaken arrest can be rectified at trial. But if war rules apply, the government is never obliged to prove a suspect's guilt. Instead, a supposed terrorist can be held for however long it takes to win the "war" against terrorism. And the consequences of error are even graver if the supposed combatant is killed, as was al-Harethi. Such mistakes are an inevitable hazard of the battlefield, where quick life-and-death decisions must be made. But when there is no such urgency, prudence and humanity dictate applying law-enforcement standards.

Washington must also remember that its conduct sets an example for governments around the world. After all, many other states would be all too eager to find an excuse to eliminate their enemies through war rules. Israel, to name one, has used this rationale to justify its assassination of terrorist suspects in Gaza and the West Bank. It is not hard to imagine Russia doing the same to Chechen leaders in Europe, Turkey using a similar pretext against Kurds in Iraq, China against Uighurs in Central Asia, or Egypt against Islamists at home.

Moreover, the Bush administration should recognize that international human rights law is not indifferent to the needs of a government facing a security crisis. Criminal trials risk disclosure of sensitive information, as the administration has discovered in prosecuting Zacarias Moussaoui. But under a concept known as "derogation," governments are permitted to suspend certain rights temporarily when they can show that it is necessary to meet a "public emergency threatening the life of the nation." The International Covenant on Civil and Political Rights, which the United States has ratified, requires governments seeking derogation to file a declaration justifying the move with the UN secretary-general. Among the many governments to have done so are Algeria, Argentina, Chile, Colombia, Peru, Poland, Russia, Sri Lanka, and the United Kingdom. Yet the United States, determined to avoid the formal scrutiny involved, has not bothered.

The Justice Department has defended the administration's use of war rules by citing a U.S. Supreme Court decision from World War II, *Ex Parte Quirin*. In that case, the Court ruled that German army saboteurs who landed in the United States could be tried as enemy combatants before military commissions. The Court distinguished its ruling from an earlier Civil War–era case, *Ex Parte Milligan*, which held that a civilian resident of Indiana could not be tried in military court because local civil courts remained open and operational. Noting that the German saboteurs had entered the United States wearing at least parts of their uniforms, the Court in *Quirin* held that the *Milligan* protections applied only to people who are not members of an enemy's armed forces.

There are several reasons, however, why *Quirin* does not justify the Bush administration's broad use of war rules. First, the saboteurs in *Quirin* were agents of a government—Germany's—with which the United States was obviously at war. Whether the United States is actually at "war" with al Qaeda, however, remains uncertain under the law. Second, although the Court in *Quirin* defined a combatant as anyone operating with hostile intent behind military lines, the case has arguably been superseded by the 1949 Geneva Conventions (ratified by the United States), which, as noted above, rule that people are combatants only if they either are members of an enemy's armed force or are taking active part in hostilities. *Quirin* thus does not help determine whether, under current law, people such as Padilla and al-Marri should be considered civilians (who, under *Milligan*, must be brought before civil courts) or combatants (who can face military treatment). Moreover, *Quirin* only establishes who can be tried before a military tribunal. The Bush administration, however, has asserted that it has the right to hold Padilla, al-Marri, and other detained "combatants" without a trial of any kind—in effect, precluding serious independent assessment of the grounds for potentially lifelong detention. Finally, whereas the government in *Quirin* was operating under a specific grant of authority from Congress, the Bush administration has acted on its own in taking the difficult decision to treat Padilla and al-Marri as combatants, without allowing the popular input that a legislative debate would provide.

STAY SAFE

THE UNITED STATES should not lightly suspend due process rights, as the Bush administration has done with its "enemy combatants"—particularly when a mistake could result in death or lengthy detention without charge or trial. Law-enforcement rules should presumptively apply to all suspects in the "war" on terror, and the burden should fall on those who want to invoke war rules to demonstrate that they are necessary and appropriate.

The best way to determine if war rules should apply would be through a three-part test. To invoke war rules, Washington should have to prove, first, that an organized group is directing repeated acts of violence against the United States, its citizens, or its interests with sufficient intensity that it can be fairly recognized as an armed conflict; second, that the suspect is an active member of an opposing armed force or is an active participant in the violence; and, third, that law-enforcement means are unavailable.

Within the United States, the third requirement would be nearly impossible to satisfy—as it should be. Given the ambiguities of terrorism, we should be guided more by *Milligan's* affirmation of the rule of law than by *Quirin's* exception to it. Outside the United States, Washington should never resort to war rules away from a traditional battlefield if local authorities can and are willing to arrest and deliver a suspect to an independent tribunal—regardless of how the tribunal then rules. War rules should be used in such cases only when no law-enforcement system exists (and the other conditions of war are present), not when the rule of law happens to produce inconvenient results. Even if military forces are used to make an arrest in such cases, law-enforcement rules can still apply; only when attempting an arrest is too dangerous should war rules be countenanced.

This approach would recognize that war rules have their place—but that, given the way they inherently compromise fundamental rights, they should be used sparingly. Away from a traditional battlefield, they should be used, even against a warlike enemy, as a tool of last resort—when there is no reasonable alternative, not when a functioning criminal justice system is available. Until there are better guidelines on when to apply war and law-enforcement rules, this three-part test, drawn from the policy consequences of the decision, offers the best way to balance security and civil rights. In the meantime, the Bush administration should abandon its excessive use of war rules. In attempting to make Americans safer, it has made all Americans, and everyone else, less free.

Combatants or Criminals?

How Washington Should Handle Terrorists

Ruth Wedgwood

FIGHTING A WAR UNDER ITS RULES

KENNETH ROTH chides the Bush administration for using armed force and the law of armed conflict to capture and detain al Qaeda's key operatives ("The Law of War in the War on Terror," January/February 2004, see page 302). It is not clear, says Roth, that the "war on terrorism" is a real war, and in any event, U.S. criminal laws should be sufficient for dealing with the terrorists.

But a war is in fact raging, and criminal law is too weak a weapon. That was the lesson the United States learned too late, on September 11, 2001, after a decade of arresting and trying terrorist suspects. As a former head of the FBI's Joint Terrorist Task Force has remarked, the U.S. government could not stop al Qaeda bombings by treating them as ordinary homicides. Using such techniques, Washington did manage to take some people off the international street, but it was not able to shut down the offshore camps that taught thousands of al Qaeda recruits how to fight or wire deadly explosives. Nor could prosecutors compel Pakistani and Saudi intelligence agencies to stop subsidizing the Taliban and al Qaeda. Destroying the infrastructure of al Qaeda's operations has required diplomacy and the use of force as well as criminal law.

The purpose of domestic criminal law is to inflict stigma and punishment, and so it must be applied cautiously. Such reticence

---

This exchange originally appeared in the May/June 2004 issue of *Foreign Affairs*.

is proper for civil government in peacetime, but it is not always appropriate in war. Different priorities come to the fore when an international foe embarks on a campaign to kill or wound thousands of people. The law of armed conflict thus allows measures, such as the preventive internment of enemy combatants during the conflict, that do not require the full-dress procedure of criminal trials.

The difficulties of relying on criminal law, especially on its cumbersome standards of proof, may not be self-evident to nonlawyers. Roth suggests that criminal justice can provide all the tools necessary to defend a democratic public against catastrophic terrorism. But few criminal cases can be built on circumstantial evidence alone, and criminal proof demands near certainty—or proof "beyond a reasonable doubt"—a very high hurdle that even first-rate intelligence cannot usually meet. In a typical case, defendants cannot be arrested or sent to trial unless the state can find eyewitnesses or co-conspirators willing to testify against them publicly, braving the dangers of retaliation. Similarly, the rules of evidence used in criminal trials keep critical information out of the courtroom. Items that were seized without a search warrant or that lack a flawless chain of custody—for example, the al Qaeda computer hard drives chock full of organizational data that a *Wall Street Journal* reporter found in a Kabul marketplace—might not be admissible, no matter how important they are. Statements made by combatants in custody might also be rejected if the fighters were denied access to counsel at the time. Any defense lawyer sent to the battlefield would advise captured combatants to stop talking, undermining chances of uncovering timely intelligence about al Qaeda's plans. And criminal law requires that sensitive methods of surveillance be disclosed when they yield information offered as evidence, even though such transparency may prevent intercepting telltale signs of future attacks.

All these restrictions make sense in a civil society, where criminal law can provide adequate deterrence even with a limited success rate in the courtroom. But in the fight against al Qaeda and its compartmentalized network, deterrence does not work. There is no obvious way to dissuade fighters programmed by extremist cults or international terrorist organizations that are not bound by the commitments of nation-states. Half-measures will not do, because the stakes in this war are higher than in many others. Mistakenly releasing a single enemy soldier means little when battles are fought en masse. But in al Qaeda's asymmetric, high-tech campaign, it takes only a few combatants to destroy scores of innocent civilians. And al Qaeda remains keenly interested in using weapons of mass destruction.

Roth may doubt that the United States is at war, but it pays to ask the other side. Al Qaeda has declared jihad against the United States, and in *fatwa* after *fatwa*, Osama bin Laden has announced that all Americans are valid targets. The U.S. Congress has understood that threat well: after the September 11 attacks, it authorized the president "to use all necessary and appropriate force against those nations, organizations, or *persons he determines* planned, authorized, committed, or aided the terrorist attacks that occurred on September 11, 2001, or harbored such organizations or persons" (emphasis added). That resolution confirmed the constitutional authority of the president, as commander-in-chief, to capture and hold enemy combatants in an armed conflict, a practice that international law also permits during active fighting.

Common sense and proportionate rules of engagement are crucial, of course. No one is advocating shootouts at the landing gates of O'Hare Airport, as Roth seems to suggest. The U.S. government should continue individualized assessments of captured combatants and gauge at regular intervals whether they have given up the fight and can be safely released. It should also continue to respect the sovereignty of allies and neutrals (but warn rogue governments and rogue leaders that sheltering international terrorists is an actionable offense).

On the face of it, Roth's three-part test sounds attractive. It allows resort to the rules of war against suspects only when the violence suffered by the United States is so intense and sustained that it amounts to an armed attack, when the suspects actively engage in plans for the attack, and when "law enforcement means are unavailable" to deal with them. But "unavailability" means different things to different people, and the foreign tribunals to which Roth proposes we defer often have idiosyncratic values or could be corrupt or intimidated. And while such ambiguities are debated, dangerous suspects might slip away.

Consider the case of Jose Padilla, a Chicago youth-gang graduate allegedly interested in "dirty bombs," who could not have been effectively countered under criminal law. According to the U.S. government affidavit filed in federal court, Padilla traveled to Afghanistan in 2001 to see a senior al Qaeda military planner named Abu Zubaydah, then went to Pakistan for explosives training. He agreed to return to the United States to stage multiple simultaneous bombings at gas stations and hotels and pick out targets for a radiological "dirty bomb" attack. Padilla flew back from Pakistan via Switzerland with agents in hot pursuit and, on landing in Chicago in May 2002, was immediately detained as a "material witness" for a federal grand jury.

The limitations of criminal law soon became clear. The Fifth Amendment privilege against self-incrimination meant that Padilla did not have to testify, and could not be held, unless the government agreed to protect him against any future criminal liability. Arresting Padilla on criminal charges was not an option, because the lead witness against him is Zubaydah, who remains in custody abroad as a crucial source of information on al Qaeda's future plans. The only alternative under standard criminal law was to open the jail door, let Padilla go, and hope that the police tail would not lose him.

TO OVERCOME THIS OBSTACLE, the Bush administration decided to detain him as an enemy combatant under the law of war. Padilla was, after all, a saboteur behind enemy lines planning an act of war against his own country in cooperation with an international terrorist network. A federal district court agreed, although it granted Padilla access to defense counsel to assist in a habeas corpus hearing. But an appellate court has reversed that decision, ruling that the Bush administration did not have the power to detain any U.S. citizen as an enemy combatant, even under these dire circumstances, without express authorization from Congress. The case is now before the Supreme Court.

Roth says we should not cavil when "the rule of law happens to produce inconvenient results." But the potential success of a dirty bomb plot is more than just an "inconvenient result." And it is a result not worth risking when, thanks to another applicable set of laws, we can protect ourselves against it.

Combatants or Criminals?

KENNETH ROTH REPLIES

RUTH WEDGWOOD attacks a straw man when she says that I find criminal law "sufficient for dealing with the terrorists." Of course force is sometimes required. And when armed conflict breaks out, as in Afghanistan or Iraq, war rules appropriately apply.

But Wedgwood also wants to invoke war rules in settings far from these traditional battlefields. In her view, the "war against terrorism" is open-ended and global, allowing the U.S. government unilaterally to designate terrorism suspects as "enemy combatants," at home or abroad, and to summarily detain or kill them. That radical proposition jettisons the most basic guarantees of criminal justice, leaving our liberty and our lives protected only by the government's professions of good faith.

Wedgwood trivializes the issue by conjuring up images of "defense lawyer[s] sent to the battlefield," which no one advocates. The real issue is whether suspects are entitled to a lawyer and due process away from the traditional battlefield, in Peoria or Manchester. The Bush administration has decided on its own that they are not. The congressional resolution that Wedgwood cites never addressed the matter.

Wedgwood contends that the U.S. government is entitled to detain Jose Padilla, the alleged dirty bomber, indefinitely, without charge or trial, because another suspect, held incommunicado under "stress and duress" interrogation, has named him. Such "evidence" would never be admitted in a U.S. court of law, let alone establish guilt beyond a reasonable doubt. Yet Wedgwood dismisses these safeguards of criminal justice as unreasonable obstacles rather than recognizing them as essential protections against government overreaching.

If Padilla were really an "enemy combatant," the government need not have detained him; it could have killed him as he stepped off the plane in Chicago. Wedgwood insists that "no one is advocating shootouts at the landing gates of O'Hare Airport." But the Bush administration has never rejected the power to kill "enemy combatants" wherever it finds them, which is precisely the treatment the rules of war allow. If we are uncomfortable applying these rules far from traditional battlefields—as even Wedgwood seems to be—

the problem lies not in these long-established norms but in the designation of non-battlefield suspects as enemy combatants.

Even summary detention without trial should give us pause. Wedgwood concedes that the U.S. government should "continue to respect the sovereignty of allies and neutrals." But Bosnia and Malawi are two countries where the U.S. government has already seized suspects despite the protests of local courts. Since these governments are hardly part of the axis of evil, Wedgwood is wrong to speak of Washington's "continue[d]" respect for their sovereignty.

Some Americans may take comfort in the fact that most terrorist suspects to date do not look like them. But exceptions to the guarantees of criminal justice, once accepted, can come back to haunt us all. If the government can unilaterally declare a global war without regard to an actual battlefield, there is nothing to stop it from, say, citing the "war" on drug trafficking—a violent enterprise that kills far more Americans than terrorism—to summarily detain or kill suspected drug dealers. And one can also imagine "wars" on crime, "wars" on corruption, and so on. Detaching the notion of "war" from a traditional battlefield is easy. But it is much too dangerous to indulge.

IV
Less or More?

What's in a Name?

How to Fight Terrorism

Michael Howard

WHEN, in the immediate aftermath of the September 11 attacks on the World Trade Center and the Pentagon, Secretary of State Colin Powell declared that the United States was "at war" with terrorism, he made a very natural but terrible and irrevocable error. Administration leaders have been trying to put it right ever since.

What Powell said made sense if one uses the term "war against terrorism" in the sense of a war against crime or against drug trafficking: that is, the mobilization of all available resources against a dangerous, antisocial activity, one that can never be entirely eliminated but can be reduced to, and kept at, a level that does not threaten social stability.

The British in their time have fought many such "wars"—in Palestine, in Ireland, in Cyprus, and in Malaya (modern-day Malaysia), to mention only a few. But they never called them wars; they called them "emergencies." This terminology meant that the police and intelligence services were provided with exceptional powers and were reinforced where necessary by the armed forces, but they continued to operate within a peacetime framework of civilian authority. If force had to be used, it was at a minimal level and so far as possible did not interrupt the normal tenor of civil life. The objectives were to isolate the terrorists from the rest of the community and to cut them off from external sources of supply. The terrorists were not dignified with the status of belligerents: they were criminals, to be regarded as such by the general public and treated as such by the authorities.

This article originally appeared in the January/February 2002 issue of *Foreign Affairs*.

What's in a Name?

To declare war on terrorists or, even more illiterately, on terrorism is at once to accord terrorists a status and dignity that they seek and that they do not deserve. It confers on them a kind of legitimacy. Do they qualify as belligerents? If so, should they not receive the protection of the laws of war? This protection was something that Irish terrorists always demanded, and it was quite properly refused. But their demands helped to muddy the waters and were given wide credence among their supporters in the United States.

But to use, or rather to misuse, the term "war" is not simply a matter of legality or pedantic semantics. It has deeper and more dangerous consequences. To declare that one is at war is immediately to create a war psychosis that may be totally counterproductive for the objective being sought. It arouses an immediate expectation, and demand, for spectacular military action against some easily identifiable adversary, preferably a hostile state—action leading to decisive results.

The use of force is seen no longer as a last resort, to be avoided if humanly possible, but as the first, and the sooner it is used the better. The news media demand immediate stories of derring-do, filling their pages with pictures of weapons, ingenious graphics, and contributions from service officers long, and probably deservedly, retired. Any suggestion that the best strategy is not to use military force at all but to employ subtler if less heroic means of destroying the adversary is dismissed as "appeasement" by politicians whose knowledge of history is about on a par with their skill at political management.

Right-wing leaders, seeing themselves cheated of what the Germans used to call a *frischer, fröhlicher Krieg* (a short, jolly war) in Afghanistan, demand one against a more accessible adversary, Iraq. This is rather like the drunk who lost his watch in a dark alley but looked for it under a lamppost because there was more light there. As for their counterparts on the left, the very word "war" brings them out on the streets to protest as a matter of principle. The qualities needed in a serious campaign against terrorists—secrecy, intelligence, political sagacity, quiet ruthlessness, covert actions that remain covert, above all infinite patience—all these are forgotten or overridden in a media-stoked frenzy for immediate results, and nagging complaints if they do not get them.

Michael Howard

CALL TO ARMS

COULD IT HAVE BEEN AVOIDED? Certainly, rather than what President George W. Bush so unfortunately termed "a crusade against evil"—that is, a military campaign conducted by an alliance dominated by the United States—many people would have preferred a police operation conducted under the auspices of the United Nations on behalf of the international community as a whole, against a criminal conspiracy whose members should be hunted down and brought before an international court, where they would receive a fair trial and, if found guilty, be awarded an appropriate sentence.

In an ideal world that is no doubt what would have happened. But we do not live in an ideal world. The suicide plane attacks that killed several thousand innocent office workers in New York, nearly two hundred military personnel in Washington, D.C., and several hundred passengers on the four hijacked flights were not seen in the United States as crimes against "the international community" to be appropriately dealt with by the United Nations, a body for which Americans have little respect. For them the attacks were outrages against the people of America, far surpassing in infamy even the Japanese attack on Pearl Harbor.

Such an insult to American honor was not to be dealt with by a long and meticulous police investigation conducted by international authorities, culminating in an even longer court case in some foreign capital, with sentences that would then no doubt be suspended to allow for further appeals. It cried for immediate and spectacular vengeance to be inflicted by America's own armed forces.

And who can blame Americans? In their position the British would have felt exactly the same way. The courage and wisdom of Bush in resisting the call for a strategy of vendetta has been admirable, but the pressure is still there, both within and beyond the administration. It is a demand that can be satisfied only by military action—if possible, rapid and decisive military action. There must be catharsis: the blood of five thousand innocent civilians demands it.

Again, Bush deserves enormous credit for his attempt to implement the alternative paradigm. He has abjured unilateral action. He has sought, and received, a United Nations mandate. He has built up an amazingly wide-ranging coalition that truly does embody "the international community" so far as such an entity exists. Within a matter of days, the United States turned its back on the unilateralism and isolationism toward which it seemed to have been steering, and it resumed its former position as leader of a world community far more extensive than the so-called free world of the Cold War.

Almost equally important, the president and his colleagues have done their best to explain to the American people that this will be a war unlike any other, and that they must adjust their expectations accordingly. But it is still a war. The "w" word has been used and now cannot be withdrawn, and its use has brought inevitable and irresistible pressure to use military force as soon, and as decisively, as possible.

BATTLE OF WITS

A STRUGGLE AGAINST TERRORISM, as the British have discovered over the past century and particularly in Northern Ireland, is unlike a war against drugs or a war against crime in one vital respect. It is fundamentally a "battle for hearts and minds"; it is worth remembering that that phrase was first coined in the context of the most successful campaign of this kind that the British armed forces have ever fought—the Malayan emergency in the 1950s (a campaign that, incidentally, took some 15 years to bring to an end). Without hearts and minds one cannot obtain intelligence, and without intelligence terrorists can never be defeated. There is not much of a constituency for criminals or drug traffickers, and in a campaign against them the government can be reasonably certain that the mass of the public will be on its side. But it is well known that one man's terrorist is another man's freedom fighter. Terrorists can be successfully destroyed only if public opinion, both at home and abroad, supports the authorities in regarding them as criminals rather than heroes.

In the intricate game of skill played between terrorists and the authorities, as the British discovered in both Palestine and Ireland, the terrorists have already won an important battle if they can provoke the authorities into using overt armed force against them. They will then be in a win-win situation: either they will escape to fight another day, or they will be defeated and celebrated as martyrs.

In the process of fighting them a lot of innocent civilians will certainly be hurt, further eroding the moral authority of the government. Who in the United Kingdom will ever forget Bloody Sunday in Northern Ireland, when in 1972 a few salvos of small-arms fire by the British army gave the Irish Republican Army a propaganda victory from which the British government would never recover? And if so much harm can be done by rifle fire, what is one to say about bombing? It is like trying to eradicate cancer cells with a blowtorch. Whatever its military justification, the bombing of Afghanistan, with the inevitable collateral damage, has whittled away the immense moral ascendancy gained as a result of the terrorist attacks in America.

Soon for much of the world that atrocity will be, if not forgotten, then remembered only as history; meanwhile, every fresh picture on television of a hospital hit, or children crippled by land mines, or refugees driven from their homes by Western military action will strengthen the hatred and recruit for the ranks of the terrorists, as well as sow fresh doubts in the minds of America's supporters.

There is no reason to doubt that the campaign in Afghanistan was undertaken only on the best available political and military advice, in full realization of the military difficulties and political dangers and in the sincere belief that there was no alternative. It was, as the Americans so nicely put it, an "AOS" situation: "all options stink." But in compelling the allies to undertake it at all, the terrorists took the first and all-important trick.

The understandable military reasoning that drove the campaign was based on the political assumption that the terrorist network had to be destroyed as quickly as possible before it could do more damage. It further assumed that the network was masterminded by a single evil genius, Osama bin Laden, whose elimination would demoralize if not destroy his organization. Bin Laden operated out of a country the rulers of which refused to yield him up to the forces of international justice. Those rulers had to be compelled to change their minds. The quickest way to break their will was by aerial bombardment, especially since a physical invasion of their territory presented such huge if not insoluble logistical problems. Given these assumptions, what alternative was there?

What's in a Name?

BUT THE BEST REASONING, and the most flawless logic, is of little value if it starts from false assumptions. I have no doubt that voices were raised both in Washington and in Whitehall questioning the need and pointing out the dangers of immediate military action, but if they were, they were at once drowned out by the thunderous political imperative: "Something must be done." The same voices no doubt also questioned the wisdom, if not the accuracy, of identifying bin Laden as the central and indispensable figure in the terrorist network—demonizing him for some people, but for others giving him the heroic status enjoyed by "freedom fighters" throughout the ages.

The allies are now in a horrible dilemma. If they "bring him to justice" and put him on trial they will provide bin Laden with a platform for global propaganda. If, instead, he is assassinated—perhaps "shot while trying to escape"—he will become a martyr. If he escapes he will become a Robin Hood. Bin Laden cannot lose. And even if he is eliminated, it is hard to believe that his global network, apparently consisting of people as intelligent and well educated as they are dedicated and ruthless, will not continue to function effectively until they are traced and dug out by patient and long-term operations of police and intelligence forces, whose activities will not, and certainly should not, make headlines. Such a process, as the British defense chief Admiral Sir Michael Boyce has rightly pointed out, may well take decades, perhaps as long as the Cold War.

Now that the operation has begun it must be pressed to a successful conclusion—successful enough for the allies to be able to disengage with honor and for the tabloid headlines to claim victory (though the very demand for victory and the sub-Churchillian rhetoric that accompanies this battle cry show how profoundly press and politicians still misunderstand the nature of the terrorist problem). Only after achieving an honorable disengagement will it be possible to continue with the real struggle described above, one in which there will be no spectacular battles and no clear victory.

Boyce's analogy with the Cold War is valuable in another respect. Not only did it go on for a very long time, but it had to be kept cold. There was a constant danger that it would be inadvertently toppled into a "hot" nuclear war, which everyone would catastrophically lose. The danger of nuclear war, at least on a global scale, has now ebbed, if only for the moment, but it has been replaced by another threat, and one no less alarming: the likelihood of an ongoing and continuous confrontation of cultures that will not only divide the world but shatter the internal cohesion of our increasingly multi-cultural societies. And the longer the overt war continues against terrorism, in Afghanistan or anywhere else, the greater is the danger of that confrontation happening.

There is no reason to suppose that Osama bin Laden enjoys any more sympathy in the Islamic world than, say, Northern Ireland's Ian Paisley does in Christendom. The type is a phenomenon that has cropped up several times in British history: a charismatic religious leader fanatically hostile to the West leading a cult that has sometimes gripped an entire nation. There was the Mahdi in the Sudan in the late nineteenth century, and the so-called Mad Mullah in Somaliland in the early twentieth. Admittedly they presented purely local problems, although a substantial proportion of the British army had to be mobilized to deal with the Mahdi and his followers.

CULTURAL UNDERPINNINGS

THE DIFFERENCE TODAY is that such leaders can recruit followers from all over the world and can strike back anywhere on the globe. They are neither representative of Islam nor approved by Islam, but the roots of their appeal lie in a peculiarly Islamic predicament that only intensified over the last half of the twentieth century: the challenge to Islamic culture and values posed by the secular and materialistic culture of the West, and the inability to come to terms with it.

This is a vast subject that must be understood if there is to be any hope, not so much of winning the new cold war as of preventing it from becoming hot. In retrospect, it is quite astonishing how little the West has understood, or empathized with, the huge crisis that has faced that vast and populous section of the world stretching from the Maghreb through the Middle East and Central Asia into

South and Southeast Asia and beyond to the Philippines: overpopulated, underdeveloped, being dragged headlong by the West into the postmodern age before their populations have come to terms with modernity.

This is not a problem of poverty as against wealth, and it is symptomatic of Western materialism to suppose that it is. It is the far more profound and intractable confrontation between a theistic, land-based, and traditional culture, in places little different from the Europe of the Middle Ages, and the secular material values of the Enlightenment. The British and the French, given their imperial experiences, ought to understand these problems. But for most Americans it must be said that Islam remains one vast terra incognita—and one, like those blank areas on medieval maps, inhabited very largely by dragons.

This is the region where the struggle for hearts and minds must be waged and won if the struggle against terrorism is to succeed. The front line in the struggle is not in Afghanistan. It is in the Islamic states where modernizing governments are threatened by a traditionalist backlash: Turkey, Egypt, and Pakistan, to name only the most obvious. The front line also runs through the streets of the multicultural cities in the West. For Muslims in Ankara or Cairo, Paris or Berlin, the events of September 11 were terrible, but they happened a long way away and in another world. By contrast, those whose sufferings as a result of Western air raids or of Israeli incursions are nightly depicted on television are people, however geographically distant, with whom Muslims around the world can easily identify.

That is why prolonging the war is likely to be so disastrous. Even more disastrous would be its extension, as U.S. opinion seems increasingly to demand, in a long march through other "rogue states" beginning with Iraq, in order to eradicate terrorism for good so that the world can live at peace. No policy is more likely not just to indefinitely prolong the war but to ensure that it can never be won.

The British prime minister and the American president have been exhorting their citizens to keep their nerve. It is no less important that we should keep our heads.

The Wrong War

Grenville Byford

WHAT'S IN A NAME?

WARS HAVE TYPICALLY been fought against proper nouns (Germany, say) for the good reason that proper nouns can surrender and promise not to do it again. Wars against common nouns (poverty, crime, drugs) have been less successful. Such opponents never give up. The war on terrorism, unfortunately, falls into the second category. Victory is possible only if the United States confines itself to fighting individual terrorists rather than the tactic of terrorism itself. Yet defining who is a terrorist is more complicated than it might seem—and even if it were not, choosing one's enemies on the basis of their tactics alone has little to recommend it.

The *Oxford English Dictionary* says that a terrorist is someone who "attempts to further his views by a system of coercive intimidation. ... The term now usually refers to a member of a clandestine or expatriate organization aiming to coerce an established government by acts of violence against it or its subjects." This definition is fine as far as it goes, but in practice the use of the term is more problematic. The dictionary's citations describe the following "terrorists" or groups involved in "terrorism": the Russian government of Tsar Alexander III, the French Resistance during World War II, the Zionist Irgun in Palestine, the Kenyan "Mau Mau" independence movement, the African National Congress (ANC), Irish nationalists, and Greek Cypriots. At least some of these groups are widely admired, and it is telling that the citations referring to the Greek Cypriots and the ANC raise questions as to whether the "terrorist" label was properly applied. Like beauty, it would seem, terrorism is in the eye of the beholder.

This article originally appeared in the July/August 2002 issue of *Foreign Affairs*.

Terrorists, it is usually agreed, are defined not by their goals but by how they elect to pursue them. If terrorism is never to be countenanced, terrorists must employ some means that no end can justify. But how exactly are unjustifiable means to be identified?

One school favors a legal approach. Both domestic and international law concede to the state a monopoly on organized violence. A simple definition of a terrorist might therefore be a nonstate actor employing violence for political ends. Yet by this logic, the violence Saddam Hussein inflicts on his own people is not terrorism, whereas that inflicted by his domestic opponents in case of a revolt would be—hardly a satisfactory start.

Another school highlights the fear that terrorism seeks to instill. This is the original use of the word "terror" in a political context. It entered the language during the later stages of the French Revolution, when Edmund Burke called the Jacobins "terrorists" for their enthusiastic resort to the guillotine. The Jacobins agreed: they had decided to secure their hold on power (with the best intentions, of course) by terrorizing the populace.

By this logic, terrorists are people who aim to get their way by frightening opponents into submission. But consider the dropping of the atomic bomb on Hiroshima: it was less a military mission than a warning—the most dramatic "submit, or else" in recorded history. Consider, too, General William Tecumseh Sherman's "march to the sea" 80 years earlier, which was specifically intended to cow the civilians of the Confederacy. The sad fact is that the use of force for political ends, whether in the context of a declared war or otherwise, is inextricably bound up with terror. The object is not to kill every opponent but merely to do away with a sufficiently large number that those who remain fear carrying on more than they fear giving up. Inducing terror is not necessarily terrorism.

A third school looks at tactics, arguing that certain methods are just plain wrong and should not be employed. Status quo powers, heavily invested in the old way of doing things, often view tactical innovation as immoral. Thus, the French knights thought Henry V's use of the longbow at Agincourt despicable, and the Japanese samurai felt much the same about gunpowder. In the nineteenth century, the British Royal Navy angrily rejected the submarine, and at the end of World War II, Germany's V-1 and V-2 missiles were widely regarded as "terror weapons." The general embrace of successful innovations over time, however, undercuts such usage.

Unconventional military methods are commonly proscribed, usually by those able to rely on conventional military power. The civilian resistance movements against Hitler's Germany, for example, operated outside of the accepted rules of war, and the Germans certainly thought of them as terrorists. Yet today we view these resistance fighters as heroes, and rightly so. Wearing uniforms used to be thought a good test of who was a terrorist, but too many admirable people—the Afghans who opposed the Soviets, for example—have now fought without them. Suicide attacks are generally frowned on, but all military heroes are willing to die. The fact that most combatants cling to the hope that they will somehow survive tells us more about human psychology than about the relationship between heroes, terrorists, and suicide.

Some behavior does seem hard to excuse: killing prisoners, for example. And yet Henry V killed his prisoners before the Battle of Agincourt, and Shakespeare lionized him all the same. The problem with cataloguing the behaviors unique to those we wish to single out as terrorists is that such a list would necessarily be short and would leave outside its bounds a great deal that smacks of terrorism. Al Qaeda, a terrorist organization if ever there was one, has not killed large numbers of prisoners, whereas U.S. allies in the Northern Alliance have.

WHAT PRICE HONOR?

WHAT ABOUT TARGETS, THEN? Are terrorists those who deliberately set out to kill civilians? This inquiry raises the politically incorrect question of what is wrong with killing civilians. Civilians are not always mere bystanders and are crucial to any war effort. U.S. military power is based on America's economic success. This relationship holds for any halfway modern economy and provides the justification for attacking industrial targets in a war—whether in Hamburg half a century ago, or in Belgrade more recently. The United States, furthermore, is a democracy; its citizens help decide how its military power is used. Are they truly innocent?

Return, though, to conventional wisdom and accept that killing civilians is wrong. It does happen, nevertheless. Serbs under Slobodan Miloÿsevic and Iraqis under Saddam Hussein, some of whom must have had a better claim on the word "innocent" than the citizens of democratic America, have been killed in recent years by American bombs. The pilots who dropped those bombs, however, are not terrorists in any meaningful sense of the word.

Still, drawing the line can be difficult. Are civilian deaths defensible if they are known to be a likely consequence of violent action—unwanted, certainly, but eminently predictable? How hard does a principled warrior have to try to avoid killing civilians, and does everyone have to try equally hard? At least part of the answer surely lies in assessing the costs of a scrupulous attempt to avoid civilian casualties. In Kosovo, the United States was willing to invest billions of dollars in advanced weaponry and tolerate delays in accomplishing its objective in order to reduce civilian casualties. Washington drew the line, however, at hazarding the lives of U.S. pilots by ordering low-level attacks. This policy was not especially immoral. The problem with using it as a model, however, is that no other power on earth has the resources to act in a like manner. Must everyone without access to the latest technologies require their pilots to run risks that the Pentagon deems unacceptable in order to fight honorably? This hardly seems a reasonable proposition.

And consider the case of those opposing a government so ruthless and powerful that any attack on its armed forces is tantamount to suicide. Can we say that in such a situation no armed struggle against the regime is legitimate, since the opposition would have to employ force against civilian targets and would certainly kill the innocent? The sad truth is that for many people—some of them decent—a scrupulously honorable struggle is an unaffordable luxury. Recognizing this reality, most of us will not pass moral judgment on any combatants without also considering the ends they pursue.

Fighters with a halfway decent cause may be forgiven much. Fighters with a noble objective and no alternatives may perhaps be forgiven everything. It is hard to think of any means, for example, that would have been unacceptable if used by the inhabitants of the Warsaw ghetto in 1943. The members of the Irgun from 1946–48, however, faced a much less dire situation and had more choices available. Their actions can be judged with this context in mind. Today's Israeli government can surely be held to a still higher standard.

How much moral latitude should be allowed is an issue about which reasonable people can differ. The argument, however, will generally center not merely on the morality of the tactics themselves but on the justice of the cause and the nature of the alternatives available. Few statues are built in remembrance of people who fought honorably for a rotten cause; most celebrate those who made moral compromises for a good one. Ends and means are hopelessly conflated.

TERROR FIRMA

To UNTANGLE THE KNOT, it is useful to think of a graph with the morality of means running along one axis and the morality of ends running along the other. Asking where different pairs of belligerents would be located on that graph is an instructive exercise.

Mohandas Gandhi's Quit India movement and the ANC in apartheid South Africa, for example, had comparable objectives—noble ones, it is usually agreed today. On means, though, a clear difference emerges. The ANC had a military wing that acted outside the generally accepted laws of war, whereas the Quit India movement did not. Some might feel that this gives the latter a distinct moral edge. Yet the ANC had few alternatives, since passive resistance would not have impressed the Afrikaners. And Gandhi himself ultimately admitted that he did not believe nonviolence would have worked against any imperial power other than the United Kingdom (an epitaph of which the Raj should be proud). Should not the difference between the situations affect our moral judgments?

Starting in October 1952, the Mau Mau rebellion in Kenya was directed against British rule and European land ownership. The movement was confined to the Kikuyu tribe, then about 20 percent of the colony's population of five million. The purpose was, quite literally, to terrorize the white settlers into leaving. Some 100 of the settlers were killed, many in grisly fashion. By the end of the ensuing struggle, 11,000 rebels and 2,000 soldiers in British uniform (most of them African enlisted men) were dead. Today the Mau Mau's anticolonial efforts seem noble, although with a troubling caveat: 80 percent of the local population did not join in. Surely the level of popular support a cause enjoys must affect its legitimacy. If a majority is willing to be patient or to accept a compromise but a small splinter group is not, how can persistent violence by that group be legitimate?

A modern analogue to the Mau Mau situation can be found in Northern Ireland. Many people believe that the Provisional IRA (the main republican paramilitary organization, often referred to as simply the Irish Republican Army, or IRA), with its widespread support among local Catholics, is on balance pursuing a legitimate goal—that of a united Ireland—even if it has used questionable means to do so. By approving the Sinn Fein party president's signing of the Good Friday agreement, which provided for an elected Northern Ireland Assembly and for the decommissioning of paramilitary weapons, it chose to compromise. The Real IRA and Continuity IRA, in contrast, are splinter groups with little popular support that continue to pursue the original goal and violently oppose any deal short of a united Ireland. Their struggle is clearly less legitimate, because the majority of Ulster's Catholics have declined to embrace it.

Looking at means rather than ends, however, the Mau Mau are on weaker ground. The British had already demonstrated in India that they were willing to leave their colonial possessions without the threat of violence, and some progress had already been made in bringing Africans into the colonial government. Alternatives to terror were available; Mau Mau leader Jomo Kenyatta was no Gandhi. And the British army, although it was fighting for a less defensible cause, generally behaved well. Some might therefore, on balance, detect a moral equivalence between the two sides in Kenya.

Usually a correlation exists between the morality of ends and means. People who pursue noble goals tend to be scrupulous about how they achieve them, whereas unscrupulous people and rotten causes often go together. This fact generally makes it possible to have a sensible discussion about political morality without distinguishing clearly between the acceptability of means and ends. The case of terrorism, however, is often an exception and can force us to make difficult moral judgments—

weighing the relative merits, for example, of those who pursue a noble end through questionable or downright horrendous means and those who pursue a dubious aim with great integrity.

WHY WE FIGHT

THE BUSH ADMINISTRATION's war against terrorism is destined to be morally unsatisfying because, if the phrase is taken at face value, it flies in the face of the multifaceted way most people really think about right and wrong. Framing U.S. foreign policy around the proposition that terrorism can be defined and must be opposed, moreover, may well run counter to American national interests. Around the world, the United States now finds itself caught between the policies it needs to adopt and the language it is using to describe them.

In their conflict with the Palestinians, for example, the Israelis claim the moral high ground by pointing to the means their opponents employ, notably suicide bombings. This is all that matters, they say; nothing else can even be discussed. The Palestinians, in contrast, focus on ends. Israel, they argue, is intent on continuing its occupation of the West Bank and the Gaza Strip. Opposing this occupation is legitimate, in their eyes, and the huge disparities in strength leave them no alternative to terrorism. Despite the absolutism on each side, both dimensions of the conflict clearly exist and have a certain moral validity. Unless the Israelis and the Palestinians begin to recognize this fact, they will never engage each other, and progress toward a resolution of the conflict will not take place. Yet the concept of a war on terrorism privileges the Israeli view, thus creating a gap between Bush administration statements and the inevitable realities of Mideast diplomacy.

A few thousand miles to the east, the future governance of Kashmir is a legitimate topic for debate. It may be possible to stifle the Kashmiri insurgent organizations that the Indian government stigmatizes as terrorists, but they will not stay in check for long absent a political settlement. And if the United States lends its weight to the attempt to squash the insurgents, it will become a de facto party to the dispute and may well contribute to destabilizing the Pakistani government— something Washington has been rightly striving to avoid.

The Wrong War

Among the prisoners captured during the military operations in Afghanistan are a number of Uighur separatists who want to hive off predominantly Muslim Xinjiang from the rest of China. Beijing considers them terrorists and wants them sent back—back, that is, to certain death. The Bush administration will probably do nothing of the kind, nor should it, but in the process it will leave itself open to the charge of applying its new doctrine selectively.

In Uzbekistan, America's new ally President Islam Karimov extended his term earlier this year in yet another crooked election. He is grooming his son for succession and does not care for opposition, often locking up his opponents and torturing them. His enemies, he says, are terrorists. Some are, but many are not, and the United States is caught in a jam. And then there are the Russians in Chechnya, the Indonesians in Aceh—the line stretches on, as it always will.

In each of these cases, the United States has to make complex decisions about which parties to support, which to oppose, and which to leave alone. In practice, those decisions will be based on judgments about America's interests, the justice of the causes in question, and how the various parties have behaved—in that order. Making the third and least important of these factors the sole criterion for decision would be absurd, yet that is what the rhetoric of the war on terrorism demands. The Bush administration's continued embrace of that language, therefore, will lead to disappointments, charges of hypocrisy, and unnecessary ill will around the globe.

It is necessary to be equally clear about the U.S. reaction to the September 11 attacks. American anger does not stem from the fact that it was terrorism. Americans would be just as furious if the carnage had been inflicted by the Afghan air force instead of a shadowy subnational group. And their outrage does not relate solely to the death of civilians. If it did, greater distinction would be made between the attacks on the World Trade Center and on the Pentagon, and certainly between both of these and the October 2000 attack on the U.S.S. *Cole* in Yemen. No, what matters is quite simple: America was attacked and Americans were killed. The details of how it happened are horrifying but relatively unimportant.

This means that rather than proclaiming itself to be engaged in a necessarily nebulous war on terrorism, the United States should instead accept that it is dealing with a less grandiose and more specific question of national security. Its challenge is to protect itself in the future while demonstrating that attacks on Americans will be met with an implacable response. The government must show that it will brook no opposition in extirpating those responsible and anyone who helps them. If the country's enemies wish to surrender, they can have a fair trial. If not, they will be killed.

To accomplish its objectives, the United States will need the active help of some countries and the passive acquiescence of others. Such cooperation will not come from goodwill alone, nor will it emerge in response to peremptory commands. It will generally have to be purchased, in the usual coin of international politics. In other words, just as America is not about to give a blanket endorsement of how the Chinese, Russians, Indians, Israelis, and others handle their local "terrorist" problems, so the rest of the world is not about to do the same for America. Acknowledging this fact frankly would be useful; it would stave off a great deal of hypocrisy, confusion, and resentment while focusing attention on the real bargains that need to be cut.

Americans now realize that they have enemies and must deal with them seriously. The "moral clarity" in the rhetoric of the "war on terrorism" is more apparent than real. It takes a one-dimensional view of a multidimensional problem, and the sooner that rhetoric is retired the better. Interests first, ends second, means third—this is how America thinks. It should be how it talks as well.

The End of Appeasement

Bush's Opportunity to Redeem America's Past Failures in the Middle East

Max Boot

FOLLOWING HANS BLIX's devastating report and President Bush's compelling State of the Union address, Saddam Hussein looks more and more like a dead man walking. In all likelihood, Baghdad will be liberated by April. This may turn out to be one of those hinge moments in history—events like the storming of the Bastille or the fall of the Berlin Wall—after which everything is different. If the occupation goes well (admittedly a big if), it may mark the moment when the powerful antibiotic known as democracy was introduced into the diseased environment of the Middle East, and began to transform the region for the better. For the United States, this represents perhaps the last, best chance to do what it has singularly failed to do since World War II—to provide the Middle East with effective imperial oversight. It is not entirely America's fault, but our mismanagement and misconceptions have allowed a backward, once insignificant region to become arguably the main threat to the security of the United States and the entire West.

In centuries past, the wild and unruly passions of the Islamic world were kept within tight confines by firm, often ruthless imperial authority, mainly Ottoman, but, starting in the late 19th century, increasingly British and French. These distant masters did not always rule wisely or well, but they generally prevented the region from

---

This article originally appeared in the February 10, 2003, issue of *The Weekly Standard* and has been reprinted with permission of the author.

menacing the security of the outside world. When the pirates of the Barbary Coast (as Europeans called North Africa) could not be dealt with by the payment of ransom, the new American republic, and then the Europeans, took matters into their own hands. Ultimately, Algiers, Tripoli, Morocco, and Tunis were colonized, and thus ended their piratical threat. When a group of Egyptian army officers led by an early-day Nasser named Arabi Pasha tried to seize power in 1882, the British occupied the country, and wound up administering it from behind the scenes for decades to come. When a fanatical Islamic sect led by a self-proclaimed Mahdi (or messiah) took over the Sudan, and threatened to spread its extremist violence throughout the Islamic world, Gen. Horatio Herbert Kitchener snuffed out the movement in a hail of gunfire at the Battle of Omdurman in 1898. When a pro-Nazi regime took power in Baghdad in 1941, the British intervened to topple the offending dictator, Rashid Ali.

Strong medicine, that. And no longer considered acceptable in today's post-colonial world. As America slowly took over Britain's over-sight role after 1945, Washington tried self-consciously to carve out a different style of leadership, one that was meant to distinguish the virtuous Americans from the grasping, greedy imperialists who had come before. America wanted to show that it sympathized with the Arabs, Persians, and Muslims, had no designs on their lands or oil wealth, and would not even choose sides in their struggle to eradicate the nascent state of Israel. Unfortunately America showed something else—that we were weak, and could be attacked, economically and physically and rhetorically, with impunity. That we were a paper tiger—or, to use Osama bin Laden's metaphor, a "weak horse." "When people see a strong horse and a weak horse," the leader of al Qaeda has said, "by nature they will like the strong horse." It is no wonder that America today has so few real friends in the region. Why would anyone ride alongside a weak horse?

This may seem an odd statement to make, since America is often accused of being a bully, in the Mideast as elsewhere. Yet the record shows precious little bullying—indeed not enough. Note that the last time the United States played a pivotal role in a Mideast change of government (if one overlooks Bill Clinton's campaign against Benjamin Netanyahu in Israel's 1999 election) was in 1953, when the CIA, along with Britain's MI6, helped to depose Iranian prime minister Mohammed Mossadegh.

Considering how many violently anti-American regimes have existed in the Middle East since World War II, America's failure to overthrow more of them is a testament to our passivity and forbearance.

This is not to suggest that the U.S. record in the Mideast during the past 50 years has been exclusively weak and pusillanimous. There have been occasional flashes of principle and infrequent displays of strength. Some of the more prominent include: Truman's ultimatum that forced the Soviets to evacuate Iran in 1946 and his decision two years later to override all his foreign policy advisers by recognizing Israel; Eisenhower's dispatch of Marines to support the Lebanese government in 1958; Nixon and Kissinger's backing of Israel with emergency arms shipments during the 1973 Yom Kippur War; Reagan's bombing of Libya in 1986 and protection of Gulf shipping from Iranian attacks in 1987–88; and, most recently, George H.W. Bush's resounding victory in the Persian Gulf War of 1991. All these actions are very much to America's credit, and have done much to serve U.S. interests in the region.

Unfortunately America's record of failure is more glaring, starting with the Suez Crisis, continuing in the run-up to the Six Day War, the oil crisis of the 1970s, the Iranian revolution, subsequent terrorist attacks against the United States by radical Islamists, and the failure to depose Saddam Hussein. A broad generalization may stretch the truth but not break it: America was strong in resisting Soviet designs on the region but weak in the face of Arab nationalism and Islamic extremism. Indeed, the United States usually sought to make common cause with Arabs and Persians against the Soviet Union. This may have been a sound short-term strategy—it did contribute to the defeat of the Evil Empire—but its unintended long-term consequence has been to leave behind a poisonous legacy of anti-Americanism, despotism, and corruption that poses a stark challenge to the 21st-century world.

NASSER

THE PATTERN of American weakness was set early on, during the 1956 Suez Crisis, which serves as a kind of template for everything the United States has done wrong in the region for the past several decades. In the immediate run-up to the crisis, the United States tried unsuccessfully to court Gamal Abdel Nasser, who had emerged as the leader of the group of Egyptian army officers that overthrew King Farouk in 1952. President Eisenhower thought he could lure Nasser to the Western camp by offering him support, such as loans to build the Aswan Dam, which would supply most of his country's electricity. But Nasser spurned the West by taking a prominent role at the Bandung Conference of nonaligned nations and by extending diplomatic recognition to the People's Republic of China. His radio station, the Voice of the Arabs, blared out a daily stream of vituperation against the West and its friends in the region, while Nasser's agents tried to subvert these "lackeys of imperialism." Like most dictators, Nasser gave top priority to getting his hands on copious stockpiles of weapons. When Washington, not wanting to fuel a regional arms race, refused to provide them, he turned to the Soviet bloc.

In 1955 the Kremlin agreed, through its Czech puppets, to supply Nasser with an awesome array of weaponry including 200 jet airplanes and 100 tanks. This would have tilted the regional balance of power sharply against Israel, which possessed only 20 jet aircraft of its own. Prime Minister David Ben Gurion asked Washington to guarantee Israel's security and supply it with weapons to counter the growing Egyptian threat. Eisenhower and his secretary of state, John Foster Dulles, refused. Their policy was centered on the Alpha Project, one of countless American attempts to broker peace between Israel and its enemies. In their pursuit of this chimerical goal, Eisenhower and Dulles decided that Israel would get no security assistance from the United States until a full settlement had been reached with the Arabs.

Such a settlement is still elusive almost 50 years later, but in the meantime Israel faced a pressing danger. The Israel Defense Forces estimated that Czech weapons would begin flowing to Egypt by November 1955, and that it would take six to eight months for the Egyptians to assimilate the inflow. Chief of Staff Moshe Dayan calculated that Egypt would be ready to attack Israel by late spring 1956. Already the danger loomed; Nasser was sponsoring guerrilla raids into Israel, blockading the southern Israeli port of Eilat, and not allowing Israeli shipping access to the Suez Canal.

The End of Appeasement

Since Washington would not help, Israel turned to states that would—first France and then Britain. They had their own beef with Nasser, who on July 26, 1956, nationalized the Suez Canal Company. The canal, which was owned (and had been built) by an Anglo-French consortium, was the transit point for two-thirds of Europe's oil supplies. Neither London nor Paris was willing to cede control of this vital waterway to a power-mad dictator who was increasingly allied with the Communist bloc. Since Washington was not interested in helping its closest allies, they got together with Israel, and in the secret Protocol of Sèvres, agreed on a joint operation to seize the canal and overthrow Nasser.

The plan began to unfold on October 29, 1956, when Israeli forces moved into the Sinai desert, effortlessly overrunning Egyptian positions. France and Britain issued an ultimatum calling on both sides to stop fighting and pull back 10 miles from the canal. Israel agreed, but Egypt didn't, and on October 31, Anglo-French forces began bombing Egyptian military positions. A few days later, on November 5, they occupied Port Said, which controlled the Mediterranean entrance to the canal, with little resistance. Nasser responded by scuttling old ships filled with cement to block the canal. His allies in Damascus sabotaged the oil pipeline linking Iraq to the Mediterranean, thus interrupting a major source of Europe's oil supplies. Saudi Arabia embargoed oil shipments to France and Britain, and acts of sabotage shut down Kuwait's supply system.

A looming oil shortage could have been averted with continued military action by Israel, France, and Britain to open the canal and overthrow Nasser. The inept Egyptian armed forces posed little obstacle. But the allies could not cope with the overwhelming pressure brought by President Eisenhower, who didn't want to "get the Arabs sore at all of us" and who was eager to paint the United States as opposed to imperialism, whether conducted by the Soviet Union in Hungary or by France and Britain in Egypt. There was little Washington could or would do to force the Soviet Union to disgorge Hungary, but America had plenty of leverage with its allies, and didn't hesitate to use it.

Ike began by pushing a resolution through the United Nations demanding the British, Israeli, and French troops withdraw immediately.

When Britain balked, Eisenhower tightened the economic screws. The crisis was causing a run on sterling and a major depletion of Britain's scant oil reserves, which, if allowed to continue, would lead to an economic meltdown. The United States had contingency plans to provide loans and emergency oil supplies to Britain, but Eisenhower refused to activate them as long as British troops remained in Egypt. He wanted to force the British and French "to work out their own oil problem—to boil in their own oil, so to speak." Faced with unremitting pressure from their most powerful benefactor, Britain, France, and Israel had no choice but to withdraw.

British prime minister Anthony Eden complained in his memoirs, with considerable justice, "In recent years the United States has sometimes failed to put its weight behind its friends, in the hope of being popular with their foes." At first this cynical gambit—precisely what the United States often accuses its European allies of doing—seemed to pay dividends. U.N. ambassador Henry Cabot Lodge reported to Eisenhower that he was deluged with support from Third World countries—and not just from their diplomats. Even U.N. busboys, typists, and elevator operators, Lodge crowed, "have been offering their congratulations." But the outpourings of support quickly faded, to be replaced by the same sullen resentment, envy, and hatred that had once been directed against the British and the French.

The immediate impact of the Suez Crisis was to give a major impetus to Nasser in his grandiose plans to unite the entire Arab world under his tyrannical rule. He was seen as the first Arab in hundreds of years to have defeated the forces of Christendom. Britain, France, and America were perceived to be on the run. Pro-Western rulers were deemed to be puppets ripe for elimination.

In the spring of 1957, Nasserite army officers tried, and failed, to overthrow King Hussein of Jordan. Arab nationalists were more successful in Iraq, where the Hashemite royal family was murdered in a 1958 coup d'état. That same year Egypt and Syria combined to form the United Arab Republic, which received substantial military support from the USSR. Eisenhower sensed, too late, the Nasserite danger, and proclaimed the Eisenhower Doctrine to help friendly Middle Eastern regimes. In 1958, as part of this doctrine, he landed 15,000 Marines in Beirut to stabilize the Christian government against a Muslim uprising. But while this may have helped keep Lebanon out of Nasserite hands, it did not discourage Nasser from further adventurism. In 1962 he dispatched 50,000 troops to Yemen, where they became embroiled in a civil war against the Saudi-backed monarchy.

A few years later Nasser turned his attention back to the "Zionist entity." Following the 1956 war, the United States had forced Israel to disgorge its territorial gains in the Sinai. To assuage Israel's security concerns, a U.N. peacekeeping force was inserted into the area. On May 16, 1967, Nasser asked the U.N. to remove its troops, and Secretary General U Thant cravenly complied. Nothing now stood in the way of Egyptian troops, who massed near Israel's border. Five days later, Nasser announced that he was closing the Straits of Tiran, thus keeping Israeli shipping out of the Gulf of Aqaba, its only outlet to the Red Sea. This was a blatant violation of international law. But although President Johnson declared Nasser's action illegal, he did not order the U.S. Navy to run the blockade and preserve the freedom of the seas—as Eisenhower had pledged ten years before that America would do if the straits were ever closed. Johnson counseled Levi Eshkol not to take matters into his own hands, either, but the Israeli prime minister decided he had no choice. On June 5, Israel launched a series of lightning strikes against its neighbors that delivered a resounding victory in just six days. This was the second straight Arab-Israeli war that the United States had failed to prevent by not offering firm support to Israel beforehand. By jollying Nasser along, Washington had only encouraged his far-flung designs.

The United States likewise did little to forestall Egypt's next attempt to wipe Israel off the map, which occurred during the Yom Kippur holiday in 1973. But at least the Nixon administration, to its great credit, rushed emergency deliveries of arms to Israel when it appeared that the Jewish state stood on the brink of annihilation. Nixon and his secretary of state, Henry Kissinger, hoped to maintain a public stance of neutrality by hiding these arms shipments from the Arab states. But the ruse fell apart when foul weather delayed some giant C-5A transport planes laden with U.S. military supplies. They were supposed to land in Israel under cover of darkness; instead they descended in the middle of the day on October 14, their insignia clear for all to see. Before long America was embroiled in its next Middle East crisis—this one centered on the oil-producing states of the Persian Gulf.

Just as the United States had done a poor job of assuming Britain's imperial role in Egypt, so now it did an equally poor job in the Gulf.

THE SHEIKHS

PRIME MINISTER HAROLD WILSON announced in 1968 that Britain was withdrawing from its military commitments "east of Suez." The Pax Britannica was defunct, the Pax Americana did not yet exist. The small Gulf states—Kuwait, Oman, Qatar, Bahrain, and what would become the United Arab Emirates—were on their own. Deprived, against their will, of British protection, the sheikhs had to make common cause with their large, dangerous neighbors. It is perhaps no coincidence that within two years of the final British pullout in 1971, these Gulf states were presenting a major challenge to the West. The British pullout had left a power vacuum that the United States, embroiled in Vietnam and, before long, Watergate, was unable to fill. Instead President Nixon outsourced the protection of the Gulf to America's great friends, the shah of Iran and the king of Saudi Arabia, who became two of the world's biggest buyers of U.S. arms. Nixon saw them as "Twin Pillars" of stability in the region, but they were also twin pillars of the Organization of Petroleum Exporting Countries.

OPEC, formed in 1960, had little success in controlling oil prices, because non-OPEC oil reserves, especially in the United States, had produced a lot of excess capacity. But by the early 1970s, fast economic growth in Japan, Western Europe, and the United States had strained oil stocks. Now there was little give in the market, leaving the oil-producing states maximum leverage to raise prices.

The OPEC countries were ready to seize the moment, having already nationalized their oil industries. Oil fields across the world had been developed at great risk and expense by Western oil companies. At the stroke of a pen, various dictators in effect stole these assets—and heard nary a peep of protest from Washington. The trend had begun in Mexico in the 1930s and spread to the Middle East in 1951, when Prime Minister Mossadegh crafted, and the shah signed, a law nationalizing Iran's oil industry. All British oil company employees were summarily booted out of the country.

This decision, which occurred amid turmoil and violence (a previous, anti-nationalization prime minister had been assassinated by Islamic terrorists), caused great consternation in London, since a British company (Anglo-Iranian, forerunner of British Petroleum) held the Iranian oil concession. But Washington nixed Prime Minister Clement Atlee's plans for military intervention to take back Anglo-Iranian's refineries. The United States got involved in toppling Mossadegh by covert means only when efforts to work out a diplomatic solution had gotten nowhere, and it appeared that "Mossy's" chaotic rule might provide an opening for Tudeh, as the Iranian Communist party was known. The combined CIA-MI6 operation (code-named Ajax, and run by Kermit Roosevelt) wouldn't have worked had it not been for declining popular support for Mossadegh and a resurgence of backing for the shah, who, under Iran's constitution, was well within his rights to sack his prime minister.

But the return of Muhammad Reza Shah Pahlavi to real power did not result in the privatization of the Iranian oil industry. The shah did sign a contract with a multinational consortium of oil companies (including Anglo-Iranian) to manage Iran's production, but his government retained ownership. As Daniel Yergin recounts in his invaluable history "The Prize," this helped establish the principle that oil assets would not be privately held, a principle that other states enthusiastically applied in the years ahead. By the mid-1970s, Algeria, Libya, Iraq, Saudi Arabia, Kuwait, and Venezuela had nationalized their oil industries, usually offering the previous owners a pittance in compensation. This was not just a financial loss for the West; it turned into a major strategic problem, for it created the "oil weapon" that OPEC wielded with great gusto.

In 1973 the Arab members of OPEC announced an embargo on oil shipments to the United States and the Netherlands to punish America for its support of Israel. This produced an immediate shock in America, with lines snaking around the block at many gas stations—when gas was available at all. Two ironies made this especially humiliating: The Gulf states were cutting off oil shipments to the U.S. Navy, which protected them; and the embargo had to be carried out by American companies, which still ran many oil fields under contract to the exporting states. Painful as it was, the selective embargo did not work very well. Oil is a fungible commodity, and America and the Netherlands were able to buy most of what they needed from other sources. Realizing that the embargo was failing, OPEC abandoned it in 1974.

But the oil cartel, led by the shah, was more successful in its attempts to ratchet up prices by ratcheting down production: Prices spiked from $3 a barrel in 1970 to a whopping $30 a barrel in 1980. As oil prices went up, the U.S. economy went down, afflicted by a horrible combination of stagnation and inflation that came to be known as "stagflation." These economic woes were exacerbated by the ham-handed U.S. government response, which under Presidents Nixon, Ford, and Carter primarily consisted of government-imposed rationing, price controls, and a "windfall profits" tax that interfered with the functioning of the market. But there was no question that the primary culprits were to be found around a meeting table in Vienna. OPEC held the Western economy hostage.

Rather pitifully, Washington pleaded with its friends in the region to exert their influence to bring down prices, but the Twin Pillars, the Saudi king and the shah, usually turned a deaf ear to American entreaties. "There are some people who thought—and perhaps some who still think—that I am a toy in the Americans' hands," the shah said in 1975. "Why would I accept to be a toy? There are reasons for our power which will make us stronger, so why would we be content to be someone else's catspaw?" Odd talk coming from a man whose survival—like that of the Saudi royal family—depended, in the final instance, on American military protection. But the shah and the Saudis were more eager to appease nationalist and Islamic radicals who called for a united Arab front against the "Zionist oppressors" and "Western imperialists." The cost of crossing the extremists was too great; the Saudis got a taste of what they could expect when, in the spring of 1973, terrorists attacked one of their refineries and pipelines. The royal family decided to buy off the extremists, even if it meant offending Washington. But then they did not especially fear the wrath of the Americans. They figured—rightly, as it turned out—that the United States would do little to undermine their governments because it feared that the alternative, whether Nasserite or fundamentalist, would be worse.

Just as the OPEC potentates expected, the United States submitted supinely to economic blackmail. The U.S. government made no attempt to take back by force the oil fields confiscated by various Middle Eastern despots. Washington did not even try to prosecute OPEC for blatant violations of antitrust law, as it has done with other overseas cartels such as De Beers. Doing so might have required legislation to lift the "sovereign immunity" provision that protects foreign governments, under most circumstances, from being sued in U.S. courts. This would have been perfectly possible for Congress to do—if any administration had pushed for such legislation. But none did. Numerous bills to allow OPEC to be sued have died in Congress, the most recent being legislation sponsored in 2001 by Rep. Ben Gilman. The result is that De Beers executives are afraid to visit the United States for fear of being arrested or served with legal papers. But OPEC sheikhs, who rig the price of a commodity far more important than diamonds, are able to come to the United States whenever they desire access to physicians, chefs, or prostitutes superior to those available in the Arab world. They also feel free to keep vast amounts of money in the U.S. financial system without fear of having their assets frozen.

By the 1980s, the oil crisis had passed, having inflicted great damage on the economies of the West. Saudi Arabia, with the largest oil reserves in the world, earned Washington's gratitude for moderating prices, much as a local Mafia boss might earn the gratitude of a bodega owner whose shop he refrained from destroying. But the Saudi pressure on fellow OPEC states not to raise prices too high, while presented to credulous Washington policymakers as a great favor to America, was in reality self-serving: Riyadh was afraid that if it priced its oil out of the market the result would be a slackening of demand and the development of alternative energy sources. That is precisely what happened during the 1970s oil crisis, which made it profitable for Britain and Norway to extract high-cost oil from the North Sea.

Generations of Washington policymakers have fooled themselves into thinking that Saudi oil revenues could be directed for friendly purposes. This illusion was easy to sustain in the 1980s when the Saudis, for their own theological purposes, bankrolled anti-Soviet mujahedeen in Afghanistan. Again, this was presented by Riyadh as a great favor to Washington, but was actually in the Saudis' interest, since it was designed to court favor with Islamic extremists both at home and abroad. Since September 11, 2001, it has become obvious that significant sums in petrodollars have gone to fund virulently anti-Western *madrassas* around the world or have found their way into the pockets of outright terrorists like Osama bin Laden, himself a Saudi. This places OPEC's activities—previously seen merely as greed run amok—in a rather more sinister light. The Saudis and the rest weren't just out to make a buck; they were also out, like Nasser before them, to assert Arab and Islamic power at the expense of the West. And successive American administrations—obsessed, understandably, with the Soviet threat—did little to stop them.

THE MULLAHS

BY THE LATE 1970S, Nasserite pan-Arabism was a spent force; Anwar Sadat, Nasser's successor, conceded as much by reaching a peace agreement with Israel. But there now arose a new and even more virulent threat to the United States in the form of Islamism, a violent creed that blended elements of fundamentalist Islam with a power-centered ideology inspired by fascism and communism. The catalyst for its rise was the 1979 Iranian revolution which overthrew America's great friend, the shah. The Carter administration did little to help the shah, hoping thereby to woo support among the revolutionaries. But the hard-liners effectively foreclosed this possibility on November 4, 1979, when they invaded the U.S. embassy in Tehran.

Seventy-nine years earlier, when hordes of fanatical Boxers had invaded the Legation Quarter in Peking, America, Japan, and the leading nations of Europe had dispatched a large expeditionary force to march on the Chinese capital and liberate the besieged diplomats. But Ayatollah Ruhollah Khomeini had no fear of an American army marching on Tehran. "Our youth should be confident that America cannot do a damn thing," he told his followers three days after the embassy takeover. "America is far too impotent to interfere in a military way here. If they could have interfered, they would have retained the shah."

The ayatollah was right. Jimmy Carter contented himself with imposing ineffectual diplomatic and economic sanctions. Only after nearly five months of "America held hostage" did Carter attempt a rescue mission, and the pathetic Eagle Claw expedition had to be aborted on April 25, 1980, after two aircraft collided at a rendezvous point code-named Desert One. The president rejected suggestions to invade Iran, or at the very least, bombard or capture its oil facilities and other important targets. This, it was feared, would lead to the hostages' being killed.

Carter's gambit paid off to the extent that all 52 hostages were released alive. But by showing such restraint, Carter ensured that many more Americans would be kidnapped and killed in the future.

Years later, one of the embassy guards, former Marine Sgt. Rodney Sickmann, regretted that he'd been ordered not to fire so much as a tear gas canister at the embassy invaders. "Had we opened fire on them maybe we would only have lasted an hour," he told *The New York Times* in 2002. But "we could have changed history" by showing that Americans could not be attacked with impunity. Instead the embassy surrender showed that Americans were easy targets. "If you look back, it started in 1979; it's just escalated," Sickmann says.

The escalation occurred first in Saudi Arabia and Egypt. In 1979 Islamist radicals briefly seized the Grand Mosque in Mecca, and in 1981 they assassinated Anwar Sadat. The Levant soon became a major focus of their operations.

In the late 1970s and early 1980s, the Palestine Liberation Organization—a secular organization but one that often cooperated with Islamist groups—used southern Lebanon as a base from which to attack Israel. Israel responded by invading Lebanon in 1982, putting the PLO fighters on the run and trapping them in Beirut. At this point, the United States, as so often in the past, intervened to prevent Israel from winning a complete victory against its sworn enemies. President Reagan pressured Prime Minister Menachem Begin to rein in his troops and let Yasser Arafat and his followers leave Lebanon, preserving them to fight another day. To supervise the evacuation of 8,000 Fatah fighters, the United States, along with

France and Italy, landed a small peacekeeping force in Beirut. Though this force was soon evacuated, the three countries decided to send a larger force back after the massacre at the Sabra and Shatila refugee camps to help the Lebanese government restore some semblance of control over a country torn by civil war. Unfortunately this only increased the number of targets available for Iranian-backed Islamists who were openly waging war on the Great Satan.

The death toll mounted fast. On April 18, 1983, a Shiite suicide bomber struck the U.S. embassy in Beirut, killing 63 people, 17 Americans among them, including both the CIA station chief and his deputy. On October 23 of that year, another Shiite suicide bomber hit the U.S. Marine barracks in Beirut, killing 241 soldiers. In the face of this attack, the Reagan administration revealed itself to be no more muscular than its Democratic predecessor had been. After the battleship *New Jersey* hurled a few Volkswagen-sized shells into the hills above Beirut, President Reagan announced that the remaining Marines would be "redeployed" to ships offshore. This sent a loud and clear message to America's enemies: The Americans are weak. Kill a few of them, and you can chase them out of your country.

The image of American impotence was reinforced by the continuing hostage crisis in Lebanon. Having learned in 1979 that taking American hostages pays, the Iranians decided to turn this into a major business. With the complicity of Syria, the Iranians directed their Hezbollah proxies to kidnap and kill a steady stream of Westerners. Among those seized and murdered were William Buckley, the new CIA station chief in Beirut, and Marine Colonel William Higgins, chief of a U.N. peacekeeping force.

It did not require Hercule Poirot to see Iranian fingerprints all over these operations. Many of the kidnap victims were held at the Sheik Abdallah Barracks in the Lebanese town of Baalbek, which had been taken over as a base of operations by uniformed members of the Iranian Revolutionary Guard Corps, the Pasdaran. One of the early hostages—David Dodge, acting president of the American University, Beirut, who was abducted on July 19, 1982—was transported first to Damascus, and then, from there, to Tehran via Iran Air. He was held in the Iranian capital for six months before being released. None of this was a secret at the time; Robert Baer, a former CIA case officer, recounts in his gripping memoir, "See No Evil," how in October 1984 he visited Baalbek and even saw the barracks where he suspected (rightly, as it turned out) that Buckley and five other Westerners were imprisoned.

Washington's ineffectual response in the face of this aggression boggles the mind. The Reagan administration did briefly bomb Libya in 1986, in response to an attack on a Berlin disco, but these pinprick airstrikes only enraged Muammar Qaddafi, whose agents, in retaliation, destroyed Pan Am flight 103 in 1988, killing 270 people. More significantly, the Reagan administration did not punish Damascus or Tehran, which were bigger sponsors of anti-American terrorism than Tripoli. It did not even dispatch Delta Force to Baalbek to free the captives and kill their kidnappers. Instead it provided the Iranian mullahs with arms in exchange for hostages, making a mockery of America's traditional policy of not dealing with terrorists. This policy was not even very successful on its face: Repeated American deliveries of thousands of missiles induced Iran to release just three hostages.

SADDAM

AMERICA was an equal opportunity appeaser. While trying to buy off Iran, it was also backing Iran's mortal enemy, Iraq, during their war in the 1980s. This was a justifiable realpolitik policy designed to forestall Iranian domination of the Persian Gulf, and included a limited war to protect Kuwaiti tankers from Iranian attacks in 1987–88. As part of this "tanker war," the *USS Vincennes* shot down an Iranian passenger airliner on July 3, 1988. It was an accident, but conspiracy-minded Iranians thought it a deliberate expression of a new get-tough approach by that cowboy Ronald Reagan. Within a month, Tehran had concluded a cease-fire with Iraq—an odd testament to the far-reaching results that even the inadvertent and misguided flexing of American muscle could achieve in the Middle East.

Unfortunately, America continued catering to Saddam Hussein even after the Iran-Iraq War was over. On July 25, 1990, U.S. Ambassador April Glaspie had an infamous meeting with Saddam in which she informed the Iraqi dictator that the United States had "no opinion on Arab-Arab conflicts, like your border disagreement with Kuwait." Saddam took this as a green light for his invasion of his tiny neighbor, which began a week later. It turned out that his expectation of American acquiescence—based not only on his conversation with Glaspie but also on his reading of events of the previous three decades, going all the way back to Suez in 1956—was not justified. President Bush, with a prompt from Margaret Thatcher, mobilized an impressive coalition to kick Iraq out of Kuwait. Desert Storm turned into one of the most one-sided wars in history.

It was America's shining hour—a victory that might have erased years of failure in the Middle East. Except that Bush refused to follow the logic of military victory to its natural political outcome; he ended the ground war after just 100 hours, while the Republican Guard remained intact and Saddam remained in power. In the cease-fire that followed, General Norman Schwarzkopf unwisely allowed Saddam's forces to fly helicopters over the parts of Iraq they still controlled. Those helicopters helped Saddam slaughter Shiites and Kurds who had risen up against his rule—at American instigation—in great numbers. American prestige instantly plummeted from the heights it had attained just a few weeks before. And no wonder. Here was the mighty American army sitting idle, while nearby rivers ran red with the blood of their allies.

This inaction in the face of Saddam's provocations would be repeated time and again in the 1990s. Saddam plotted to kill George H.W. Bush in 1993; in retaliation, President Clinton unleashed America's full wrath . . . to flatten an empty intelligence headquarters. The U.S. government hatched a plot to overthrow Saddam in 1995, only to pull out at the last minute, and leave its Kurdish friends to either cut deals with the dictator, flee, or be killed. Saddam stopped cooperating with U.N. weapons inspectors in 1998; in response, the United States and Britain bombed Iraq for all of four days. None of this made an appreciable dent in Saddam's dictatorship. This failure suggested to conspiracy-minded Middle Easterners either that the United States secretly wanted to maintain Saddam in power for some nefarious purpose, or that it feared the Iraqi dictator. Either way, the vacillating U.S. policy on Iraq signaled a fatal lack of seriousness on America's part.

The End of Appeasement

AL QAEDA

THIS IMPRESSION was reinforced in the 1990s by America's failure to take stern steps against the terrorists who waged war against it. Continuing a campaign that began in 1979, Islamist operatives bombed the World Trade Center in 1993, two U.S. embassies in Africa in 1998, and the *USS Cole* in 2000. Hezbollah attacked a Saudi National Guard facility in Riyadh in 1995, killing five Americans, and the Khobar Towers barracks in 1996, killing 19 Americans. Al Qaeda also claimed credit for working with local tribesmen to kill 18 American soldiers in Mogadishu in 1993, driving U.S. forces out of Somalia. Daniel Pipes estimates that even before the costliest terrorist strike in history occurred on September 11, 2001, Islamist violence directed at Americans had killed 800 people—"more than killed by any other enemy since the Vietnam War."

Yet, as Pipes notes, "these murders hardly registered." Successive administrations, Republican and Democratic alike, treated them not as an ongoing war but as a matter for the criminal justice system. Bob Woodward's new book, "Bush at War," reveals that during the Clinton administration, a group of Afghan agents hired by the CIA to shadow Osama bin Laden offered to kill the al Qaeda leader. The agency refused to authorize the mission, because it would have violated the executive ban on assassinations.

Such unwarranted restraint demoralized America's friends in the region and emboldened our enemies. Looking at how America was chased out of Vietnam, Lebanon, and Somalia, bin Laden and his minions thought they saw an explanation for America's inaction: The United States was too weak and decadent to resist the jihadists. "We no longer fear the so-called Great Powers," bin Laden proclaimed in a 2000 recruitment video for al Qaeda.

> We believe that America is much weaker than Russia; and our brothers who fought in Somalia told us they were astonished to observe how weak, impotent and cowardly the American soldier is. As soon as eighty [sic] American troops were killed, they fled in the dark as fast as they could, after making a great noise about the new international order. America's nightmares in Vietnam and Lebanon will pale by comparison with the forthcoming victory in al-Hijaz.

Max Boot

Presumably the campaign in Afghanistan disabused al Qaeda of some of these illusions—but not all. The toppling of the Taliban was a good start, but only a start. A bigger test now awaits us in Iraq. America's "friends" in the region fear that American troops will march on Baghdad and install a democratic government, something that would undermine their own grip on power. They couch this fear in the language of "stability"—toppling Saddam, they counsel, would foster "instability" in the region. This is actually the best reason to liberate Iraq. The "stability" of the region produced September 11. There is no guarantee what will come out of post-invasion "instability," but if the United States remains a strong player in the region, it should be considerably better than the status quo antebellum.

Beyond Iraq loom other challenges—especially Syria and Iran, which have been waging undeclared war on the United States for 20 years, but also Saudi Arabia, which has abetted this war even as it has benefited from American protection. It is possible that a U.S. victory in Iraq will intimidate these regimes into better behavior. If not, the United States will have to take more vigorous steps to align our relationships with these countries with our interests and principles. This is a major undertaking, and the necessity for it might have been averted by wiser action years ago, but the long record of U.S. futility in the Middle East now presents us with this defining task.

V
The State of Play

The Protean Enemy

Jessica Stern

WHAT'S NEXT FROM AL QAEDA?

HAVING SUFFERED the destruction of its sanctuary in Afghanistan two years ago, al Qaeda's already decentralized organization has become more decentralized still. The group's leaders have largely dispersed to Pakistan, Iran, Iraq, and elsewhere around the world (only a few still remain in Afghanistan's lawless border regions). And with many of the planet's intelligence agencies now focusing on destroying its network, al Qaeda's ability to carry out large-scale attacks has been degraded.

Yet despite these setbacks, al Qaeda and its affiliates remain among the most significant threats to U.S. national security today. In fact, according to George Tenet, the CIA's director, they will continue to be this dangerous for the next two to five years. An alleged al Qaeda spokesperson has warned that the group is planning another strike similar to those of September 11. On May 12, simultaneous bombings of three housing complexes in Riyadh, Saudi Arabia, killed at least 29 people and injured over 200, many of them Westerners. Intelligence officials in the United States, Europe, and Africa report that al Qaeda has stepped up its recruitment drive in response to the war in Iraq. And the target audience for its recruitment has also changed. They are now younger, with an even more "menacing attitude," as France's top investigative judge on terrorism-related cases, Jean-Louis Bruguière, describes them. More of them are converts to Islam. And more of them are women.

What accounts for al Qaeda's ongoing effectiveness in the face of an unprecedented onslaught? The answer lies in the organization's

---

This article originally appeared in the July/August 2003 issue of *Foreign Affairs*.

remarkably protean nature. Over its life span, al Qaeda has constantly evolved and shown a surprising willingness to adapt its mission. This capacity for change has consistently made the group more appealing to recruits, attracted surprising new allies, and—most worrisome from a Western perspective—made it harder to detect and destroy. Unless Washington and its allies show a similar adaptability, the war on terrorism won't be won anytime soon, and the death toll is likely to mount.

MALLEABLE MISSIONS

WHY DO RELIGIOUS TERRORISTS KILL? In interviews over the last five years, many terrorists and their supporters have suggested to me that people first join such groups to make the world a better place—at least for the particular populations they aim to serve. Over time, however, militants have told me, terrorism can become a career as much as a passion. Leaders harness humiliation and anomie and turn them into weapons. Jihad becomes addictive, militants report, and with some individuals or groups—the "professional" terrorists—grievances can evolve into greed: for money, political power, status, or attention.

In such "professional" terrorist groups, simply perpetuating their cadres becomes a central goal, and what started out as a moral crusade becomes a sophisticated organization. Ensuring the survival of the group demands flexibility in many areas, but especially in terms of mission. Objectives thus evolve in a variety of ways. Some groups find a new cause once their first one is achieved—much as the March of Dimes broadened its mission from finding a cure for polio to fighting birth defects after the Salk vaccine was developed. Other groups broaden their goals in order to attract a wider variety of recruits. Still other organizations transform themselves into profit-driven organized criminals, or form alliances with groups that have ideologies different from their own, forcing both to adapt. Some terrorist groups hold fast to their original missions. But only the spry survive.

Consider, for example, Egyptian Islamic Jihad (EIJ). EIJ's original objective was to fight the oppressive, secular rulers of Egypt and turn the country into an Islamic state. But the group fell on hard times after its leader, Sheikh Omar Abdel Rahman, was imprisoned in the United States and other EIJ leaders were killed or forced into exile. Thus in the early 1990s, Ayman al-Zawahiri decided to shift the group's sights from its "near enemy"—the secular rulers of Egypt—to the "far enemy," namely the United States and other Western countries. Switching goals in this way allowed the group to align itself with another terrorist aiming to attack the West and able to provide a significant influx of cash: Osama bin Laden. In return for bin Laden's financial assistance, Zawahiri provided some 200 loyal, disciplined, and well-trained followers, who became the core of al Qaeda's leadership.

A second group that has changed its mission over time to secure a more reliable source of funding is the Islamic Movement of Uzbekistan (IMU), which, like EIJ, eventually joined forces with the Taliban and al Qaeda. The IMU's original mission was to topple Uzbekistan's corrupt and repressive post-Soviet dictator, Islam Karimov. Once the IMU formed an alliance with the Taliban's leader, Mullah Omar, however, it began promoting the Taliban's anti-American and anti-Western agenda, also condemning music, cigarettes, sex, and alcohol. This new puritanism reduced its appeal among its original, less-ideological supporters in Uzbekistan—one downside to switching missions.

Even Osama bin Laden himself has changed his objectives over time. The Saudi terrorist inherited an organization devoted to fighting Soviet forces in Afghanistan. But he turned it into a flexible group of ruthless warriors ready to fight on behalf of multiple causes. His first call to holy war, issued in 1992, urged believers to kill American soldiers in Saudi Arabia and the Horn of Africa but barely mentioned Palestine. The second, issued in 1996, was a 40-page document listing atrocities and injustices committed against Muslims, mainly by Western powers. With the release of his third manifesto in February 1998, however, bin Laden began urging his followers to start deliberately targeting American civilians, rather than soldiers. (Some al Qaeda members were reportedly distressed by this shift to civilian targets and left the group.) Although this third declaration mentioned the Palestinian struggle, it was still only one among a litany of grievances. Only in bin Laden's fourth call to arms—issued to the al Jazeera network on October 7, 2001, to coincide with the U.S. aerial bombardment of Afghanistan—did he emphasize Israel's occupation of Palestinian lands and the suffering of Iraqi children under UN sanctions, concerns broadly shared in the Islamic world. By extending his appeal, bin Laden sought to turn the war on terrorism into a war between all of Islam and the West. The events of September 11, he charged, split the world into two camps—believers and infidels—and the time had come for "every Muslim to defend his religion."

One of the masterminds of the September 11 attacks, Ramzi bin al-Shibh, later described violence as "the tax" that Muslims must pay "for gaining authority on earth." This comment points to yet another way that al Qaeda's ends have mutated over the years. In his putative autobiography, Zawahiri calls the "New World Order" a source of humiliation for Muslims. It is better, he says, for the youth of Islam to carry arms and defend their religion with pride and dignity than to submit to this humiliation. One of al Qaeda's aims in fighting the West, in other words, has become to restore the dignity of humiliated young Muslims. This idea is similar to the anticolonialist theoretician Frantz Fanon's notion that violence is a "cleansing force" that frees oppressed youth from "inferiority complexes," "despair," and "inaction," making them fearless and restoring their self-respect. The real target audience of violent attacks is therefore not necessarily the victims and their sympathizers, but the perpetrators and their sympathizers. Violence becomes a way to bolster support for the organization and the movement it represents. Hence, among the justifications for "special operations" listed in al Qaeda's terrorist manual are "bringing new members to the organization's ranks" and "boosting Islamic morale and lowering that of the enemy." The United States may have become al Qaeda's principal enemy, but raising the morale of Islamist fighters and their sympathizers is now one of its principal goals.

FRIENDS OF CONVENIENCE

APART FROM THE FLEXIBILITY of its mission, another explanation for al Qaeda's remarkable staying power is its willingness to forge broad—and sometimes unlikely—alliances. In an effort to expand his network, bin Laden created the International Islamic Front for

Jihad Against the Jews and Crusaders (IIF) in February 1998. In addition to bin Laden and EIJ's Zawahiri, members included the head of Egypt's Gama'a al Islamiya, the secretary-general of the Pakistani religious party known as the Jamiat-ul-Ulema-e-Islam (JUI), and the head of Bangladesh's Jihad Movement. Later, the IIF was expanded to include the Pakistani jihadi organizations Lashkar-e-Taiba, Harkat-ul-Mujahideen, and Sipah-e-Sahaba Pakistan, the last an anti-Shi'a sectarian party. Senior al Qaeda lieutenant Abu Zubaydah was captured at a Lashkar-e-Taiba safe house in Faisalabad in March 2002, suggesting that some of Lashkar-e-Taiba's members are facilitating and assisting the movement of al Qaeda members in Pakistan. And Indian sources claim that Lashkar-e-Taiba is now trying to play a role similar to that once played by al Qaeda itself, coordinating and in some cases funding pro-bin Laden networks, especially in Southeast Asia and the Persian Gulf.

In addition to its formal alliances through the IIF, bin Laden's organization has also nurtured ties and now works closely with a variety of still other groups around the world, including Ansar al Islam, based mainly in Iraq and Europe; Jemaah Islamiah in Southeast Asia; Abu Sayyaf and the Moro Islamic Liberation Front in the Philippines; and many Pakistani jihadi groups. In some cases, al Qaeda has provided these allies with funding and direction. In others, the groups have shared camps, operatives, and logistics. Some "franchise groups," such as Jemaah Islamiah, have raised money for joint operations with al Qaeda.

Perhaps most surprising (and alarming) is the increasing evidence that al Qaeda, a Sunni organization, is now cooperating with the Shi'a group Hezbollah, considered to be the most sophisticated terrorist group in the world. Hezbollah, which enjoys backing from Syria and Iran, is based in southern Lebanon and in the lawless "triborder" region of South America, where Paraguay, Brazil, and Argentina meet. The group has also maintained a fundraising presence in the United States since the 1980s. According to the CIA's Tenet, however, the group has lately stepped up its U.S. activities and was recently spotted "casing and surveilling American facilities." Although low-level cooperation between al Qaeda and Hezbollah has been evident for some time—their logistical cooperation was revealed in the trial of al Qaeda operatives involved in the 1998 embassy bombing attacks in east Africa—the two groups have formed a much closer relationship since al Qaeda was evicted from its base in Afghanistan. Representatives of the two groups have lately met up in Lebanon, Paraguay, and an unidentified African country. According to a report in Israel's *Ha'aretz* newspaper, Imad Mughniyah, who directs Hezbollah in the triborder area, has also been appointed by Iran to coordinate the group's activities with Hamas and Palestinian Islamic Jihad.

The triborder region of South America has become the world's new Libya, a place where terrorists with widely disparate ideologies— Marxist Colombian rebels, American white supremacists, Hamas, Hezbollah, and others—meet to swap tradecraft. Authorities now worry that the more sophisticated groups will invite the American radicals to help them. Moneys raised for terrorist organizations in the United States are often funneled through Latin America, which has also become an important stopover point for operatives entering the United States. Reports that Venezuela's President Hugo Chávez is allowing Colombian rebels and militant Islamist groups to operate in his country are meanwhile becoming more credible, as are claims that Venezuela's Margarita Island has become a terrorist haven.

As these developments suggest and Tenet confirms, "mixing and matching of capabilities, swapping of training, and the use of common facilities" have become the hallmark of professional terrorists today. This fact has been borne out by the leader of a Pakistani jihadi group affiliated with al Qaeda, who recently told me that informal contacts between his group and Hezbollah, Hamas, and others have become common. Operatives with particular skills loan themselves out to different groups, with expenses being covered by the charities that formed to fund the fight against the Soviet Union in Afghanistan.

Meanwhile, the Bush administration's claims that al Qaeda cooperated with the "infidel" (read: secular) Saddam Hussein while he was still in office are now also gaining support, and from a surprising source. Hamid Mir, bin Laden's "official biographer" and an analyst for al Jazeera, spent two weeks filming in Iraq during the war. Unlike most reporters, Mir wandered the country freely and was not embedded with U.S. troops. He reports that he has "personal knowledge" that one of Saddam's intelligence operatives, Farooq Hijazi, tried to contact bin Laden in Afghanistan as early as 1998. At that time, bin Laden was publicly still quite critical of the Iraqi leader, but he had become far more circumspect by November 2001, when Mir interviewed him for the third time. Mir also reports that he met a number of Hezbollah operatives while in Iraq and was taken to a recruitment center there.

NEW-STYLE NETWORKS

AL QAEDA seems to have learned that in order to evade detection in the West, it must adopt some of the qualities of a "virtual network": a style of organization used by American right-wing extremists for operating in environments (such as the United States) that have effective law enforcement agencies. American antigovernment groups refer to this style as "leaderless resistance." The idea was popularized by Louis Beam, the self-described ambassador-at-large, staff propagandist, and "computer terrorist to the Chosen" for Aryan Nations, an American neo-Nazi group. Beam writes that hierarchical organization is extremely dangerous for insurgents, especially in "technologically advanced societies where electronic surveillance can often penetrate the structure, revealing its chain of command." In leaderless organizations, however, "individuals and groups operate independently of each other, and never report to a central headquarters or single leader for direction or instruction, as would those who belong to a typical pyramid organization." Leaders do not issue orders or pay operatives; instead, they inspire small cells or individuals to take action on their own initiative.

Lone-wolf terrorists typically act out of a mixture of ideology and personal grievances. For example, Mir Aimal Kansi, the Pakistani national who shot several CIA employees in 1993, described his actions as "between jihad and tribal revenge"—jihad against America for its support of Israel and revenge against the CIA, which he apparently felt had mistreated his father during Afghanistan's war against the Soviets. Meanwhile, John Allen Muhammad, one of the alleged "Washington snipers," reportedly told a friend that he endorsed the September 11 attacks and disapproved of U.S. policy toward Muslim states, but he appears to have been principally motivated by anger at his ex-wife for keeping him from seeing their children, and some of his victims seem to have been personal enemies. As increasingly powerful weapons become more and more available, lone wolves, who face few political constraints, will become more of a threat, whatever their primary motivation.

The Internet has also greatly facilitated the spread of "virtual" subcultures and has substantially increased the capacity of loosely networked terrorist organizations. For example, Beam's essay on the virtues of "leaderless resistance" has long been available on the Web and, according to researcher Michael Reynolds, has been highlighted by radical Muslim sites. Islamist Web sites also offer on-line training courses in the production of explosives and urge visitors to take action on their own. The "encyclopedia of jihad," parts of which are available on-line, provides instructions for creating "clandestine activity cells," with units for intelligence, supply, planning and preparation, and implementation.

The obstacles these Web sites pose for Western law enforcement are obvious. In one article on the "culture of jihad" available on-line, a Saudi Islamist urges bin Laden's sympathizers to take action without waiting for instructions. "I do not need to meet the Sheikh and ask his permission to carry out some operation," he writes, "the same as I do not need permission to pray, or to think about killing the Jews and the Crusaders that gather on our lands." Nor does it make any difference whether bin Laden is alive or dead: "There are a thousand bin Ladens in this nation. We should not abandon our way, which the Sheikh has paved for you, regardless of the existence of the Sheikh or his absence." And according to U.S. government officials, al Qaeda now uses chat rooms to recruit Latino Muslims with U.S. passports, in the belief that they will arouse less suspicion as operatives than would Arab-Americans. Finally, as the late neo-Nazi William Pierce once told me, using the Web to recruit "leaderless resisters" offers still another advantage: it attracts better-educated young people than do more traditional methods, such as radio programs.

Already the effects of these leaderless cells have been felt. In February 2002, Ahmed Omar Saeed Sheikh, the British national who was recently sentenced to death for his involvement in the abduction and murder of *Wall Street Journal* reporter Daniel Pearl, warned his Pakistani interrogators that they would soon confront the threat of small cells, working independently of the known organizations that Pakistani President Pervez Musharraf had vowed to shut down. Sure enough, soon after Omar Sheikh made this threat, unidentified terrorists killed 5 people in an Islamabad church known to be frequented by U.S. embassy personnel, and another group killed 11 French military personnel in Karachi in May. And in July, still other unidentified terrorists detonated a truck bomb at the entrance of the U.S. consulate in Karachi, killing 12 Pakistanis.

JOINING THE FAMILY

VIRTUAL LINKS are only part of the problem; terrorists, including members of bin Laden's IIF, have also started to forge ties with traditional organized crime groups, especially in India. One particularly troubling example is the relationship established between Omar Sheikh and an ambitious Indian gangster named Aftab Ansari. Asif Reza Khan, the "chief executive" for Ansari's Indian operations, told interrogators that he received military training at a camp in Khost, Afghanistan, belonging to Lashkar-e-Taiba, and that "leaders of different militant outfits in Pakistan were trying to use his network for the purpose of jihad, whereas [Ansari] was trying to use the militants' networks for underworld operations."

Khan told his interrogators that the don provided money and hideouts to his new partners, in one case transferring $100,000 to Omar Sheikh—money that Omar Sheikh, in turn, wired to Muhammad Atta, the lead hijacker in the September 11 attacks. According to Khan, Ansari viewed the $100,000 gift as an "investment" in a valuable relationship.

Still another set of unlikely links has sprung up in American prisons, where Saudi charities now fund organizations that preach radical Islam. According to Warith Deen Umar, who hired most of the Muslim chaplains currently active in New York State prisons, prisoners who are recent Muslim converts are natural recruits for Islamist organizations. Umar, incidentally, told *The Wall Street Journal* that the September 11 hijackers should be honored as martyrs, and he traveled to Saudi Arabia twice as part of an outreach program designed to spread Salafism (a radical Muslim movement) in U.S. prisons.

Another organization now active in U.S. prisons is Jamaat ul-Fuqra, a terrorist group committed to purifying Islam through violence. (Daniel Pearl was abducted and murdered in Pakistan while attempting to interview the group's leader, Sheikh Gilani, to investigate the claim that Richard Reid—who attempted to blow up an international flight with explosives hidden in his shoes—was acting under Gilani's orders.) The group functions much like a cult in the United States; members live in poverty in compounds, some of which are heavily armed. Its members have been convicted of fraud, murder, and several bombings, but so far, most of their crimes have been relatively small scale. Clement Rodney Hampton-El, however, convicted of participating with Omar Abdel Rahman in a 1993 plot to blow up New York City landmarks, was linked to the group, and U.S. law enforcement authorities worry that the Fuqra has since come under the influence of al Qaeda.

Still another surprising source of al Qaeda recruits is Tablighi Jamaat (TJ), a revivalist organization that aims at creating better Muslims through "spiritual jihad": good deeds, contemplation, and proselytizing. According to the historian Barbara Metcalf, TJ has traditionally functioned as a self-help group, much like Alcoholics Anonymous, and most specialists claim that it is no more prone to violence than are the Seventh-Day Adventists, with whom TJ is frequently compared. But several Americans known to have trained in al Qaeda camps were brought to Southwest Asia by TJ and appear to have been recruited into jihadi organizations while traveling under TJ auspices. For example, Jose Padilla (an American now being held as an "enemy combatant" for planning to set off a "dirty" radiological bomb in the United States) was a member of TJ, as were Richard Reid and John Walker Lindh (the so-called American Taliban). According to prosecutors, the "Lackawanna Six" group (an alleged al Qaeda sleeper cell from a Buffalo, New York, suburb) similarly first went to Pakistan to receive TJ religious training before proceeding to the al Farooq training camp in Afghanistan. A Pakistani TJ member told me that jihadi groups openly recruit at the organization's central headquarters in Raiwind, Pakistan, including at the mosque. And TJ members in Boston say that a lot of Muslims end up treating the group, which is now active in American inner cities and prisons, as a gateway to jihadi organizations.

As such evidence suggests, although it may have been founded to create better individuals, TJ has produced offshoots that have evolved into more militant outfits. In October 1995, Pakistani authorities uncovered a military plot to assassinate Prime Minister Benazir Bhutto and establish a theocracy. Most of the officers involved in the attempted coup were members of TJ. The group is said to have been strongly influenced by retired Lieutenant General Javed Nasir, who served as Pakistan's intelligence chief from 1990 to 1993 but was sacked under pressure from the United States for his support of militant Islamists around the world.

Totalitarian Islamist revivalism has become the ideology of the dystopian new world order. In an earlier era, radicals might have described their grievances through other ideological lenses, perhaps anarchism, Marxism, or Nazism. Today they choose extreme Islamism.

Radical transnational Islam, divorced from its countries of origin, appeals to some jobless youths in depressed parts of Europe and the United States. As the French scholar Olivier Roy points out, leaders of radical Islamic groups often come from the middle classes, many of them having trained in technical fields, but their followers tend be working-class dropouts.

Focusing on economic and social alienation may help explain why such a surprising array of groups has proved willing to join forces with al Qaeda. Some white supremacists and extremist Christians applaud al Qaeda's rejectionist goals and may eventually contribute to al Qaeda missions. Already a Swiss neo-Nazi named Albert Huber has called for his followers to join forces with Islamists. Indeed, Huber sat on the board of directors of the Bank al Taqwa, which the U.S. government accuses of being a major donor to al Qaeda. Meanwhile, Matt Hale, leader of the white-supremacist World Church of the Creator, has published a book indicting Jews and Israelis as the real culprits behind the attacks of September 11. These groups, along with Horst Mahler (a founder of the radical leftist German group the Red Army Faction), view the September 11 attacks as the first shot in a war against globalization, a phenomenon that they fear will exterminate national cultures. Leaderless resisters drawn from the ranks of white supremacists or other groups are not currently capable of carrying out massive attacks on their own, but they may be if they join forces with al Qaeda.

MODERN METHODOLOGY

AL QAEDA has lately adopted innovative tactics as well as new alliances. Two new approaches are particularly alarming to intelligence officials: efforts to use surface-to-air missiles to shoot down aircraft and attempts to acquire chemical, nuclear, or biological weapons.

In November 2002, terrorists launched two shoulder-fired SA-7 missiles at an Israeli passenger jet taking off from Mombasa, Kenya, with 271 passengers on board. Investigators say that the missiles came from the same batch as those used in an earlier, also unsuccessful attack on a U.S. military jet in Saudi Arabia. And intelligence officials believe that Hezbollah contacts were used to smuggle the missiles into Kenya from Somalia.

Meanwhile, according to Barton Gellman of *The Washington Post*, documents seized in Pakistan in March 2003 reveal that al Qaeda has acquired the necessary materials for producing botulinum and salmonella toxins and the chemical agent cyanide—and is close to developing a workable plan for producing anthrax, a far more lethal agent. Even more worrisome is the possibility that al Qaeda, perhaps working with Hezbollah or other terrorist groups, will recruit scientists with access to sophisticated nuclear or biological weapons programs, possibly, but not necessarily, ones that are state-run.

To fight such dangerous tactics, Western governments will also need to adapt. In addition to military, intelligence, and law enforcement responses, Washington should start thinking about how U.S. policies are perceived by potential recruits to terrorist organizations. The United States too often ignores the unintended consequences of its actions, disregarding, for example, the negative message sent by Washington's ongoing neglect of Afghanistan and of the chaos in postwar Iraq. If the United States allows Iraq to become another failed state, groups both inside and outside the country that support al Qaeda's goals will benefit.

Terrorists, after all, depend on the broader population for support, and the right U.S. policies could do much to diminish the appeal of rejectionist groups. It does not make sense in such an atmosphere to keep U.S. markets closed to Pakistani textiles or to insist on protecting intellectual property with regard to drugs that needy populations in developing countries cannot hope to afford.

In countries where extremist religious schools promote terrorism, Washington should help develop alternative schools rather than attempt to persuade the local government to shut down radical madrasahs. In Pakistan, many children end up at extremist schools because their parents cannot afford the alternatives; better funding for secular education could therefore make a positive difference.

The appeal of radical Islam to alienated youth living in the West is perhaps an even more difficult problem to address. Uneasiness with liberal values, discomfort with uncertain identities, and resentment of the privileged are perennial problems in modern societies. What is new today is that radical leaders are using the tools of globalization to construct new, transnational identities based on death cults, turning grievances and alienation into powerful weapons. To fight these tactics will require getting the input not just of moderate Muslims, but of radical Islamist revivalists who oppose violence.

To prevent terrorists from acquiring new weapons, meanwhile, Western governments must make it harder for radicals to get their hands on them. Especially important is the need to continue upgrading security at vulnerable nuclear sites, many of which, in Russia and other former Soviet states, are still vulnerable to theft. The global system of disease monitoring—a system sorely tested during the SARS epidemic—should also be upgraded, since biological attacks may be difficult to distinguish from natural outbreaks. Only by matching the radical innovation shown by professional terrorists such as al Qaeda— and by showing a similar willingness to adapt and adopt new methods and new ways of thinking—can the United States and its allies make themselves safe from the ongoing threat of terrorist attack.

Counterterrorism After Al Qaeda

Paul R. Pillar

THE FIGHT AGAINST Osama bin Laden's Al Qaeda, the principal terrorist menace to U.S. interests since the mid-1990s, has come a long way. The disciplined, centralized organization that carried out the September 11 attacks is no more. Most of the group's senior and midlevel leaders are either incarcerated or dead, while the majority of those still at large are on the run and focused at least as much on survival as on offensive operations. Bin Laden and his senior deputy, Ayman al-Zawahiri, have survived to this point but have been kept on the run and in hiding, impairing their command and control of what remains of the organization. Al Qaeda still has the capacity to inflict lethal damage, but the key challenges for current counterterrorism efforts are not as much Al Qaeda as what will follow Al Qaeda.

This emerging primary terrorist threat has much in common with Al Qaeda in that it involves the same global network of mostly Sunni Islamic extremists of which bin Laden has been the best known voice. "Al Qaeda" is often broadly applied to the entire terrorist network that threatens U.S. interests although, in fact, the network extends beyond members of this particular organization. The roots of this brand of extremism, if not its most visible advocates and centralized structure, remain very much alive and in some cases are growing deeper. They include the closed economic and political

This article originally appeared in the Summer 2004 issue of *The Washington Quarterly*. ©2003 by the Center for Strategic and International Studies (CSIS) and the Massachusetts Institute of Technology.

systems in much of the Muslim world that deny many young adults the opportunity to build better lives for themselves and, often, the political representation to voice their grievances peacefully over the lack of such opportunity. Among other lasting causal factors behind the rise of Islamist terrorism are the paucity of credible alternatives to militant Islam as vehicles of opposition to the established order as well as widespread opposition toward U.S. policies within and toward the Muslim world, especially the U.S. position on the Israeli-Palestinian conflict and, more recently, the invasion and occupation of Iraq. In short, even with Al Qaeda waning, the larger terrorist threat from radical Islamists is not.

That radical Islamist threat will come from an eclectic array of groups, cells, and individuals. Those fragments of Al Qaeda that continue to carry on bin Laden's malevolent cause and operate under local leaders as central direction weakens will remain part of the mix. Also increasingly part of the greater terrorist network are like-minded but nameless groups associated with Al Qaeda, such as the Middle Eastern organization headed by Abu Musab al-Zarqawi, and regionally based groups with established identities such as the Iraq-centered Ansar al-Islam and the Southeast Asian Jemaah Islamiya. Many of these groups have local objectives but share the transnational anti-Americanism of the larger network. Finally, individuals best labeled simply as jihadists, who carry no group membership card but move through and draw support from the global network of like-minded radical Islamists, are also part of the picture. From their ranks, some will likely emerge with the leadership skills needed to organize operational cells and conduct terrorist attacks.

In a word, the transformation of the terrorist threat from the Al Qaeda of September 11, 2001, to the mixture described above is one of decentralization. The initiative, direction, and support for anti-U.S. terrorism will come from more, and more widely scattered, locations than it did before. Although the breaking up of Al Qaeda lessens but does not eliminate the risks posed by particularly large, well-organized, and well-financed terrorist operations, the decentralization of the threat poses offsetting problems for collecting and analyzing related intelligence, enlisting foreign support to counter it, and sustaining the United States' own commitment to combat it while avoiding further damage to U.S. relations with the Muslim world. For these reasons, the counterterrorism challenges after the defeat of Al Qaeda may very well be even more complex than they were before.

UNCERTAIN TARGETS FOR INTELLIGENCE

THE SMALL, SECRETIVE NATURE of terrorist plots and the indeterminate nature of the target—likely to become an even greater problem as the Islamic terrorist threat further decentralizes—have always made terrorism a particularly difficult target subject. The mission of intelligence in counterterrorism is not only to monitor known terrorists and terrorist groups but also to uncover any individuals or groups who might conduct a terrorist attack against the United States and its interests. The greater the number of independent actors and centers of terrorist planning and operations, the more difficult that mission becomes. Exhortations to the intelligence community to penetrate terrorist groups are useless if the groups that need to be penetrated have not even been identified.

The U.S. intelligence community's experience a decade ago may help it adjust to the transformation currently underway. Prior to the 1993 World Trade Center (WTC) bombing, the terrorist threat against the United States was thought of chiefly in terms of known, named, discrete groups such as the Lebanese Hizballah. The principal analytical challenges involved identifying the structure and strength of each group as well as making sense of the pseudonymous "claim names" commonly used to assume responsibility for attacks. The 1993 WTC bombing and the subsequent rolled-up plot to bomb several other New York City landmarks introduced the concept of ad hoc terrorists: nameless cells of radicals who come together for the sole purpose of carrying out a specific attack.

The term "ad hoc" was subsequently discarded as too casual and as not reflecting the links to the wider network that intelligence work through the mid-1990s gradually uncovered. Even with those links, however, the New York plots were examples of a decentralized threat in that they were evidently initiated locally. As demonstrated by the shoestring budget on which the 1993 WTC bombers operated, the plots were not directed and financed by bin Laden from a lair in Sudan or South Asia but rather by the operation's ringleader, Ramzi Yousef, and his still unknown financial patrons. Now, in 2004, with Al Qaeda having risen and mostly fallen, the threats that U.S. intelligence must monitor in the current decade have in a sense returned to what existed in the early 1990s; only now the threat has many more moving parts, more geographically disparate operations, and more ideological momentum.

Much, though not all, of the intelligence community's counter-terrorism efforts over the past several years can be applied to the increasingly decentralized threat the world now faces. Even the intelligence work narrowly focused on Al Qaeda has unearthed many leads and links, involving anything from telephone calls to shared apartments, that are useful in uncovering other possible centers of terrorist planning and operations. These links are central to intelligence counterterrorism efforts because linkages with known terrorists can uncover other individuals who may be terrorists themselves. Most successful U.S. efforts to disrupt terrorist organizations in the past, including the capture of most of the Al Qaeda leadership since September 11, 2001, have resulted from such link analysis.

The danger now lies in the fact that the looser the operational connections become and the less Islamist terrorism is instigated by a single figure, the harder it will be to uncover exploitable links and the more likely that the instigators of future terrorist attacks will escape the notice of U.S. intelligence. In a more decentralized network, these individuals will go unnoticed not because data on analysts' screens are misinterpreted but because they will never appear on those screens in the first place.

The September 11 plot helps to illustrate the point. Retrospective inquiries have given a great deal of attention to the tardiness in placing two of the hijackers, Khalid al-Mihdhar and Nawaf al-Hazmi, on U.S. government watch lists. Had these individuals been identified, they might have been prevented from entering the United States and launching the attack. Ironically, less attention has been paid to what made al-Mihdhar and al-Hazmi candidates for a watch list in the first place: their participation in a meeting with an Al Qaeda operative in Kuala Lumpur. U.S. intelligence acquired information about the meeting by piecing together Al Qaeda's activities in the Far East and by developing rosters of Al Qaeda intermediaries whose activities could be tracked to gain information that would provide new leads. Although skillful and creative intelligence work, it relied on linkages to a known terrorist group, Al Qaeda— linkages that existed because bin Laden and senior Al Qaeda leadership in South Asia ultimately directed and financed the terrorist operation in question. A decentralized version of the threat will not necessarily leave such a trail.

Muhammad Atta and some of the other September 11 hijackers were never even considered candidates for the watch lists because intelligence reporting had not previously associated them with known terrorists. In fact, one of Al Qaeda's criteria for selecting the hijackers almost certainly was that they were relatively clean, in that they did not have any such associations. In a more decentralized future network, such connections are even less likely.

Yet, even a decentralized terrorist threat has some linkages that can be exploited, and this will be key to intelligence community counterterrorist efforts from here on out. Within the networks of Sunni Islamic extremists, almost everyone can be linked at least indirectly, such as through their past common experiences in camps in Afghanistan, to almost everyone else. The overwhelming majority of these linkages, however, consists of only casual contacts and do not involve preparations for terrorist operations directed against the United States, as the meeting in Kuala Lumpur evidently did. No intelligence service has the resources to monitor all of these contacts, to compile the life history of every extremist who has the potential to become a terrorist, or to construct comprehensive sociograms of the radical Islamist scene. Detecting the perpetrators of the next terrorist attack against the United States will therefore have to go beyond link analysis and increasingly rely on other techniques for picking terrorists out of a crowd.

Mining of financial, travel, and other data on personal actions and circumstances other than mere association with questionable individuals and groups[1] is one such technique. The potential for such data mining goes well beyond current usage. Yet, data mining for counterterrorism purposes will always require a major investment in obtaining and manipulating the data in return for only a modest narrowing of the search for terrorists. Numerous practical difficulties in gaining access to personal information, significant privacy issues, and the lack of a reliable algorithm for processing the data all inhibit the effectiveness of this technique. The September 11 attacks, however, significantly lowered the threshold for all investments in counterterrorist operations, including data mining, making this technique worth trying even if it appears no more cost effective than it did before September 11, 2001. The Transportation Security Administration already uses profiling to screen air passengers; the intelligence community might reasonably extend this technique to include profiling of foreigners to identify possible terrorists even before they buy an airplane ticket.

It is the U.S. population and the U.S. government, not the intelligence community, that will have to make the most important adjustment concerning intelligence operations. The reality is that they will have to lower their expectations of just how much of the burden of stopping terrorists that intelligence can carry. An increasingly decentralized terrorist threat and indeterminate intelligence target will mean that an even greater number of terrorists and terrorist plots may escape the notice of intelligence services altogether. The transformation in the threat itself coupled with the inherent limits of intelligence operations implies that more of the counterterrorist burden will have to be borne by other policy instruments, from initiatives to address the reasons individuals gravitate toward terrorism in the first place to physical security measures to defeat attempted attacks.

FRAGILE INTERNATIONAL COOPERATION

THE WILLINGNESS of governments worldwide to join the campaign against terrorism has increased significantly over the last two decades—a welcome change from earlier days when many regimes, through their representatives at the United Nations General Assembly and elsewhere, were more apt to condone terrorism than to condemn it because of their support for "national liberation movements." The September 11 attacks further strengthened an apparent global antiterrorism consensus. This apparent collective commitment to counterterrorism should not be taken for granted. Despite many governments' declarations that they stand with the United States in combating terrorism, each decision by a foreign government on whether to cooperate with the United States reflects calculations about the threat that nation faces from particular terrorist groups, its relations with the United States, any incentives Washington offers for its cooperation, domestic opinion, and the potential effect of enhanced counterterrorist measures on its domestic interests. Such calculations can change, and the perceived net advantage of cooperating may be slim. In short, global cooperation against terrorism is already fragile.

Much of foreign governments' willingness to help has depended on Al Qaeda's record and menacing capabilities. The sheer enormity of the September 11 attacks and the unprecedented impact they had on the U.S. government's priorities and policies have accounted for much of the increased willingness among foreign governments to assist in efforts to combat terrorism. The threat Al Qaeda has posed to some of the governments themselves, particularly the Saudi regime, also has helped the United States gain cooperation. The bombings in Riyadh in May and November 2003 were wake-up calls that partly nullified the numerous reasons for the Saudis' sluggishness in cracking down on Islamic extremists in their midst. Most of the victims of the November bombing were Arabs of modest means; this sloppy targeting undoubtedly cost Al Qaeda some of its support in the kingdom.

Foreign cooperation will become more problematic as the issue moves beyond Al Qaeda. How will governments respond to a U.S. appeal to move against groups that have never inflicted comparable horrors on the United States or on any other nation or against groups that do not conspicuously pose the kind of threat that Al Qaeda has posed to Saudi Arabia? How can regimes be motivated to tackle Islamic groups that may represent an emerging terrorist threat but have not yet resorted to terrorism, such as the Central Asian–based Hizb al-Tahrir? Without the special glue that the attacks of September 11 provide against a centralized and directed Al Qaeda, many of the past reasons for foot-dragging in counterterrorist efforts are likely to reassert themselves. These reasons include the sympathy that governments or their populations feel for many of the anti-Western or anti-imperialist themes in whose name terrorists claim to act, an aversion to doing Washington's bidding against interests closer to home, and a general reluctance to rock local boats.

Problems that the United States has already encountered in dealing with Lebanese Hizballah[2] illustrate some of the difficulties in more generally enlisting foreign help against terrorist groups—even highly capable groups—other than Al Qaeda. Deputy Secretary of State Richard Armitage once called Hizballah the "A-team" of international terrorism;[3] the group's 1983 bombing of U.S. Marine barracks in Beirut is second only to the events of September 11, 2001, in the number of American deaths attributable to a terrorist attack. Hizballah's terrorist apparatus, led by its longtime chief Imad Mughniyah, remains formidable today. The dominant view of Hizballah in Lebanon and elsewhere in the Middle East, however, is that the group is a legitimate participant in Lebanese politics: the group holds seats in Parliament and provides social services within the country. Despite the events two decades ago in Lebanon, including other bombings and a series of kidnappings of Westerners, Hizballah's accepted political status has prevented U.S. officials from effectively appealing for cooperation against Hizballah in the way that the September 11 attacks have allowed them to appeal for cooperation against Al Qaeda. Notwithstanding the major potential terrorist threat it poses, Hizballah has not been clearly implicated in any attack on Americans since the bombing of Khobar Towers eight years ago.

An underlying limitation to foreign willingness to cooperate with the United States on antiterrorist efforts is the skepticism among foreign publics and even elites that the most powerful nation on the planet needs to be preoccupied with small bands of radicals. Even the depth of the trauma that the September 11 attacks caused the American public does not seem to be fully appreciated in many areas overseas, particularly in the Middle East. In addition, the skepticism is likely to be much greater when the U.S. preoccupation is no longer with the group that carried out the September 11 attacks.

Any reduced foreign support for the campaign against terrorism will not be clear or sudden. Certainly, no foreign government will declare that it now supports the terrorists. Instead, foreign governments may be a little slower to act, a little less forthcoming with information, or slightly more apt to cite domestic impediments to cooperation. Whether counterterrorism cooperation weakens, therefore, will rest largely on whether and how Washington responds to the concerns and needs of its foreign partners. As antiterrorist cooperation becomes increasingly more difficult to obtain and more vulnerable to frictions over other issues, sustaining such cooperation will require increased sensitivity to foreign interests.

MUSLIMS' SUSPICIONS

SKEPTICISM AND DISTRUST among Muslims across the world about U.S. counterterrorist efforts have impeded international cooperation and may become an even bigger problem in the post–Al Qaeda era. With the perpetrators of the September 11 attacks disabled and Muslims—especially Muslims claiming to act in the name of their religion—still dominating international terrorism, Muslims will still dominate Washington's counterterrorist target list. This fact will continue to encourage questions about whether the so-called U.S. war on terrorism is really a war on Islam. Many Muslims will ask whether a sustained counterterrorist campaign has less to do with fighting terrorism than with maintaining the political status quo in countries with pro-U.S. regimes. Other Muslims will see the campaign as many already see it: as part of a religiously based war between the Muslim world and a Judeo-Christian West.

The "war on terrorism" terminology exacerbates this problem, partly because a war is most clearly understood as a war against somebody rather than a metaphorical war against a tactic. The fact that counterterrorist operations have been aimed primarily at a particular group, Al Qaeda, has minimized this problem thus far. The less the fight is conducted against a single named foe, the greater the problem of misinterpreting the term "war." The problem has been exacerbated by extension of the "war on terrorism" label to the invasion and occupation of Iraq. Even though much of the violence that has plagued Iraq since the operation began is unmistakably attributable to terrorism, the U.S. government undertook the military operation in Iraq primarily for reasons other than counterterrorism, feeding Muslim misperceptions and fears that the United States also has ulterior motives every other time it talks about fighting terrorism.

Such perceptions among Muslims will strengthen the roots of the very Islamist terrorism that already poses the principal threat to U.S. interests. They will encourage a sense that the Muslim world as a whole is in a struggle with the Judeo-Christian West and foster a view of the United States as the chief adversary of Muslims worldwide. Given the fact that Islamist extremism is likely to continue to be the driving force behind significant terrorist threats to U.S. interests, fighting terrorism without the effort being perceived simply as a war against Muslims may be a challenge that can only be lessened and not altogether avoided. President George W. Bush and senior U.S. officials have been careful to disavow any antipathy toward Muslims, which has helped to a certain extent. Most Muslims' attitudes will be shaped more by deeds than by words, however, which means that U.S. policies toward Iraq and the Arab-Israeli conflict in particular will be especially influential.

MAINTAINING THE COMMITMENT

THE GREATEST FUTURE CHALLENGE to the U.S. counterterrorist efforts that may emerge with a more decentralized terrorist threat is the ability to sustain the country's own determination to fight it. The American public has shown that its commitment to counterterrorism can be just as fickle as that of foreign publics. Over the past quarter century, the U.S. population and government has given variable attention, priority, and resources to U.S. counterterrorist programs, with interest and efforts spiking in the aftermath of a major terrorist incident and declining as time passes without an attack.

Important to keep in mind about the strong U.S. attention to counterterrorism during the last three years is that it took a disaster of the dimensions of September 11, 2001, to generate. Although intended to topple the twin towers and kill thousands, the 1993 WTC bombing sparked nothing near a similar amount of attention. Bin Laden and the prowess his group demonstrated with overseas attacks garnered full appreciation among U.S. government specialists of Al Qaeda's intentions and capabilities by at least the late 1990s but still remained comparably unnoticed by the greater U.S. public and government. U.S. citizens and their elected leaders and representatives respond far more readily to dramatic events in their midst than to warnings and analysis about threatening events yet to occur. The further the events of September 11 fade into the past, the more difficult it will be to keep Americans focused on the danger posed by terrorism, especially that posed by terrorists other than the perpetrators of the WTC and Pentagon attacks.

The U.S. response to the March 2004 bombing of commuter trains in Madrid suggests how difficult it is to energize or reenergize Americans about counterterrorism. (Early investigation of the attack indicated that it was also a good example of the decentralized Islamist terrorist threat, being the work of Muslim radicals with only loose associations with Al Qaeda.) Commentary in the United States focused less on the continued potency of the global terrorist threat than on inter-allied differences over the Iraq war, with charges of "appeasement" leveled against Spanish voters for ousting the governing party in an election held three days after the attack. For most Americans, the difference between terrorism inside the United States and terrorism against even a close ally is huge, with only the former capable of boosting their commitment to counterterrorism.

Here again, the "war on terrorism" metaphor appears problematic. Americans tend to think in non-Clausewitzian terms, in which war and peace are markedly different and clearly separated states of being. War entails special sacrifices and rules that the United States does not want to endure in peacetime. Peace means demobilization, relaxation of the nation's guard, and a return to nonmartial pursuits. In U.S. history, in particular, peace has usually meant either victory or withdrawal and a rejection of the reasons for having gone to war in the first place, such as with the Vietnam War. Americans are not accustomed to the concept of a war that is necessary and waged with good reason but offers no prospect of ending with a clear peace and especially a clear victory.[4]

U.S. leaders have conveyed some of the right cautions to the public. Secretary of Defense Donald Rumsfeld correctly observed that the war on terrorism will not end with a surrender on the deck of the *USS Missouri*.5 Attitudes in the United States, however, probably will be shaped less by such words of caution than by the historical conception of war and peace. Moreover, not having a clear end is not the same as having no end—and the latter is, for practical purposes, what the United States faces in countering terrorism during the years ahead.

In fact, an end, whether clear or not so clear, will be even more elusive in the fight against terrorism than it was during the Cold War. Though the Cold War did not conclude with the signing of any surrender agreement on a battleship, its end was nonetheless fairly distinct, highlighted by the dismantling of the Berlin Wall in November 1989 and the dissolution of the Soviet Union in December 1991. It also entailed an indisputable victory for the West, achieved with the collapse of a single arch foe. Success in counter-terrorism offers no such prospect.

The sense of being at war has been sustained thus far not only by war on terrorism rhetoric but also by certain practices that resemble those used in real shooting wars of the past, such as indefinite detention of prisoners without recourse to civilian courts. Although quite useful in mustering support for the invasion, the application of the "war on terrorism" label to the campaign in Iraq will compound the difficulty in sustaining domestic public support for counter-terrorism in the post–Al Qaeda era. Even if the reconstruction and democratization of Iraq go well, the fact that this campaign will not bring an end to anti-U.S. terrorist attacks elsewhere might lead many in the United States to question whether the sacrifices made in the name of fighting terrorists had been worthwhile. With so much attention having been paid to state sponsorship of terrorists, and to one (now eliminated) state sponsor in particular, further appeals to make still more sacrifices to defeat disparate and often nameless groups are apt to confuse many U.S. citizens.

More specifically, an unfavorable outcome in Iraq would mean that the Bush administration could face an increase in skepticism about the credibility of warnings concerning threats to U.S. security, including terrorist threats. Meanwhile, the existence of a specific, recognizable, hated terrorist enemy has helped the U.S. population retain its focus. As long as Al Qaeda exists, even in its current, severely weakened form, it will serve that function. Yet, when will Al Qaeda be perceived as having ceased to exist? The group's demise will be nowhere near as clear as, say, the fall of a government.

For the U.S. public, the signal that terrorism has been eliminated as a threat is likely to be the death or capture of bin Laden. Americans tend to personalize their conflicts by concentrating their animosity on a single despised leader, a role that Adolf Hitler and Saddam Hussein played at different times in history. This personalized perspective often leads to an overestimation of the effect of taking out the hated leader, as if the conflict were a game of chess in which checkmate of the king ends the contest. The euphoria following Saddam's capture in December 2003 is an example. Bin Laden, although on the run since 2001, probably has played a role in Al Qaeda's operations almost as limited and indirect as Saddam's influence was on the Iraqi insurgency during his eight months in hiding. Yet, this is where any similarities with Iraq ends. The elimination of bin Laden, if followed by several months without another major Al Qaeda operation against the United States, would lead many in the United States to believe that the time had come to declare victory in the war on terrorism and move on to other concerns. Meanwhile, bin Laden's death would not end or even cripple the radical Islamist movement. Fragments of the organization are likely to spread, subdivide, and inject themselves into other parts of the worldwide Islamist network, like a metastasizing cancer that lives on with sometimes lethal effects even after the original tumor has been excised.

CONTEXT AND CONSEQUENCES

ANY EROSION in the U.S. commitment to counterterrorism that may occur in the years ahead will depend not only on popular perceptions (or misperceptions) of the terrorist threat but also on the broader policy environment in which national security decisions are made. Available resources constitute part of that environment. The resources devoted to counterterrorist operations may decline not because of a specific decision to reduce them but because any further reductions in spending for national security would reduce funds available for counterterrorism. Recent surges in both defense spending and budget deficits make some such reductions likely during the next several years. Departmental comptrollers seeking to spread the pain of those budget cuts will inflict pain on counterterrorist programs along with everything else.

Controversies over privacy and civil liberties constitute another part of the policy environment. The United States has already experienced a backlash against some provisions of the principal post-September 11 counterterrorist legislation, the USA Patriot Act. In the wake of the attacks, the U.S. government's investigative powers expanded in some ways that would have been unthinkable earlier. As the clear danger represented by Al Qaeda appears to recede, pressures to roll back those powers will increase.

Any diminution, for whatever combination of reasons, of the priority the United States gives to counterterrorist operations will have consequences that go well beyond specific counterterrorist programs. At home, the impact would be seen in everything from reduced vigilance by baggage screeners to less tolerance by citizens for the daily inconveniences brought about by stricter security measures. Abroad, a weaker commitment to counterterrorism on the part of the U.S. public would make it more difficult for U.S. diplomats to insist on cooperation from foreign governments.

How long any reduction of the U.S. commitment to counterterrorism lasts depends on how much time passes before the next major terrorist attack against U.S. interests, especially the next such attack on U.S. soil. Time, as always, is more on the side of the terrorist, whose patience and historical sense is greater than that of the average American. Americans' perception of the threat almost certainly will decline more rapidly than the threat itself.

The United States thus faces during the next several years an unfortunate combination of a possibly premature celebration along with a continuing and complicating terrorist threat. The counterterrorist successes against Al Qaeda thus far have been impressive and important, and the capture or death of bin Laden will unleash a popular reaction that probably will be nothing short of ecstatic. That joy could be a harmful diversion, however, from attention that will be needed more than ever in the face of remaining problems: difficulty in cementing the counterterrorist cooperation of foreign partners, antagonism and alienation within the Muslim world that breeds more terrorists, and added complexity for intelligence services charged with tracking the threat.

The chief counterterrorist problem confronting U.S. leaders in the years ahead will be a variation on an old challenge: sustaining a national commitment to fighting terrorism even in the absence of a well-defined and clearly perceived danger. The demise of Al Qaeda will make the need for that commitment less apparent to most U.S. citizens, even though the danger will persist in a different form. Political leaders will bear the heavy burden of instilling that commitment, and they will have to do so with analysis, education, and their powers of persuasion, not just with symbols and war cries. No doubt, that will be a very difficult task.

Endnotes

1. Paul R. Pillar, "Statement to Joint Inquiry of the Senate Select Committee on Intelligence and the House Permanent Select Committee on Intelligence," Washington, D.C., October 8, 2002. www.cia.gov/nic/testimony_8oct2002.html (accessed March 20, 2004).

2. See Daniel Byman, "Should Hezbollah Be Next?" *Foreign Affairs* Vol. 82, no. 6 (November/December 2003): 54–66.

3. Office of International Information Programs, U.S. Department of State, "Conditions Underlying Conflict Must Be Addressed, Armitage Says," September 5, 2002. http://usinfo.state.gov/topical/pol/terror/02090504.htm (accessed March 20, 2004) (speech and question and answer session with Deputy Secretary of State Richard Armitage at the U.S. Institute of Peace, Washington, D.C., September 5, 2002).

4. One of the more thoughtful statements that looks to a "victory" against terrorism is found in Gabriel Schoenfeld, "Could September 11 Have Been Averted?" *Commentary* 112, no. 5 (December 2001): 21–29. See also *Commentary* 113, no. 2 (February 2002): 12–16 (subsequent correspondence about Schoenfeld's article).

5. Donald Rumsfeld, interview, *Face the Nation*, CBS, September 23, 2001.

Not a Diversion

Reuel Marc Gerecht

"I DON'T FAULT George Bush for doing too much in the war on terror, as some do. I believe that he's done too little and done some things that he didn't have to. When the focus of the war on terror was appropriately in Afghanistan and on breaking al Qaeda, President Bush shifted his focus to Iraq and to Saddam Hussein. He pushed away our allies at a time when we needed them the most. He hasn't pursued a strategy to win the hearts and minds of people around the world, and win the war of ideas against the radical ideology of Osama bin Laden."

So spoke Senator John Kerry on March 15. This could, of course, have been Richard Clarke, the former counterterrorism chief, or Zbigniew Brzezinski and Brent Scowcroft, the former national security advisers who often do tandem "realist" critiques. Or it could have been Al Franken, the liberal comedian-turned-less-witty-broadcaster, or Patrick Buchanan, the standard-bearer of conservative blue-collar America. From the far left to the far right, a common theme has developed among those who opposed the Iraq war: The campaign against Saddam Hussein diverted us from the battle against al Qaeda in Afghanistan and beyond. Indeed, the invasion and occupation of Iraq has made, to quote Clarke, "America less secure and strengthen[ed] the broader radical Islamic-terrorist movement."

Of course, this view did not occur to all of the above before March 2003—if John Kerry actually believed back then that the war would imperil America's national security, then his vote for it was inexcusably

---

This article originally appeared in the April 12-19, 2004, issue of *The Weekly Standard* ©2004.

reckless (Howard Dean's logic was at least impeccable). But retrospective clairvoyance, fortified by a good sense for the jugular, has won the day. If you can collapse the central pillar of the Bush war presidency, the odds are good that you can win in November. Politics aside, do these folks have a point? There are always unintended, adverse consequences to any military action. Could those from the Iraq war be the very ones that Clarke, the "realists," and the antiwar Democrats envision?

Not likely. Point by point, their case actually inverts the reality, often the history, of what has happened in Afghanistan, Iraq, and the rest of the Muslim Middle East. Let us start with the war in Afghanistan, before we get diverted by President Bush's preemptive campaign against Saddam Hussein.

There are certainly legitimate criticisms of the way the administration fought the war in Afghanistan. This magazine made a few, with which the White House took issue. It shouldn't be that hard to see now—it really wasn't that hard to see then—that the Pentagon moved too slowly south, that Defense Secretary Donald Rumsfeld's fascination with "new-age" warfare, where very small deployments of special forces, reinforced with awesome air power and what the British used to call "tribal levies," slowed the campaign at critical points. The real issue was never whether the United States was going to get bogged down in an Afghan quagmire, as did the Soviets in the 1980s and the British (briefly) in 1842. Victory for America, once President Bush made the decision to invade and destroy the Taliban state, was never in doubt. The issue was whether we would rapidly fracture Taliban power in Kandahar and possibly catch al Qaeda in disarray. The military brass chose not to throw much manpower at southeastern Afghanistan, the area bin Laden knew best, and to which, it strongly appears, he withdrew. Doing so surely would have cost many U.S. soldiers their lives, but it probably would have increased the odds of catching Osama bin Laden, his number two, Ayman al Zawahiri, and their inner circle and families. It is impossible to say, however, by how much the odds would have improved. With the possible exception of the deep jungles of the Amazon, the southeastern border region between Afghanistan and Pakistan is the worst area imaginable to play a lethal version of hide and seek. You could pour tens of thousands of troops into that terrain and only marginally improve the chances of finding your target.

Which brings us to Iraq. The tactics used in Afghanistan were not predicated on an ensuing war in Mesopotamia. Rightly or wrongly, Rumsfeld likes "new-age" warfare, regardless of the locale. There simply is no serious argument that the actions of the first campaign were diminished by the planning, logistics, and execution of the second a year later.

There is a pretty good case to be made that in 2001–02 the Bush administration didn't seriously pressure Pakistani president Pervez Musharraf to understand the urgent need to move aggressively against the unpatrolled tribal regions bordering Afghanistan. But again, that had nothing to do with Iraq, and everything to do with internal Pakistani politics. And America's second Gulf War certainly did not discourage Musharraf from becoming more aggressive against domestic and foreign holy warriors in 2003–04. It beggars the imagination to believe that al Qaeda's foreign holy warriors and their Pakistani sympathizers want to kill Musharraf for the war in Iraq more than they want to kill him for the war in Afghanistan and his current efforts to extinguish them and their Pakistani base of operations.

It is certainly true, as Clarke and others have charged, that the Bush administration should have done, and still should do, a lot more in reconstructing Afghanistan and in aiding those who want to reform, and eventually end, the warlord system that prevails outside of the capital, Kabul. The holy-warrior camps in Afghanistan that General Musharraf and his predecessors developed for the battle against India in Kashmir—the camps that starting in 1996 came under the control of bin Laden—could come back, particularly if there were a change of heart in Islamabad. If the Bush administration allowed this to develop—and this scenario remains hypothetical—then it would deserve to be damned for shortsightedness and gross negligence. But in the Pentagon, at the State Department, and in the National Security Council, they are well aware of the dangers. It is very hard to see this administration, any administration after 9/11, not doing the minimum necessary to keep Afghanistan from experiencing a Taliban renaissance where jihadist camps could operate.

Let's be honest: It was perfectly clear that the Bush administration was not going to invest massively in Afghanistan way before the White House made the decision to fight in Iraq (it strongly appears that former Treasury Secretary Paul O'Neill actually doesn't know anybody at Defense, for if he did, he would know, as we did, that the decision to fight in Iraq was neither quick nor easy nor foreordained). As Olivier Roy, the renowned French scholar of Afghanistan and Islamic militancy, has pointed out, the average Afghan certainly wanted us to play the *khan,* the overlord who takes care of the family. But this runs against the American grain, be it liberal or conservative. Wipe the Iraq war from history, and it remains hard to imagine Secretary Rumsfeld, the Joint Chiefs of Staff, Secretary of State Colin Powell, or President Al Gore if he were in power, putting tens of thousands of troops and tens of billions of dollars into a country that is, in virtually every way, nondeveloped. It is easy, and maybe wise, to throw large amounts of money and manpower at a developed or even developing country after it's been blown to bits by years of war and civil strife. It is much more difficult, and far less wise, to invest too quickly and too massively in a place like Afghanistan.

Baseline point: The Americans aren't going to run away from Afghanistan—odds are we will be in that country for far longer than we will be, in any force, in Iraq. With a little luck, a bit more money and manpower, and a willingness to play hardball with Pakistan in case it returns to its former ways, Afghanistan will muddle through. Certainly, we won't want to use it as an ideal case study at a Harvard seminar on American-led postwar reconstruction in the third world. But it will do. And by the time we leave, it will be perfectly clear to both Democrats and Republicans that neither the time nor the money the United States spent in Afghanistan had much to do at all with George Bush's decision to invade and occupy Iraq.

NEXT CRITICISM

WHAT ABOUT OUR ALLIES, the ones critical to our war on terror, whom we've angered and dissed? Have we not, as General Scowcroft predicted in August 2002 and as Senator Kerry regularly reminds us from the stump, just shot to hell the international system? As Scowcroft wrote in the *Wall Street Journal,* "And make no mistake, we simply cannot win that war [against bin Laden] without enthusiastic international cooperation, especially on intelligence." According to the *Washington Post,* Rand Beers, who was President Bush's senior director for counterterrorism, resigned just before the Iraq war because he thought the president's decision to invade had, among other things, "created fissures in the United States' counterterrorism alliances."

Okay, name an important intelligence service in the Middle East that doesn't have a *stronger* liaison relationship with the United States today than it had on, say, the day after Kandahar fell? Though the Central Intelligence Agency likes to think of itself as an airtight shop, we all know, given what's happened since the end of the Iraq war, that unhappy employees who don't get the foreign policies they prefer leak. And the senior grades of the Clandestine Service in particular love to leak, especially via their retired friends, when they are upset. Can anybody recall, even in the vaguest way, a planted story about anti–al Qaeda operations getting aborted because an Arab service didn't want to touch us?

Anybody hear about the French DST (internal security) or the DGSE (foreign intelligence) turning off a spigot of information about Islamic extremists? According to a senior French intelligence officer, the first and principal exchange point for the United States and continental European security services is Paris. Does this sound like the French elite (which really would like to see George Bush get demolished in Iraq and John Kerry elected) has a problem with intelligence cooperation? Anybody heard of any problems with the Spanish, who just got scorched, so the theory goes, because of their alliance with us in Iraq? How about the Russians, Pakistanis, Uzbeks, or Chinese?

A pretty good argument could be made that we would be better off if the CIA didn't have such friendly relationships with its counterparts in Tashkent, Cairo, Islamabad, or Algiers; that the short-term gain from these relationships, though undoubtedly vital at times of great urgency, fundamentally compromises us in the long-term and ultimately more important task of opening up these societies so that domestically generated Islamic extremism doesn't attack us. In any case, our intelligence and security liaison relationships have never been better. For our Middle Eastern "allies" in particular, it's as if they'd died and gone to heaven. The CIA, often more accurately addressed as Sugar Daddy, has never before come calling with so many gifts. Egypt's president-for-life Hosni Mubarak, who would strongly prefer that the United States not create a functioning democracy in Iraq, knows that his intelligence-liaison relationship with the United States is an ace in the hole. That fraternal tie will certainly stay warm as long as Mubarak thinks there's a chance that President Bush might be serious about transforming the dictatorial politics of the Middle East.

NEXT CRITICISM

GEORGE BUSH'S WAR in Iraq has inflamed Islamic opinion, radicalized more Muslim youth, and created a new legion of anti-American holy warriors. This is probably the most damning, if the most ethereal, of the charges against President Bush. Odds are, this will be the charge that Senator Kerry and his minions hurl most often at the president (the possible exception being the gravamen that George W. has neglected homeland defense).

Now, the first thing that ought to be said is that we really don't know how many jihadists got born during the first Bush presidency and the eight years of Bill Clinton. Al Qaeda slowly evolved from the Maktab al-Khadamat ("The Office of Services"), an organization started during the Soviet-Afghan War to transport Muslims, primarily Arabs, to Pakistan to join the battle against the Red Army. We really don't know how many Muslims went. If one tracks down the figures for the Maktab, all one can say for sure is that the sources on the numbers are all Pakistani and that Pakistani sources are notoriously unreliable. We have no firm idea how many of the Muslims who did go actually ever crossed into Afghanistan and fought, or how many of them stayed in Pakistan, living lives often more comfortable than those they'd had at home. (This was particularly true when it came to having wives. The cult of the Afghan woman—and there were hundreds of thousands of Afghan women in distress in Pakistan during the war—was very popular among the "jihadists.") And it is difficult to say precisely when al Qaeda became an independent, self-conscious organization developing anti-American holy warriors. This may have happened as early as 1989, or it could have been only two or three years later that a real organization developed with a clear raison d'être and a full-time staff.

The afterword of Daniel Benjamin and Steven Simon's *The Age of Sacred Terror,* which is easily the best book about the rise of bin Ladenism and the Clinton administration's response to it, tells us the following: "U.S. officials have spoken of 'tens of thousands' of individuals who were trained in the camps of Afghanistan, and Germany's intelligence chief put the number at seventy thousand, though many were trained as soldiers to fight alongside the Taliban, not as terrorists. Still the number of operatives at large is probably multiples greater than that on any other terrorist group in memory."

Benjamin and Simon were once the director and senior director for counterterrorism in the Clinton administration's National Security Council, and they, too, are highly critical of the Bush administration. I strongly suspect the numbers above are grossly exaggerated. When I visited Ahmed Shah Massoud, the legendary Tajik leader of the Northern Alliance, in the fall of 1999, he told me that he was then facing around 700 Arab Afghans. This figure fluctuated a bit, perhaps, but the Taliban never deployed more than 1,000 Arab Afghans against him.

But, for the sake of argument, let's accept the numbers suggested by Benjamin and Simon. In other words, during the eight years of Bill Clinton's presidency, when the United States studiously avoided invading Iraq, the number of Islamic holy warriors fully formed in the Afghan training camps skyrocketed. Let us recall these were the glory years of the Israeli-Palestinian peace process, when the president often worked night and day to bring conciliation and settlement to the two sides. These were the years, too, when the Americans went to the rescue of the Bosnian Muslims. And these were the times when President Clinton tried to make nice-nice with President Mohammad Khatami of Iran (of course, Sunni Muslim holy warriors might not care for this too much; but since bin Laden knew *he* hadn't blown up the American barracks at Khobar Towers in 1996, and since his contacts inside the Saudi royal family were pretty good, he might have drawn the right conclusion when the Clinton administration didn't retaliate against the real perpetrator of the Khobar bombing, the regime in Tehran—to wit, Clinton wasn't tough).

So, during the best of years—or at least, according to Clarke and Kerry, vastly better years than what followed—al Qaeda grew from scratch to an umbrella organization, drawing into its apocalyptic designs holy warriors from the Middle East, America, Europe, Africa, Latin America, and the Orient. These were the years when bin Laden promised the faithful that they, not the Americans, were the "stronger horse."

And now, according to the "realists" and antiwar Democrats, the Bush administration has made things worse. It's theoretically possible, of course. It's possible the Clinton years were less energizing to the enemy than the Bush years, when the Taliban were destroyed, bin Laden was put to chase, and al Qaeda as an organization was badly battered. It is possible that America's invasion and (temporary) occupation of Iraq will galvanize holy warriors as did the first Gulf War for an earlier generation. Professor Bernard Lewis's textual analysis showing that bin Laden used the first Gulf War as a clarion call for holy war is undeniable. (And was not the first Gulf War worth angering Islamic militants?)

But we should be enormously cautious in suggesting, as Bush's critics eagerly do, that apocalyptic holy warriors come into being primarily because of specific American actions. We know this is certainly not true for the deadliest of the Wahhabi jihadists—the highly Westernized ones reared or educated in Western Europe. These men are born from their troubled assimilation into Europe's secularized societies. And killer Sunni fundamentalism predates the first Gulf War by decades. Its evolution is attached to no specific Western event—certainly not to the creation of Israel, which in fundamentalist literature is just one more proof, a particularly painful proof since Jews are among the weakest of people in Islamic history, that civilization has gone to hell. But the primary culprits for this fall are not Europeans or Americans—"Christendom," to the fundamentalists. Christendom has been there, in one shape or another, since the beginning of the Islamic era. The real villains, according to the first few generations of fundamentalists, are the Muslims who ape Western ways. The new breed of Muslim activists, the killer elite of bin Laden's deracinated young men who know not love of country or father, have elevated the old disgust at the despotic Westernizing rulers of the Middle East—the men many "realists" still see as our friends—into a global hatred of the West and its cutting edge, the United States. These young men were coming for us, regardless of whether the Bush administration invaded Iraq. Or whether the Clinton administration quarantined and bombed Iraq for eight years. They live to kill. The most devout live to die. It is not surprising at all that Americans, particularly those who work in Washington, who are mostly good secular sorts, view so mundanely the causes of holy war.

On the biggest of issues, Benjamin and Simon are definitely right: "Democratization, however hazardous and unpredictable the process may be, is the key to eliminating sacred terror over the long term." Which is why, of course, the war in Iraq—the attempt to build a democracy on the ruins of the Middle East's most despicable regime—has been worth the blood and treasure. There were many reasons to go to war; as Robert Kagan and William Kristol recently pointed out in these pages, President Clinton and his national security adviser Sandy Berger did a very convincing job of enumerating them in their finest speeches. But a compelling reason, even if it is not one that many in the Bush administration fully understand, was bin Ladenism itself and the need to strike boldly to give us, and Muslims in the Middle East, a way out.

We should be skeptical of those voices who tell us that success in Iraq won't have serious repercussions for the rest of the Middle East (the same voices that are usually quick to point out the adverse effects of failure). The trial of Saddam Hussein, in whom many Muslims of the Middle East will see the image of their own rulers, will make gripping television, even on the anti-American Al Jazeera satellite channel. Iraq's coming great debates, for all the country's enormous problems and attendant violence, will echo through the region on television and radio. The Sunni Arabs of the region will watch Shiite Arabs, long cursed creatures, moving forward, however fitfully and slowly, toward more democracy than they themselves have ever imagined. The shame could be unbearably provocative. The now famous letter to al Qaeda from Abu Musab al Zarqawi, a Jordanian holy warrior operating in Iraq, tells, we can hope, the future of the entire region. Jihadism cannot survive people power. When the common Muslim man is responsible for his own fate, human decency and civility will win out.

The liberal *Washington Post* columnist Jackson Diehl, who writes often on the Arab world, recently provided the most honest description of what George W. Bush has wrought in the Middle East:

> The most underreported and encouraging story in the Middle East in the past year has been the emergence in public of homegrown civic movements demanding political change. Two years ago they were nonexistent or in jail. Now they are out in the open even in the most politically backward places in the region: Egypt, Saudi Arabia, and Syria. They are made up not only of intellectuals but of businessmen, women, students, teachers, and journalists. Unlike their governments—and the old school of U.S. and European Arabists—they don't believe that change should be gradual, and they reject the dictators' claim that democracy would only empower Islamic extremists. It is the delay of change, they say, that is increasingly dangerous.
>
> These people weren't created by George W. Bush. They are the homegrown answer to a decadent political order, and they ride a powerful historical current. But they will tell you frankly: The new U.S. democratization policy, far from being an unwanted imposition, has given them a voice, an audience and at least a partial shield against repression—three things they didn't have one year ago.

These words are the best retort to Richard Clarke and John Kerry. But we have no time to waste. Under any circumstances, building democracy in the Muslim Middle East will be slow. And bin Ladenism is a resilient, captivating disease. We should pray, however, that it will not take generations. It certainly won't happen at all if the Bush administration pulls back from its "forward strategy of freedom." Voluntary change in the Middle East is no change at all. But we are off to a good beginning. The war on terror had, thank God, a second act. We will all have to wait until after November to see if there will be a third. Everyone in the Middle East, but especially the holy warriors, will be watching.

Bush's Lost Year

James Fallows

I REMEMBER distinctly the way 2002 began in Washington. New Year's Day was below freezing and blustery. The next day was worse. That day, January 2, I trudged several hundred yards across the vast parking lots of the Pentagon. I was being pulled apart by the wind and was ready to feel sorry for myself, until I was shamed by the sight of miserable, frozen Army sentries at the numerous outdoor security posts that had been manned non-stop since the September 11 attacks.

I was going for an interview with Paul Wolfowitz, the deputy secretary of defense. At the time, Wolfowitz's name and face were not yet familiar worldwide. He was known in Washington for offering big-picture explanations of the Administration's foreign-policy goals—a task for which the President was unsuited, the Vice President was unavailable, and most other senior Administration officials were, for various reasons, inappropriate. The National Security Adviser, Condoleezza Rice, was still playing a background role; the Secretary of Defense, Donald Rumsfeld, was mainly dealing with immediate operational questions in his daily briefings about the war in Afghanistan; the Secretary of State, Colin Powell, was already known to be on the losing side of most internal policy struggles.

After the interview I wrote a short article about Wolfowitz and his views for the March 2002 issue of this magazine. In some ways the outlook and choices he described then still fit the world situation two and a half years later. Even at the time, the possibility that the Administration's next move in the war on terror would be against Iraq, whether or not Iraq proved to be involved in the 9/11 hijackings, was under active discussion. When talking with me Wolfowitz touched

---

This article originally appeared in the October 2004 issue of *The Atlantic Monthly.*

briefly on the case for removing Saddam Hussein, in the context of the general need to reduce tyranny in the Arab-Islamic world.

But in most ways the assumptions and tone of the conversation now seem impossibly remote. At the beginning of 2002 the United States still operated in a climate of worldwide sympathy and solidarity. A broad range of allies supported its anti-Taliban efforts in Afghanistan, and virtually no international Muslim leaders had denounced them. President Bush was still being celebrated for his eloquent speech expressing American resolve, before a joint session of Congress on September 20. His deftness in managing domestic and international symbols was typified by his hosting an end-of-Ramadan ceremony at the White House in mid-December, even as battle raged in the Tora Bora region of Afghanistan, on the Pakistani border. At the start of 2002 fewer than 10,000 U.S. soldiers were deployed overseas as part of the war on terror, and a dozen Americans had died in combat. The United States had not captured Osama bin Laden, but it had routed the Taliban leadership that sheltered him, and seemed to have put al-Qaeda on the run.

Because of the quick and, for Americans, nearly bloodless victory over the Taliban, the Administration's national-security team had come to epitomize competence. During our talk Wolfowitz referred to "one reason this group of people work very well together," by which he meant that Cheney, Rumsfeld, Powell, and many others, including himself, had collaborated for years, from the Reagan Administration through the 1991 Gulf War and afterward. From this experience they had developed a shared understanding of the nuances of "how to use force effectively," which they were now applying. In retrospect, the remarkable thing about Wolfowitz's comment was the assumption—which I then had no reason to challenge—that Bush's foreign-policy team was like a great business or sporting dynasty, which should be examined for secrets of success.

As I listen to the tape of that interview now, something else stands out: how expansive and unhurried even Wolfowitz sounded. "Even" Wolfowitz because since then he has become the symbol of an unrelenting drive toward war with Iraq. We now know that within the Administration he was urging the case for "regime change" there immediately after 9/11. But when speaking for the record, more than a year before that war began, he stressed how broad a range of challenges the United States would have to address, and over how many years, if it wanted to contain the sources of terrorism. It would need to find ways to "lance the boil" of growing anti-Americanism, as it had done during the Reagan years by supporting democratic reform in South Korea and the Philippines. It would have to lead the Western world in celebrating and welcoming Turkey as the most successfully modernized Muslim country. It would need to understand that in the long run the most important part of America's policy was its moral example—that America stands for things "the rest of the world wants for itself."

I also remember the way 2002 ended. By late December some 200,000 members of the U.S. armed forces were en route to staging areas surrounding Iraq. Hundreds of thousands of people had turned out on the streets of London, Rome, Madrid, and other cities to protest the impending war. That it was impending was obvious, despite ongoing negotiations at the United Nations. Within weeks of the 9/11 attacks President Bush and Secretary Rumsfeld had asked to see plans for a possible invasion of Iraq. Congress voted to authorize the war in October. Immediately after the vote, planning bureaus inside the Pentagon were told to be ready for combat at any point between then and the following April. (Operation Iraqi Freedom actually began on March 19.) Declaring that it was impossible to make predictions about a war that might not occur, the Administration refused to discuss plans for the war's aftermath—or its potential cost. In December the President fired Lawrence Lindsey, his chief economic adviser, after Lindsey offered a guess that the total cost might be $100 billion to $200 billion. As it happened, Lindsey's controversial estimate held up very well. By this summer, fifteen months after fighting began in Iraq, appropriations for war and occupation there totaled about $150 billion. With more than 100,000 U.S. soldiers still based in Iraq, the outlays will continue indefinitely at a rate of about $5 billion a month—much of it for fuel, ammunition, spare parts, and other operational needs. All this is at striking variance with the pre-war insistence by Donald Rumsfeld and Paul Wolfowitz that Iraq's oil money, plus contributions from allies, would minimize the financial burden on Americans.

Despite the rout of al-Qaeda in Afghanistan, terror attacks, especially against Americans and Europeans, were rising at the end of 2002 and would continue to rise through 2003. Some 400 people worldwide had died in terror attacks in 2000, and some 300 in 2001, apart from the 3,000-plus killed on September 11. In 2002 more than 700 were killed, including 200 when a bomb exploded outside a Bali nightclub in October.

Whereas at the beginning of the year Paul Wolfowitz had sounded expansive about the many avenues the United States had to pursue in order to meet the terror threat, by the end of the year the focus was solely on Iraq, and the Administration's tone was urgent. "Simply stated, there is no doubt that Saddam Hussein now has weapons of mass destruction," Vice President Cheney said in a major speech to the Veterans of Foreign Wars just before Labor Day. "There is no doubt he is amassing them to use against our friends, against our allies, and against us." Two weeks later, as Congress prepared for its vote to authorize the war, Condoleezza Rice said on CNN, "We do know that [Saddam Hussein] is actively pursuing a nuclear weapon ...We don't want the smoking gun to be a mushroom cloud."

On the last day of the year President Bush told reporters at his ranch in Texas, "I hope this Iraq situation will be resolved peacefully. One of my New Year's resolutions is to work to deal with these situations in a way so that they're resolved peacefully." As he spoke, every operating branch of the government was preparing for war.

September 11, 2001, has so often been described as a "hinge event" that it is tempting to think no other events could rival its significance. Indeed, as a single shocking moment that changed Americans' previous assumptions, the only modern comparisons are Pearl Harbor and the assassination of John F. Kennedy. But as 9/11 enters history, it seems likely that the aftermath, especially the decisions made during 2002, will prove to be as significant as the attack itself. It is obviously too early to know the full historical effect of the Iraq campaign. The biggest question about post-Saddam Iraq—whether it is headed toward stability or toward new tyranny and chaos—may not be answered for years.

But the biggest question about the United States—whether its response to 9/11 has made it safer or more vulnerable—can begin to be answered. Over the past two years I have been talking with a group of people at the working level of America's anti-terrorism efforts. Most are in the military, the intelligence agencies, and the diplomatic service; some are in think tanks and nongovernmental agencies. I have come to trust them, because most of them have no partisan ax to grind with the Administration (in the nature of things, soldiers and spies are mainly Republicans), and because they have so far been proved right. In the year before combat started in Iraq, they warned that occupying the country would be far harder than conquering it. As the occupation began, they pointed out the existence of plans and warnings the Administration seemed determined to ignore.

As a political matter, whether the United States is now safer or more vulnerable is of course ferociously controversial. That the war was necessary—and beneficial—is the Bush Administration's central claim. That it was not is the central claim of its critics. But among national-security professionals there is surprisingly little controversy. Except for those in government and in the opinion industries whose job it is to defend the Administration's record, they tend to see America's response to 9/11 as a catastrophe. I have sat through arguments among soldiers and scholars about whether the invasion of Iraq should be considered the worst strategic error in American history—or only the worst since Vietnam. Some of these people argue that the United States had no choice but to fight, given a pre-war consensus among its intelligence agencies that Iraq actually had WMD supplies. Many say that things in Iraq will eventually look much better than they do now. But about the conduct and effect of the war in Iraq one view prevails: it has increased the threats America faces, and has reduced the military, financial, and diplomatic tools with which we can respond.

"Let me tell you my gut feeling," a senior figure at one of America's military-sponsored think tanks told me recently, after we had talked for twenty minutes about details of the campaigns in Afghanistan and Iraq. "If I can be blunt, the Administration is full of shit. In my view we are much, much worse off now than when we went into Iraq. That is not a partisan position. I voted for these guys. But I think they are incompetent, and I have had a very close perspective on what is happening. Certainly in the long run we have harmed ourselves. We are playing to the enemy's political advantage. What- ever tactical victories we may gain along the way, this will prove to be a strategic blunder."

This man will not let me use his name, because he is still involved in military policy. He cited the experiences of Joseph Wilson, Richard Clarke, and Generals Eric Shinseki and Anthony Zinni to illustrate the personal risks of openly expressing his dissenting view. But I am quoting him anonymously—as I will quote some others—because his words are representative of what one hears at the working level.

To a surprising extent their indictment doesn't concentrate on the aspect of the problem most often discussed in public: exactly why the United States got the WMD threat so wrong. Nor does it involve a problem I have previously discussed in this magazine (see "Blind Into Baghdad," January/February *Atlantic*): the Administration's failure, whether deliberate or inadvertent, to make use of the care- ful and extensive planning for postwar Iraq that had been carried out by the State Department, the CIA, various branches of the mil- itary, and many other organizations. Rather, these professionals argue that by the end of 2002 the decisions the Administration had made—and avoided making—through the course of the year had left the nation less safe, with fewer positive options. Step by step through 2002 America's war on terror became little more than its preparation for war in Iraq.

Because of that shift, the United States succeeded in removing Saddam Hussein, but at this cost: The first front in the war on ter- ror, Afghanistan, was left to fester, as attention and money were drained toward Iraq. This in turn left more havens in Afghanistan in which terrorist groups could reconstitute themselves; a resurgent opium-poppy economy to finance them; and more of the disorder and brutality the United States had hoped to eliminate. Whether or not the strong international alliance that began the assault on the Taliban might have brought real order to Afghanistan is im- possible to say. It never had the chance, because America's pre- mature withdrawal soon fractured the alliance and curtailed postwar reconstruction. Indeed, the campaign in Afghanistan was warped and limited from the start, by a pre-existing desire to save troops for Iraq.

James Fallows

A full inventory of the costs of war in Iraq goes on. President Bush began 2002 with a warning that North Korea and Iran, not just Iraq, threatened the world because of the nuclear weapons they were developing. With the United States preoccupied by Iraq, these other two countries surged ahead. They have been playing a game of chess, or nerves, against America—and if they have not exactly won, they have advanced by several moves. Because it lost time and squandered resources, the United States now has no good options for dealing with either country. It has fewer deployable soldiers and weapons; it has less international leverage through the "soft power" of its alliances and treaties; it even has worse intelligence, because so many resources are directed toward Iraq.

At the beginning of 2002 the United States imported over 50 percent of its oil. In two years we have increased that figure by nearly 10 percent. The need for imported oil is the fundamental reason the United States must be deferential in its relationship with Saudi Arabia. Revenue from that oil is the fundamental reason that extremist groups based in Saudi Arabia were so rich. After the first oil shocks, in the mid-1970s, the United States took steps that reduced its imports of Persian Gulf oil. The Bush Administration could have made similar steps a basic part of its anti-terrorism strategy, and could have counted on making progress: through most of 2002 the Administration could assume bipartisan support for nearly anything it proposed. But its only such suggestion was drilling in the Arctic National Wildlife Refuge.

Before America went to war in Iraq, its military power seemed limitless. There was less need to actually apply it when all adversaries knew that any time we did so we would win. Now the limits on our military's manpower and sustainability are all too obvious. For example, the Administration announced this summer that in order to maintain troop levels in Iraq, it would withdraw 12,500 soldiers from South Korea. The North Koreans, the Chinese, the Iranians, the Syrians, and others who have always needed to take into account the chance of U.S. military intervention now realize that America has no stomach for additional wars. Before Iraq the U.S. military was turning away qualified applicants. Now it applies "stop-loss" policies that forbid retirement or resignation by volunteers, and it has mobilized the National Guard and Reserves in a way not seen since World War II.

Because of outlays for Iraq, the United States cannot spend $150 billion for other defensive purposes. Some nine million shipping containers enter American ports each year; only two percent of them are physically inspected, because inspecting more would be too expensive. The Department of Homeland Security, created after 9/11, is a vast grab-bag of federal agencies, from the Coast Guard to the Border Patrol to the former Immigration and Naturalization Service; ongoing operations in Iraq cost significantly more each month than all Homeland Security expenses combined. The department has sought to help cities large and small to improve their "first responder" systems, especially with better communications for their fire and emergency medical services. This summer a survey by the U.S. Conference of Mayors found that fewer than a quarter of 231 major cities under review had received any of the aid they expected. An internal budget memo from the Administration was leaked this past spring. It said that outlays for virtually all domestic programs, including homeland security, would have to be cut in 2005—and the federal budget deficit would still be more than $450 billion.

Worst of all, the government-wide effort to wage war in Iraq crowded out efforts to design a broader strategy against Islamic extremists and terrorists; to this day the Administration has articulated no comprehensive long-term plan. It dismissed out of hand any connection between policies toward the Israeli-Palestinian conflict and increasing tension with many Islamic states. Regime change in Iraq, it said, would have a sweeping symbolic effect on worldwide sources of terror. That seems to have been true—but in the opposite way from what the President intended. It is hard to find a counterterrorism specialist who thinks that the Iraq War has reduced rather than increased the threat to the United States.

And here is the startling part. There is no evidence that the President and those closest to him ever talked systematically about the "opportunity costs" and tradeoffs in their decision to invade Iraq. No one has pointed to a meeting, a memo, a full set of discussions, about what America would gain and lose.

James Fallows

SUCCESS IN WAR requires an understanding of who the enemy is, what resources can be used against him, and how victory will be defined. In the immediate aftermath of 9/11 America's expert agencies concluded that Osama bin Laden and al-Qaeda were almost certainly responsible for the attacks—and that the Taliban regime in Afghanistan was providing them with sanctuary. Within the government there was almost no dispute, then or later, about the legitimacy and importance of destroying that stronghold. Indeed, the main criticism of the initial anti-Taliban campaign was that it took so long to start.

In his book *Against All Enemies* the former terrorism adviser Richard Clarke says it was "plainly obvious" after September 11 that "al Qaeda's sanctuary in Taliban-run Afghanistan had to be occupied by U.S. forces and the al Qaeda leaders killed." It was therefore unfortunate that the move against the Taliban was "slow and small." Soon after the attacks President Bush created an interagency Campaign Coordination Committee to devise responses to al-Qaeda, and named Clarke its co-chairman. Clarke told me that this group urged a "rapid, no-holds-barred" retaliation in Afghanistan—including an immediate dispatch of troops to Afghanistan's borders to cut off al-Qaeda escape routes.

But the Administration was unwilling to use overwhelming power in Afghanistan. The only authorized account of how the "principals"— the big shots of the Administration—felt and thought at this time is in Bob Woodward's books *Bush at War* (2002) and *Plan of Attack* (2004), both based on interviews with the President and his senior advisers. To judge by *Bush at War*, Woodward's more laudatory account, a major reason for delay in attacking the Taliban had to do with "CSAR"—combat search and rescue teams. These were meant to be in place before the first aerial missions, so that they could go to the aid of any American pilot who might be downed. Preparations took weeks. They involved negotiations with the governments of Tajikistan and Uzbekistan for basing rights, the slow process of creating and equipping support airstrips in remote mountainous regions, and the redeployment of far-flung aircraft carriers to the Persian Gulf.

"The slowness was in part because the military weren't ready and they needed to move in the logistics support, the refueling aircraft, all of that," Richard Clarke told me. "But through this time the President kept saying to the Taliban, 'You still have an opportunity to come clean with us.' Which I thought—and the State Department thought—was silly. We'd already told them in advance that if this happened we were going to hold them personally responsible." Laurence Pope, a former ambassador to Chad, made a similar point when I spoke with him. Through the late 1990s Pope was the political adviser to General Zinni, who as the head of U.S. Central Command was responsible for Iraq and Afghanistan. Pope had run war games concerning assaults on both countries. "We had warned the Taliban repeatedly about Osama bin Laden," he told me, referring to the late Clinton years. "There was no question [after 9/11] that we had to take them on and deny that sanctuary to al-Qaeda. We should have focused like a laser on bin Laden and taking down al-Qaeda, breaking crockery in the neighborhood if necessary."

The crockery he was referring to included the government of Pakistan, which viewed the Pashtun tribal areas along the Afghan border as ungovernable. In the view of Pope and some others, the United States should have insisted on going into these areas right away, either with Pakistani troops or on its own—equipped with money to buy support, weapons, or both. This might have caused some regional and international disruption—but less than later invading Iraq.

It was on October 6, three and a half weeks after the attacks, that President Bush issued his final warning that "time was running out" for the Taliban to turn over bin Laden. The first cruise-missile strikes occurred the next day. The first paramilitary teams from the CIA and Special Forces arrived shortly thereafter; the first regular U.S. combat troops were deployed in late November. Thus, while the United States prepared for its response, Osama bin Laden, his deputy Ayman al-Zawahiri, and the rest of their ruling Shura Council had almost two months to flee and hide.

Opinions vary about exactly how much difference it would have made if the United States had killed or captured al-Qaeda's leaders while the World Trade Center ruins were still smoldering. But no one disputes that the United States needed to move immediately against al-Qaeda, and in the most complete and decisive way possible. And there is little disagreement about what happened next. The military and diplomatic effort in Afghanistan was handicapped from the start because the Administration had other concerns, and it ended badly even though it started well.

WINTER 2001–2002: WAR ON THE CHEAP

BY THE BEGINNING of 2002 U.S. and Northern Alliance forces had beaten the Taliban but lost bin Laden. At that point the United States faced a consequential choice: to bear down even harder in Afghanistan, or to shift the emphasis in the global war on terror (GWOT, as it is known in the trade) somewhere else.

A version of this choice between Afghanistan and "somewhere else" had in fact been made at the very start of the Administration's response to the 9/11 attacks. As Clarke, Woodward, and others have reported, during the top-level meetings at Camp David immediately after the attacks Paul Wolfowitz forcefully argued that Saddam Hussein was so threatening, and his overthrow was so "doable," that he had to be included in the initial military response. "The 'Afghanistan first' argument prevailed, basically for the reasons that Colin Powell advocated," Richard Clarke told me. "He said that the American people just aren't going to understand if you don't do something in Afghanistan right away—and that the lack of causal connection between Iraq and 9/11 would make it difficult to make the case for that war."

But Afghanistan first did not mean Afghanistan only. Clarke reminded me that he had prepared a memo on anti-terrorism strategy for the President's review before September 11. When it came back, on September 17, Clarke noticed only one significant change: the addition of a paragraph asking the Defense Department to prepare war plans for Iraq. Throughout the fall and winter, as U.S. troops were deployed in Afghanistan, Bush asked for and received increasingly detailed briefings from General Tommy Franks about the forces that might later be necessary in Iraq. According to many people who observed the process, the stated and unstated need to be ready for Saddam Hussein put a serious crimp in the U.S. effort against bin Laden and the Taliban.

The need to reserve troops for a likely second front in Iraq was one factor, though not the only one, in the design of the U.S. battle plan for Afghanistan. Many in the press (including me) marveled at America's rapid move against the Taliban for the ingenuity of its tactics. Instead of sending in many thousands of soldiers, the Administration left much of the actual fighting to the tribes of the Northern Alliance. Although the U.S. forces proved unable to go in fast, they certainly went in light—the Special Forces soldiers who chose targets for circling B-52s while picking their way through mountains on horseback being the most famous example. And they very quickly won. All this was exactly in keeping with the "transformation" doctrine that Donald Rumsfeld had been emphasizing in the Pentagon, and it reflected Rumsfeld's determination to show that a transformed military could substitute precision, technology, and imagination for sheer manpower.

But as would later become so obvious in Iraq, ousting a regime is one thing, and controlling or even pacifying a country is something else. For a significant group of military and diplomatic officials within the U.S. government, winning this "second war," for post-combat stability in Afghanistan, was a crucial step in the Administration's long-term efforts against al-Qaeda. Afghanistan had, after all, been the site of al-Qaeda's main training camps. The Taliban who harbored al-Qaeda had originally come to power as an alternative to warlordism and an economy based on extortion and drugs, so the United States could ill afford to let the country revert to the same rule and economy.

In removing the Taliban, the United States had acted as a genuine liberator. It came to the task with clean hands and broad international support. It had learned from the Soviet Union the folly of trying to hold Afghanistan by force. But it did not have to control the entire country to show that U.S. intervention could have lasting positive effects. What it needed, according to the "second war" group, was a sustained military, financial, and diplomatic effort to keep Afghanistan from sinking back toward chaos and thus becoming a terrorist haven once again.

"Had we seen Afghanistan as anything other than a sideshow," says Larry Goodson, a scholar at the Army War College who spent much of 2002 in Afghanistan, "we could have stepped up both the economic and security presence much more quickly than we did. Had Iraq not been what we were ginning up for in 2002, when the security situation in Afghanistan was collapsing, we might have come much more quickly to the peacekeeping and 'nation-building' strategy we're beginning to employ now." Iraq, of course, was what we were ginning up for, and the effects on Afghanistan were more important, if subtler, than has generally been discussed.

I asked officials, soldiers, and spies whether they had witnessed tradeoffs—specific transfers of manpower—that materially affected U.S. success in Afghanistan, and the response of Thomas White was typical: not really. During the wars in Afghanistan and Iraq, White was Secretary of the Army. Like most other people I spoke with, he offered an example or two of Iraq-Afghanistan tradeoffs, mainly involving strain on Special Forces or limits on electronic intelligence from the National Security Agency. Another man told me that NSA satellites had to be "boreholed" in a different direction— that is, aimed directly at sites in Iraq, rather than at Afghanistan. But no one said that changes like these had really been decisive. What did matter, according to White and nearly everyone else I spoke with, was the knowledge that the "center of gravity" of the anti-terrorism campaign was about to shift to Iraq. That dictated not just the vaunted "lightness" of the invasion but also the decision to designate allies for crucial tasks: the Northern Alliance for initial combat, and the Pakistanis for closing the border so that al-Qaeda leaders would not escape. In the end neither ally performed its duty the way the Americans had hoped. The Northern Alliance was far more motivated to seize Kabul than to hunt for bin Laden. The Pakistanis barely pretended to patrol the border. In its recent "after-action reports" the U.S. military has been increasingly critical of its own management of this campaign, but delegating the real work to less motivated allies seems to have been the uncorrectable error.

The desire to limit U.S. commitment had at least as great an effect on what happened after the fall of the Taliban. James Dobbins, who was the Bush Administration's special envoy for Afghanistan and its first representative in liberated Kabul, told me that three decisions in the early months "really shaped" the outcome in

Afghanistan. "One was that U.S. forces were not going to do peace-keeping of any sort, under any circumstances. They would remain available to hunt down Osama bin Laden and find renegade Taliban, but they were not going to have any role in providing security for the country at large. The second was that we would oppose anybody else's playing this role outside Kabul. And this was at a time when there was a good deal of interest from other countries in doing so." A significant reason for refusing help, according to Dobbins, was that accepting it would inevitably have tied up more American resources in Afghanistan, especially for airlifting donated supplies to foreign-led peacekeeping stations in the hinterland. The third decision was that U.S. forces would not engage in any counter-narcotics activities. One effect these policies had was to prolong the disorder in Afghanistan and increase the odds against a stable government. The absence of American or international peacekeepers guaranteed that the writ of the new Karzai government would extend, at best, to Kabul itself.

"I can't prove this, but I believe they didn't want to put in a lot of regular infantry because they wanted to hold it in reserve," Richard Clarke explains. "And the issue is the infantry. A rational military planner who was told to stabilize Afghanistan after the Taliban was gone, and who was not told that we might soon be doing Iraq, would probably have put in three times the number of infantry, plus all the logistics support 'tail.' He would have put in more civil-affairs units, too. Based on everything I heard at the time, I believe I can make a good guess that the plan for Afghanistan was affected by a predisposition to go into Iraq. The result of that is that they didn't have enough people to go in and stabilize the country, nor enough people to make sure these guys didn't get out."

The Administration later placed great emphasis on making Iraq a showcase of Islamic progress: a society that, once freed from tyranny, would demonstrate steady advancement toward civil order, economic improvement, and, ultimately, democracy. Although Afghanistan is a far wilder, poorer country, it might have provided a better showcase, and sooner. There was no controversy about America's involvement; the rest of the world was ready to provide aid; if it wasn't going to become rich, it could become demonstrably less poor. The amount of money and manpower sufficient to transform Afghanistan would have been a tiny fraction of what America decided to commit in Iraq. But the opportunity was missed, and Afghanistan began a descent to its pre-Taliban warlord state.

SPRING 2002: CHAOS AND CLOSED MINDS

EARLY 2002 was the Administration's first chance to look beyond its initial retaliation in Afghanistan. This could have been a time to think broadly about America's vulnerabilities and to ask what problems might have been overlooked in the immediate response to 9/11. At this point the United States still had comfortable reserves of all elements of international power, "hard" and "soft" alike.

As the fighting wound down in Tora Bora, the Administration could in principle have matched a list of serious problems with a list of possible solutions. In his State of the Union speech, in late January, President Bush had named Iran, Iraq, and North Korea as an "axis of evil." The Administration might have weighed the relative urgency of those three threats, including uncontested evidence that North Korea was furthest along in developing nuclear weapons. It might have launched an all-out effort to understand al-Qaeda's strengths and weaknesses—and to exploit the weak points. It might have asked whether relations with Pakistan, Egypt, and Saudi Arabia needed fundamental reconsideration. For decades we had struck an inglorious bargain with the regimes in those countries: we would overlook their internal repression and their role as havens for Islamic extremists; they would not oppose us on first-order foreign-policy issues—demonstrating, for instance, a relative moderation toward Israel. And the Saudis would be cooperative about providing oil. Maybe, after serious examination, this bargain would still seem to be the right one, despite the newly manifest dangers of Islamic extremism. But the time to ask the question was early in 2002.

The Administration might also have asked whether its approach to Israel and the Palestinians needed reconsideration. Before 9/11 it had declared a hands-off policy toward Israel and the PLO, but sooner or later all Bush's predecessors had come around to a "land for peace" bargain as the only plausible solution in the Middle East. The new

Administration would never have more leverage or a more opportune moment for imposing such a deal than soon after it was attacked.

Conceivably the Administration could have asked other questions—about energy policy, about manpower in the military, about the fiscal base for a sustained war. This was an opportunity created by crisis. At the top level of the Administration attention swung fast, and with little discussion, exclusively to Iraq. This sent a signal to the working levels, where daily routines increasingly gave way to preparations for war, steadily denuding the organizations that might have been thinking about other challenges.

The Administration apparently did not consider questions like "If we pursue the war on terror by invading Iraq, might we incite even more terror in the long run?" and "If we commit so many of our troops this way, what possibilities will we be giving up?" But Bush "did not think of this, intellectually, as a comparative decision," I was told by Senator Bob Graham, of Florida, who voted against the war resolution for fear it would hurt the fight against terrorism. "It was a single decision: he saw Saddam Hussein as an evil person who had to be removed." The firsthand accounts of the Administration's decision-making indicate that the President spent most of his time looking at evidence of Saddam Hussein's threat, and significant but smaller amounts of time trying to build his coalition and hearing about the invasion plans. A man who participated in high-level planning for both Afghanistan and Iraq—and who is unnamed here because he still works for the government—told me, "There was absolutely no debate in the normal sense. There are only six or eight of them who make the decisions, and they only talk to each other. And if you disagree with them in public, they'll come after you, the way they did with Shinseki."

The three known exceptions to this pattern actually underscore the limits on top-level talks. One was the discussions at Camp David just after 9/11: they led to "Afghanistan first," which delayed rather than forestalled the concentration on Iraq. The second was Colin Powell's "You break it, you've bought it" warning to the President in the summer of 2002: far from leading to serious questions about the war, it did not even persuade the Administration to use the postwar plans devised by the State Department, the Army, and the CIA. The third was a long memo from Rumsfeld to Bush a few months before the war began, when a campaign against Iraq was a foregone conclusion. As excerpted in *Plan of Attack*, it listed twenty-nine ways in which an invasion could backfire. "Iraq could successfully best the U.S. in public relations and persuade the world that it was a war against Muslims" was one. "There could be higher than expected collateral damage" was another. But even this memo was couched in terms of "making sure that we had done everything humanly possible to prepare [the President] for what could go wrong, to prepare so things would go right," Rumsfeld explained to Bob Woodward. And its only apparent effect was that Bush called in his military commanders to look at the war plans.

Discussions at the top were distorted in yet another way—by an unspoken effect of disagreements over the Middle East. Some connections between Iraq policy and the Israeli-Palestinian dispute are obvious. One pro-war argument was "The road to Jerusalem runs through Baghdad"—that is, once the United States had removed Saddam Hussein and the threat he posed to Israel, it could lean more effectively on Ariel Sharon and the Likud government to accept the right deal. According to this logic, America could also lean more effectively on the Palestinians and their supporters, because of the new strength it would have demonstrated by liberating Iraq. The contrary argument—"The road to Baghdad leads through Jerusalem"—appears to have been raised mainly by Tony Blair. Its point was that if the United States first took a tougher line with Sharon and recognized that the Palestinians, too, had grievances, it would have a much easier time getting allied support and Arab acquiescence for removing Saddam Hussein. There is no evidence that this was ever significantly discussed inside the Administration.

"The groups on either side of the Iraq debate basically didn't trust each other," a former senior official in the Administration told me—and the people "on either side" he was speaking of all worked for George Bush. (He, too, insisted on anonymity because he has ongoing dealings with the government.) "If it wasn't clear why you were saying these skeptical things about invading Iraq, there was naturally the suspicion that you were saying [them] because you opposed the Israeli position. So any argument became suspect."

Suspicion ran just as strongly the other way—that officials were steadfast for war because they supported the Israeli position. In this (admittedly oversimplified) schema, the CIA, the State Department, and the uniformed military were the most skeptical of war—and, in the view of war supporters, were also the most critical of Israel. The White House (Bush, Cheney, Rice) and the Defense Department's civilian leadership were the most pro-war-and the most pro-Israel. Objectively, all these people agreed far more than they differed, but their mutual suspicions further muted dissenting views.

At the next level down, different problems had the same effect: difficulty in thinking broadly about threats and responses. An obscure-sounding bureaucratic change contributed. At the start of his second term Bill Clinton had signed PDD 56, a presidential decision directive about handling international emergencies. The idea was that, like it or not, a chaotic world would continually involve the United States in "complex contingency operations." These were efforts, like the ones in the Balkans and East Africa, in which soldiers, diplomats, relief workers, reconstruction experts, economists, legal authorities, and many other officials from many different institutions would need to work together if any of them were to succeed. The directive set up a system for coordinating these campaigns, so that no one organization dominated the others or operated unilaterally.

When it took office, the Bush Administration revoked this plan and began working on a replacement. But nothing was on hand as of September 11. For months the response to the attacks was managed by a variety of ad hoc groups. The Campaign Coordination Committee, run by Richard Clarke and his colleague Franklin Miller, oversaw strategies against al-Qaeda. The new Domestic Preparedness Committee, run by John Ashcroft's deputy, Larry Thompson, oversaw internal-security measures. And the "principals"—Bush, Cheney, Rumsfeld, Powell, Rice, Director of Central Intelligence George Tenet, and a few others, including Wolfowitz, Powell's deputy Richard Armitage, and Cheney's aide Lewis "Scooter" Libby—met frequently to plan the showdown with Iraq. There was no established way to make sure that State knew what Defense was doing and vice versa, as became disastrously obvious after the fall of Baghdad. And there was no recognized venue for opportunity-cost discussions about the emerging Iraq policy, even if anyone had wanted them.

In the absence of other plans, initiative on every issue was increasingly taken in the Pentagon. And within the Pentagon the emphasis increasingly moved toward Iraq. In March of 2002, when U.S. troops were still engaged in Operation Anaconda on the Afghan-Pakistani border, and combat in Iraq was still a year away, inside the government Afghanistan had begun to seem like yesterday's problem. When asked about Iraq at a press conference on March 13, Bush said merely, "All options are on the table." By that time Tommy Franks had answered Bush's request for battle plans and lists of potential bombing targets in Iraq.

The more experienced in government the people I interviewed were, the more likely they were to stress the importance of the mental shift in the spring of 2002. When I asked Richard Clarke whether preparations for Iraq had really taken anything crucial from Afghanistan or other efforts, he said yes, unquestionably. "They took one thing that people on the outside find hard to believe or appreciate," he said. "Management time. We're a huge government, and we have hundreds of thousands of people involved in national security. Therefore you would think we could walk and chew gum at the same time. I've never found that to be true. You've got one National Security Adviser and one CIA director, and they each have one deputy. The same is true in Defense. Interestingly in terms of the military, both of these wars took place in the same 'CINCdom'"—by which Clarke meant that both were in the realm of Tommy Franks's Central Command, rather than in two different theaters. "It just is not credible that the principals and the deputies paid as much attention to Afghanistan or the war against al-Qaeda as they should have."

According to Michael Scheuer, a career CIA officer who spent the late 1990s as head of the agency's anti–bin Laden team, the shift of attention had another destructive effect on efforts to battle al-Qaeda: the diversion of members of that team and the Agency's limited supply of Arabic speakers and Middle East specialists to support the mounting demand for intelligence on Iraq. (Because Scheuer is still on active duty at the CIA, the Agency allowed him to publish his recent book, *Imperial Hubris*, a harsh criticism of U.S. approaches to controlling terrorism, only as "Anonymous." After we spoke, his identity was disclosed by Jason Vest, in the *Boston Phoenix;* when I met him, he declined to give his name and was introduced simply as "Mike.") "With a finite number of people who have any kind of pertinent experience," Scheuer told me, "there is unquestionably a sucking away of resources from Afghanistan and al-Qaeda to Iraq, just because it was a much bigger effort."

Scheuer observed that George Tenet had claimed early in 2003 that there was enough expertise and manpower to handle both Iraq and al-Qaeda. "From inside the system that sounded like a very questionable judgment," Scheuer said. "You start with a large group of people who have worked bin Laden and al-Qaeda and Sunni terrorism for years—and worked it every day since 9/11. Then you move a lot of people out to work the Iraq issue, and instead you have a lot of people who come in for ninety days or one hundred and twenty days, then leave. It's like any other profession. Over time you make connections. A name comes up, and there's nothing on file in the last two years—but you remember that five years ago there was a guy with that name doing acts in the Philippines. If you don't have an institutional memory, you don't make the connection. When they talk about connecting the dots, the computers are important. But at the end of the day, the most important thing is that human being who's been working this issue for five or six years. You can have the best computers in the world, and you can have an ocean of information, but if you have a guy who's only been there for three weeks or three months, you're very weak."

Laurence Pope, the former ambassador, told me that Iraq monomania was particularly destructive in the spring of 2002 because of the opportunity that came and went in Afghanistan. "There was a moment of six months or so when we could have put much more pressure on the tribal areas [to get al-Qaeda], and on Pakistan, and done a better job of reconstruction in Afghanistan," he said. "In reality, the Beltway can only do one thing at a time, and because of the attention to Iraq, what should have happened in Afghanistan didn't."

So by the spring, after six months in which to consider its strategy, the Administration had radically narrowed its choices. Its expert staffers were deflected toward Iraq—and away from Afghanistan, Iran, North Korea, Israel-Palestine, the hunt for bin Laden, the assault on al-Qaeda, even China and Taiwan. Its diplomats were not squeezing Pakistan as hard as possible about chasing al-Qaeda, or Saudi Arabia about cracking down on extremists, because the United States needed their help—or at least acquiescence—in the coming war with Iraq. Its most senior officials were working out the operational details of a plan whose fundamental wisdom they had seldom, if ever, stopped to examine.

SUMMER AND FALL: THE ONE-FRONT WAR

PRESIDENT BUSH'S first major statement about his post 9/11 foreign policy had come in his State of the Union address. His second came on June 1, when he gave the graduation speech at West Point. It carefully laid out the case for a new doctrine of "pre-emptive" war. Bush didn't say "Iraq" or "Saddam Hussein," but his meaning was unmistakable. "Containment is not possible when unbalanced dictators with weapons of mass destruction can deliver those weapons on missiles or secretly provide them to terrorist allies," he said. "We cannot put our faith in the word of tyrants who solemnly sign non-proliferation treaties and then systemically break them. If we wait for threats to fully materialize, we will have waited too long." A few weeks later Condoleezza Rice presented a fuller version of the concept, and Dick Cheney hammered home his warnings that Saddam Hussein had, beyond all doubt, acquired weapons of mass destruction. In September, Donald Rumsfeld said at a news conference that the link between Saddam Hussein and al-Qaeda was "not debatable." By October, Bush had practically stopped referring to Osama bin Laden in his press statements; he said of Saddam Hussein, "This is the guy that tried to kill my dad."

The Democrats still controlled the Senate, but on October 11 Majority Leader Tom Daschle led John Kerry, John Edwards, and twenty-six other Democrats in voting to authorize the war. (Authorization passed the Senate 77-23; most Democrats in the House voted against it, but it still carried there, by 296 to 133.) Democratic officials were desperate to get the vote behind them, so that in the impending midterm elections they could not be blamed for hampering the war on terrorism—in which, the Administration said, war in Iraq played an integral part.

The Cyclops-like nature of the Administration's perception of risk became more evident. Uncertain evidence about Iraq was read in the most pessimistic fashion; much more reliable evidence about other threats was ignored. Of the three members of the "axis of evil," Iraq had made the sketchiest progress toward developing nuclear weapons. In October, just before the Iraq War vote, a delegation of Americans in Pyongyang found that North Korea's nuclear-weapons program was actually up and running. As the weeks wore on, North Korea became more and more brazen. In December it reactivated a nuclear processing plant it had closed eight years earlier as part of a deal with the United States. Soon thereafter it kicked out inspectors from the International Atomic Energy Agency and announced that it would withdraw from the Nuclear Non-Proliferation Treaty. North Korea was dropping even the pretense that it was not developing nuclear bombs.

Meanwhile, in August of 2002, an Iranian opposition group revealed the existence of two previously secret nuclear facilities, in Natanz and Arak. The first was devoted to uranium enrichment, the second to heavy-water production, which is a step toward producing plutonium. Months before the vote on war with Iraq, then, the United States had very strong indications that Iran was pursuing two paths toward atomic weaponry: uranium and plutonium. The indications from North Korea were at least as strong. If the very worst pre-war suspicions about Saddam Hussein's weapons of mass destruction had turned out to be true, the nuclear stakes would still have been lower than those in North Korea or Iran.

"How will history judge this period, in terms of the opportunity costs of invading Iraq?" said John Pike, the director of GlobalSecurity.org, when we spoke. "I think the opportunity cost is going to be North Korea and Iran. I mean, in 2002 it became obvious that Iran has a full-blown nuclear-weapons program under way, no ifs or buts. For the next eighteen months or so, before it's running, we have the opportunity to blow it up. But this Iraq adventure will give blowing up your enemies a bad name. The concern now has to be that the 'Iraq syndrome' will make us flinch from blowing up people who really need to be blown up."

Bombing North Korea's reactor has never been an option, since North Korea has so many retaliatory forces so close to Seoul. But whatever choices the United States had at the beginning of 2002, it has fewer and worse ones now. The North Koreans are that much further along in their program; the U.S. military is under that much more strain; international hostility to U.S. policies is that much greater. "At the rate North Korea is pumping out bomb material," Pike said, "the Japanese will realize that the missile defense we've sold them will not save them. And they will conclude that only weaponizing their plutonium will enable them to sleep easily at night. And then you'll have South Korea and Taiwan..." and on through other ripple-effect scenarios. Pike says that the United States has little leverage to prevent any of this, and therefore can't afford to waste any more time in acting against North Korea.

"Are we better off in basic security than before we invaded Iraq?" asks Jeffrey Record, a professor of strategy at the Air War College and the author of the recent *Dark Victory*, a book about the Iraq War. "The answer is no. An unnecessary war has consumed American Army and other ground resources, to the point where we have nothing left in the cupboard for another contingency—for instance, should the North Koreans decide that with the Americans completely absorbed in Iraq, now is the time to do something."

"We really have four armies," an Army officer involved in Pentagon planning for the Iraq War told me. "There's the one that's deployed in Afghanistan and Iraq. There's the one that's left back home in Fort Hood and other places. There's the 'modular Army,' of new brigade-sized units that are supposed to be rotated in and out of locations easily. There's the Guard and Reserve. And every one of them is being chewed up by the ops tempo." "Ops tempo" means the pace of operations, and when it is too high, equipment and supplies are being used faster than they can be replaced, troops are being deployed far longer than they expected, and training is being pared back further than it should. "We're really in dire straits with resourcing," he said. "There's not enough armor for Humvees. There's not enough fifty-caliber machine guns for the Hundred and First Airborne or the Tenth Mountain Division. A country that can't field heavy machine guns for its army—there's something wrong with the way we're doing business."

"The stress of war has hit all the services, but none harder than the Army," Sydney Freedberg wrote recently in *National Journal.* "The crucial shortfall is not in money or machines, but in manpower." More than a third of the Army's 500,000 active-duty soldiers are in Iraq or Kuwait. Freedberg referred to a study showing that fifteen of the Army's thirty-four active-duty combat units were currently deployed overseas, and wrote, "That means that nearly as many units are abroad as at home, when historical experience shows that a long-term commitment, as with the British in Northern Ireland, requires three or four units recuperating and training for each one deployed." In the long run the U.S. military needs either more people or fewer responsibilities. At the moment, because of Iraq, it has very little slack for dealing with other emergencies that might arise.

WINTER: MISLEADING THE ENEMY

PRESIDENT BUSH'S first major speech after 9/11, on September 20, 2001, was one of the outstanding addresses given by a modern President. But it introduced a destructive concept that Bush used more and more insistently through 2002. "Why do they hate us?" he asked about the terrorists. He answered that they hate what is best in us: "They hate what we see right here in this chamber—a democratically elected government... They hate our freedoms—our freedom of religion, our freedom of speech, our freedom to vote and assemble and disagree with each other." As he boiled down this thought in subsequent comments it became "They hate us for who we are" and "They hate us because we are free."

There may be people who have studied, fought against, or tried to infiltrate al-Qaeda and who agree with Bush's statement. But I have never met any. The soldiers, spies, academics, and diplomats I have interviewed are unanimous in saying that "They hate us for who we are" is dangerous claptrap. Dangerous because it is so lazily self-justifying and self-deluding: the only thing we could possibly be doing wrong is being so excellent. Claptrap because it reflects so little knowledge of how Islamic extremism has evolved.

"There are very few people in the world who are going to kill themselves so we can't vote in the Iowa caucuses," Michael Scheuer said to me. "But there's a lot of them who are willing to die because we're helping the Israelis, or because we're helping Putin against the Chechens, or because we keep oil prices low so Muslims lose money." Jeffrey Record said, "Clearly they do not like American society. They think it's far too libertine, democratic, Christian. But that's not the reason they attack us. If it were, they would have attacked a lot of other Western countries too. I don't notice them putting bombs in Norway. It's a combination of who we are and also our behavior."

This summer's report of the 9/11 Commission, without associating this view with Bush, was emphatic in rejecting the "hate us for who we are" view. The commission said this about the motivation of Khalid Sheikh Muhammad, whom it identified as the "mastermind of the 9/11 attacks": "KSM's animus toward the United States stemmed not from his experiences there as a student, but rather from his violent disagreement with U.S. foreign policy favoring Israel." In discussing long-term strategies for dealing with extremist groups the commission said, "America's policy choices have consequences. Right or wrong, it is simply a fact that American policy regarding the Israeli-Palestinian conflict and American actions in Iraq are dominant staples of popular commentary across the Arab and Muslim world." The most striking aspect of the commission's analysis is that it offered any thoughts at all about the right long-term response to Islamic extremists. The 9/11 Commission was one of several groups seeking to fill the void left by the Administration's failure to put forward any comprehensive battle plan for a long-term campaign against terrorism. By its actions the Administration showed that the only terrorism problem it recognized was Saddam Hussein's regime, plus the al-Qaeda leaders shown on its "most wanted" lists.

The distinction between who we are and what we do matters, because it bears on the largest question about the Iraq War: Will it bring less or more Islamic terrorism? If violent extremism is purely vengeful and irrational, there is no hope except to crush it. Any brutality along the way is an unavoidable cost. But if it is based on logic of any sort, a clear understanding of its principles could help us to weaken its appeal—and to choose tactics that are not self-defeating.

A later article will describe insights about controlling terrorism. For now the point is the strong working-level consensus that terrorists are "logical," if hideously brutal, and that the steps in 2002 that led to war have broadened the extremists' base. In March of 2003, just after combat began in Iraq, President Hosni Mubarak of Egypt warned that if the United States invaded, "instead of having one bin Laden, we will have one hundred bin Ladens." Six months later, when the combat was over, Rumsfeld wrote in a confidential memo quoted in *Plan of Attack*, "We lack metrics to know if we are winning or losing the global war on terror. Are we capturing, killing or deterring and dissuading more terrorists every day than the *madrassas* [Islamic schools] and the radical clerics are recruiting, training and deploying against us? ... The cost-benefit ratio is against us! Our cost is billions against the terrorists' costs of millions." Six months after that, as violence surged in occupied Iraq, the International Institute for Strategic Studies, in London, reported that al-Qaeda was galvanized by the wars in Afghanistan and Iraq. As of mid-2004 it had at least 18,000 operatives in sixty countries. "Al Qaeda has fully reconstituted [and] set its sights firmly on the USA and its closest Western allies in Europe," the report said. Meanwhile, a British parliamentary report warns that Afghanistan is likely to "implode" for lack of support.

"I have been saying for years, Osama bin Laden could never have done it without us," a civilian adviser to the Pentagon told me this summer. "We have continued to play to his political advantage and to confirm, in the eyes of his constituency, the very claims he made about us." Those claims are that the United States will travel far to suppress Muslims, that it will occupy their holy sites, that it will oppose the rise of Islamic governments, and that it will take their resources. "We got to Baghdad," Michael Scheuer said, "and the first thing Rumsfeld said is, 'We'll accept any government as long as it's not Islamic.' It draws their attention to bin Laden's argument that the United States is leading the West to annihilate Islam." The Administration had come a long way from the end-of-Ramadan ceremony at the White House.

James Fallows

WHAT HAPPENED IN A YEAR

TO GOVERN IS TO CHOOSE, and the choices made in 2002 were fateful. The United States began that year shocked and wounded, but with tremendous strategic advantages. Its population was more closely united behind its leadership than it had been in fifty years. World opinion was strongly sympathetic. Longtime allies were eager to help; longtime antagonists were silent. The federal budget was nearly in balance, making ambitious projects feasible. The U.S. military was superbly equipped, trained, and prepared. An immediate foe was evident—and vulnerable—in Afghanistan. For the longer-term effort against Islamic extremism the Administration could draw on a mature school of thought from academics, regional specialists, and its own intelligence agencies. All that was required was to think broadly about the threats to the country, and creatively about the responses.

The Bush Administration chose another path. Implicitly at the beginning of 2002, and as a matter of formal policy by the end, it placed all other considerations second to regime change in Iraq. It hampered the campaign in Afghanistan before fighting began and wound it down prematurely, along the way losing the chance to capture Osama bin Laden. It turned a blind eye to misdeeds in Saudi Arabia and Pakistan, and to WMD threats from North Korea and Iran far more serious than any posed by Saddam Hussein, all in the name of moving toward a showdown with Iraq. It overused and wore out its army in invading Iraq—without committing enough troops for a successful occupation. It saddled the United States with ongoing costs that dwarf its spending for domestic security. And by every available measure it only worsened the risk of future terrorism. In every sense 2002 was a lost year.

Afghanistan, Iraq: Two Wars Collide

Barton Gellman and Dafna Linzer

IN THE SECOND HALF of March 2002, as the Bush administration mapped its next steps against al Qaeda, Deputy CIA Director John E. McLaughlin brought an unexpected message to the White House Situation Room. According to two people with firsthand knowledge, he told senior members of the president's national security team that the CIA was scaling back operations in Afghanistan.

That announcement marked a year-long drawdown of specialized military and intelligence resources from the geographic center of combat with Osama bin Laden. As jihadist enemies reorganized, slipping back and forth from Pakistan and Iran, the CIA closed forward bases in the cities of Herat, Mazar-e Sharif and Kandahar. The agency put off an $80 million plan to train and equip a friendly intelligence service for the new U.S.-installed Afghan government. Replacements did not keep pace with departures as case officers finished six-week tours. And Task Force 5—a covert commando team that led the hunt for bin Laden and his lieutenants in the border region—lost more than two-thirds of its fighting strength.

The commandos, their high-tech surveillance equipment and other assets would instead surge toward Iraq through 2002 and early 2003, as President Bush prepared for the March invasion that would extend the field of battle in the nation's response to the Sept. 11, 2001, attacks.

Bush has shaped his presidency, and his reelection campaign, around the threat that announced itself in the wreckage of the

---

This article originally appeared in the October 22, 2004, issue of *The Washington Post* ©2004. Reprinted with permission.

World Trade Center and the Pentagon. Five days after the attacks, he made it clear that he conceived a broader war. Impromptu remarks on the White House South Lawn were the first in which he named "this war on terrorism," and he cast it as a struggle with "a new kind of evil." Under that banner he toppled two governments, eased traditional restraints on intelligence and law enforcement agencies, and reshaped the landscape of the federal government.

As the war on terrorism enters its fourth year, its results are sufficiently diffuse—and obscured in secrecy—to resist easy measure. Interpretations of the public record are also polarized by the claims and counterclaims of the presidential campaign. Bush has staked his reelection on an argument that defense of the U.S. homeland requires unyielding resolve to take the fight to the terrorists. His opponent, Sen. John F. Kerry (D-Mass.), portrays the Bush strategy as based on false assumptions and poor choices, particularly when it came to Iraq.

The contention that the Iraq invasion was an unwise diversion in confronting terrorism has been central to Kerry's critique of Bush's performance. But this account—drawn largely from interviews with those who have helped manage Bush's offensive—shows how the debate over that question has echoed within the ranks of the administration as well, even among those who support much of the president's agenda.

Interviews with those advisers also highlight an internal debate over Bush's strategy against al Qaeda and allied jihadists, which has stressed the "decapitation" of the network by capturing or killing leaders, but which has had less success in thwarting recruitment of new militants.

At the core of Bush's approach is an offensive strategy abroad that Homeland Security Secretary Tom Ridge said complements the defensive efforts he oversees at home. In an interview, Ridge said Bush's priority is to "play as hard and strong an offense as possible," most of it "offshore, overseas."

Published and classified documents and interviews with officials at many levels portray a war plan that scored major victories in its first months. Notable among them were the destruction of al Qaeda's Afghan sanctuary, the death or capture of leading jihadists, and effective U.S. demands for action by reluctant foreign governments.

But at least a dozen current and former officials who have held key positions in conducting the war now say they see diminishing returns in Bush's decapitation strategy. Current and former leaders of that effort, three of whom departed in frustration from the top White House terrorism post, said the manhunt is important but cannot defeat the threat of jihadist terrorism. Classified government tallies, moreover, suggest that Bush and Vice President Cheney have inflated the manhunt's success in their reelection bid.

Bush's focus on the instruments of force, the officials said, has been slow to adapt to a swiftly changing enemy. Al Qaeda, they said, no longer exerts centralized control over a network of operational cells. It has rather become the inspirational hub of a global movement, fomenting terrorism that it neither funds nor directs. Internal government assessments describe this change with a disquieting metaphor: They say jihadist terrorism is "metastasizing."

The war has sometimes taken unexpected turns, one of which brought the Bush administration into hesitant contact with Iran. For a time the two governments made tentative common cause, and Iran delivered hundreds of low-level al Qaeda figures to U.S. allies. Participants in Washington and overseas said Bush's deadlocked advisers—unable to transmit instructions—closed that channel before testing Iran's willingness to take more substantial steps. Some of al Qaeda's most wanted leaders now live in Iran under ambiguous conditions of house arrest.

Twenty months after the invasion of Iraq, the question of whether Americans are safer from terrorism because Saddam Hussein is no longer in power hinges on subjective judgment about might-have-beens. What is not in dispute, among scores of career national security officials and political appointees interviewed periodically since 2002, is that Bush's choice had opportunity costs—first in postwar Afghanistan, then elsewhere. Iraq, they said, became a voracious consumer of time, money, personnel and diplomatic capital—as well as the scarce tools of covert force on which Bush prefers to rely—that until then were engaged against al Qaeda and its sources of direct support.

'WHAT DOES IT MEAN TO BE SAFER?'

BUSH CONDUCTS the war on terrorism above all as a global hunt for a cast of evil men he knows by name and photograph. He tracks progress in daily half-hour meetings that Richard A. Falkenrath, who sometimes attended them before departing recently as deputy homeland security adviser, described as "extremely granular, about individual guys." Frances Fragos Townsend, who took the post of White House counterterrorism and homeland security adviser in May, said in an interview that Bush's strategy—now, as in the war's first days—is to "decapitate the beast."

The president is also focused on states that sponsor terrorism. The danger he sees is a "great nexus," thus far hypothetical, in which an enemy nation might hand terrorists a nuclear, biological or chemical weapon. That danger is what Bush said drove him to war in Iraq.

Bush emphasizes force of will—determination to prosecute the enemy, and equally to stand up to allies who disapprove. Bush and his aides most often deflect questions about recent global polls that have found sharply rising anti-U.S. sentiment in Arab and Muslim countries and in Europe, but one of them addressed it in a recent interview. Speaking for the president by White House arrangement, but declining to be identified, a high-ranking national security official said of the hostility detected in surveys: "I don't think it matters. It's about keeping the country safe, and I don't think that matters."

That view is at odds with the view of many career military and intelligence officials, who spoke with increasing alarm about al Qaeda's success in winning recruits to its cause and defining its struggle with the United States.

Retired Army Gen. Wayne A. Downing, who was summoned to lead the White House Office for Combating Terrorism a few weeks after the Sept. 11 attacks, said the war has been least successful where it has the highest stakes: slowing the growth of jihadist sympathies in populations that can provide the terrorists with money, concealment and recruits. Bin Laden has worked effectively to "convince the Islamic world the U.S. is the common enemy," Downing said. He added, "We have done little or nothing. That is the big failure."

Townsend, who inherited Downing's duties this spring, said the best evidence of Bush's success "is every day that goes by that America doesn't suffer another attack."

"By any measure, to me, we're winning, they're losing," she said. "We know for a fact that it's very difficult for them to raise money and move money around. We've made it increasingly difficult to communicate. It is harder for them to travel without risk. . . . Is there something that they absolutely, 100 percent guaranteed, can't do? I'm not going to say that. The point is we have degraded their capability to act across the board."

John A. Gordon, Townsend's immediate predecessor, said in his first interview since leaving government in June that those measures of tactical success are no longer enough.

"People in the business would say, 'We've done all this stuff, we know we've pushed back some attacks,' but what does it mean to be safer?" he asked. "You decrease the probability of a major attack, but you haven't pushed it to anywhere near zero. If it happens, nobody's going to care whether we 'significantly affected' [the threat] or not."

'A MANAGEABLE PROBLEM'

TWO YEARS AGO, Gordon thought better of the strategy. He helped direct it.

Born in Jefferson City, Mo., Gordon spent a career in the Cold War Air Force, rising to four-star general in the missile and bomber force. Bush tapped him in June 2002 as chief of the Office for Combating Terrorism, with a rank just below that of national security adviser Condoleezza Rice.

From his vantage in Room 313 of the Old Executive Office Building, Gordon saw a colossal mismatch of strength between the global superpower and its stateless enemy. He sat down for an interview, after six months on the job, in a cautiously optimistic frame of mind.

With al Qaeda's Afghan training camps demolished and its troops dispersed, he said in 2002, the network's deadliest capabilities relied on "fewer than three dozen" uniquely dangerous men. "Where we're focusing is on the manhunt," he said. "That's still job number one, to break down and capture and kill . . . the inner core of Osama and his very, very closest advisers."

At the CIA's Counterterrorist Center in Langley, which then as now maintained wall-size charts of al Qaeda's global network, the approximately 30 names at the top were known as "high-value targets." At the time, a year into the manhunt, many of Gordon's peers agreed that "leadership targets," in the argot of U.S. military and intelligence agencies, were a "center of gravity" for al Qaeda—a singular source of strength without which the enemy could be brought to collapse.

Hunting al Qaeda's leaders cut them off from their followers, Gordon said then, and "layers of interdiction" stood between would-be attackers and their targets. Some could be stopped in their country of origin, others as they crossed the U.S. border, and still others as they neared the point of attack. Each defensive measure, in theory, created U.S. opportunities to strike.

"If I can cut him in half every time he comes through," he said, "now I can give the FBI and local law enforcement a manageable problem."

'THE SAME PEOPLE, OVER AND OVER'

THAT DID NOT HAPPEN. On its own terms—as a manhunt, measured in "high-value" captures and kills—the president's strategy produced its peak results the first year.

Classified tallies made available to *The Washington Post* have identified 28 of the approximately 30 names on the unpublished HVT List. Half—14—are known to be dead or in custody. Those at large include three of the five men on the highest echelon: bin Laden, his deputy Ayman Zawahiri and operational planner Saif al-Adel.

More significant than the bottom line, government analysts said, is the trend. Of the al Qaeda leaders accounted for, eight were killed or captured by the end of 2002. Five followed in 2003—notably Khalid Sheik Mohammed, the principal planner of the Sept. 11 attack. This year only one more name—Hassan Ghul, a senior courier captured infiltrating Iraq—could be crossed off.

"I'll be pretty frank," Gordon said this fall after leaving the administration. "Obviously we would have liked to pick up more of the high-value targets than have been done. There have been strong initiatives. They just haven't all panned out."

As the manhunt results declined, the Bush administration has portrayed growing success. Early last year, the president's top advisers generally said in public that more than one-third of those most wanted had been found. Late this year it became a staple of presidential campaign rhetoric that, as Bush put it in the Sept. 30 debate with Kerry, "75 percent of known al Qaeda leaders have been brought to justice."

Although some of the administration's assertions are too broadly stated to measure, some are not. Townsend, Bush's homeland security and counterterrorism adviser, said "three-quarters" of "the known al Qaeda leaders on 9/11" were dead or in custody. Asked to elaborate, she said she would have to consult a list. White House spokeswoman Erin Healy referred follow-up questions to the FBI. Spokesmen for the FBI, the National Security Council and the CIA did not respond to multiple telephone calls and e-mails.

Whatever its results, the manhunt remains at the center of Bush's war. He mentions little else, save the Taliban's expulsion from power, when describing progress against al Qaeda. According to people who have briefed him, Bush still marks changes by hand on a copy of the HVT list.

"This is a conversation he's been having every day, more or less, with his senior advisers since September 11th," Falkenrath said. It covers "the same people, over and over again."

When Townsend was asked to describe the most important milestones of the war, she cited individual captures and kills. She named Khalid Sheik Mohammed; Abu Issa al Hindi, accused of surveying U.S. financial targets for al Qaeda in 2000 and 2001; Riduan Isamuddin, the alleged Southeast Asia coordinator; Abu Bakar Bashir, the spiritual leader of an al Qaeda affiliate in Indonesia; and Yazid Sufaat of Malaysia, who led efforts to develop a biological weapon.

Each of those men had significance "in a greater sense than just the individual," Townsend said, because they had "unique expertise, experience or access." Al Qaeda may replace them, "but does that person have the same strength and leadership and capability? The answer is no. Maybe he acquires it on the job, but maybe not."

UNLIKELY ALLIES

DAYS AFTER BUSH declared an "axis of evil," one of its members dispatched an envoy to New York. Javad Zarif, Iran's deputy foreign minister, arrived at John F. Kennedy International Airport in the first week of February 2002 with a thick sheaf of papers. According to sources involved in the transaction, Zarif passed the papers to U.N. Secretary General Kofi Annan, who passed them in turn to Washington.

Neatly arranged inside were photos of 290 men and copies of their travel documents. Iran said they were al Qaeda members, arrested as they tried to cross the rugged border from Afghanistan. Most were Saudi, a fact that two officials said Saudi Arabia's government asked Iran to conceal. All had been expelled to their home countries.

"They did not coordinate with us, but as long as the bad guys were going—fine," a senior U.S. national security official said.

Diplomats from Tehran and Washington had been meeting quietly all winter in New York and Bonn. They found common interests against the Taliban, Iran's bitter enemy. Iranian envoys notified their U.S. counterparts about the 290 arrests and proposed to cooperate against al Qaeda as well. The U.S. delegation sought instructions from Washington.

The delegation's room to maneuver, however, was limited by a policy guideline set shortly after the Sept. 11 attacks.

In late November 2001, the State Department's policy planning staff wrote a paper arguing that "we have a real opportunity here" to work more closely with Iran in fighting al Qaeda, according to Flynt Leverett, a career CIA analyst then assigned to State, who is now at the Brookings Institution and has provided advice to Kerry's campaign. Participants in the ensuing interagency debate said the CIA joined the proposal to exchange information and coordinate border sweeps against al Qaeda. Some of the most elusive high-value targets were living in or transiting Iran, including bin Laden's son Saad, al-Adel and Abu Hafs the Mauritanian.

Representatives of Cheney and Defense Secretary Donald H. Rumsfeld fought back. Any engagement, they argued, would legitimate Iran and other historic state sponsors of terrorism such as Syria. In the last weeks of 2001, the Deputies Committee adopted what came to be called "Hadley Rules," after deputy national security adviser Stephen J. Hadley, who chaired the meeting. The document said the United States would accept tactical information about terrorists from countries on the "state sponsors" list but offer nothing in return. Bush's State of the Union speech the next month linked Iran to Iraq and North Korea as "terrorist allies."

Twice in the coming year, Washington passed requests for Tehran to deliver al Qaeda suspects to the Afghan government.

Iran transferred two of the suspects and sought more information about others.

Iran, in turn, asked the United States, among other things, to question four Taliban prisoners held at Guantanamo Bay. They were suspects in the 1998 slayings of nine Iranian diplomats in Kabul.

Participants said Bush's divided national security team was unable to agree on an answer. Some believe important opportunities were lost.

"I sided with the Langley guys on that," Downing said. "I was willing to make a deal with the devil if we could clip somebody important off or stop an attack."

BACK TO AFGHANISTAN

TWO MONTHS AGO, a team of soldiers from a highly classified special operations squadron arrived in the southeastern mountains of Afghanistan, along the Pakistani border. They were back to hunt bin Laden, many of them after a two-year gap.

"We finally settled in at our 'permanent' location 8 days ago after moving twice in three weeks," one team member wrote to a friend. "New territory, right at the border, up in the mountains. Interesting place. We need to start from scratch, nothing operational in place. Guess we'll spend our whole time developing a basic structure for our ops."

At the peak of the hunt for bin Laden and his lieutenants, in early 2002, about 150 commandos operated along Afghanistan's borders with Pakistan and Iran in a top-secret team known as Task Force 5. The task force included a few CIA paramilitaries, but most of its personnel came from military "special mission units," or SMUs, whose existence is not officially acknowledged. One is the Army squadron once known as Delta Force. The other—specializing in human and technical intelligence operations—has not been described before in public. Its capabilities include close-in electronic surveillance and, uniquely in the U.S. military, the conduct of "low-level source operations"—recruiting and managing spies.

These elite forces, along with the battlefield intelligence technology of Predator and Global Hawk drone aircraft, were the scarcest tools of the hunt for jihadists along the Afghanistan-Pakistan border. With

Bush's shift of focus to Iraq, the special mission units called most of their troops home to prepare for a new set of high-value targets in Baghdad.

"There is a direct consequence for us having taken these guys out prematurely," said Leverett, who then worked as senior director for Middle Eastern affairs on Bush's NSC staff. "There were people on the staff level raising questions about what that meant for getting al Qaeda, for creating an Afghan security and intelligence service [to help combat jihadists]. Those questions didn't get above staff level, because clearly there had been a strategic decision taken."

Task Force 5 dropped in strength at times to as few as 30 men. Its counterpart in Iraq, by early 2003, burgeoned to more than 200 as an insurgency grew and Hussein proved difficult to find. Late last year, the Defense Department merged the two commando teams and headquartered the reflagged Task Force 121 under Rear Adm. William H. McRaven in Baghdad.

"I support the decision to go into Iraq and topple Saddam Hussein's regime," said Downing, a former U.S. Special Operations Command chief. "But in fact it was a gamble of sorts because Iraq did take focus and energy away from the Afghanistan campaign."

"It's been extraordinarily painful, very frustrating," said a member of one elite military unit who watched what he considered the main enemy slip away. Even now, with a modest resurgence in U.S. efforts in Afghanistan, the task force "is not getting as much attention from the home office as Iraq."

Much the same drawdown took place in the CIA.

With the closing of forward bases, the remaining case officers formed mobile teams of four or five, traveling in SUVs with translators, a medic and tribal allies they recruited. In some posts with former full-time presence, according to an operations officer who served there, they left empty safe houses for "almost a circuit riding thing—just bring your communications equipment in" for each visit. Others shut down altogether.

In 2002, the CIA transferred its station chief in Islamabad, Pakistan, to lead the new Iraq Issue Group. At least 30 case officers, a knowledgeable official said, joined the parallel Iraq Operations Task Force by mid-2002. By the time war came in Iraq nearly 150 case officers filled the task force and issue group on the "A Corridor" of Langley's top management. The Baghdad station became the largest since the Vietnam War, with more than 300.

Early this year, the CIA's then-station chief in Kabul reported a resurgence of Taliban and al Qaeda forces in three border provinces. He proposed a spring intelligence offensive in South Waziristan and in and around Kunar province farther north. The chief, whose first name is Peter, estimated he would need 25 case officers in the field and an additional five for the station. A national security official who tracked the proposal said CIA headquarters replied that it did not have the resources to make the surge. Peter finished his year as station chief in June.

'A LOT OF LITTLE CANCERS'

TOWNSEND, the White House terrorism and homeland security adviser, gives two framed courtroom sketches from a former life a place of honor on her West Wing wall. The color portraits, from 1990, depict her as lead prosecutor in a case against New York's Gambino crime family. When she took her White House job in May, she told the Associated Press that the transition from organized crime to terrorism "actually turns out not to be that big a leap." She added, "Really in many ways you're talking about a group with a command-and-control structure."

Jihadist terrorism has always posed what strategists call an "asymmetric threat," capable of inflicting catastrophic harm against a much stronger foe. But the way it operates, they said, is changing. Students of al Qaeda used to speak of it as a network with "key nodes" that could be attacked. More recently they have described the growth of "franchises." Gordon and Falkenrath pioneered an analogy, before leaving government, with an even less encouraging prognosis.

Jihadists "metastasized into a lot of little cancers in a lot of different countries," Gordon said recently. They formed "groups, operating under the terms of a movement, who don't have to rely on al Qaeda itself for funding, for training or for authority. [They operate] at a level that doesn't require as many people, doesn't require them to be as well-trained, and it's going to be damned hard to get in front of that."

Bruce Hoffman of the government-funded Rand Corp., who consults with participants in the war in classified forums, said U.S. analysts see clearly that "you can only have an effective top-down strategy if you're also drying up recruitment and sources of support."

Marc Sageman, a psychologist and former CIA case officer who studies the formation of jihadist cells, said the inspirational power of the Sept. 11 attacks—and rage in the Islamic world against U.S. steps taken since—has created a new phenomenon. Groups of young men gather in common outrage, he said, and a violent plan takes form without the need for an outside leader to identify, persuade or train those who carry it out.

The brutal challenge for U.S. intelligence, Sageman said, is that "you don't know who's going to be a terrorist" anymore. Citing the 15 men who killed 190 passengers on March 11 in synchronized bombings of the Spanish rail system, he said "if you had gone to those guys in Madrid six months prior, they'd say 'We're not terrorists,' and they weren't. Madrid took like five weeks from inception."

Much the same pattern, officials said, preceded deadly attacks in Indonesia, Turkey, Kenya, Morocco and elsewhere. There is no reason to believe, they said, that the phenomenon will remain overseas.

Such attacks do not rely on leaders as the Bush administration strategy has conceived them. New jihadists can acquire much of the know-how they need, Sageman and his counterparts still in government said, in al Qaeda's Saudi-published magazines, Al Baatar and the Voice of Jihad, available online.

Townsend acknowledged in an interview this month that "as you put more pressure on the center" of al Qaeda, "it pushes power out." That does not change the strategy, she said: "While you want to decapitate the beast, you also want to be able to cut the tentacles off. . . . Do we find there are others who emerge on the screen as leaders of their operational cadre? Of course. We capture and kill them, too."

'TEST OF WILLS'

DOWNING, BUSH's first counterterrorism adviser after Sept. 11, said in a 2002 interview that hunting down al Qaeda leaders could do no more than "buy time" for longer-term efforts to stem the jihadist tide. This month he said, "Time is not on our side."

"This is not a war," he said. "What we're faced with is an Islamic insurgency that is spreading throughout the world, not just the Islamic world." Because it is "a political struggle," he said, "the military is not the key factor. The military has to be coordinated with the other elements of national power."

Many of Downing's peers—and strong majorities of several dozen officers and officials who were interviewed—agree. They cite a long list of proposals to address terrorism at its roots that have not been carried out. Among them was a plan by Wendy Chamberlin, then ambassador to Pakistan, to offer President Pervez Musharraf a substitute for Saudi funding of a radical network of Islamist schools known as madrasas. Downing backed Chamberlin in the interagency debate, describing education as "the root of many of the recruits for the Islamist movement." Bush promised such support to Musharraf in a meeting soon after Sept. 11, said an official who accompanied him, but the $300 million plan did not survive the White House budget request.

The formal White House strategy for combating terrorism says that the United States will "use every instrument of national power— diplomatic, economic, law enforcement, financial, information, intelligence, and military" to triumph. A central criticism in the Sept. 11 commission's report is that the efforts at nonmilitary suasion overseas lack funding, energy from top leaders and what the commission's executive director, Philip D. Zelikow, called "gravitas."

Most officials interviewed said Bush has not devised an answer to a problem then-CIA Director George J. Tenet identified publicly on Feb. 11, 2003—"the numbers of societies and peoples excluded from the benefits of an expanding global economy, where the daily lot is hunger, disease, and displacement—and that produce large populations of disaffected youth who are prime recruits for our extremist foes."

The president and his most influential advisers, many officials said, do not see those factors—or U.S. policy overseas—as primary contributors to the terrorism threat. Bush's explanation, in private and public, is that terrorists hate America for its freedom.

Sageman, who supports some of Bush's approach, said that analysis is "nonsense, complete nonsense. They obviously haven't looked at any surveys." The central findings of polling by the Pew Charitable Trust and others, he said, is that large majorities in much of the world "view us as a hypocritical huge beast throwing our weight around in the Middle East."

When Bush speaks of al Qaeda's supporters, he refers to the leaders, not the citizens, of foreign nations. In a May 2003 speech about the Middle East, he said the "hateful ideology of terrorism is shaped and nurtured and protected by oppressive regimes." His approach centers not on winning support for U.S. values and policy, but on confronting evil without flinching.

Citing two governments he toppled by force and promising to "confront governments that support terrorists," Bush said in a speech on Oct. 6: "America is always more secure when freedom is on the march, and freedom is on the march in Afghanistan and Iraq and elsewhere."

Thomas W. O'Connell, who is assistant defense secretary in charge of special operations and low-intensity conflict, said Rumsfeld sometimes gathers Pentagon leaders to discuss the nature of the threat. After one such discussion recently, O'Connell concluded that "battle of ideas" is a poor term for the conflict underway.

"Perhaps the term 'test of wills,'" he said, "is more like what we're up against." Battles, he said, are "short, sharp events" against an external enemy. A test is "something that's internal" and "more reflective of a long, drawn-out ordeal."

Staff writer Craig Whitlock and researchers Robert Thomason and Julie Tate contributed to this report.

Contributors

RICHARD K. BETTS is Director of the Saltzman Institute of War and Peace Studies at Columbia University and Co-editor of *Paradoxes of Strategic Intelligence*. He previously served on the staff of the Senate's Church Committee investigation of U.S. intelligence agencies and as a consultant in the intelligence community.

MAX BOOT is Senior Fellow of National Security Studies at the Council on Foreign Relations.

LADAN BOROUMAND, a former visiting fellow at the International Forum for Democratic Studies, is a historian from Iran, and Director of the Abdorrahman Boroumand Foundation for the Promotion of Human Rights and Democracy in Iran.

ROYA BOROUMAND, a historian from Iran, is a specialist in Iran's contemporary history and has been a consultant for Human Rights Watch. She is Co-Director of the Abdorrahman Boroumand Foundation for the Promotion of Human Rights and Democracy in Iran.

GEORGE W. BUSH is the 43rd president of the United States.

GRENVILLE BYFORD is a Boston-based entrepreneur and independent analyst of international relations. He is also an affiliate of Caspian studies at the Belfer Center for Science and International Affairs at the John F. Kennedy School of Government at Harvard University.

Contributors

THOMAS CAROTHERS is Senior Associate and Director of the Democracy and Rule of Law Project at the Carnegie Endowment for International Peace.

STEPHEN PHILIP COHEN is Senior Fellow in Foreign Policy Studies at the Brookings Institution.

ALAN CULLISON is a Moscow correspondent for *The Wall Street Journal* and a Nieman fellow at Harvard University.

MICHAEL SCOTT DORAN is Assistant Professor of Near Eastern Studies at Princeton University.

PAULA J. DOBRIANSKY is Undersecretary of State for Global Affairs.

JAMES FALLOWS is National Correspondent for *The Atlantic Monthly* and founding Chairman of New America Board of Directors.

STEPHEN E. FLYNN is the Jeane J. Kirkpatrick Senior Fellow for National Security Studies at the Council on Foreign Relations.

F. GREGORY GAUSE III is Associate Professor of Political Science at the University of Vermont.

BARTON GELLMAN is a staff writer for the *Washington Post*.

REUEL MARC GERECHT is a resident fellow at the American Enterprise Institute and a contributing editor to *The Weekly Standard*. He is Senior Fellow at the project for the New American Century.

JOHN GERSHMAN is Senior Analyst at the Interhemispheric Resource Center and the Co-Director for Foreign Policy in Focus (www.fpif.org).

Contributors

MICHAEL HOWARD has been Professor of the History of War at Oxford and Robert A. Lovett Professor of Military and Naval History at Yale.

WALTER LAQUEUR is co-Chairman of the International Research Council at the Center for Strategic and International Studies. He is founder and editor of the *Journal of Contemporary History*.

DAFNA LINZER is a staff writer for the *Washington Post*.

MICHAEL E. O'HANLON is a Senior Fellow at the Brookings Institution. He has written several books on U.S. foreign policy, including *Defense Policy Choices for the Bush Administration*.

PAUL PILLAR was deputy chief of the Counterterrorist Center at the CIA.

GIDEON ROSE is the managing editor of *Foreign Affairs*.

KENNETH ROTH is Executive Director of Human Rights Watch.

JESSICA STERN is Lecturer in public policy and a faculty affiliate at the Belfer Center for Science and International Affairs at Harvard's John F. Kennedy School of Government.

RUTH WEDGWOOD is the Edward B. Burling Professor of International Law and Diplomacy and Director of the International Law and Organization Program at the Paul H. Nitze School of Advanced International Studies at Johns Hopkins University.

FAREED ZAKARIA is Editor of *Newsweek* International.